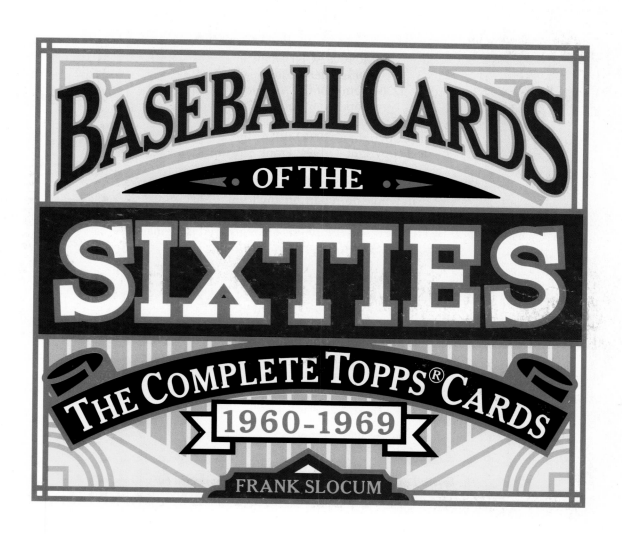

Baseball Cards

OF THE

SIXTIES

THE COMPLETE TOPPS® CARDS

1960-1969

FRANK SLOCUM

SIMON & SCHUSTER

New York   London   Toronto   Sydney   Tokyo   Singapore

SIMON & SCHUSTER
Rockefeller Center
1230 Avenue of the Americas
New York, New York 10020

AN MBKA PRODUCTION
1725 York Avenue
New York, New York 10128

Manufactured in Hong Kong

10 9 8 7 6 5 4 3 2 1

ISBN 0-671-89223-1

*The baseball cards reproduced on the cover were provided by
Alex's MVP Cards & Comics, 256 E. 89th St., New York, NY 10128*

FOREWORD
by
Willie Mays

Baseball cards probably aren't the kind of things most people give much thought to as they go about their daily lives. In fact, although I was exposed to them just about every day of my life since Topps issued their first card of me in 1952, I never gave them much thought either.

But a few years ago I was asked to participate in a baseball card show, and it was there that I came to the realization that these little pieces of cardboard were an integral part of so many people's lives. Yes, literally thousands of people, both young and old, paid their way in and lined up to get autographs of the big-league players (past and present) who were invited. These good folks moved in and out among the stalls, checking out the baseball memorabilia and above all looking for cards to enhance their collections. And from what I could see, the cards that were being shown—the cards that were being bought and traded—were mostly the Topps baseball cards.

You see, I was truly familiar with the Topps cards, since I appeared on fifty-seven different ones during and after my playing days in the majors. I certainly have seen enough of them. Although I never counted, I must have signed over a million of them. The Topps logo is indelibly impressed on me. In another respect they always reminded me of one of the closest friendships I made in baseball, going back to 1951. I was just a raw rookie in the New York Giants clubhouse looking for a friendly face. I found it when Sy Berger came along, and it's been the same for forty-four years.

I'm sure to many of you this book will recall memories of a happy childhood in which baseball cards played a significant role. I never collected these cards as a boy, only because I never saw a baseball card, or ever heard of such a thing. But once I got to the big leagues and walked through the streets of New York, San Francisco, etc., I knew there was a magic in the Topps cards. I could sense the joy of the youngsters as they unwrapped the gum packages to see their new treasures.

I was a happy young man when I saw my first picture printed on the Topps card, and I admit I liked my last one too. In the clubhouse I know how much the players enjoyed seeing themselves on these cards. I remember the young players beaming proudly when they saw their faces on the Rookie Cards that Topps published and how they looked forward to the day when they would be featured all by themselves on their own card.

Such fond memories—all from looking at an advance copy of this marvelous collection. I'm sure you who are lucky enough to own this book will find that it will bring back many memories of happy moments, as well as the material and information all of us baseball fans relish.

1960

Expansion became a reality, the classic swing of Ted Williams became a memory, the always puzzling world of managers took some new turns, and the World Series was a topsy-turvey example of the unimportance of statistics.

After a maelstrom of confusion that involved the demise of the proposed Continental League, jockeying between the two leagues for choice territories, and an unbelievable amount of last-minute roadblocks from just about everyone involved, the two major leagues finally decided on the hows, whens, and wheres of their expansions.

The National League decided on it first, but the American League moved first. After the National League announced they would enlarge to ten clubs in 1962, the American League said they were doing the same thing, but in 1961. The existing Washington franchise finally made their long-awaited move to Minneappolis/St. Paul. In its place a new franchise was put in the nation's capitol, headed by the former chief of the Federal Aviation Agency, Lt. Gen. Elwood Quesada. Cowboy movie star, Gene Autry, rode in out of the west, and then back out again with the Los Angeles Angels in his saddlebag.

The sale of an existing franchise resulted in a new face, and a new voice, in American League owners. The 52 per cent of the Kansas City franchise owned by the recently deceased Arnold Johnson was bought by a Gary, Indiana , insurance man named Charles O. Finley.

After the World Series, the most successful field–front office combination in baseball history made news. First, the Yankees called a press conference to announce the retirement of Casey Stengel (227), at which Stengel said, "I wasn't retired – they fired me." Two weeks later, General Manager George Weiss announced his resignation. It had been at the instigation of Weiss that Stengel had been hired 12 years earlier, during which time the team won ten pennants.

On September 28th, in the final home game of the year for the Boston Red Sox, Ted Williams came up for the last time. The pitcher was Baltimore's Jack Fisher (46), and Williams hit his 29th home run of the season, and his 521st lifetime. He immediately announced that he would forego the team's weekend road trip to New York and call it a career. Only Babe Ruth and Jimmy Foxx had hit more career home runs than the one they called "Teddy Ballgame."

The baseball cliché that says "managers are hired to be fired," was certainly true in 1960, with some fascinating variations on the theme. There was Billy Jurges (220) in Boston. First it was announced that because of ill health, he was being replaced by Del Baker (456) as interim manager. Two days later it was announced that Jurges had been fired. Jurges, who had replaced Mike Higgins as Red Sox manager a year before was being replaced by – Mike Higgins.

Then there was Chicago, where the Cubs decided to replace Charley Grimm (217) as manager. They reached into their broadcasting booth, picked out Lou Boudreau, gave him a uniform, and made him manager. His replacement in the booth? Why, Charley Grimm.

On August 3rd, two general managers decided to make a trade. Not players, but managers. Cleveland GM, Frank Lane, sent manager Joe Gordon (216) to Detroit, and in exchange Bill DeWitt of the Tigers sent Jimmy Dykes (214) to Cleveland. Both were gone shortly after the season ended.

Pittsburgh won the National League flag by seven games, and the Yankees won in the A.L. by eight. They met in a World Series that was, to put it mildly, "unique." The Pirates won the first game, and the Yankees won the second. In New York, the Yankees won game three, the Pirates games four and five. Back to Pittsburgh, the Yankees won game six to tie the Series.

If that sounds like a seesaw, listen to how game seven went. After four innings, the Pirates led, 4–0. After six, the Yankees led, 5–4. After seven and a half, the Yankees led 7–4. In the bottom of the eighth, thanks to a three-run home run by Hal Smith (48), the Pirates went ahead, 9–7. The Yankees tied it up in the top of the ninth, and in the bottom of the ninth, Bill Mazeroski (55) hit Ralph Terry's (96) second pitch over the left field wall, and Pittsburgh went crazy.

The Cards

This 572-card collection is the only Topps set in the 2½ by 3½-inch size to utilize a horizontal design. World Series cards (385 to 391) – 1959 Dodgers/White Sox – and 16 cards (455 to 470) picturing Major League Team Coaches are two Topps "firsts." The set also has 16 Manager Cards (212 to 227), 11 Combination Cards (down from 1959), and the *Sport* Magazine All-Star Teams (553 to 572). There is also a group of Rookie Cards (117 to 148), which includes the first baseball cards published of Jim Kaat (136) and Carl Yastrzemski (148). The Mickey Mantle (350) card is the top-valued card in the series at $450.

QUIZ

On May 7th, he and his brother became the 10th battery to appear together in a big league game. He hit a home run in the 11th, to give his brother the victory. Who? (529)

He began the year with the Cubs, but was traded to the Phillies before the season began. In June the Phillies traded him to the Braves, and in October the Braves traded him to the Giants, who named him manager. Who? (472)

An All-American basketball player, he passed up the pros for baseball and led the league in hitting and was chosen MVP. Who? (258)

The MVP in the other league had an outstanding year, but few remember because of the great year that followed. Who? (377)

On Easter Sunday, he became the second youngest ever to hit 300 home runs. Who? (420)

On the Fourth of July, he became the third youngest ever to hit 300 home runs. Who? (350)

Traded to the Cubs on May 13th, he pitched a no-hitter on the 15th. Who? (384)

He drove in seven runs from the All-Star break to the end of the season, and 12 in the World Series, six in one game. Who? (405)

After this Cincinnati infielder punched a Cubs pitcher, the Cubs filed a $1,040,000 lawsuit against him. Who? (173)

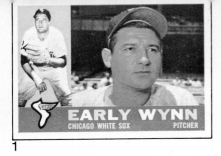
1 EARLY WYNN — CHICAGO WHITE SOX — PITCHER

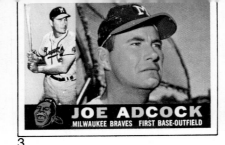
2 ROMAN MEJIAS — PITTSBURGH PIRATES — OUTFIELD

3 JOE ADCOCK — MILWAUKEE BRAVES — FIRST BASE-OUTFIELD

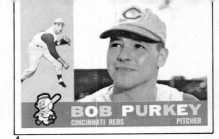
4 BOB PURKEY — CINCINNATI REDS — PITCHER

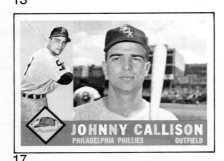
5 WALLY MOON — LOS ANGELES DODGERS — OUTFIELD

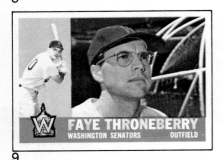
6 LOU BERBERET — DETROIT TIGERS — CATCHER

7 MASTER & MENTOR — GIANTS — MAYS—RIGNEY

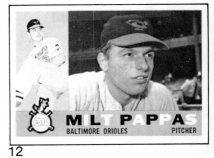
8 BUD DALEY — KANSAS CITY ATHLETICS — PITCHER

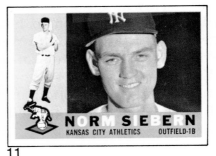
9 FAYE THRONEBERRY — WASHINGTON SENATORS — OUTFIELD

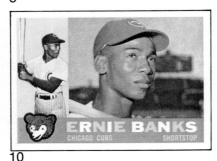
10 ERNIE BANKS — CHICAGO CUBS — SHORTSTOP

11 NORM SIEBERN — KANSAS CITY ATHLETICS — OUTFIELD-1B

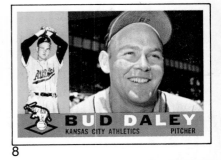
12 MILT PAPPAS — BALTIMORE ORIOLES — PITCHER

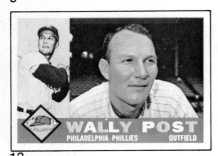
13 WALLY POST — PHILADELPHIA PHILLIES — OUTFIELD

14 JIM GRANT — CLEVELAND INDIANS — PITCHER

15 PETE RUNNELS — BOSTON RED SOX — SECOND BASE-FIRST BASE

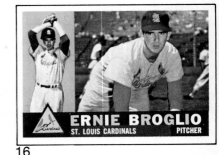
16 ERNIE BROGLIO — ST. LOUIS CARDINALS — PITCHER

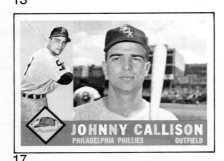

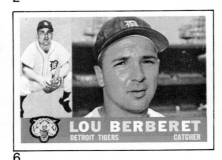
18 LOS ANGELES DODGERS

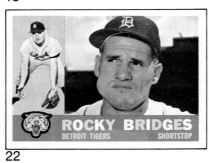
19 FELIX MANTILLA — MILWAUKEE BRAVES — 2nd BASE-SHORTSTOP

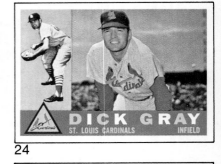
20 ROY FACE — PITTSBURGH PIRATES — PITCHER

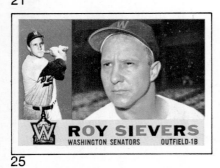
17 JOHNNY CALLISON — PHILADELPHIA PHILLIES — OUTFIELD

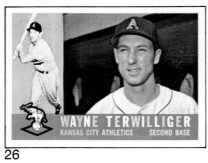
21 DUTCH DOTTERER — CINCINNATI REDS — CATCHER

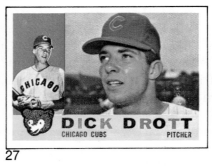
22 ROCKY BRIDGES — DETROIT TIGERS — SHORTSTOP

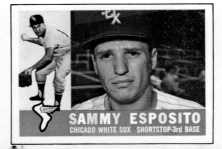
23 EDDIE FISHER — SAN FRANCISCO GIANTS — PITCHER

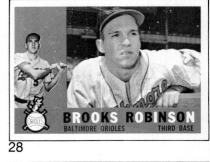
24 DICK GRAY — ST. LOUIS CARDINALS — INFIELD

25 ROY SIEVERS — WASHINGTON SENATORS — OUTFIELD-1B

26 WAYNE TERWILLIGER — KANSAS CITY ATHLETICS — SECOND BASE

27 DICK DROTT — CHICAGO CUBS — PITCHER

28 BROOKS ROBINSON — BALTIMORE ORIOLES — THIRD BASE

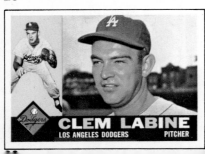
CLEM LABINE — LOS ANGELES DODGERS — PITCHER

TITO FRANCONA — CLEVELAND INDIANS — OUTFIELD

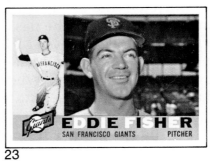
SAMMY ESPOSITO — CHICAGO WHITE SOX — SHORTSTOP-3rd BASE

SOPHOMORE STALWARTS — O'TOOLE—PINSON

TOM MORGAN — Detroit Tigers — PITCHER — 33	GEORGE ANDERSON — Philadelphia Phillies — SECOND BASE — 34	WHITEY FORD — New York Yankees — PITCHER — 35	RUSS NIXON — Cleveland Indians — CATCHER — 36
BILL BRUTON — Milwaukee Braves — OUTFIELD — 37	JERRY CASALE — Boston Red Sox — PITCHER — 38	EARL AVERILL — Chicago Cubs — CATCHER-THIRD BASE — 39	JOE CUNNINGHAM — St. Louis Cardinals — FIRST BASE-OUTFIELD — 40
BARRY LATMAN — Chicago White Sox — PITCHER — 41	HOBIE LANDRITH — San Francisco Giants — CATCHER — 42	WASHINGTON SENATORS — 43	BOBBY LOCKE — Cleveland Indians — PITCHER — 44
ROY McMILLAN — Cincinnati Reds — SHORTSTOP — 45	JACK FISHER — Baltimore Orioles — PITCHER — 46	DON ZIMMER — Los Angeles Dodgers — SHORTSTOP — 47	HAL SMITH — Pittsburgh Pirates — 3d Base-Catcher — 48
CURT RAYDON — Pittsburgh Pirates — PITCHER — 49	AL KALINE — Detroit Tigers — OUTFIELD — 50	JIM COATES — New York Yankees — PITCHER — 51	DAVE PHILLEY — Philadelphia Phillies — INFIELD-OUTFIELD — 52
JACKIE BRANDT — Baltimore Orioles — OUTFIELD — 53	MIKE FORNIELES — Boston Red Sox — PITCHER — 54	BILL MAZEROSKI — Pittsburgh Pirates — SECOND BASE — 55	STEVE KORCHECK — Washington Senators — CATCHER — 56
WIN-SAVERS — LOWN-STALEY — 57	GINO CIMOLI — Pittsburgh Pirates — OUTFIELD — 58	JUAN PIZARRO — Milwaukee Braves — PITCHER — 59	GUS TRIANDOS — Baltimore Orioles — CATCHER — 60
EDDIE KASKO — Cincinnati Reds — SHORTSTOP-THIRD BASE — 61	ROGER CRAIG — Los Angeles Dodgers — PITCHER —	GEORGE STRICKLAND — Cleveland Indians — THIRD BASE —	JACK MEYER — Philadelphia Phillies — PITCHER —

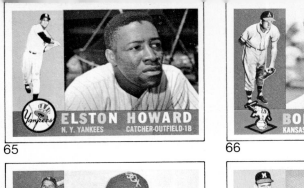
ELSTON HOWARD
N. Y. Yankees
CATCHER-OUTFIELD-1B

BOB TROWBRIDGE
KANSAS CITY ATHLETICS
PITCHER

JOSE PAGAN
SAN FRANCISCO GIANTS
INFIELD

DAVE HILLMAN
BOSTON RED SOX
PITCHER

65

66

67

68

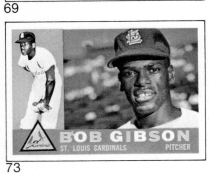
BILLY GOODMAN
CHICAGO WHITE SOX
THIRD BASE

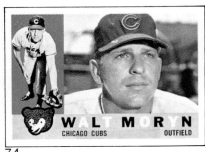
LOU BURDETTE
MILWAUKEE BRAVES
PITCHER

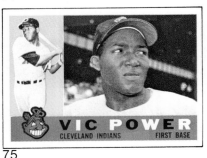
MARTY KEOUGH
BOSTON RED SOX
OUTFIELD

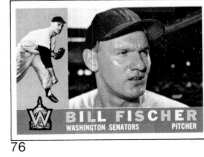
DETROIT
TIGERS

69

70

71

72

BOB GIBSON
ST. LOUIS CARDINALS
PITCHER

WALT MORYN
CHICAGO CUBS
OUTFIELD

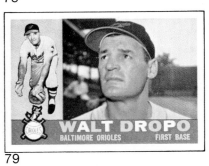
VIC POWER
CLEVELAND INDIANS
FIRST BASE

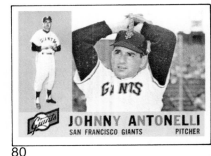
BILL FISCHER
WASHINGTON SENATORS
PITCHER

73

74

75

76

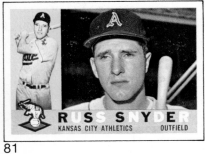
HANK FOILES
KANSAS CITY ATHLETICS
CATCHER

BOB GRIM
KANSAS CITY ATHLETICS
PITCHER

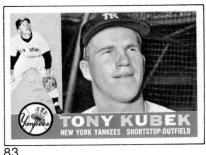
WALT DROPO
BALTIMORE ORIOLES
FIRST BASE

JOHNNY ANTONELLI
SAN FRANCISCO GIANTS
PITCHER

77

78

79

80

RUSS SNYDER
KANSAS CITY ATHLETICS
OUTFIELD

RUBEN GOMEZ
PHILADELPHIA PHILLIES
PITCHER

TONY KUBEK
NEW YORK YANKEES
SHORTSTOP-OUTFIELD

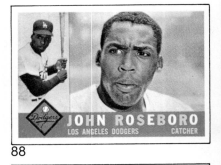
HAL SMITH
ST. LOUIS CARDINALS
CATCHER

81

82

83

84

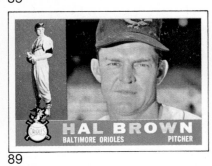
FRANK LARY
DETROIT TIGERS
PITCHER

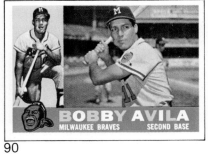
DICK GERNERT
CHICAGO CUBS
FIRST BASE-OUTFIELD

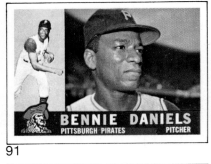
JOHN ROMONOSKY
WASHINGTON SENATORS
PITCHER

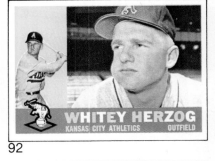
JOHN ROSEBORO
LOS ANGELES DODGERS
CATCHER

85

86

87

88

HAL BROWN
BALTIMORE ORIOLES
PITCHER

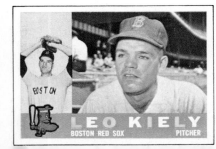
BOBBY AVILA
MILWAUKEE BRAVES
SECOND BASE

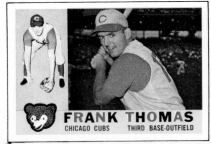
BENNIE DANIELS
PITTSBURGH PIRATES
PITCHER

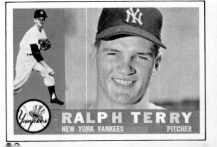
WHITEY HERZOG
KANSAS CITY ATHLETICS
OUTFIELD

89

90

91

92

ART SCHULT
CHICAGO CUBS
FIRST BASE-OUTFIELD

LEO KIELY
BOSTON RED SOX
PITCHER

FRANK THOMAS
CHICAGO CUBS
THIRD BASE-OUTFIELD

RALPH TERRY
NEW YORK YANKEES
PITCHER

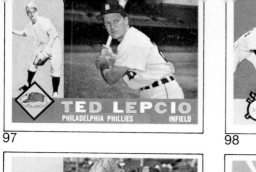
TED LEPCIO PHILADELPHIA PHILLIES INFIELD
97

GORDON JONES BALTIMORE ORIOLES PITCHER
98

LENNY GREEN WASHINGTON SENATORS OUTFIELD
99

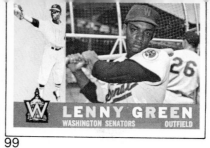
NELLIE FOX CHICAGO WHITE SOX SECOND BASE
100

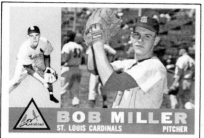
BOB MILLER ST. LOUIS CARDINALS PITCHER
101

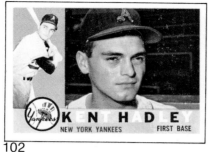
KENT HADLEY NEW YORK YANKEES FIRST BASE
102

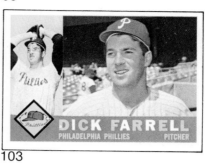
DICK FARRELL PHILADELPHIA PHILLIES PITCHER
103

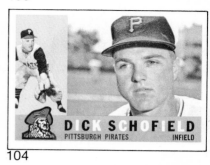
DICK SCHOFIELD PITTSBURGH PIRATES INFIELD
104

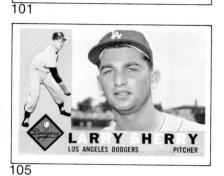
LARRY SHERRY LOS ANGELES DODGERS PITCHER
105

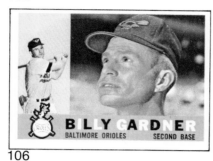
BILLY GARDNER BALTIMORE ORIOLES SECOND BASE
106

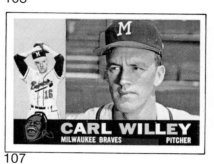
CARL WILLEY MILWAUKEE BRAVES PITCHER
107

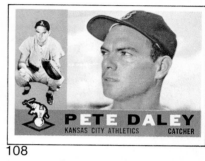
PETE DALEY KANSAS CITY ATHLETICS CATCHER
108

CLETIS BOYER NEW YORK YANKEES SHORTSTOP
109

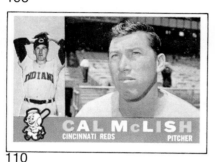
CAL McLISH CINCINNATI REDS PITCHER
110

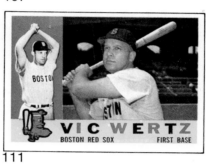
VIC WERTZ BOSTON RED SOX FIRST BASE
111

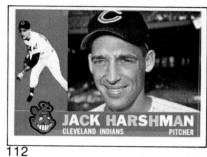
JACK HARSHMAN CLEVELAND INDIANS PITCHER
112

BOB SKINNER PITTSBURGH PIRATES OUTFIELD
113

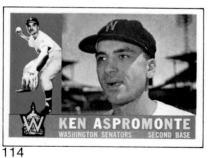
KEN ASPROMONTE WASHINGTON SENATORS SECOND BASE
114

FORK & KNUCKLER

FACE & WILHELM
115

JIM RIVERA CHICAGO WHITE SOX OUTFIELD
116

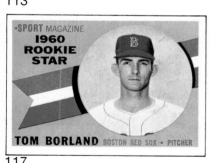
SPORT MAGAZINE
1960 ROOKIE STAR
TOM BORLAND BOSTON RED SOX · PITCHER
117

SPORT MAGAZINE
1960 ROOKIE STAR
BOB BRUCE DETROIT TIGERS · PITCHER
118

SPORT MAGAZINE
1960 ROOKIE STAR
CHICO CARDENAS CINN. REDS · SHORTSTOP
119

SPORT MAGAZINE
1960 ROOKIE STAR
DUKE CARMEL ST. LOUIS CARDS · 1B-O.F.
120

SPORT MAGAZINE
1960 ROOKIE STAR
CAMILO CARREON CHIC. WHITE SOX · CATCHER
121

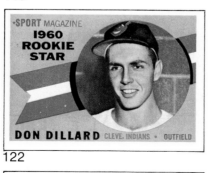
SPORT MAGAZINE
1960 ROOKIE STAR
DON DILLARD CLEVE. INDIANS · OUTFIELD
122

SPORT MAGAZINE
1960 ROOKIE STAR
DAN DOBBEK WASH. SENATORS · Outfield
123

SPORT MAGAZINE
1960 ROOKIE STAR
JIM DONOHUE ST. LOUIS CARDS · PITCHER
124

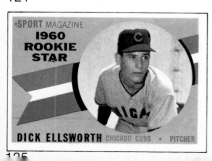
SPORT MAGAZINE
1960 ROOKIE STAR
DICK ELLSWORTH CHICAGO CUBS · PITCHER
125

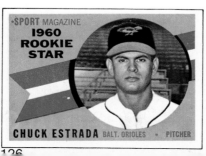
SPORT MAGAZINE
1960 ROOKIE STAR
CHUCK ESTRADA BALT. ORIOLES · PITCHER
126

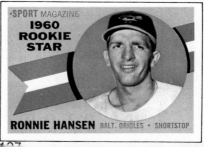
SPORT MAGAZINE
1960 ROOKIE STAR
RONNIE HANSEN BALT. ORIOLES · SHORTSTOP
127

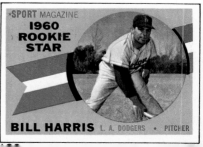
SPORT MAGAZINE
1960 ROOKIE STAR
BILL HARRIS L. A. DODGERS · PITCHER
128

BOB HARTMAN MIL. BRAVES · PITCHER
129

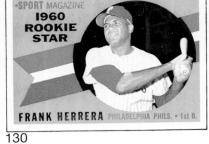
FRANK HERRERA Philadelphia Phils. · 1st B.
130

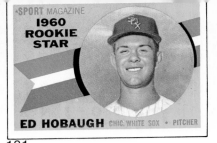
ED HOBAUGH CHIC. WHITE SOX · PITCHER
131

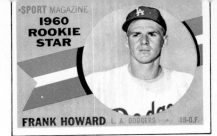
FRANK HOWARD L. A. DODGERS · 1B-O.F.
132

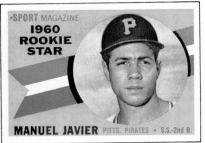
MANUEL JAVIER PITTS. PIRATES · S.S.-2nd B.
133

DERON JOHNSON N.Y. YANKEES · Outfield
134

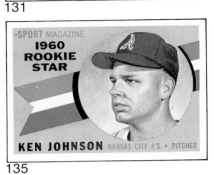
KEN JOHNSON KANSAS CITY A'S · PITCHER
135

JIM KAAT WASH. SENATORS · PITCHER
136

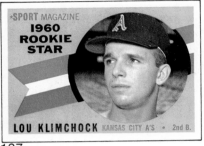
LOU KLIMCHOCK KANSAS CITY A'S · 2nd B.
137

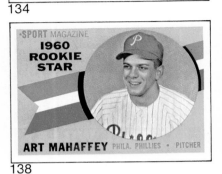
ART MAHAFFEY PHILA. PHILLIES · PITCHER
138

CARL MATHIAS CLEVE. INDIANS · PITCHER
139

JULIO NAVARRO S.F. GIANTS · PITCHER
140

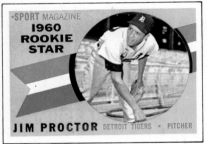
JIM PROCTOR DETROIT TIGERS · PITCHER
141

BILL SHORT N.Y. YANKEES · PITCHER
142

AL SPANGLER MIL. BRAVES · OUTFIELD
143

AL STIEGLITZ S.F. GIANTS · CATCHER
144

JIM UMBRICHT PITTS. PIRATES · PITCHER
145

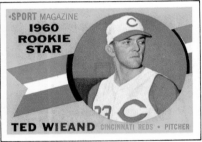
TED WIEAND CINCINNATI REDS · PITCHER
146

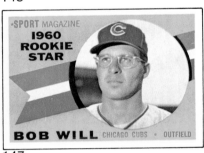
BOB WILL CHICAGO CUBS · OUTFIELD
147

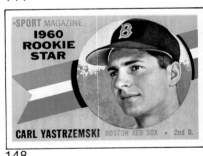
CARL YASTRZEMSKI BOSTON RED SOX · 2nd B.
148

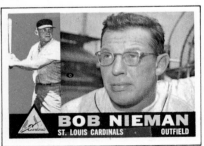
BOB NIEMAN ST. LOUIS CARDINALS OUTFIELD
149

BILLY PIERCE CHICAGO WHITE SOX PITCHER
150

SAN FRANCISCO
GIANTS
151

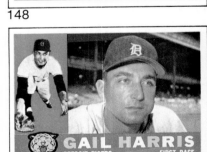
GAIL HARRIS DETROIT TIGERS FIRST BASE
152

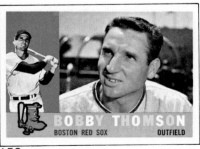
BOBBY THOMSON BOSTON RED SOX OUTFIELD
153

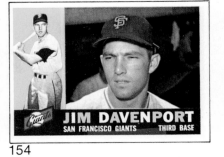
JIM DAVENPORT SAN FRANCISCO GIANTS THIRD BASE
154

CHARLIE NEAL LOS ANGELES DODGERS SECOND BASE
155

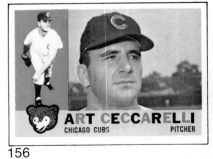
ART CECCARELLI CHICAGO CUBS PITCHER
156

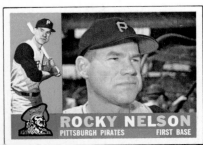
ROCKY NELSON PITTSBURGH PIRATES FIRST BASE

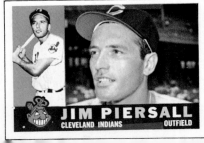
WES COVINGTON MILWAUKEE BRAVES OUTFIELD

JIM PIERSALL CLEVELAND INDIANS OUTFIELD

RIVAL ALL STARS
MANTLE & BOYER

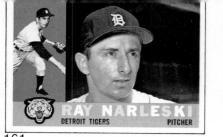

RAY NARLESKI — DETROIT TIGERS — PITCHER
161

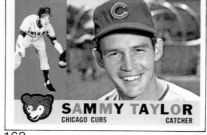

SAMMY TAYLOR — CHICAGO CUBS — CATCHER
162

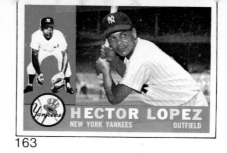

HECTOR LOPEZ — NEW YORK YANKEES — OUTFIELD
163

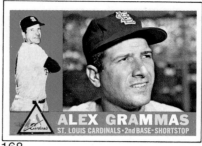

CINCINNATI REDS
164

JACK SANFORD — SAN FRANCISCO GIANTS — PITCHER
165

CHUCK ESSEGIAN — LOS ANGELES DODGERS — OUTFIELD
166

VALMY THOMAS — PHILADELPHIA PHILLIES — CATCHER
167

ALEX GRAMMAS — ST. LOUIS CARDINALS · 2nd BASE-SHORTSTOP
168

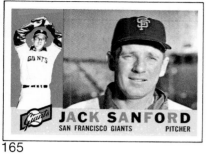

JAKE STRIKER — CHICAGO WHITE SOX — PITCHER
169

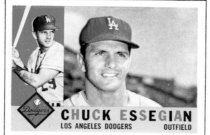

DEL CRANDALL — MILWAUKEE BRAVES — CATCHER
170

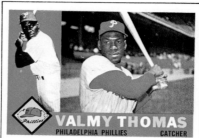

JOHNNY GROTH — DETROIT TIGERS — OUTFIELD
171

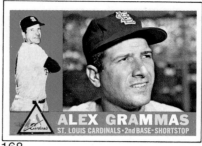

WILLIE KIRKLAND — SAN FRANCISCO GIANTS — OUTFIELD
172

BILLY MARTIN — CINCINNATI REDS — SECOND BASE
173

CLEVELAND INDIANS
174

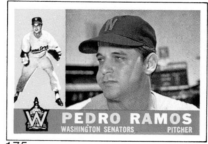

PEDRO RAMOS — WASHINGTON SENATORS — PITCHER
175

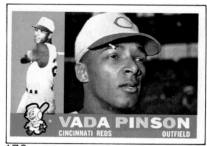

VADA PINSON — CINCINNATI REDS — OUTFIELD
176

JOHNNY KUCKS — KANSAS CITY ATHLETICS — PITCHER
177

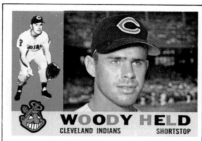

WOODY HELD — CLEVELAND INDIANS — SHORTSTOP
178

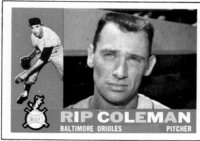

RIP COLEMAN — BALTIMORE ORIOLES — PITCHER
179

HARRY SIMPSON — CHICAGO WHITE SOX — OUTFIELD-1st BASE
180

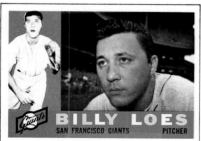

BILLY LOES — SAN FRANCISCO GIANTS — PITCHER
181

GLEN HOBBIE — CHICAGO CUBS — PITCHER
182

ELI GRBA — NEW YORK YANKEES — PITCHER
183

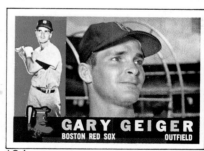

GARY GEIGER — BOSTON RED SOX — OUTFIELD
184

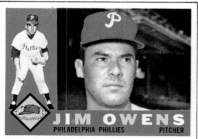

JIM OWENS — PHILADELPHIA PHILLIES — PITCHER
185

DAVE SISLER — DETROIT TIGERS — PITCHER
186

JAY HOOK — CINCINNATI REDS — PITCHER
187

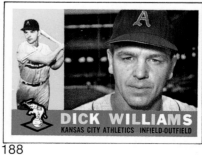

DICK WILLIAMS — KANSAS CITY ATHLETICS — INFIELD-OUTFIELD
188

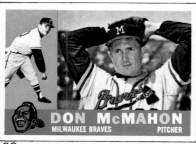

DON McMAHON — MILWAUKEE BRAVES — PITCHER
189

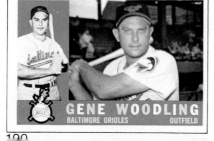

GENE WOODLING — BALTIMORE ORIOLES — OUTFIELD
190

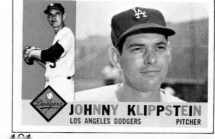

JOHNNY KLIPPSTEIN — LOS ANGELES DODGERS — PITCHER
191

DANNY O'CONNELL — SAN FRANCISCO GIANTS — INFIELD

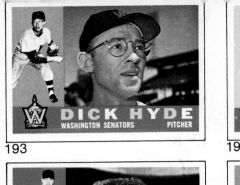
DICK HYDE
WASHINGTON SENATORS PITCHER
193

BOBBY GENE SMITH
PHILADELPHIA PHILLIES OUTFIELD
194

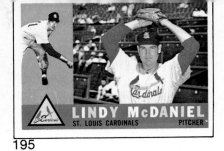
LINDY McDANIEL
ST. LOUIS CARDINALS PITCHER
195

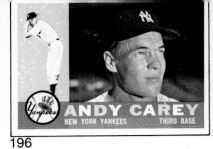
ANDY CAREY
NEW YORK YANKEES THIRD BASE
196

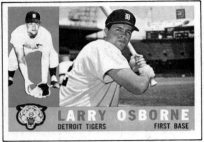
RON KLINE
ST. LOUIS CARDINALS PITCHER
197

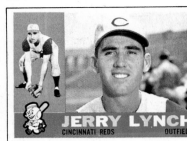
JERRY LYNCH
CINCINNATI REDS OUTFIELD
198

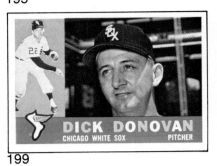
DICK DONOVAN
CHICAGO WHITE SOX PITCHER
199

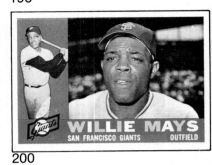
WILLIE MAYS
SAN FRANCISCO GIANTS OUTFIELD
200

LARRY OSBORNE
DETROIT TIGERS FIRST BASE
201

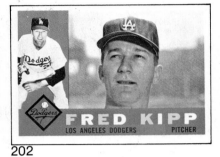
FRED KIPP
LOS ANGELES DODGERS PITCHER
202

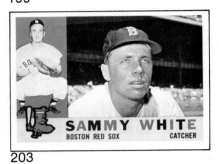
SAMMY WHITE
BOSTON RED SOX CATCHER
203

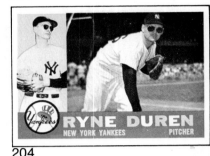
RYNE DUREN
NEW YORK YANKEES PITCHER
204

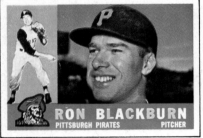
JOHNNY LOGAN
MILWAUKEE BRAVES SHORTSTOP
205

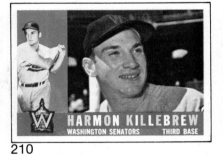
CLAUDE OSTEEN
CINCINNATI REDS PITCHER
206

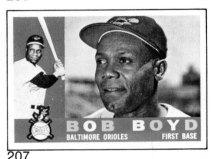
BOB BOYD
BALTIMORE ORIOLES FIRST BASE
207

CHICAGO
WHITE SOX
208

RON BLACKBURN
PITTSBURGH PIRATES PITCHER
209

HARMON KILLEBREW
WASHINGTON SENATORS THIRD BASE
210

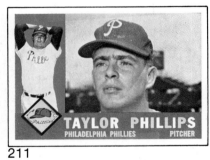
TAYLOR PHILLIPS
PHILADELPHIA PHILLIES PITCHER
211

WALT ALSTON
MANAGER • LOS ANGELES
Dodgers
212

CHUCK DRESSEN
MANAGER • MILWAUKEE
BRAVES
213

JIMMIE DYKES
MANAGER • DETROIT
TIGERS
214

BOB ELLIOTT
MANAGER • KANSAS CITY
ATHLETICS
215

JOE GORDON
MANAGER • CLEVELAND
INDIANS
216

CHARLEY GRIMM
MANAGER • CHICAGO (N.L.)
CUBS
217

SOLLY HEMUS
MANAGER • ST. LOUIS
CARDS
218

FRED HUTCHINSON
MANAGER • CINCINNATI
REDS
219

BILLY JURGES
MANAGER • BOSTON
RED SOX
220

COOKIE LAVAGETTO
MANAGER • WASHINGTON
SENATORS
221

AL LOPEZ
MANAGER • CHICAGO (A.L.)
WHITE SOX
222

DANNY MURTAUGH
MANAGER • PITTSBURGH
PIRATES
223

PAUL RICHARDS
MANAGER • BALTIMORE
ORIOLES
224

BILL RIGNEY · MANAGER · SAN FRANCISCO
225

EDDIE SAWYER · MANAGER · PHILADELPHIA
226

CASEY STENGEL · MANAGER · NEW YORK
227

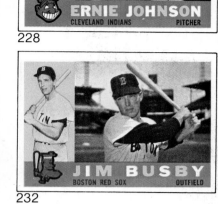
ERNIE JOHNSON
CLEVELAND INDIANS — PITCHER
228

JOE MORGAN
KANSAS CITY ATHLETICS — SECOND BASE
229

MOUND MAGICIANS
BURDETTE-SPAHN-BUHL
230

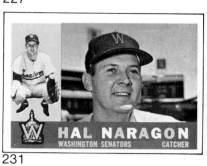
HAL NARAGON
WASHINGTON SENATORS — CATCHER
231

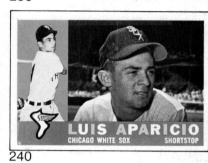
JIM BUSBY
BOSTON RED SOX — OUTFIELD
232

DON ELSTON
CHICAGO CUBS — PITCHER
233

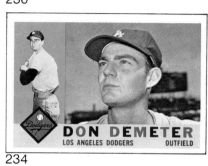
DON DEMETER
LOS ANGELES DODGERS — OUTFIELD
234

GUS BELL
CINCINNATI REDS — OUTFIELD
235

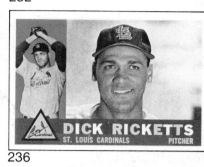
DICK RICKETTS
ST. LOUIS CARDINALS — PITCHER
236

ELMER VALO
NEW YORK YANKEES — OUTFIELD
237

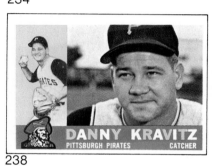
DANNY KRAVITZ
PITTSBURGH PIRATES — CATCHER
238

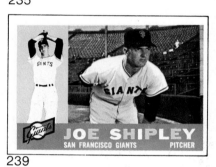
JOE SHIPLEY
SAN FRANCISCO GIANTS — PITCHER
239

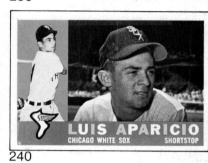
LUIS APARICIO
CHICAGO WHITE SOX — SHORTSTOP
240

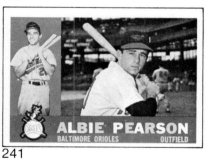
ALBIE PEARSON
BALTIMORE ORIOLES — OUTFIELD
241

ST. LOUIS
CARDINALS
242

BUBBA PHILLIPS
CLEVELAND INDIANS — 3rd BASE-OUTFIELD
243

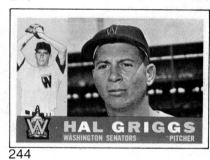
HAL GRIGGS
WASHINGTON SENATORS — PITCHER
244

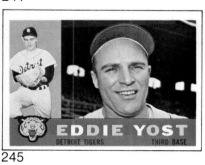
EDDIE YOST
DETROIT TIGERS — THIRD BASE
245

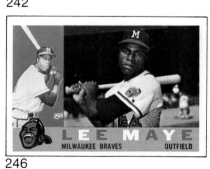
LEE MAYE
MILWAUKEE BRAVES — OUTFIELD
246

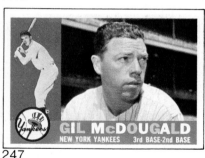
GIL McDOUGALD
NEW YORK YANKEES — 3rd BASE-2nd BASE
247

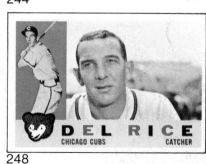
DEL RICE
CHICAGO CUBS — CATCHER
248

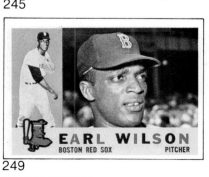
EARL WILSON
BOSTON RED SOX — PITCHER
249

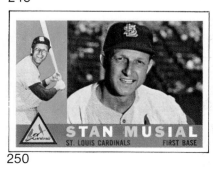
STAN MUSIAL
ST. LOUIS CARDINALS — FIRST BASE
250

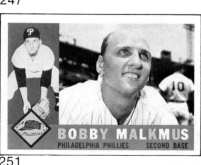
BOBBY MALKMUS
PHILADELPHIA PHILLIES — SECOND BASE
251

RAY HERBERT
KANSAS CITY ATHLETICS — PITCHER
252

EDDIE BRESSOUD
SAN FRANCISCO GIANTS — SHORTSTOP
253

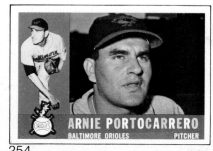
ARNIE PORTOCARRERO
BALTIMORE ORIOLES — PITCHER
254

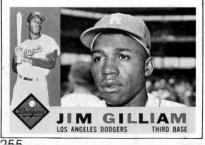
JIM GILLIAM
LOS ANGELES DODGERS — THIRD BASE
255

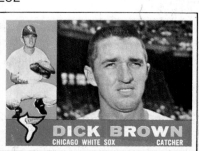
DICK BROWN
CHICAGO WHITE SOX — CATCHER
256

GORDY COLEMAN
CINCINNATI REDS FIRST BASE
257

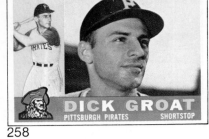
DICK GROAT
PITTSBURGH PIRATES SHORTSTOP
258

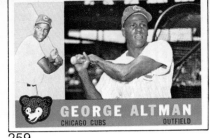
GEORGE ALTMAN
CHICAGO CUBS OUTFIELD
259

POWER PLUS
COLAVITO — FRANCONA
260

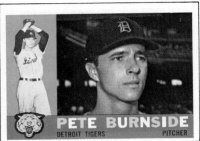
PETE BURNSIDE
DETROIT TIGERS PITCHER
261

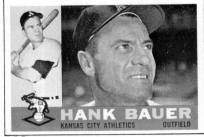
HANK BAUER
KANSAS CITY ATHLETICS OUTFIELD
262

DARRELL JOHNSON
ST. LOUIS CARDINALS CATCHER
263

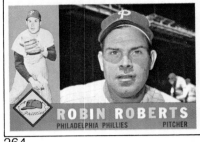
ROBIN ROBERTS
PHILADELPHIA PHILLIES PITCHER
264

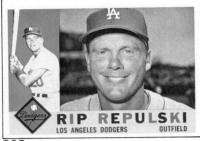
RIP REPULSKI
LOS ANGELES DODGERS OUTFIELD
265

JOE JAY
MILWAUKEE BRAVES PITCHER
266

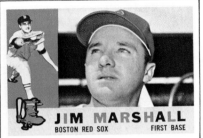
JIM MARSHALL
BOSTON RED SOX FIRST BASE
267

AL WORTHINGTON
SAN FRANCISCO GIANTS PITCHER
268

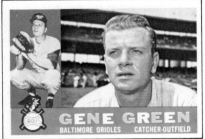
GENE GREEN
BALTIMORE ORIOLES CATCHER-OUTFIELD
269

BOB TURLEY
NEW YORK YANKEES PITCHER
270

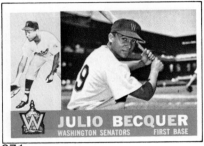
JULIO BECQUER
WASHINGTON SENATORS FIRST BASE
271

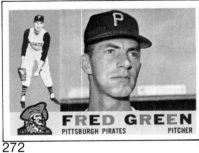
FRED GREEN
PITTSBURGH PIRATES PITCHER
272

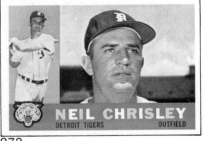
NEIL CHRISLEY
DETROIT TIGERS OUTFIELD
273

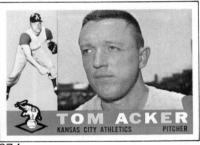
TOM ACKER
KANSAS CITY ATHLETICS PITCHER
274

CURT FLOOD
ST. LOUIS CARDINALS OUTFIELD
275

KEN McBRIDE
CHICAGO WHITE SOX PITCHER
276

HARRY BRIGHT
CHICAGO CUBS INFIELD
277

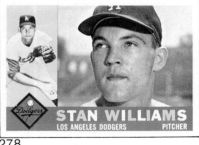
STAN WILLIAMS
LOS ANGELES DODGERS PITCHER
278

CHUCK TANNER
CLEVELAND INDIANS OUTFIELD
279

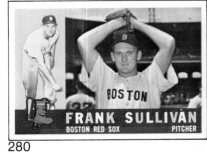
FRANK SULLIVAN
BOSTON RED SOX PITCHER
280

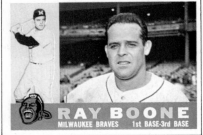
RAY BOONE
MILWAUKEE BRAVES 1st BASE-3rd BASE
281

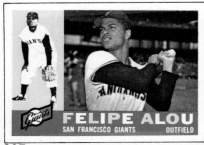
JOE NUXHALL
CINCINNATI REDS PITCHER
282

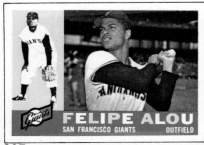
JOHN BLANCHARD
NEW YORK YANKEES CATCHER
283

DON GROSS
PITTSBURGH PIRATES PITCHER
284

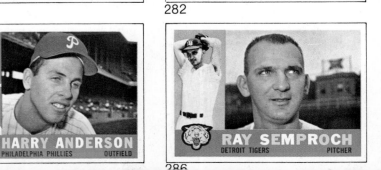
HARRY ANDERSON
PHILADELPHIA PHILLIES OUTFIELD
285

RAY SEMPROCH
DETROIT TIGERS PITCHER
286

FELIPE ALOU
SAN FRANCISCO GIANTS OUTFIELD
287

BOB MABE
BALTIMORE ORIOLES PITCHER
288

WILLIE JONES
CINCINNATI REDS — THIRD BASE
289

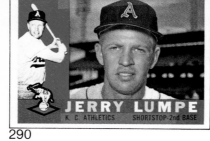
JERRY LUMPE
K. C. ATHLETICS — SHORTSTOP-2nd BASE
290

BOB KEEGAN
ST. LOUIS CARDINALS — PITCHER
291

DODGER BACKSTOPS
PIGNATANO—ROSEBORO
292

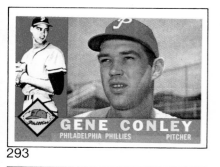
GENE CONLEY
PHILADELPHIA PHILLIES — PITCHER
293

TONY TAYLOR
CHICAGO CUBS — SECOND BASE
294

GIL HODGES
LOS ANGELES DODGERS — 1st BASE
295

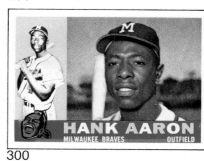
NELSON CHITTUM
BOSTON RED SOX — PITCHER
296

RENO BERTOIA
WASH. SENATORS — 2nd BASE-3rd BASE
297

GEORGE WITT
PITTSBURGH PIRATES — PITCHER
298

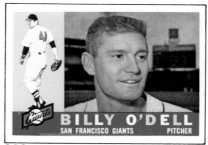
EARL TORGESON
CHICAGO WHITE SOX — FIRST BASE
299

HANK AARON
MILWAUKEE BRAVES — OUTFIELD
300

JERRY DAVIE
DETROIT TIGERS — PITCHER
301

PHILADELPHIA
PHILLIES
302

BILLY O'DELL
SAN FRANCISCO GIANTS — PITCHER
303

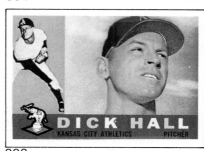
JOE GINSBERG
BALTIMORE ORIOLES — CATCHER
304

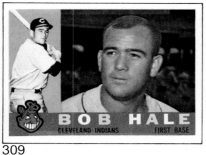
RICHIE ASHBURN
CHICAGO CUBS — OUTFIELD
305

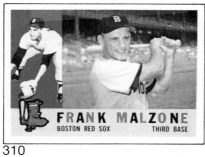
FRANK BAUMANN
CHICAGO WHITE SOX — PITCHER
306

GENE OLIVER
ST. LOUIS CARDINALS — OUTFIELD-CATCHER
307

DICK HALL
KANSAS CITY ATHLETICS — PITCHER
308

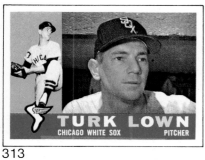
BOB HALE
CLEVELAND INDIANS — FIRST BASE
309

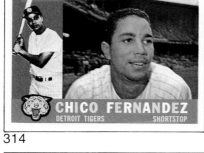
FRANK MALZONE
BOSTON RED SOX — THIRD BASE
310

RAUL SANCHEZ
CINCINNATI REDS — PITCHER
311

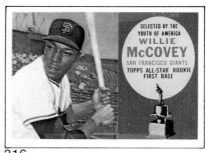
CHARLIE LAU
MILWAUKEE BRAVES — CATCHER
312

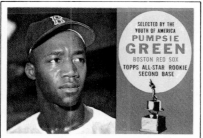
TURK LOWN
CHICAGO WHITE SOX — PITCHER
313

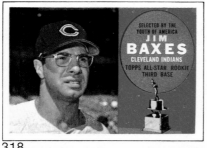
CHICO FERNANDEZ
DETROIT TIGERS — SHORTSTOP
314

BOBBY SHANTZ
NEW YORK YANKEES — PITCHER
315

SELECTED BY THE YOUTH OF AMERICA
WILLIE McCOVEY
SAN FRANCISCO GIANTS
TOPPS ALL-STAR ROOKIE
FIRST BASE
316

SELECTED BY THE YOUTH OF AMERICA
PUMPSIE GREEN
BOSTON RED SOX
TOPPS ALL-STAR ROOKIE
SECOND BASE
317

SELECTED BY THE YOUTH OF AMERICA
JIM BAXES
CLEVELAND INDIANS
TOPPS ALL-STAR ROOKIE
THIRD BASE
318

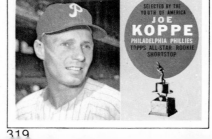
SELECTED BY THE YOUTH OF AMERICA
JOE KOPPE
PHILADELPHIA PHILLIES
TOPPS ALL-STAR ROOKIE
SHORTSTOP
319

SELECTED BY THE YOUTH OF AMERICA
BOB ALLISON
WASHINGTON SENATORS
TOPPS ALL-STAR ROOKIE
OUTFIELD
320

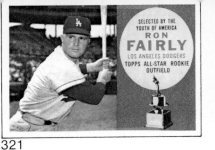
321

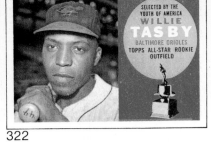
322

323

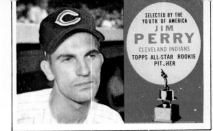
324

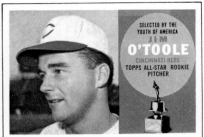
325

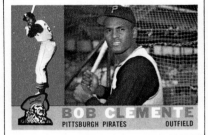
326

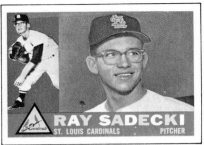
327

328

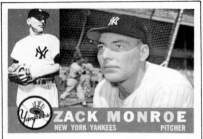
329

330

331

332

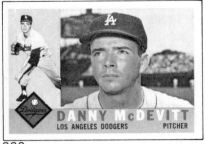
333

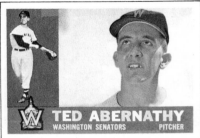
334

335

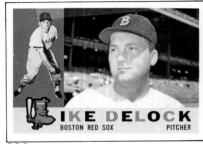
336

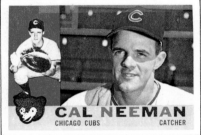
337

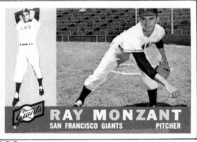
338

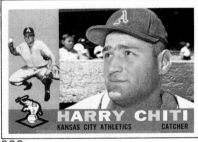
339

340

341

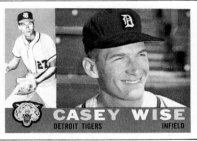
342

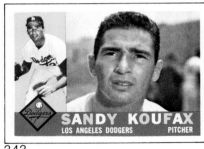
343

344

345

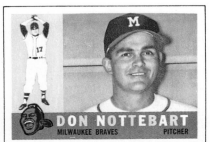
346

347

348

349

350

351

352

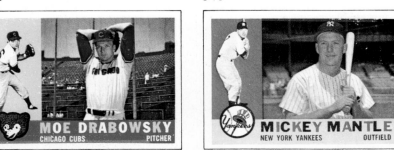

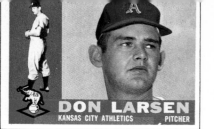
DON LARSEN
KANSAS CITY ATHLETICS PITCHER
353

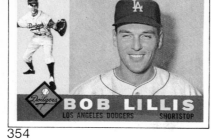
BOB LILLIS
LOS ANGELES DODGERS SHORTSTOP
354

BILL WHITE
ST. LOUIS CARDINALS OUTFIELD-1st BASE
355

JOE AMALFITANO
SAN FRANCISCO GIANTS INFIELD
356

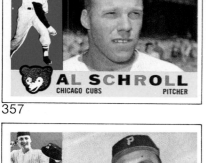
AL SCHROLL
CHICAGO CUBS PITCHER
357

JOE DE MAESTRI
NEW YORK YANKEES SHORTSTOP
358

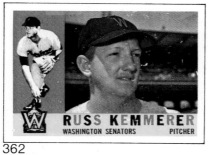
BUDDY GILBERT
CINCINNATI REDS OUTFIELD
359

HERB SCORE
CLEVELAND INDIANS PITCHER
360

BOB OLDIS
PITTSBURGH PIRATES CATCHER
361

RUSS KEMMERER
WASHINGTON SENATORS PITCHER
362

GENE STEPHENS
BOSTON RED SOX OUTFIELD
363

PAUL FOYTACK
DETROIT TIGERS PITCHER
364

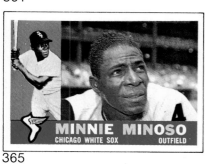
MINNIE MINOSO
CHICAGO WHITE SOX OUTFIELD
365

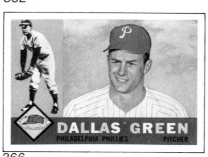
DALLAS GREEN
PHILADELPHIA PHILLIES PITCHER
366

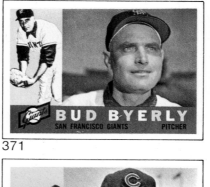
BILL TUTTLE
KANSAS CITY ATHLETICS OUTFIELD
367

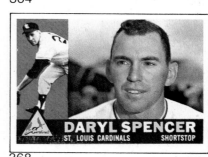
DARYL SPENCER
ST. LOUIS CARDINALS SHORTSTOP
368

BILLY HOEFT
BALTIMORE ORIOLES PITCHER
369

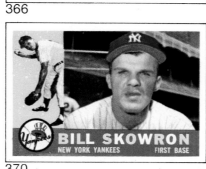
BILL SKOWRON
NEW YORK YANKEES FIRST BASE
370

BUD BYERLY
SAN FRANCISCO GIANTS PITCHER
371

FRANK HOUSE
CINCINNATI REDS CATCHER
372

DON HOAK
PITTSBURGH PIRATES THIRD BASE
373

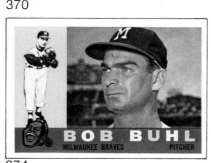
BOB BUHL
MILWAUKEE BRAVES PITCHER
374

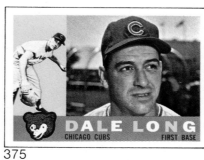
DALE LONG
CHICAGO CUBS FIRST BASE
375

JOHNNY BRIGGS
CLEVELAND INDIANS PITCHER
376

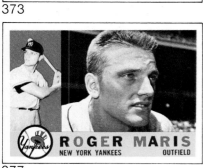
ROGER MARIS
NEW YORK YANKEES OUTFIELD
377

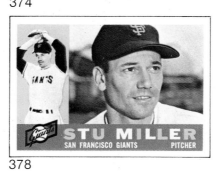
STU MILLER
SAN FRANCISCO GIANTS PITCHER
378

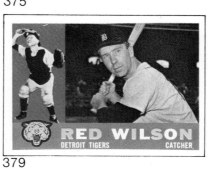
RED WILSON
DETROIT TIGERS CATCHER
379

BOB SHAW
CHICAGO WHITE SOX PITCHER
380

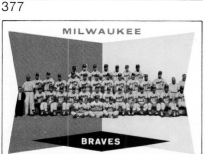
MILWAUKEE

BRAVES
381

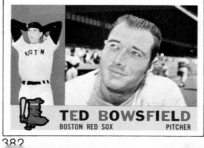
TED BOWSFIELD
BOSTON RED SOX PITCHER
382

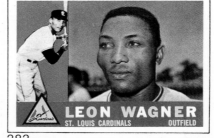
LEON WAGNER
ST. LOUIS CARDINALS OUTFIELD
383

DON CARDWELL
PHILADELPHIA PHILLIES PITCHER
384

1959 WORLD SERIES GAME #1 SOX 11—L.A. 0 **NEAL STEALS SECOND**
385

1959 WORLD SERIES GAME #2 L.A. 4—SOX 3 **NEAL BELTS 2nd HOMER**
386

1959 WORLD SERIES GAME #3 L.A. 3—SOX 1 **FURILLO BREAKS UP GAME**
387

1959 WORLD SERIES GAME #4 L.A. 5—SOX 4 **HODGES' WINNING HOMER**
388

1959 WORLD SERIES GAME #5 SOX 1—L.A. 0 **LUIS SWIPES BASE**
389

1959 WORLD SERIES GAME #6 L.A. 9—SOX 3 **SCRAMBLING AFTER BALL**
390

1959 WORLD SERIES **THE CHAMPS CELEBRATE**
391

TEX CLEVENGER WASHINGTON SENATORS PITCHER
392

SMOKY BURGESS PITTSBURGH PIRATES CATCHER
393

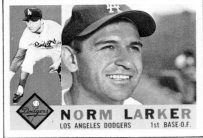
NORM LARKER LOS ANGELES DODGERS 1st BASE-O.F.
394

HOYT WILHELM BALTIMORE ORIOLES PITCHER
395

STEVE BILKO DETROIT TIGERS FIRST BASE
396

DON BLASINGAME SAN FRANCISCO GIANTS SECOND BASE
397

MIKE CUELLAR CINCINNATI REDS PITCHER
398

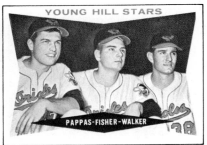
YOUNG HILL STARS **PAPPAS-FISHER-WALKER**
399

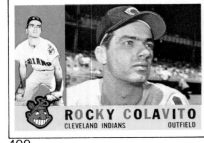
ROCKY COLAVITO CLEVELAND INDIANS OUTFIELD
400

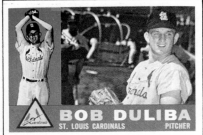
BOB DULIBA ST. LOUIS CARDINALS PITCHER
401

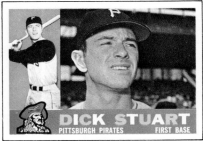
DICK STUART PITTSBURGH PIRATES FIRST BASE
402

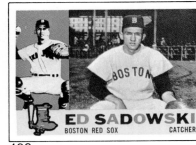
ED SADOWSKI BOSTON RED SOX CATCHER
403

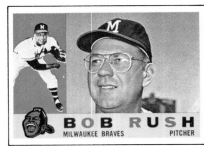
BOB RUSH MILWAUKEE BRAVES PITCHER
404

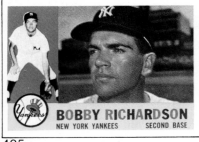
BOBBY RICHARDSON NEW YORK YANKEES SECOND BASE
405

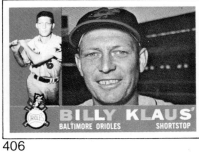
BILLY KLAUS BALTIMORE ORIOLES SHORTSTOP
406

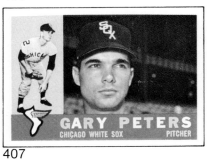
GARY PETERS CHICAGO WHITE SOX PITCHER
407

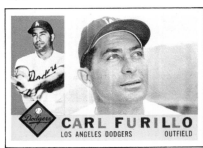
CARL FURILLO LOS ANGELES DODGERS OUTFIELD
408

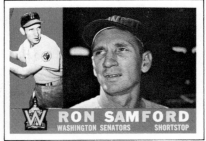
RON SAMFORD WASHINGTON SENATORS SHORTSTOP
409

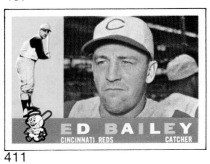
SAM JONES SAN FRANCISCO GIANTS PITCHER
410

ED BAILEY CINCINNATI REDS CATCHER
411

BOB ANDERSON CHICAGO CUBS PITCHER
412

KANSAS CITY **ATHLETICS**
413

DON WILLIAMS PITTSBURGH PIRATES PITCHER
414

BOB CERV KANSAS CITY ATHLETICS OUTFIELD
415

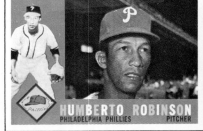
HUMBERTO ROBINSON PHILADELPHIA PHILLIES PITCHER
416

CHUCK COTTIER
MILWAUKEE BRAVES   SECOND BASE
417

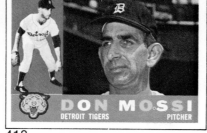
DON MOSSI
DETROIT TIGERS   PITCHER
418

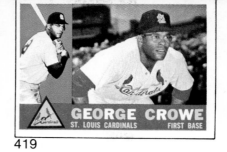
GEORGE CROWE
ST. LOUIS CARDINALS   FIRST BASE
419

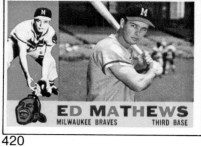
ED MATHEWS
MILWAUKEE BRAVES   THIRD BASE
420

DUKE MAAS
NEW YORK YANKEES   PITCHER
421

JOHNNY POWERS
BALTIMORE ORIOLES   OUTFIELD
422

ED FITZGERALD
CLEVELAND INDIANS   CATCHER
423

PETE WHISENANT
CINCINNATI REDS   OUTFIELD
424

JOHNNY PODRES
LOS ANGELES DODGERS   PITCHER
425

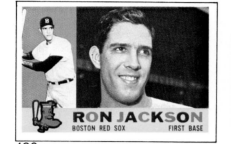
RON JACKSON
BOSTON RED SOX   FIRST BASE
426

AL GRUNWALD
KANSAS CITY ATHLETICS   PITCHER
427

AL SMITH
CHICAGO WHITE SOX   OUTFIELD
428

AMERICAN LEAGUE KINGS

FOX-KUENN
429

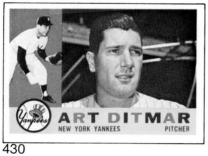
ART DITMAR
NEW YORK YANKEES   PITCHER
430

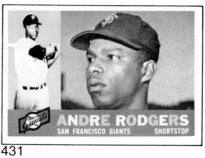
ANDRE RODGERS
SAN FRANCISCO GIANTS   SHORTSTOP
431

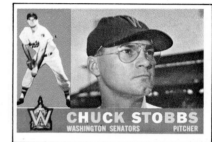
CHUCK STOBBS
WASHINGTON SENATORS   PITCHER
432

IRV NOREN
CHICAGO CUBS   OUTFIELD
433

BROOKS LAWRENCE
CINCINNATI REDS   PITCHER
434

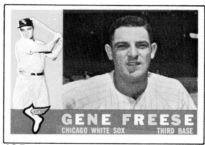
GENE FREESE
CHICAGO WHITE SOX   THIRD BASE
435

MARV THRONEBERRY
KANSAS CITY ATHLETICS   FIRST BASE
436

BOB FRIEND
PITTSBURGH PIRATES   PITCHER
437

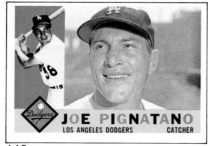
JIM COKER
PHILADELPHIA PHILLIES   CATCHER
438

TOM BREWER
BOSTON RED SOX   PITCHER
439

JIM LEMON
WASHINGTON SENATORS   OUTFIELD
440

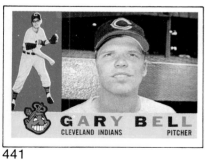
GARY BELL
CLEVELAND INDIANS   PITCHER
441

JOE PIGNATANO
LOS ANGELES DODGERS   CATCHER
442

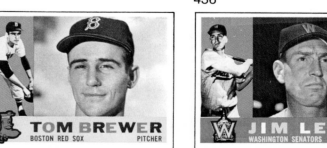
CHARLIE MAXWELL
DETROIT TIGERS   OUTFIELD
443

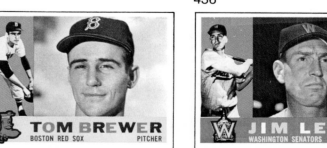
JERRY KINDALL
CHICAGO CUBS   INFIELD
444

WARREN SPAHN
MILWAUKEE BRAVES   PITCHER
445

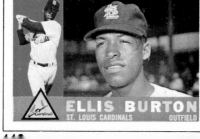
ELLIS BURTON
ST. LOUIS CARDINALS   OUTFIELD

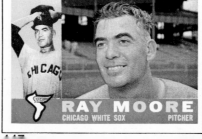
RAY MOORE
CHICAGO WHITE SOX   PITCHER

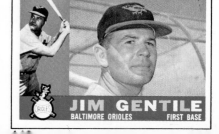
JIM GENTILE
BALTIMORE ORIOLES   FIRST BASE

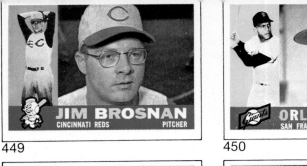
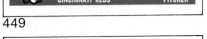
JIM BROSNAN
CINCINNATI REDS — PITCHER
449

ORLANDO CEPEDA
SAN FRANCISCO GIANTS — FIRST BASE
450

CURT SIMMONS
PHILADELPHIA PHILLIES — PITCHER
451

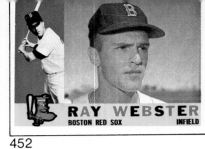
RAY WEBSTER
BOSTON RED SOX — INFIELD
452

VERN LAW
PITTSBURGH PIRATES — PITCHER
453

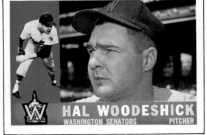
HAL WOODESHICK
WASHINGTON SENATORS — PITCHER
454

ROBINSON / HARRIS / BRECHEEN
BALTIMORE ORIOLES COACHES
455

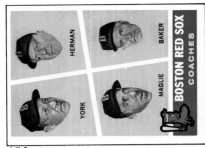
HERMAN / BAKER / YORK / MAGLIE
BOSTON RED SOX COACHES
456

ROOT / TAPPE / KLEIN
CHICAGO CUBS COACHES
457

GUTTERIDGE / BERRES / CUCCINELLO / COONEY
CHICAGO WHITE SOX COACHES
458

OTERO / MOSES / DEAL
CINCINNATI REDS COACHES
459

WHITE / KRESS / HARDER / LEMON
CLEVELAND INDIANS COACHES
460

FERRICK / HITCHCOCK / APPLING
DETROIT TIGERS COACHES
461

FITZSIMMONS / COOPER / HEFFNER
KANSAS CITY A's COACHES
462

REISER / MULLEAVY / BRAGAN / BECKER
L. A. DODGERS COACHES
463

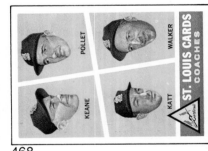
WYATT / MYATT / SCHEFFING / PAFKO
MILWAUKEE BRAVES COACHES
464

HOUK / LOPAT / DICKEY / CROSETTI
N. Y. YANKEES COACHES
465

SILVESTRI / COHEN / CARTER
PHILA. PHILS COACHES
466

OCEAK / BURWELL / VERNON / NARRON
PITTS. PIRATES COACHES
467

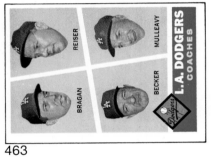
POLLET / WALKER / KEANE / KATT
ST. LOUIS CARDS COACHES
468

WESTRUM / POSEDEL / PARKER
SAN FRAN. GIANTS COACHES
469

SWIFT / MELE / CLARY
WASH. SENATORS COACHES
470

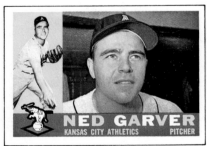
NED GARVER
KANSAS CITY ATHLETICS — PITCHER
471

AL DARK
PHILADELPHIA PHILLIES — THIRD BASE
472

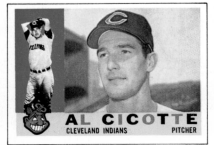
AL CICOTTE
CLEVELAND INDIANS — PITCHER
473

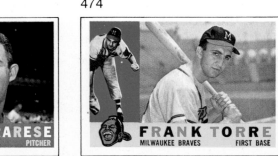
HAYWOOD SULLIVAN
BOSTON RED SOX — CATCHER
474

DON DRYSDALE
LOS ANGELES DODGERS — PITCHER
475

LOU JOHNSON
CHICAGO CUBS — OUTFIELD
476

DON FERRARESE
CHICAGO WHITE SOX — PITCHER

FRANK TORRE
MILWAUKEE BRAVES — FIRST BASE

GEORGES MARANDA
SAN FRANCISCO GIANTS — PITCHER

YOGI BERRA
NEW YORK YANKEES — CATCHER

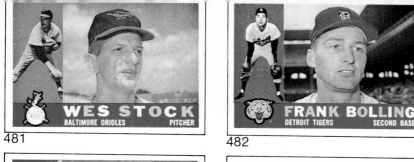
WES STOCK — BALTIMORE ORIOLES — PITCHER
481

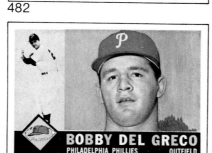
FRANK BOLLING — DETROIT TIGERS — SECOND BASE
482

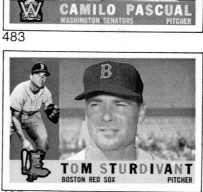
CAMILO PASCUAL — WASHINGTON SENATORS — PITCHER
483

PITTSBURGH — **PIRATES**
484

KEN BOYER — ST. LOUIS CARDINALS — THIRD BASE
485

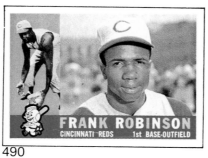
BOBBY DEL GRECO — PHILADELPHIA PHILLIES — OUTFIELD
486

TOM STURDIVANT — BOSTON RED SOX — PITCHER
487

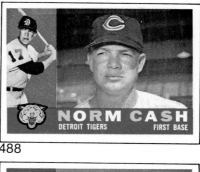
NORM CASH — DETROIT TIGERS — FIRST BASE
488

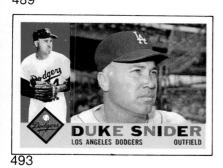
STEVE RIDZIK — CHICAGO CUBS — PITCHER
489

FRANK ROBINSON — CINCINNATI REDS — 1st BASE-OUTFIELD
490

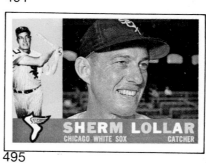
MEL ROACH — MILWAUKEE BRAVES — 2nd BASE-OUTFIELD
491

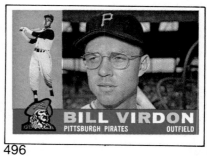
LARRY JACKSON — ST. LOUIS CARDINALS — PITCHER
492

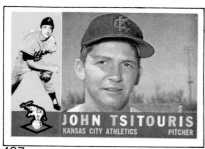
DUKE SNIDER — LOS ANGELES DODGERS — OUTFIELD
493

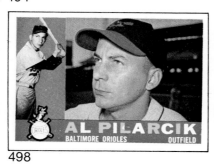
BALTIMORE — **ORIOLES**
494

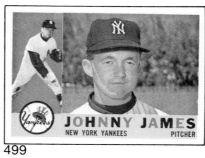
SHERM LOLLAR — CHICAGO WHITE SOX — CATCHER
495

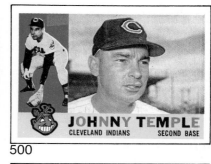
BILL VIRDON — PITTSBURGH PIRATES — OUTFIELD
496

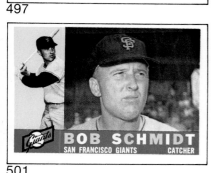
JOHN TSITOURIS — KANSAS CITY ATHLETICS — PITCHER
497

AL PILARCIK — BALTIMORE ORIOLES — OUTFIELD
498

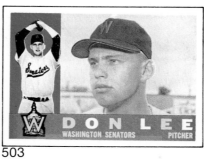
JOHNNY JAMES — NEW YORK YANKEES — PITCHER
499

JOHNNY TEMPLE — CLEVELAND INDIANS — SECOND BASE
500

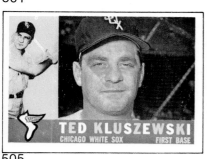
BOB SCHMIDT — SAN FRANCISCO GIANTS — CATCHER
501

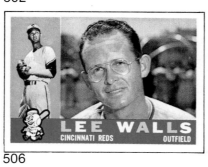
JIM BUNNING — DETROIT TIGERS — PITCHER
502

DON LEE — WASHINGTON SENATORS — PITCHER
503

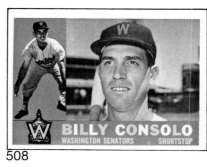
SETH MOREHEAD — CHICAGO CUBS — PITCHER
504

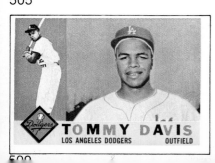
TED KLUSZEWSKI — CHICAGO WHITE SOX — FIRST BASE
505

LEE WALLS — CINCINNATI REDS — OUTFIELD
506

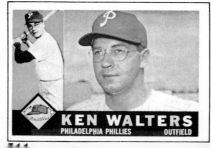
DICK STIGMAN — CLEVELAND INDIANS — PITCHER
507

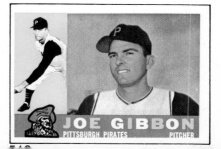
BILLY CONSOLO — WASHINGTON SENATORS — SHORTSTOP
508

TOMMY DAVIS — LOS ANGELES DODGERS — OUTFIELD
509

JERRY STALEY — CHICAGO WHITE SOX — PITCHER
510

KEN WALTERS — PHILADELPHIA PHILLIES — OUTFIELD
511

JOE GIBBON — PITTSBURGH PIRATES — PITCHER
512

513

514
STEVE BARBER
BALTIMORE ORIOLES PITCHER

515
STAN LOPATA
MILWAUKEE BRAVES CATCHER

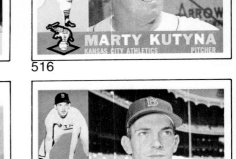
516
MARTY KUTYNA
KANSAS CITY ATHLETICS PITCHER

517
CHARLEY JAMES
ST. LOUIS CARDINALS OUTFIELD

518
TONY GONZALEZ
CINCINNATI REDS OUTFIELD

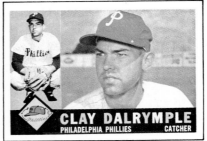
519
ED ROEBUCK
LOS ANGELES DODGERS PITCHER

520
DON BUDDIN
BOSTON RED SOX SHORTSTOP

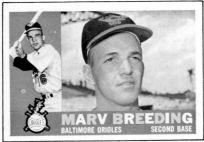
521
MIKE LEE
CLEVELAND INDIANS PITCHER

522
KEN HUNT
NEW YORK YANKEES OUTFIELD

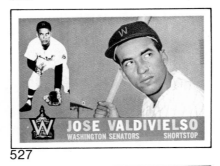
523
CLAY DALRYMPLE
PHILADELPHIA PHILLIES CATCHER

524
BILL HENRY
CINCINNATI REDS PITCHER

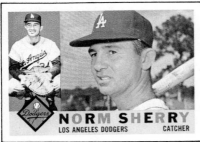
525
MARV BREEDING
BALTIMORE ORIOLES SECOND BASE

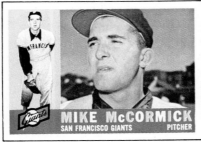
526
PAUL GIEL
PITTSBURGH PIRATES PITCHER

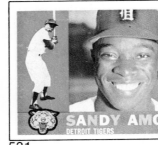
527
JOSE VALDIVIELSO
WASHINGTON SENATORS SHORTSTOP

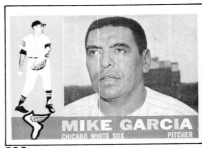
528
BEN JOHNSON
CHICAGO CUBS PITCHER

529
NORM SHERRY
LOS ANGELES DODGERS CATCHER

530
MIKE McCORMICK
SAN FRANCISCO GIANTS PITCHER

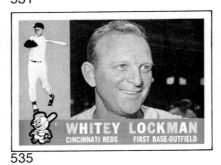
531
SANDY AMOROS
DETROIT TIGERS OUTFIELD

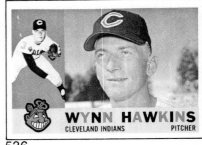
532
MIKE GARCIA
CHICAGO WHITE SOX PITCHER

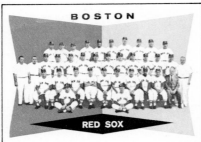
533
LU CLINTON
BOSTON RED SOX OUTFIELD

534
KEN MacKENZIE
MILWAUKEE BRAVES PITCHER

535
WHITEY LOCKMAN
CINCINNATI REDS FIRST BASE-OUTFIELD

536
WYNN HAWKINS
CLEVELAND INDIANS PITCHER

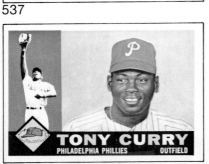
537

538
FRANK BARNES
CHICAGO WHITE SOX PITCHER

539
GENE BAKER
PITTSBURGH PIRATES INFIELD

540
JERRY WALKER
BALTIMORE ORIOLES PITCHER

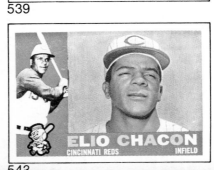
541
TONY CURRY
PHILADELPHIA PHILLIES OUTFIELD

542
KEN HAMLIN
KANSAS CITY ATHLETICS SHORTSTOP

543
ELIO CHACON
CINCINNATI REDS INFIELD

544
BILL MONBOUQUETTE
BOSTON RED SOX PITCHER

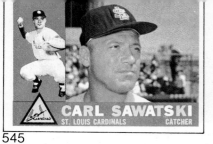

CARL SAWATSKI
ST. LOUIS CARDINALS   CATCHER

545

HANK AGUIRRE
DETROIT TIGERS   PITCHER

546

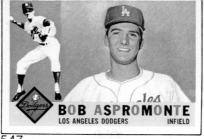

BOB ASPROMONTE
LOS ANGELES DODGERS   INFIELD

547

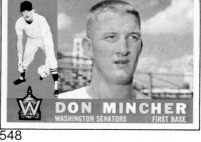

DON MINCHER
WASHINGTON SENATORS   FIRST BASE

548

JOHN BUZHARDT
PHILADELPHIA PHILLIES   PITCHER

549

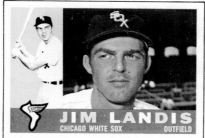

JIM LANDIS
CHICAGO WHITE SOX   OUTFIELD

550

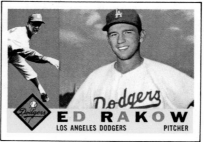

ED RAKOW
LOS ANGELES DODGERS   PITCHER

551

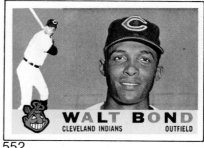

WALT BOND
CLEVELAND INDIANS   OUTFIELD

552

SPORT MAGAZINE '60 ALL-STAR SELECTION
BILL SKOWRON   1st Base/American League

553

SPORT MAGAZINE '60 ALL-STAR SELECTION
WILLIE McCOVEY   1st Base/National League

554

SPORT MAGAZINE '60 ALL-STAR SELECTION
NELLIE FOX   2nd Base/American League

555

SPORT MAGAZINE '60 ALL-STAR SELECTION
CHARLIE NEAL   2nd Base/National League

556

SPORT MAGAZINE '60 ALL-STAR SELECTION
FRANK MALZONE   3rd Base/American League

557

SPORT MAGAZINE '60 ALL-STAR SELECTION
EDDIE MATHEWS   3rd Base/National League

558

SPORT MAGAZINE '60 ALL-STAR SELECTION
LUIS APARICIO   Shortstop/American League

559

SPORT MAGAZINE '60 ALL-STAR SELECTION
ERNIE BANKS   Shortstop/National League

560

SPORT MAGAZINE '60 ALL-STAR SELECTION
AL KALINE   Outfield/American League

561

SPORT MAGAZINE '60 ALL-STAR SELECTION
JOE CUNNINGHAM   Outfield/National League

562

SPORT MAGAZINE '60 ALL-STAR SELECTION
MICKEY MANTLE   Outfield/American League

563

SPORT MAGAZINE '60 ALL-STAR SELECTION
WILLIE MAYS   Outfield/National League

564

SPORT MAGAZINE '60 ALL-STAR SELECTION
ROGER MARIS   Outfield/American League

565

SPORT MAGAZINE '60 ALL-STAR SELECTION
HANK AARON   Outfield/National League

566

SPORT MAGAZINE '60 ALL-STAR SELECTION
SHERM LOLLAR   Catcher/American League

567

SPORT MAGAZINE '60 ALL-STAR SELECTION
DEL CRANDALL   Catcher/National League

568

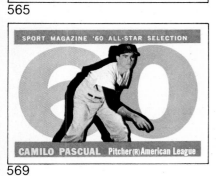

SPORT MAGAZINE '60 ALL-STAR SELECTION
CAMILO PASCUAL   Pitcher (R)/American League

569

SPORT MAGAZINE '60 ALL-STAR SELECTION
DON DRYSDALE   Pitcher (R)/National League

570

SPORT MAGAZINE '60 ALL-STAR SELECTION
BILLY PIERCE   Pitcher (L)/American League

571

SPORT MAGAZINE '60 ALL-STAR SELECTION
JOHNNY ANTONELLI   Pitcher (L)/National League

572

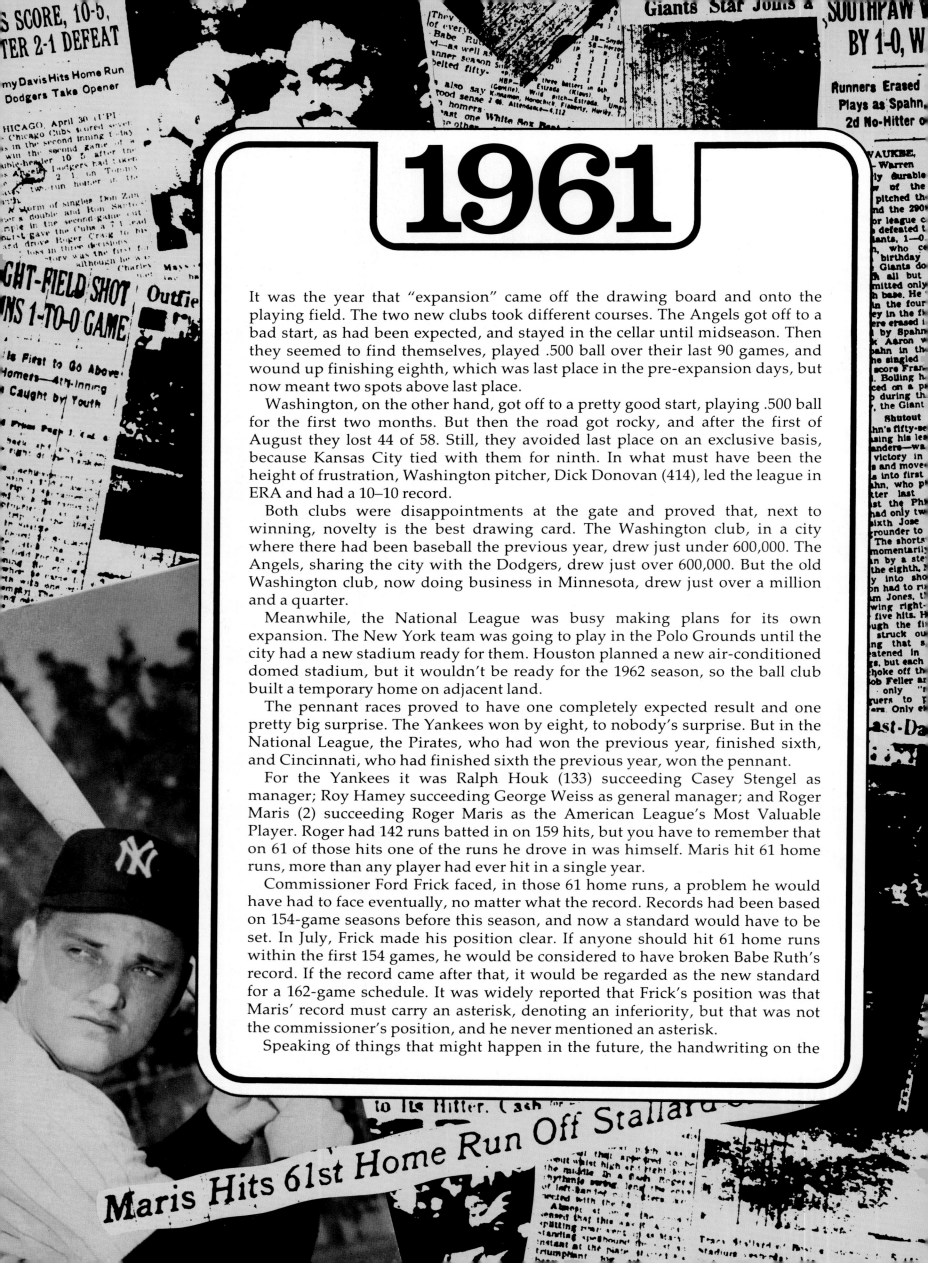

1961

It was the year that "expansion" came off the drawing board and onto the playing field. The two new clubs took different courses. The Angels got off to a bad start, as had been expected, and stayed in the cellar until midseason. Then they seemed to find themselves, played .500 ball over their last 90 games, and wound up finishing eighth, which was last place in the pre-expansion days, but now meant two spots above last place.

Washington, on the other hand, got off to a pretty good start, playing .500 ball for the first two months. But then the road got rocky, and after the first of August they lost 44 of 58. Still, they avoided last place on an exclusive basis, because Kansas City tied with them for ninth. In what must have been the height of frustration, Washington pitcher, Dick Donovan (414), led the league in ERA and had a 10–10 record.

Both clubs were disappointments at the gate and proved that, next to winning, novelty is the best drawing card. The Washington club, in a city where there had been baseball the previous year, drew just under 600,000. The Angels, sharing the city with the Dodgers, drew just over 600,000. But the old Washington club, now doing business in Minnesota, drew just over a million and a quarter.

Meanwhile, the National League was busy making plans for its own expansion. The New York team was going to play in the Polo Grounds until the city had a new stadium ready for them. Houston planned a new air-conditioned domed stadium, but it wouldn't be ready for the 1962 season, so the ball club built a temporary home on adjacent land.

The pennant races proved to have one completely expected result and one pretty big surprise. The Yankees won by eight, to nobody's surprise. But in the National League, the Pirates, who had won the previous year, finished sixth, and Cincinnati, who had finished sixth the previous year, won the pennant.

For the Yankees it was Ralph Houk (133) succeeding Casey Stengel as manager; Roy Hamey succeeding George Weiss as general manager; and Roger Maris (2) succeeding Roger Maris as the American League's Most Valuable Player. Roger had 142 runs batted in on 159 hits, but you have to remember that on 61 of those hits one of the runs he drove in was himself. Maris hit 61 home runs, more than any player had ever hit in a single year.

Commissioner Ford Frick faced, in those 61 home runs, a problem he would have had to face eventually, no matter what the record. Records had been based on 154-game seasons before this season, and now a standard would have to be set. In July, Frick made his position clear. If anyone should hit 61 home runs within the first 154 games, he would be considered to have broken Babe Ruth's record. If the record came after that, it would be regarded as the new standard for a 162-game schedule. It was widely reported that Frick's position was that Maris' record must carry an asterisk, denoting an inferiority, but that was not the commissioner's position, and he never mentioned an asterisk.

Speaking of things that might happen in the future, the handwriting on the

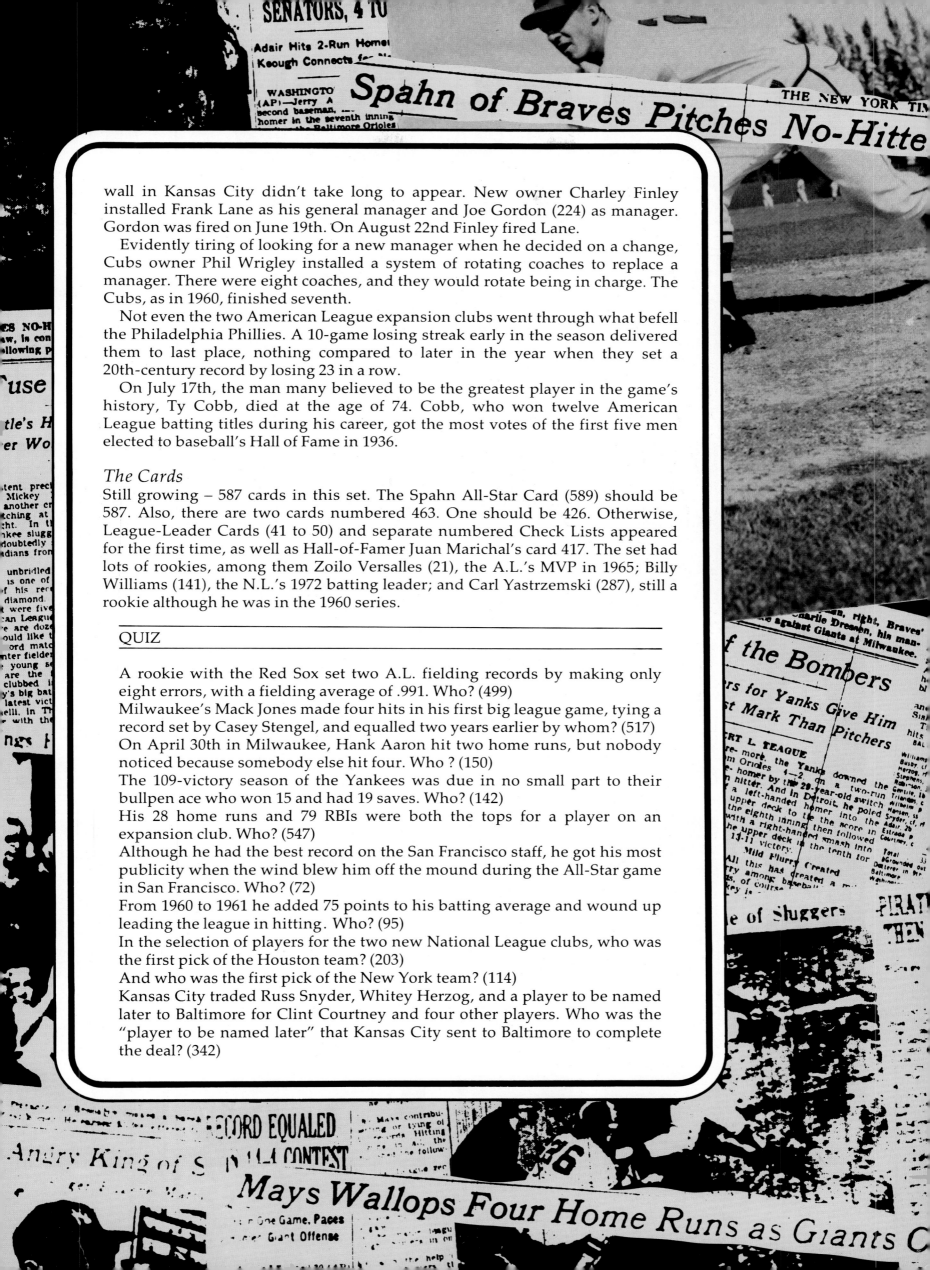

wall in Kansas City didn't take long to appear. New owner Charley Finley installed Frank Lane as his general manager and Joe Gordon (224) as manager. Gordon was fired on June 19th. On August 22nd Finley fired Lane.

Evidently tiring of looking for a new manager when he decided on a change, Cubs owner Phil Wrigley installed a system of rotating coaches to replace a manager. There were eight coaches, and they would rotate being in charge. The Cubs, as in 1960, finished seventh.

Not even the two American League expansion clubs went through what befell the Philadelphia Phillies. A 10-game losing streak early in the season delivered them to last place, nothing compared to later in the year when they set a 20th-century record by losing 23 in a row.

On July 17th, the man many believed to be the greatest player in the game's history, Ty Cobb, died at the age of 74. Cobb, who won twelve American League batting titles during his career, got the most votes of the first five men elected to baseball's Hall of Fame in 1936.

The Cards

Still growing – 587 cards in this set. The Spahn All-Star Card (589) should be 587. Also, there are two cards numbered 463. One should be 426. Otherwise, League-Leader Cards (41 to 50) and separate numbered Check Lists appeared for the first time, as well as Hall-of-Famer Juan Marichal's card 417. The set had lots of rookies, among them Zoilo Versalles (21), the A.L.'s MVP in 1965; Billy Williams (141), the N.L.'s 1972 batting leader; and Carl Yastrzemski (287), still a rookie although he was in the 1960 series.

QUIZ

A rookie with the Red Sox set two A.L. fielding records by making only eight errors, with a fielding average of .991. Who? (499)

Milwaukee's Mack Jones made four hits in his first big league game, tying a record set by Casey Stengel, and equalled two years earlier by whom? (517)

On April 30th in Milwaukee, Hank Aaron hit two home runs, but nobody noticed because somebody else hit four. Who ? (150)

The 109-victory season of the Yankees was due in no small part to their bullpen ace who won 15 and had 19 saves. Who? (142)

His 28 home runs and 79 RBIs were both the tops for a player on an expansion club. Who? (547)

Although he had the best record on the San Francisco staff, he got his most publicity when the wind blew him off the mound during the All-Star game in San Francisco. Who? (72)

From 1960 to 1961 he added 75 points to his batting average and wound up leading the league in hitting. Who? (95)

In the selection of players for the two new National League clubs, who was the first pick of the Houston team? (203)

And who was the first pick of the New York team? (114)

Kansas City traded Russ Snyder, Whitey Herzog, and a player to be named later to Baltimore for Clint Courtney and four other players. Who was the "player to be named later" that Kansas City sent to Baltimore to complete the deal? (342)

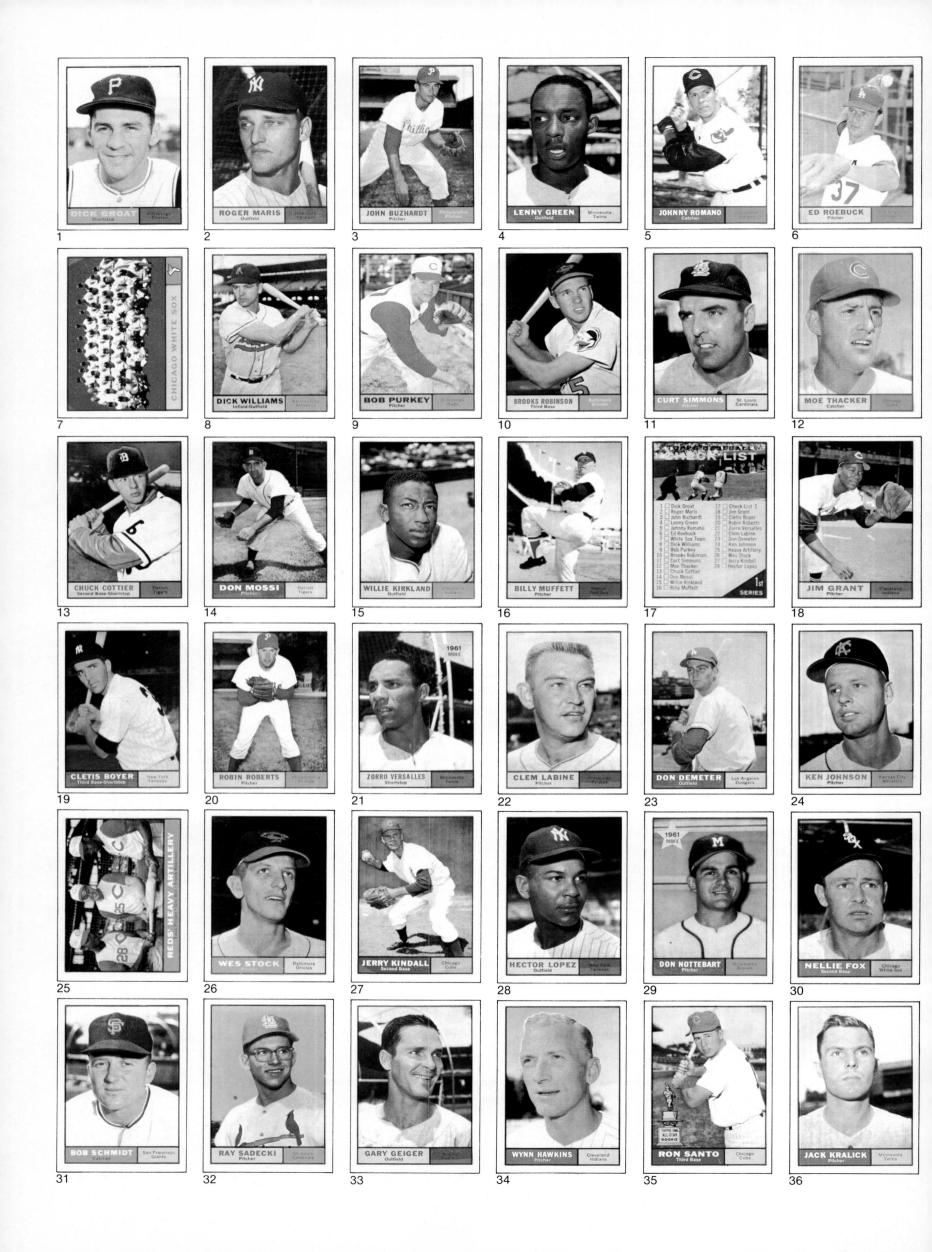

37 CHARLIE MAXWELL — Outfield — Detroit Tigers

38 BOB LILLIS — Shortstop — Los Angeles Dodgers

39 LEO POSADA — Outfield — Kansas City Athletics

40 BOB TURLEY — Pitcher

41 NATIONAL LEAGUE 1960 BATTING LEADERS

42 AMERICAN LEAGUE 1960 BATTING LEADERS

43 NATIONAL LEAGUE 1960 HOME RUN LEADERS

44 AMERICAN LEAGUE 1960 HOME RUN LEADERS

45 NATIONAL LEAGUE 1960 E.R.A. LEADERS

46 AMERICAN LEAGUE 1960 E.R.A. LEADERS

47 NATIONAL LEAGUE 1960 PITCHING LEADERS GAMES WON

48 AMERICAN LEAGUE 1960 PITCHING LEADERS GAMES WON

49 NATIONAL LEAGUE 1960 STRIKEOUT LEADERS

50 AMERICAN LEAGUE 1960 STRIKEOUT LEADERS

51 DETROIT TIGERS

52 GEORGE CROWE — First Base — St. Louis Cardinals

53 RUSS NIXON — Catcher — Boston Red Sox

54 EARL FRANCIS — Pitcher — Pittsburgh Pirates

55 JIM DAVENPORT — Third Base — San Francisco Giants

56 RUSS KEMMERER — Pitcher — Chicago White Sox

57 MARV THRONEBERRY — First Base — Kansas City Athletics

58 JOE SCHAFFERNOTH — Pitcher — Chicago Cubs

59 JIM WOODS — Third Base — Philadelphia Phillies

60 WOODIE HELD — Shortstop — Cleveland Indians

61 RON PICHE — Pitcher — Milwaukee Braves

62 AL PILARCIK — Outfield — Baltimore Orioles

63 JIM KAAT — Pitcher — Minnesota Twins

64 ALEX GRAMMAS — Second Base-Shortstop — St. Louis Cardinals

65 TED KLUSZEWSKI — First Base — Los Angeles Angels

66 BILL HENRY — Pitcher — Cincinnati Reds

67 OSSIE VIRGIL — Third Base — Detroit Tigers

68 DERON JOHNSON — Third Base-Outfield — New York Yankees

69 EARL WILSON — Pitcher — Boston Red Sox

70 BILL VIRDON — Outfield — Pittsburgh Pirates

71 JERRY ADAIR — Second Base-Shortstop — Baltimore Orioles

72 STU MILLER — Pitcher — San Francisco Giants

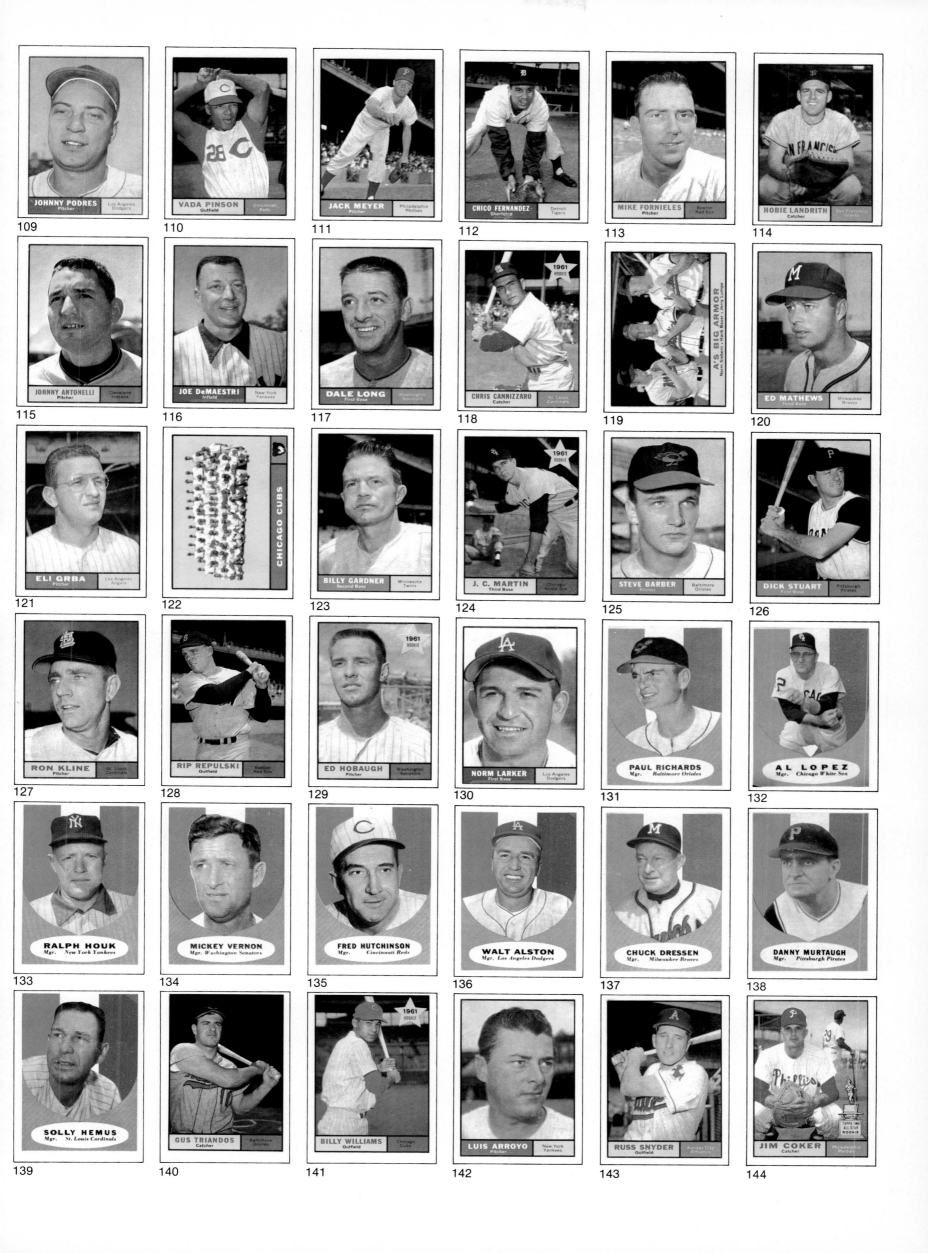

JOHNNY PODRES — Pitcher, Los Angeles Dodgers	VADA PINSON — Outfield, Cincinnati Reds	JACK MEYER — Pitcher, Philadelphia Phillies	CHICO FERNANDEZ — Shortstop, Detroit Tigers	MIKE FORNIELES — Pitcher, Boston Red Sox	HOBIE LANDRITH — Catcher, San Francisco Giants
109	110	111	112	113	114
JOHNNY ANTONELLI — Pitcher, Cleveland Indians	JOE DeMAESTRI — Infield, New York Yankees	DALE LONG — First Base, Washington Senators	CHRIS CANNIZZARO — Catcher, St. Louis Cardinals	A'S BIG ARMOR — Norm Siebern, Hank Bauer, Jerry Lumpe	ED MATHEWS — Third Base, Milwaukee Braves
115	116	117	118	119	120
ELI GRBA — Pitcher, Los Angeles Angels	CHICAGO CUBS	BILLY GARDNER — Second Base, Minnesota Twins	J. C. MARTIN — Third Base, Chicago White Sox	STEVE BARBER — Pitcher, Baltimore Orioles	DICK STUART — First Base, Pittsburgh Pirates
121	122	123	124	125	126
RON KLINE — Pitcher, St. Louis Cardinals	RIP REPULSKI — Outfield, Boston Red Sox	ED HOBAUGH — Pitcher, Washington Senators	NORM LARKER — First Base, Los Angeles Dodgers	PAUL RICHARDS — Mgr., Baltimore Orioles	AL LOPEZ — Mgr., Chicago White Sox
127	128	129	130	131	132
RALPH HOUK — Mgr., New York Yankees	MICKEY VERNON — Mgr., Washington Senators	FRED HUTCHINSON — Mgr., Cincinnati Reds	WALT ALSTON — Mgr., Los Angeles Dodgers	CHUCK DRESSEN — Mgr., Milwaukee Braves	DANNY MURTAUGH — Mgr., Pittsburgh Pirates
133	134	135	136	137	138
SOLLY HEMUS — Mgr., St. Louis Cardinals	GUS TRIANDOS — Catcher, Baltimore Orioles	BILLY WILLIAMS — Outfield, Chicago Cubs	LUIS ARROYO — Pitcher, New York Yankees	RUSS SNYDER — Outfield, Kansas City Athletics	JIM COKER — Catcher, Philadelphia Phillies
139	140	141	142	143	144

145 · 146 · 147 · 148 · 149 · 150
151 · 152 · 153 · 154 · 155 · 156
157 · 158 · 159 · 160 · 161 · 162
163 · 164 · 165 · 166 · 167 · 168
169 · 170 · 171 · 172 · 173 · 174
175 · 176 · 177 · 178 · 179 · 180

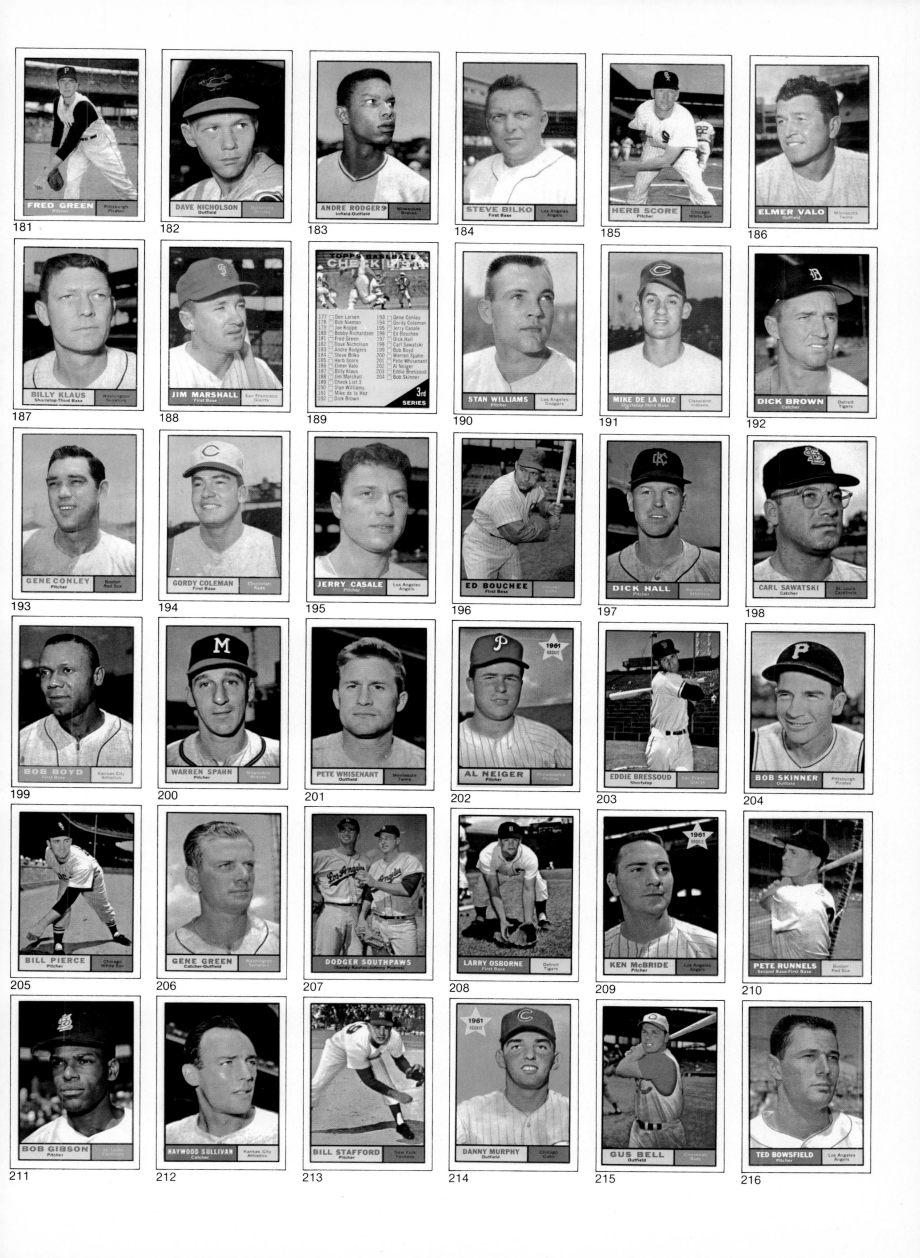

181 FRED GREEN — Pitcher — Pittsburgh Pirates

182 DAVE NICHOLSON — Outfield — Baltimore Orioles

183 ANDRE RODGERS — Infield-Outfield — Milwaukee Braves

184 STEVE BILKO — First Base — Los Angeles Angels

185 HERB SCORE — Pitcher — Chicago White Sox

186 ELMER VALO — Outfield — Minnesota Twins

187 BILLY KLAUS — Shortstop-Third Base — Washington Senators

188 JIM MARSHALL — First Base — San Francisco Giants

189 TOPPS BASEBALL CHECK LIST — 3rd SERIES

190 STAN WILLIAMS — Pitcher — Los Angeles Dodgers

191 MIKE DE LA HOZ — Shortstop-Third Base — Cleveland Indians

192 DICK BROWN — Catcher — Detroit Tigers

193 GENE CONLEY — Pitcher — Boston Red Sox

194 GORDY COLEMAN — First Base — Cincinnati Reds

195 JERRY CASALE — Pitcher — Los Angeles Angels

196 ED BOUCHEE — First Base — Chicago Cubs

197 DICK HALL — Pitcher — Kansas City Athletics

198 CARL SAWATSKI — Catcher — St. Louis Cardinals

199 BOB BOYD — First Base — Kansas City Athletics

200 WARREN SPAHN — Pitcher — Milwaukee Braves

201 PETE WHISENANT — Outfield — Minnesota Twins

202 AL NEIGER — Pitcher — Philadelphia Phillies

203 EDDIE BRESSOUD — Shortstop — San Francisco Giants

204 BOB SKINNER — Outfield — Pittsburgh Pirates

205 BILL PIERCE — Pitcher — Chicago White Sox

206 GENE GREEN — Catcher-Outfield — Washington Senators

207 DODGER SOUTHPAWS (Sandy Koufax-Johnny Podres)

208 LARRY OSBORNE — First Base — Detroit Tigers

209 KEN McBRIDE — Pitcher — Los Angeles Angels

210 PETE RUNNELS — Second Base-First Base — Boston Red Sox

211 BOB GIBSON — Pitcher — St. Louis Cardinals

212 HAYWOOD SULLIVAN — Catcher — Kansas City Athletics

213 BILL STAFFORD — Pitcher — New York Yankees

214 DANNY MURPHY — Outfield — Chicago Cubs

215 GUS BELL — Outfield — Cincinnati Reds

216 TED BOWSFIELD — Pitcher — Los Angeles Angels

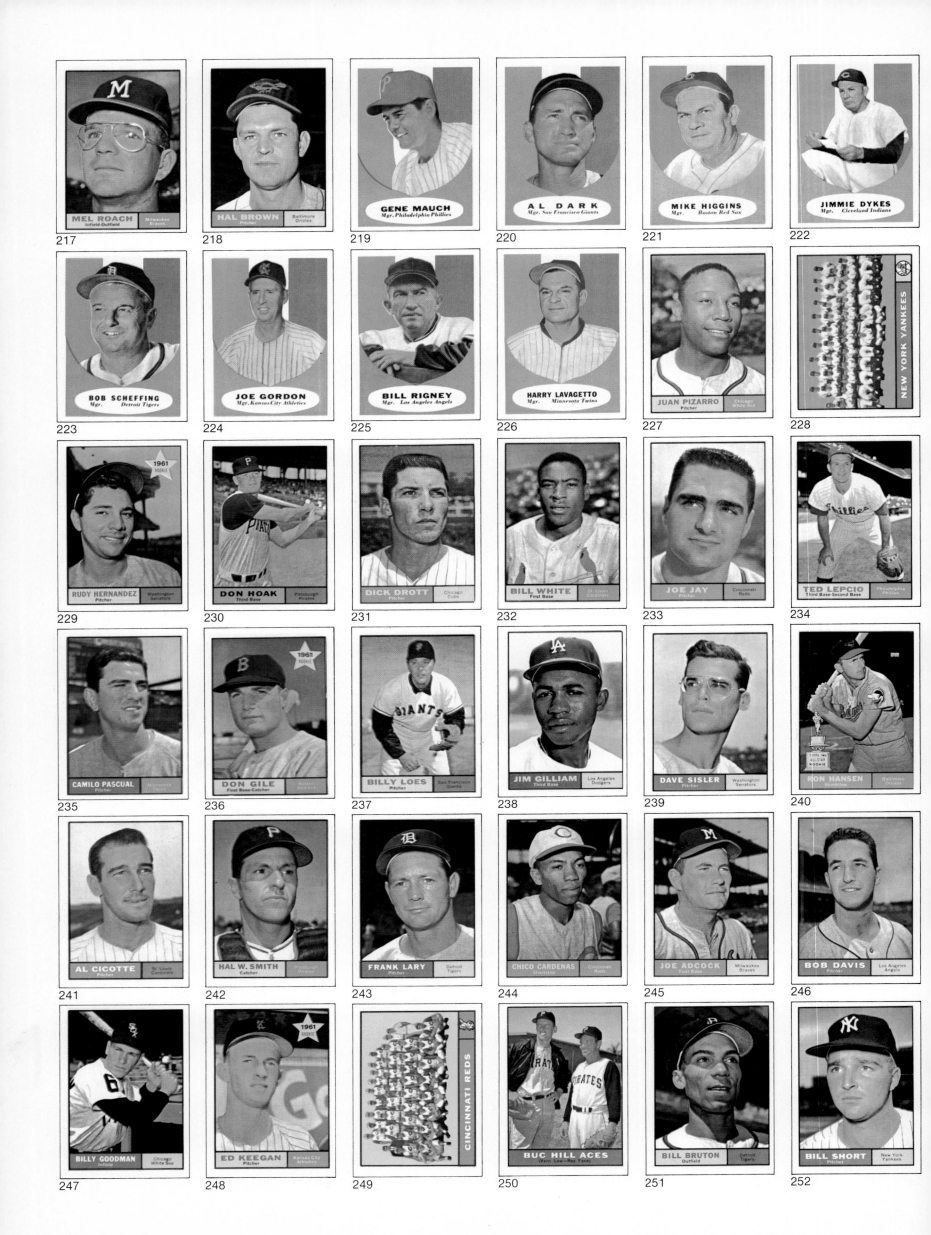

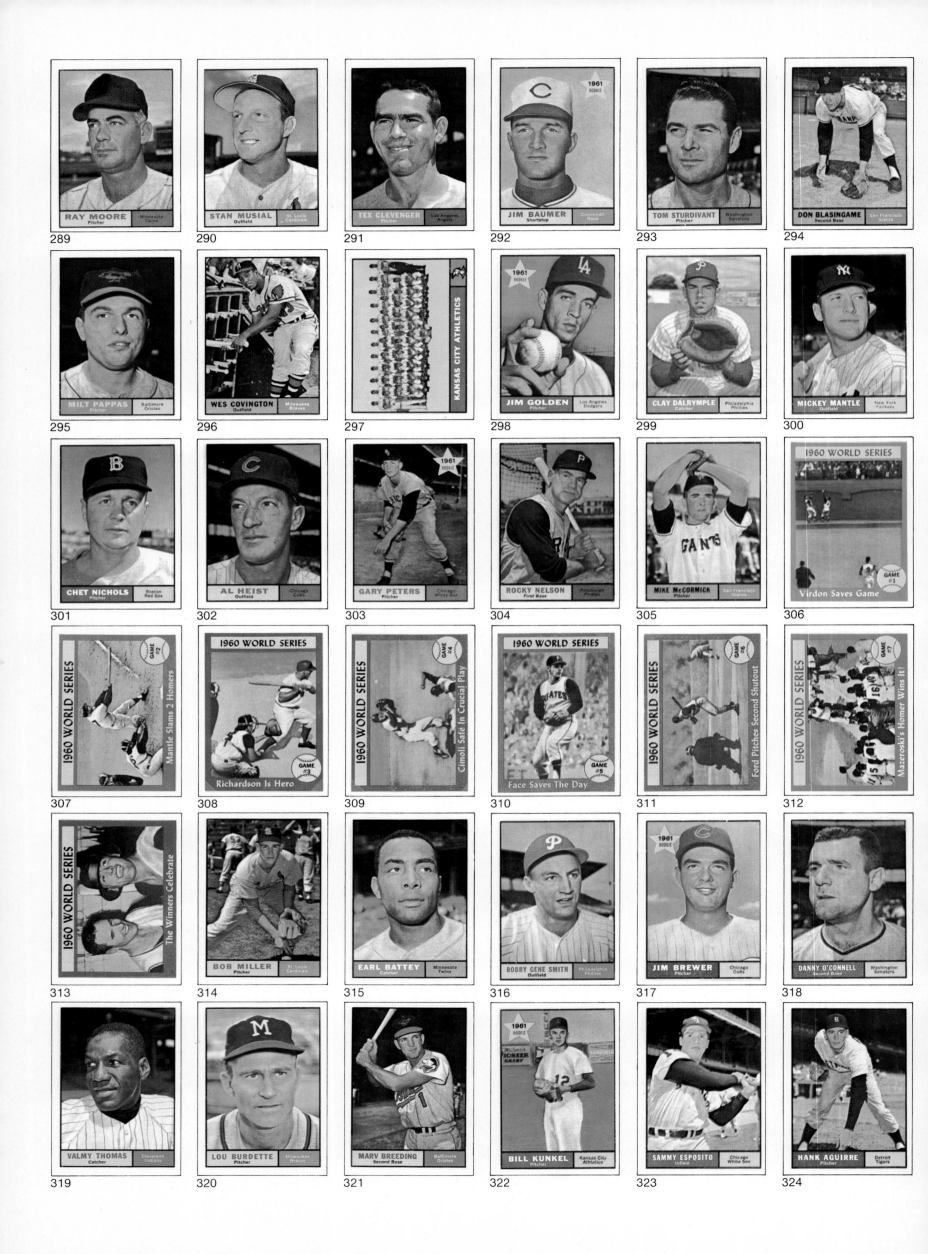

289

290

291

292

293

294

295

296

297

298

299

300

301

302

303

304

305

306

307

308

309

310

311

312

313

314

315

316

317

318

319

320

321

322

323

324

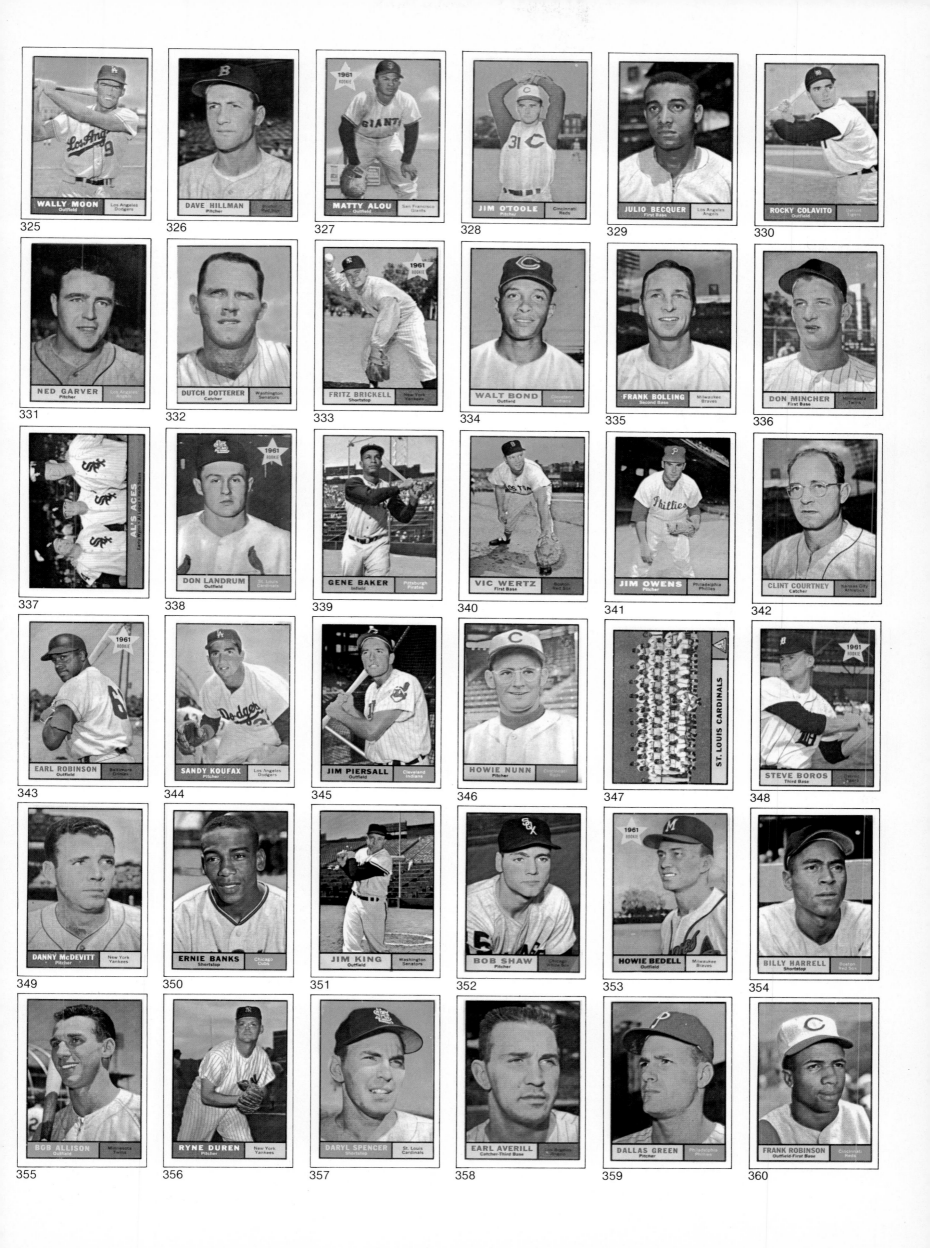

WALLY MOON Outfield Los Angeles Dodgers
325

DAVE HILLMAN Pitcher Boston Red Sox
326

MATTY ALOU Outfield San Francisco Giants
327

JIM O'TOOLE Pitcher Cincinnati Reds
328

JULIO BECQUER First Base Los Angeles Angels
329

ROCKY COLAVITO Outfield Detroit Tigers
330

NED GARVER Pitcher Los Angeles Angels
331

DUTCH DOTTERER Catcher Washington Senators
332

FRITZ BRICKELL Shortstop New York Yankees
333

WALT BOND Outfield Cleveland Indians
334

FRANK BOLLING Second Base Milwaukee Braves
335

DON MINCHER First Base Minnesota Twins
336

AL'S ACES Early Wynn / Los Angeles Angels Pitching Staff
337

DON LANDRUM Outfield St. Louis Cardinals
338

GENE BAKER Infield Pittsburgh Pirates
339

VIC WERTZ First Base Boston Red Sox
340

JIM OWENS Pitcher Philadelphia Phillies
341

CLINT COURTNEY Catcher Kansas City Athletics
342

EARL ROBINSON Outfield Baltimore Orioles
343

SANDY KOUFAX Pitcher Los Angeles Dodgers
344

JIM PIERSALL Outfield Cleveland Indians
345

HOWIE NUNN Pitcher Cincinnati Reds
346

ST. LOUIS CARDINALS
347

STEVE BOROS Third Base Detroit Tigers
348

DANNY McDEVITT Pitcher New York Yankees
349

ERNIE BANKS Shortstop Chicago Cubs
350

JIM KING Outfield Washington Senators
351

BOB SHAW Pitcher Chicago White Sox
352

HOWIE BEDELL Outfield Milwaukee Braves
353

BILLY HARRELL Shortstop Boston Red Sox
354

BOB ALLISON Outfield Minnesota Twins
355

RYNE DUREN Pitcher New York Yankees
356

DARYL SPENCER Shortstop St. Louis Cardinals
357

EARL AVERILL Catcher-Third Base Los Angeles Angels
358

DALLAS GREEN Pitcher Philadelphia Phillies
359

FRANK ROBINSON Outfield-First Base Cincinnati Reds
360

361

FRANK FUNK
Pitcher — Cleveland Indians
362

JOHN ROSEBORO
Catcher — Los Angeles Dodgers
363

MOE DRABOWSKY
Pitcher — Chicago Cubs
364

JERRY LUMPE
Second Base — Kansas City Athletics
365

EDDIE FISHER
Pitcher — San Francisco Giants
366

JIM RIVERA
Outfield — Chicago White Sox
367

BENNIE DANIELS
Pitcher — Washington Senators
368

DAVE PHILLEY
Infield-Outfield — Baltimore Orioles
369

ROY FACE
Pitcher — Pittsburgh Pirates
370

BILL SKOWRON
First Base — New York Yankees
371

BOB HENDLEY
Pitcher — Milwaukee Braves
372

BOSTON RED SOX
373

PAUL GIEL
Pitcher — Minnesota Twins
374

KEN BOYER
Third Base — St. Louis Cardinals
375

MIKE ROARKE
Catcher — Detroit Tigers
376

RUBEN GOMEZ
Pitcher — Philadelphia Phillies
377

WALLY POST
Outfield — Cincinnati Reds
378

BOBBY SHANTZ
Pitcher — Pittsburgh Pirates
379

MINNIE MINOSO
Outfield — Chicago White Sox
380

DAVE WICKERSHAM
Pitcher — Kansas City Athletics
381

FRANK THOMAS
Outfield — Chicago Cubs
382

FRISCO FIRST LINERS
383

CHUCK ESSEGIAN
Outfield — Kansas City Athletics
384

JIM PERRY
Pitcher — Cleveland Indians
385

JOE HICKS
Outfield — Washington Senators
386

DUKE MAAS
Pitcher — New York Yankees
387

BOB CLEMENTE
Outfield — Pittsburgh Pirates
388

RALPH TERRY
Pitcher — New York Yankees
389

DEL CRANDALL
Catcher — Milwaukee Braves
390

WINSTON BROWN
Pitcher — Chicago White Sox
391

RENO BERTOIA
Third Base — Minnesota Twins
392

BATTER BAFFLERS
Don Cardwell • Glen Hobbie
393

KEN WALTERS
Outfield — Philadelphia Phillies
394

CHUCK ESTRADA
Pitcher — Baltimore Orioles
395

BOB ASPROMONTE
Third Base — Los Angeles Dodgers
396

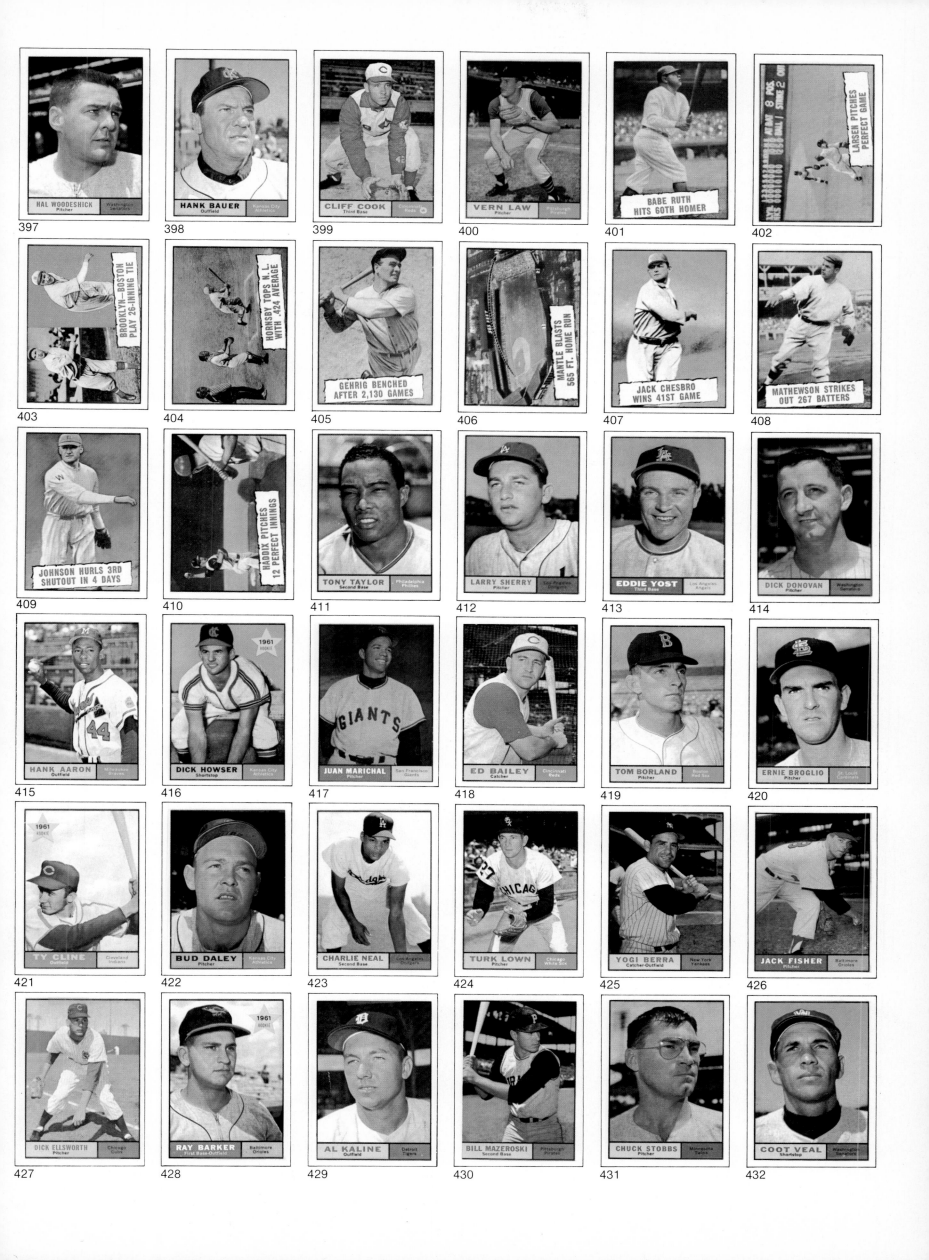

397

398

399

400

401

402

403

404

405

406

407

408

409

410

411

412

413

414

415

416

417

418

419

420

421

422

423

424

425

426

427

428

429

430

431

432

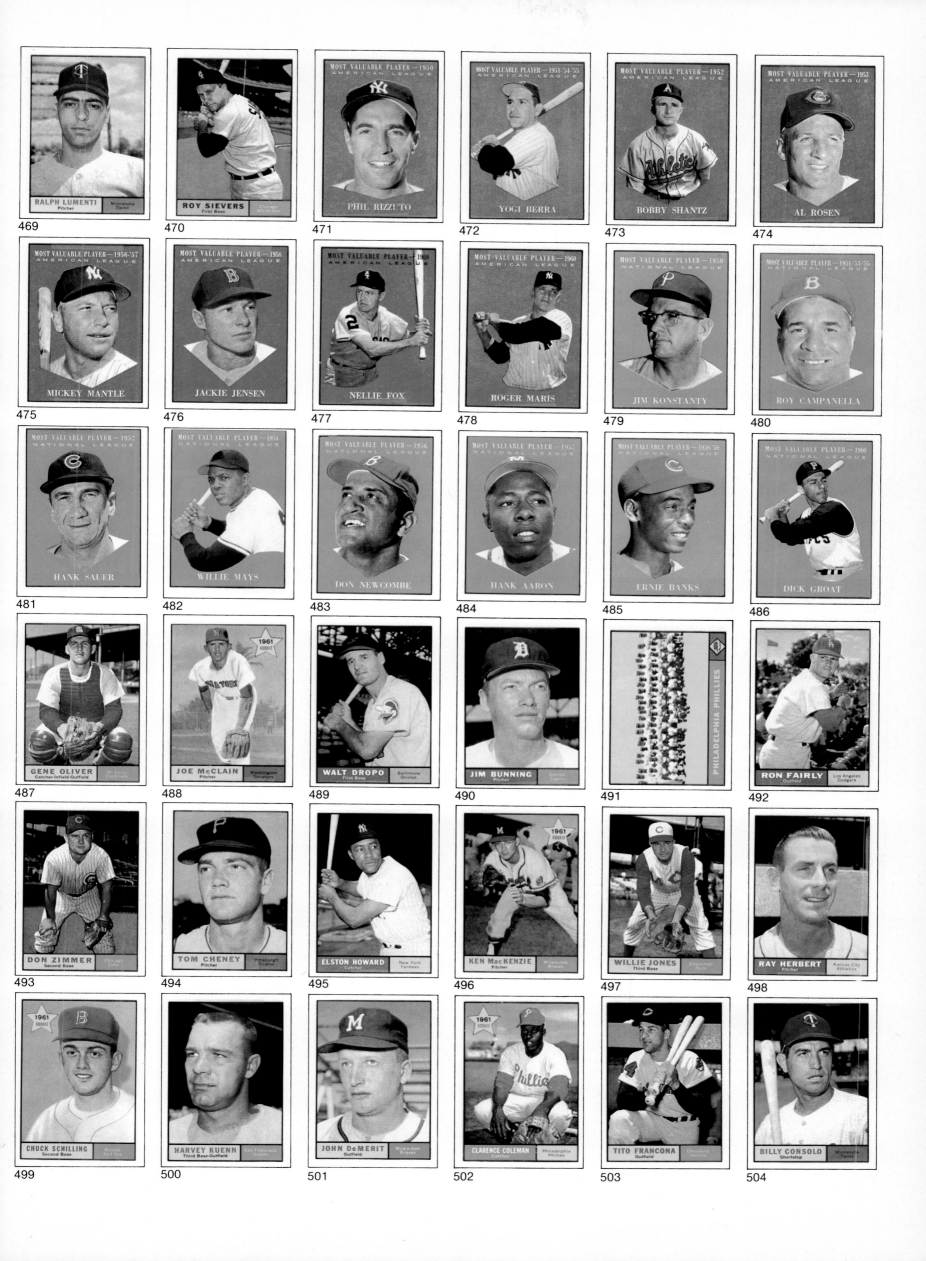

469   RALPH LUMENTI — Pitcher, Minnesota Twins

470   ROY SIEVERS — First Base, Chicago White Sox

471   MOST VALUABLE PLAYER — 1950 AMERICAN LEAGUE — PHIL RIZZUTO

472   MOST VALUABLE PLAYER — 1951-54-55 AMERICAN LEAGUE — YOGI BERRA

473   MOST VALUABLE PLAYER — 1952 AMERICAN LEAGUE — BOBBY SHANTZ

474   MOST VALUABLE PLAYER — 1953 AMERICAN LEAGUE — AL ROSEN

475   MOST VALUABLE PLAYER — 1956-'57 AMERICAN LEAGUE — MICKEY MANTLE

476   MOST VALUABLE PLAYER — 1958 AMERICAN LEAGUE — JACKIE JENSEN

477   MOST VALUABLE PLAYER — 1959 AMERICAN LEAGUE — NELLIE FOX

478   MOST VALUABLE PLAYER — 1960 AMERICAN LEAGUE — ROGER MARIS

479   MOST VALUABLE PLAYER — 1950 NATIONAL LEAGUE — JIM KONSTANTY

480   MOST VALUABLE PLAYER — 1951-53-55 NATIONAL LEAGUE — ROY CAMPANELLA

481   MOST VALUABLE PLAYER — 1952 NATIONAL LEAGUE — HANK SAUER

482   MOST VALUABLE PLAYER — 1954 NATIONAL LEAGUE — WILLIE MAYS

483   MOST VALUABLE PLAYER — 1956 NATIONAL LEAGUE — DON NEWCOMBE

484   MOST VALUABLE PLAYER — 1957 NATIONAL LEAGUE — HANK AARON

485   MOST VALUABLE PLAYER — 1958-'59 NATIONAL LEAGUE — ERNIE BANKS

486   MOST VALUABLE PLAYER — 1960 NATIONAL LEAGUE — DICK GROAT

487   GENE OLIVER — Catcher-Infield-Outfield, St. Louis Cardinals

488   JOE McCLAIN — Pitcher, Washington Senators

489   WALT DROPO — First Base, Baltimore Orioles

490   JIM BUNNING — Pitcher, Detroit Tigers

491   PHILADELPHIA PHILLIES

492   RON FAIRLY — Outfield, Los Angeles Dodgers

493   DON ZIMMER — Second Base, Chicago Cubs

494   TOM CHENEY — Pitcher, Pittsburgh Pirates

495   ELSTON HOWARD — Catcher, New York Yankees

496   KEN MacKENZIE — Pitcher, Milwaukee Braves

497   WILLIE JONES — Third Base, Cincinnati Reds

498   RAY HERBERT — Pitcher, Kansas City Athletics

499   CHUCK SCHILLING — Second Base, Boston Red Sox

500   HARVEY KUENN — Third Base-Outfield, San Francisco Giants

501   JOHN DeMERIT — Outfield, Milwaukee Braves

502   CLARENCE COLEMAN — Catcher, Philadelphia Phillies

503   TITO FRANCONA — Outfield, Cleveland Indians

504   BILLY CONSOLO — Shortstop, Minnesota Twins

505

506

507

508

509

510

511

512

513

514

515

516

517

518

519

520

521

522

523

524

525

526

527

528

529

530

531

532

533

534

535

536

537

538

539

540

541 ROLAND SHELDON Pitcher New York Yankees

542 MINNESOTA TWINS Formerly Washington Senators 1960

543 ROGER CRAIG Pitcher Los Angeles Dodgers

544 GEORGE THOMAS Outfield Detroit Tigers

545 HOYT WILHELM Pitcher Baltimore Orioles

546 MARTY KUTYNA Pitcher Washington Senators

547 LEON WAGNER Outfield Los Angeles Angels

548 TED WILLS Pitcher Boston Red Sox

549 HAL R. SMITH Catcher St. Louis Cardinals

550 FRANK BAUMANN Pitcher Chicago White Sox

551 GEORGE ALTMAN Outfield-First Base Chicago Cubs

552 JIM ARCHER Pitcher Kansas City Athletics

553 BILL FISCHER Pitcher Detroit Tigers

554 PITTSBURGH PIRATES

555 SAM JONES Pitcher San Francisco Giants

556 KEN R. HUNT Pitcher Cincinnati Reds

557 JOSE VALDIVIELSO Shortstop Minnesota Twins

558 DON FERRARESE Pitcher Philadelphia Phillies

559 JIM GENTILE First Base Baltimore Orioles

560 BARRY LATMAN Pitcher Cleveland Indians

561 CHARLEY JAMES Outfield St. Louis Cardinals

562 BILL MONBOUQUETTE Pitcher Boston Red Sox

563 BOB CERV Outfield New York Yankees

564 DON CARDWELL Pitcher Chicago Cubs

565 FELIPE ALOU Outfield San Francisco Giants

566 PAUL RICHARDS—MGR.

567 DANNY MURTAUGH—MGR.

568 BILL SKOWRON—1B

569 FRANK HERRERA—1B

570 NELLIE FOX—2B

571 BILL MAZEROSKI—2B

572 BROOKS ROBINSON—3B

573 KEN BOYER—3B

574 LUIS APARICIO—SS

575 ERNIE BANKS—SS

576 ROGER MARIS—RF

577

578

579

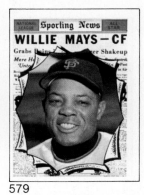
580

581

582

583

584

585

586

589

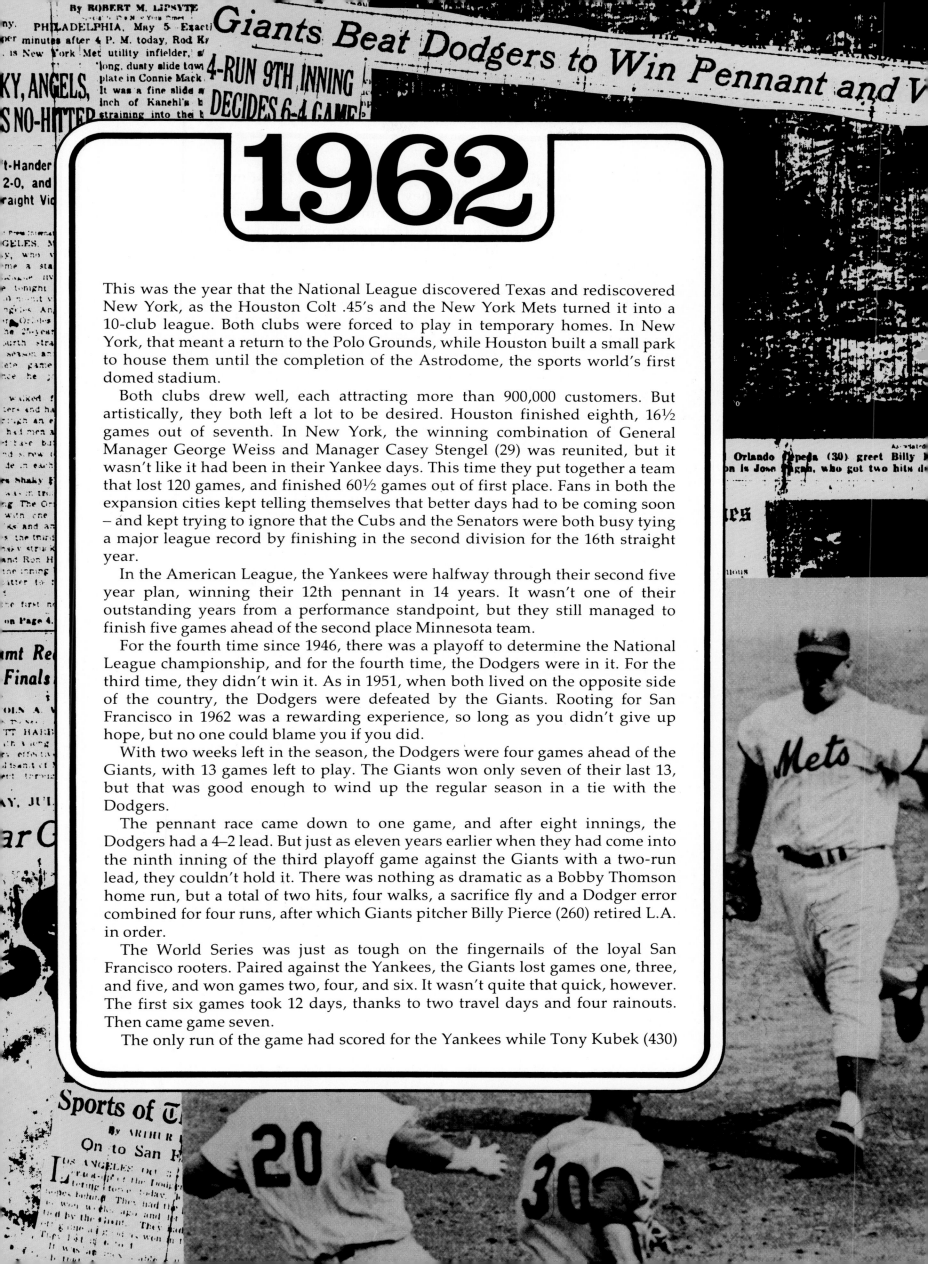

1962

This was the year that the National League discovered Texas and rediscovered New York, as the Houston Colt .45's and the New York Mets turned it into a 10-club league. Both clubs were forced to play in temporary homes. In New York, that meant a return to the Polo Grounds, while Houston built a small park to house them until the completion of the Astrodome, the sports world's first domed stadium.

Both clubs drew well, each attracting more than 900,000 customers. But artistically, they both left a lot to be desired. Houston finished eighth, 16½ games out of seventh. In New York, the winning combination of General Manager George Weiss and Manager Casey Stengel (29) was reunited, but it wasn't like it had been in their Yankee days. This time they put together a team that lost 120 games, and finished 60½ games out of first place. Fans in both the expansion cities kept telling themselves that better days had to be coming soon – and kept trying to ignore that the Cubs and the Senators were both busy tying a major league record by finishing in the second division for the 16th straight year.

In the American League, the Yankees were halfway through their second five year plan, winning their 12th pennant in 14 years. It wasn't one of their outstanding years from a performance standpoint, but they still managed to finish five games ahead of the second place Minnesota team.

For the fourth time since 1946, there was a playoff to determine the National League championship, and for the fourth time, the Dodgers were in it. For the third time, they didn't win it. As in 1951, when both lived on the opposite side of the country, the Dodgers were defeated by the Giants. Rooting for San Francisco in 1962 was a rewarding experience, so long as you didn't give up hope, but no one could blame you if you did.

With two weeks left in the season, the Dodgers were four games ahead of the Giants, with 13 games left to play. The Giants won only seven of their last 13, but that was good enough to wind up the regular season in a tie with the Dodgers.

The pennant race came down to one game, and after eight innings, the Dodgers had a 4–2 lead. But just as eleven years earlier when they had come into the ninth inning of the third playoff game against the Giants with a two-run lead, they couldn't hold it. There was nothing as dramatic as a Bobby Thomson home run, but a total of two hits, four walks, a sacrifice fly and a Dodger error combined for four runs, after which Giants pitcher Billy Pierce (260) retired L.A. in order.

The World Series was just as tough on the fingernails of the loyal San Francisco rooters. Paired against the Yankees, the Giants lost games one, three, and five, and won games two, four, and six. It wasn't quite that quick, however. The first six games took 12 days, thanks to two travel days and four rainouts. Then came game seven.

The only run of the game had scored for the Yankees while Tony Kubek (430) was hitting into a double play, and the Giants came to bat in the ninth, behind by only that run. With two out, they had men on second and third and Willie McCovey (544) at bat. McCovey's screaming line drive was a couple of steps to the left of second baseman Bobby Richardson (65), who took those couple of steps, caught the ball, which first knocked him backward slightly, and held it to end the Series.

Milwaukee, the last club to be a holdout against televising their games, finally made television unanimous, sort of. They agreed to telecasts of 15 road games.

Stan Musial (50), became the new proprietor of the record for most base hits by a National League player on May 19th, when he got lifetime hit number 3,431 off lefty Ron Perranoski (297) in Dodger Stadium. Maury Wills broke Ty Cobb's mark for stolen bases in a single season, 96, when he managed 104 successful larcenies, four of them coming in the playoff. Musial also broke Mel Ott's record for career RBIs, and set new marks for games played and runs scored.

Two of modern baseball's greatest players, and biggest gate attractions, Bobby Feller and Jackie Robinson, were made members of the Hall of Fame.

The Cards
Two new concepts were tried by Topps in this largest set yet – 598 cards: (1) In Action Cards (311 to 319), showing among others Spahn, Mantle, and Musial in game action, and (2) Rookie Cards by Position (591 to 598) with four and five players on a card. The Lou Brock Rookie Card (387) is also in this set, which also has a special feature on Babe Ruth (135 to 144) and 10 Combination Cards (18 pictures Mantle and Mays). There are 9 cards which, when reprinted, had different pictures. These reprinted cards have greater value. Also there are some Hal Reniff cards numbered 139, which should be 159.

QUIZ

Which Detroit left-hander had the best ERA in the American League? (407)
He broke the major league record for second basemen by going 78 games and 418 chances without an error, although only a rookie. Who? (461)
At 39, this switch-hitting second baseman ties the National League record for pinch-hits in a season. Who? (575)
He led the league in home runs and runs batted in, despite a batting average of only .243. Who is this Hall-of-Famer to be? (70)
Washington pitcher Tom Cheney set an all-time mark by striking out 21 Orioles in a 16-inning game. The game-ending strikeout was against a man who would manage teams from both leagues in World Series play. Who? (382)
Although he had never won more than 14 games in a season before, his 20–9 record gave him the best percentage of any A.L. pitcher. Who? (8)
One reason the Giants won the pennant was that one of their pitchers won 16 games in a row. Who? (538)
He started the season as Tony Kubek's replacement at shortstop. When Kubek came out of the service, he moved into the outfield and was named A.L. Rookie of the Year. Who? (31)
In later years he was to say that if he hadn't been a good pitcher, he wouldn't have gotten enough chances to lose 24 games. Who? (183)

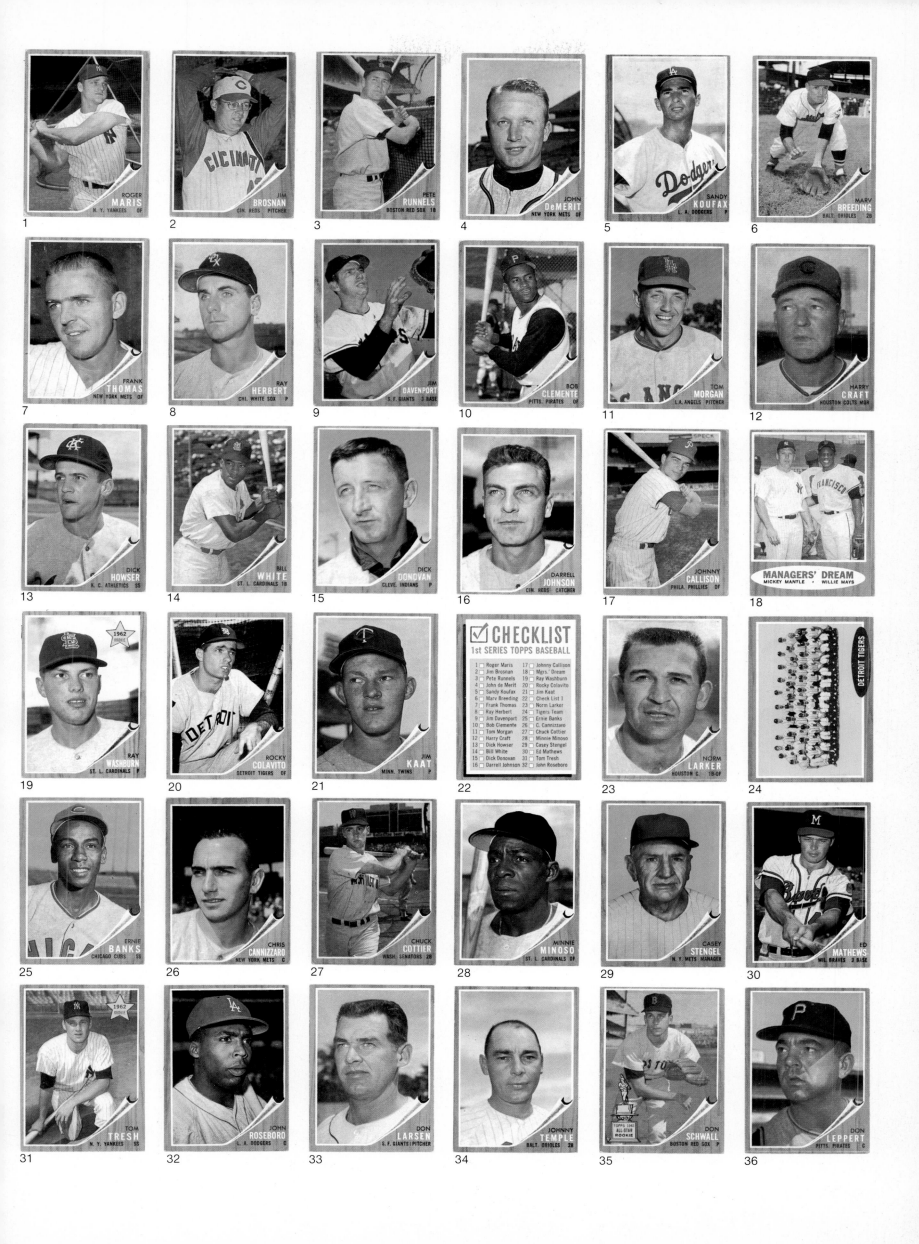

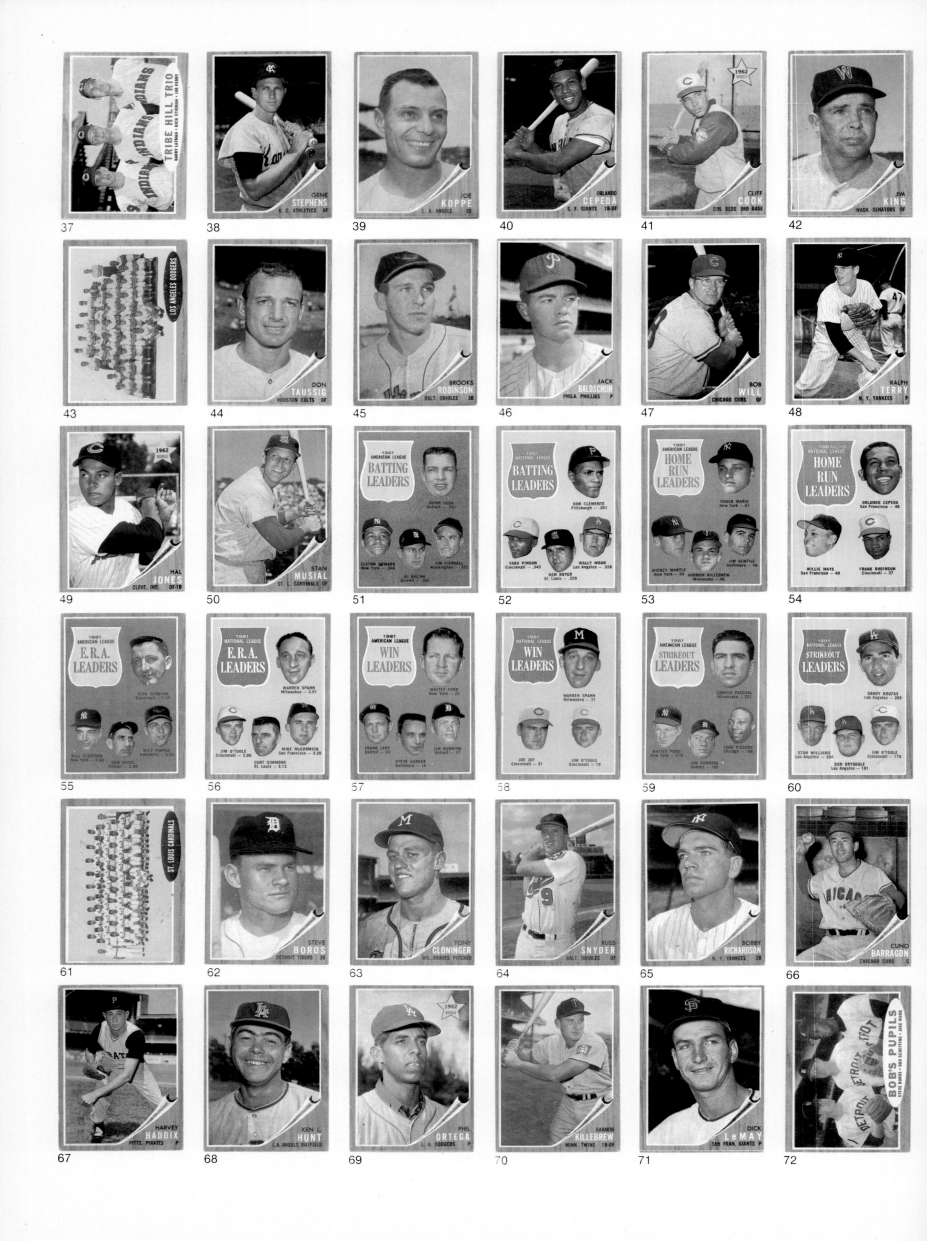

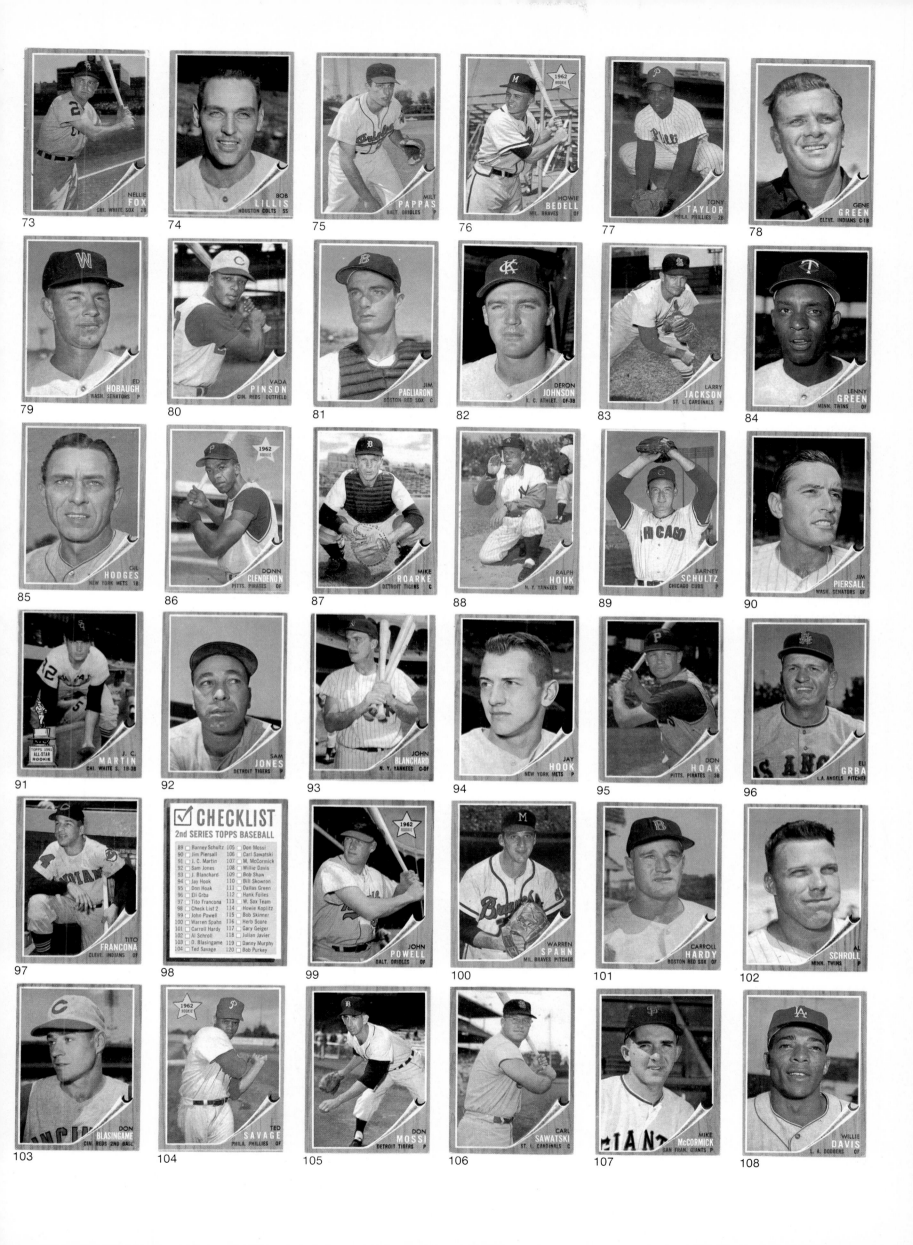

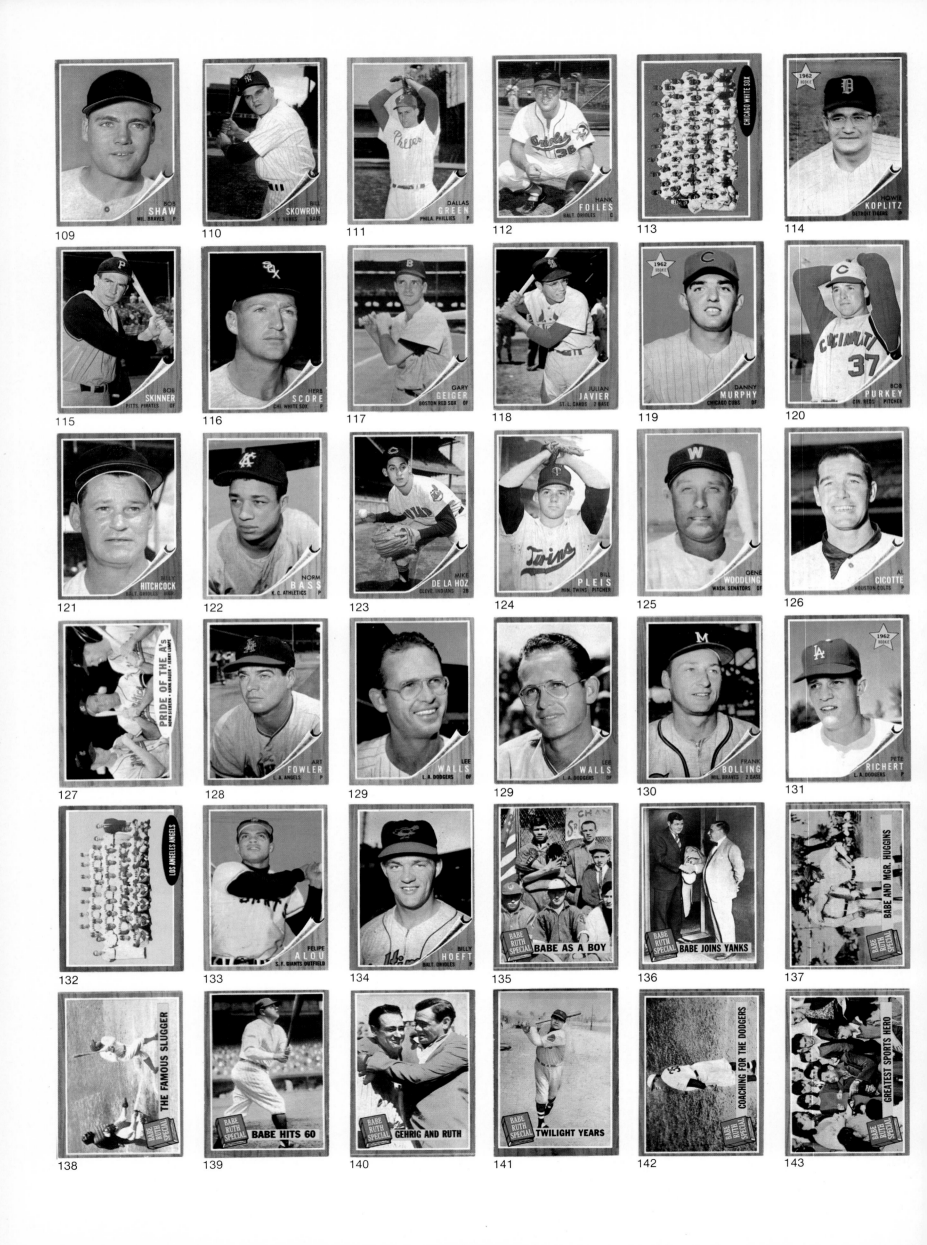

109 BOB SHAW MIL. BRAVES P

110 BILL SKOWRON N.Y. YANKS 1 BASE

111 DALLAS GREEN PHILA. PHILLIES P

112 HANK FOILES BALT. ORIOLES C

113 CHICAGO WHITE SOX

114 HOWIE KOPLITZ Detroit Tigers

115 BOB SKINNER PITTS. PIRATES OF

116 HERB SCORE CHI. WHITE SOX P

117 GARY GEIGER BOSTON RED SOX OF

118 JULIAN JAVIER ST. L. CARDS 2 BASE

119 DANNY MURPHY CHICAGO CUBS OF

120 BOB PURKEY CIN. REDS PITCHER

121 BILLY HITCHCOCK BALT. ORIOLES MGR.

122 NORM BASS K. C. ATHLETICS P

123 MIKE DE LA HOZ CLEVE. INDIANS 2B

124 BILL PLEIS MIN. TWINS PITCHER

125 GENE WOODLING WASH. SENATORS OF

126 AL CICOTTE HOUSTON COLTS

127 PRIDE OF THE A's NORM SIEBERN • HANK BAUER • JERRY LUMPE

128 ART FOWLER L. A. ANGELS P

129 LEE WALLS L. A. DODGERS OF

129 LEE WALLS L. A. DODGERS OF

130 FRANK BOLLING MIL. BRAVES 2 BASE

131 PETE RICHERT L. A. DODGERS

132 LOS ANGELES ANGELS

133 FELIPE ALOU S. F. GIANTS OUTFIELD

134 BILLY HOEFT BALT. ORIOLES P

135 BABE AS A BOY

136 BABE JOINS YANKS

137 BABE AND MGR. HUGGINS

138 THE FAMOUS SLUGGER

139 BABE HITS 60

140 GEHRIG AND RUTH

141 TWILIGHT YEARS

142 COACHING FOR THE DODGERS

143 GREATEST SPORTS HERO

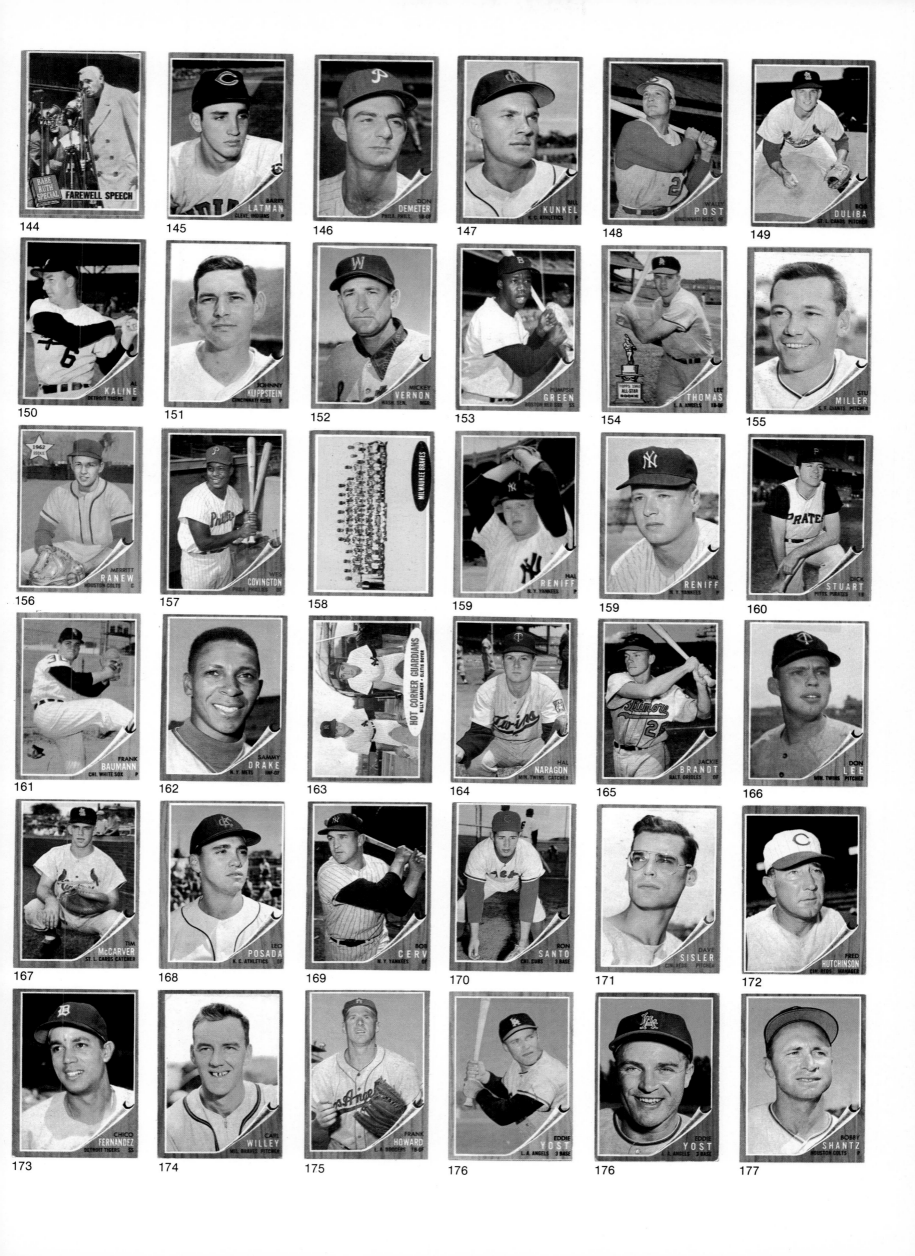

144

145

146

147

148

149

150

151

152

153

154

155

156

157

158

159

159

160

161

162

163

164

165

166

167

168

169

170

171

172

173

174

175

176

176

177

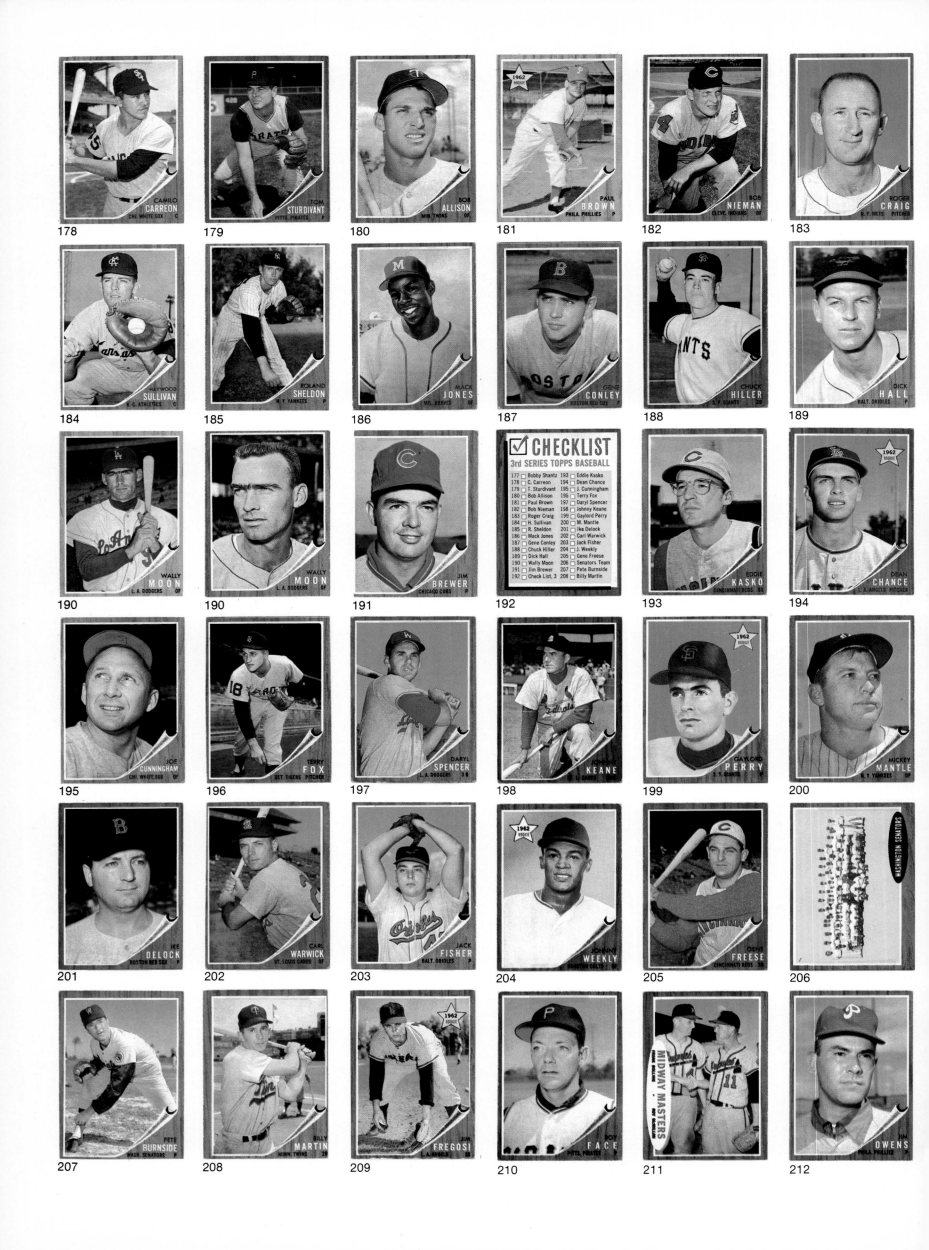

178

179

180

181

182

183

184

185

186

187

188

189

190

190

191

CHECKLIST
3rd SERIES TOPPS BASEBALL

177 ☐ Bobby Shantz   193 ☐ Eddie Kasko
178 ☐ C. Carreon   194 ☐ Dean Chance
179 ☐ T. Sturdivant   195 ☐ J. Cunningham
180 ☐ Bob Allison   196 ☐ Terry Fox
181 ☐ Paul Brown   197 ☐ Daryl Spencer
182 ☐ Bob Nieman   198 ☐ Johnny Keane
183 ☐ Roger Craig   199 ☐ Gaylord Perry
184 ☐ H. Sullivan   200 ☐ M. Mantle
185 ☐ R. Sheldon   201 ☐ Ike Delock
186 ☐ Mack Jones   202 ☐ Carl Warwick
187 ☐ Gene Conley   203 ☐ Jack Fisher
188 ☐ Chuck Hiller   204 ☐ J. Weekly
189 ☐ Dick Hall   205 ☐ Gene Freese
190 ☐ Wally Moon   206 ☐ Senators Team
191 ☐ Jim Brewer   207 ☐ Pete Burnside
192 ☐ Check List, 3   208 ☐ Billy Martin

192

193

194

195

196

197

198

199

200

201

202

203

204

205

206

207

208

209

210

211

212

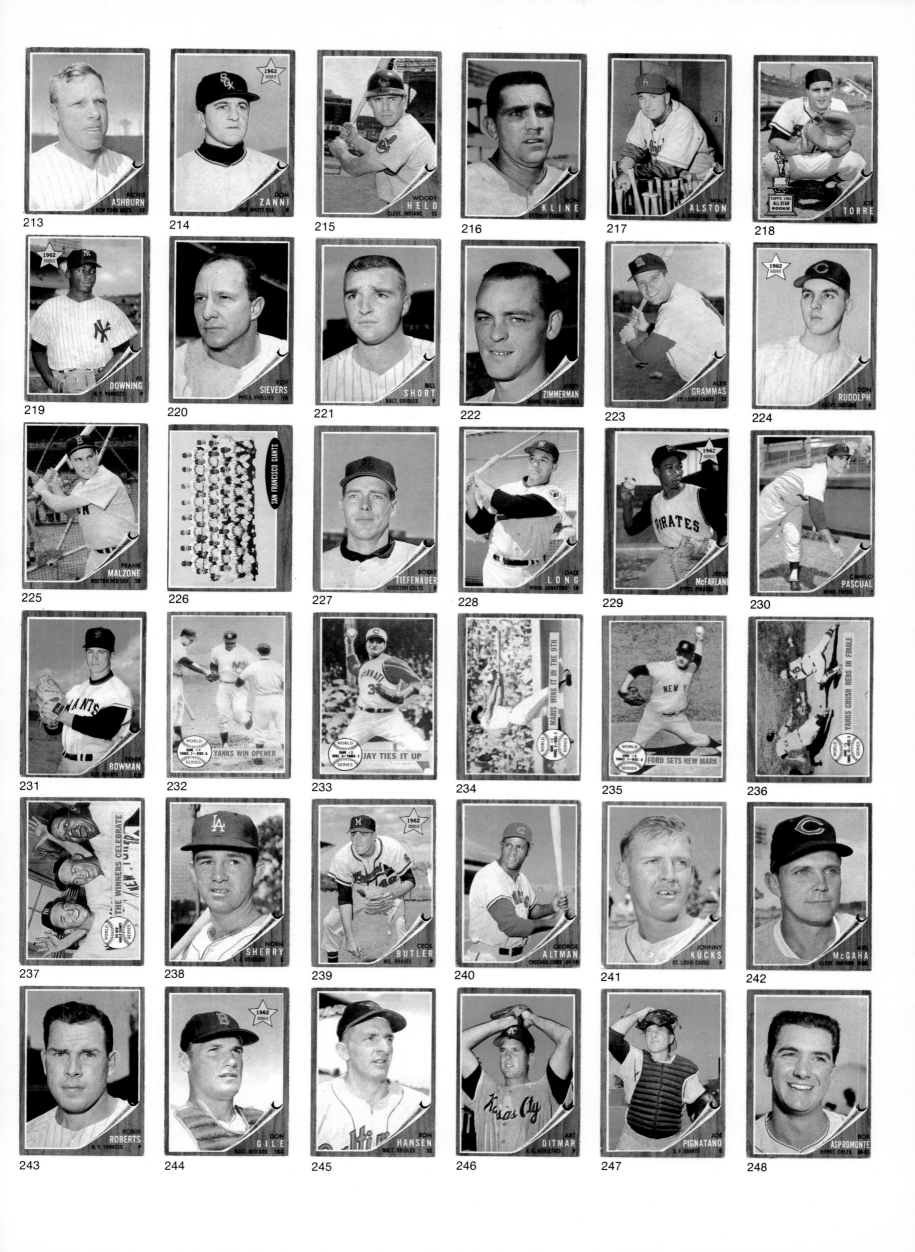

213

214

215

216

217

218

219

220

221

222

223

224

225

226

227

228

229

230

231

232

233

234

235

236

237

238

239

240

241

242

243

244

245

246

247

248

249

250

251

252

253

254

255

256

257

258

259

260

261

262

263

264

265

266

267

268

269

270

271

272

273

274

275

276

277

278

279

280

281

282

283

284

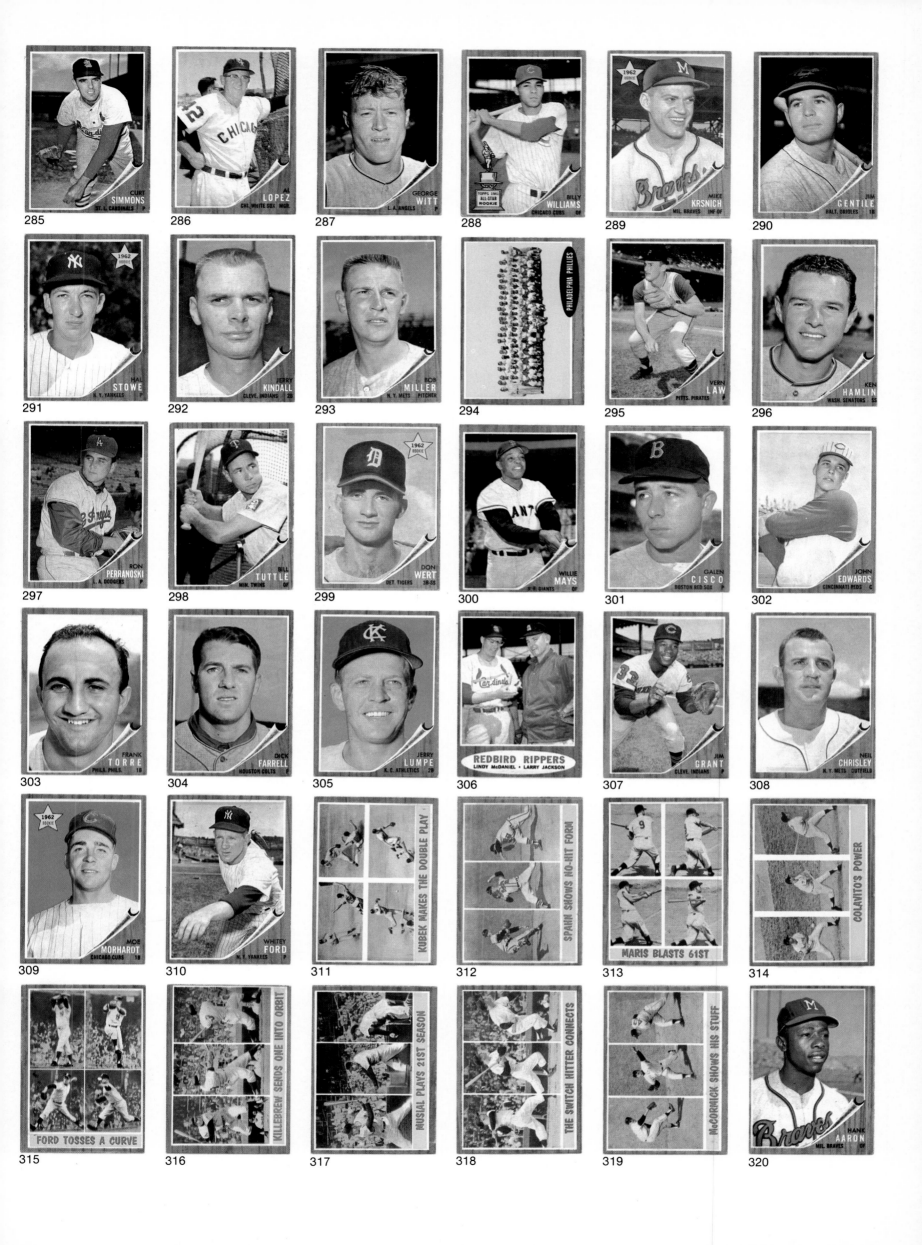

321

322

323

324

325

326

327

328

329

330

331

332

333

334

335

336

337

338

339

340

341

342

343

344

345

346

347

348

349

350

351

352

353

354

355

356

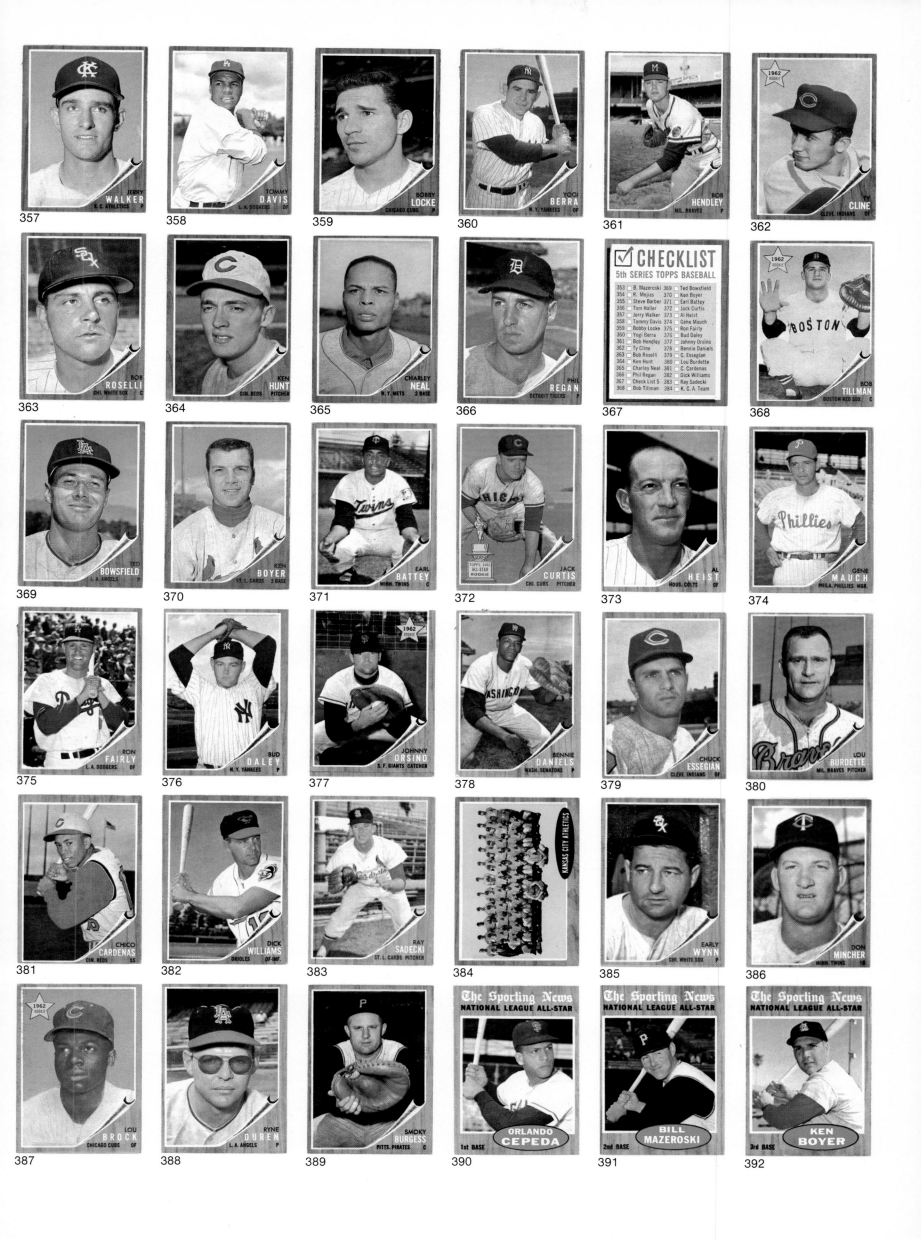

357 JERRY WALKER K.C. ATHLETICS P

358 TOMMY DAVIS L.A. DODGERS

359 BOBBY LOCKE CHICAGO CUBS P

360 YOGI BERRA N.Y. YANKEES OF

361 BOB HENDLEY MIL. BRAVES P

362 TY CLINE CLEVE. INDIANS OF

363 BOB ROSELLI CHI. WHITE SOX C

364 KEN HUNT CIN. REDS

365 CHARLEY NEAL N.Y. METS 2 BASE

366 PHIL REGAN DETROIT TIGERS P

367 CHECKLIST
5th SERIES TOPPS BASEBALL

353	B. Mazeroski	369	Ted Bowsfield
354	R. Mejias	370	Ken Boyer
355	Steve Barber	371	Earl Battey
356	Tom Haller	372	Jack Curtis
357	Jerry Walker	373	Al Heist
358	Tommy Davis	374	Gene Mauch
359	Bobby Locke	375	Ron Fairly
360	Yogi Berra	376	Bud Daley
361	Bob Hendley	377	Johnny Orsino
362	Ty Cline	378	Bennie Daniels
363	Bob Roselli	379	C. Essegian
364	Ken Hunt	380	Lou Burdette
365	Charley Neal	381	C. Cardenas
366	Phil Regan	382	Dick Williams
367	Check List 5	383	Ray Sadecki
368	Bob Tillman	384	K. C. A. Team

368 BOB TILLMAN BOSTON RED SOX C

369 TED BOWSFIELD L.A. ANGELS P

370 KEN BOYER ST. L. CARDS 3 BASE

371 EARL BATTEY MINN. TWINS C

372 JACK CURTIS CHI. CUBS PITCHER

373 AL HEIST HOUS. COLTS OF

374 GENE MAUCH PHILA. PHILLIES MGR.

375 RON FAIRLY L.A. DODGERS OF

376 BUD DALEY N.Y. YANKEES P

377 JOHNNY ORSINO S.F. GIANTS CATCHER

378 BENNIE DANIELS WASH. SENATORS P

379 CHUCK ESSEGIAN CLEVE. INDIANS OF

380 LOU BURDETTE MIL. BRAVES PITCHER

381 CHICO CARDENAS CIN. REDS SS

382 DICK WILLIAMS ORIOLES OF-INF.

383 RAY SADECKI ST. L. CARDS PITCHER

384 KANSAS CITY ATHLETICS

385 EARLY WYNN CHI. WHITE SOX P

386 DON MINCHER MINN. TWINS 1B

387 LOU BROCK CHICAGO CUBS OF

388 RYNE DUREN L.A. ANGELS P

389 SMOKY BURGESS PITTS. PIRATES C

390 The Sporting News NATIONAL LEAGUE ALL-STAR ORLANDO CEPEDA 1st BASE

391 The Sporting News NATIONAL LEAGUE ALL-STAR BILL MAZEROSKI 2nd BASE

392 The Sporting News NATIONAL LEAGUE ALL-STAR KEN BOYER 3rd BASE

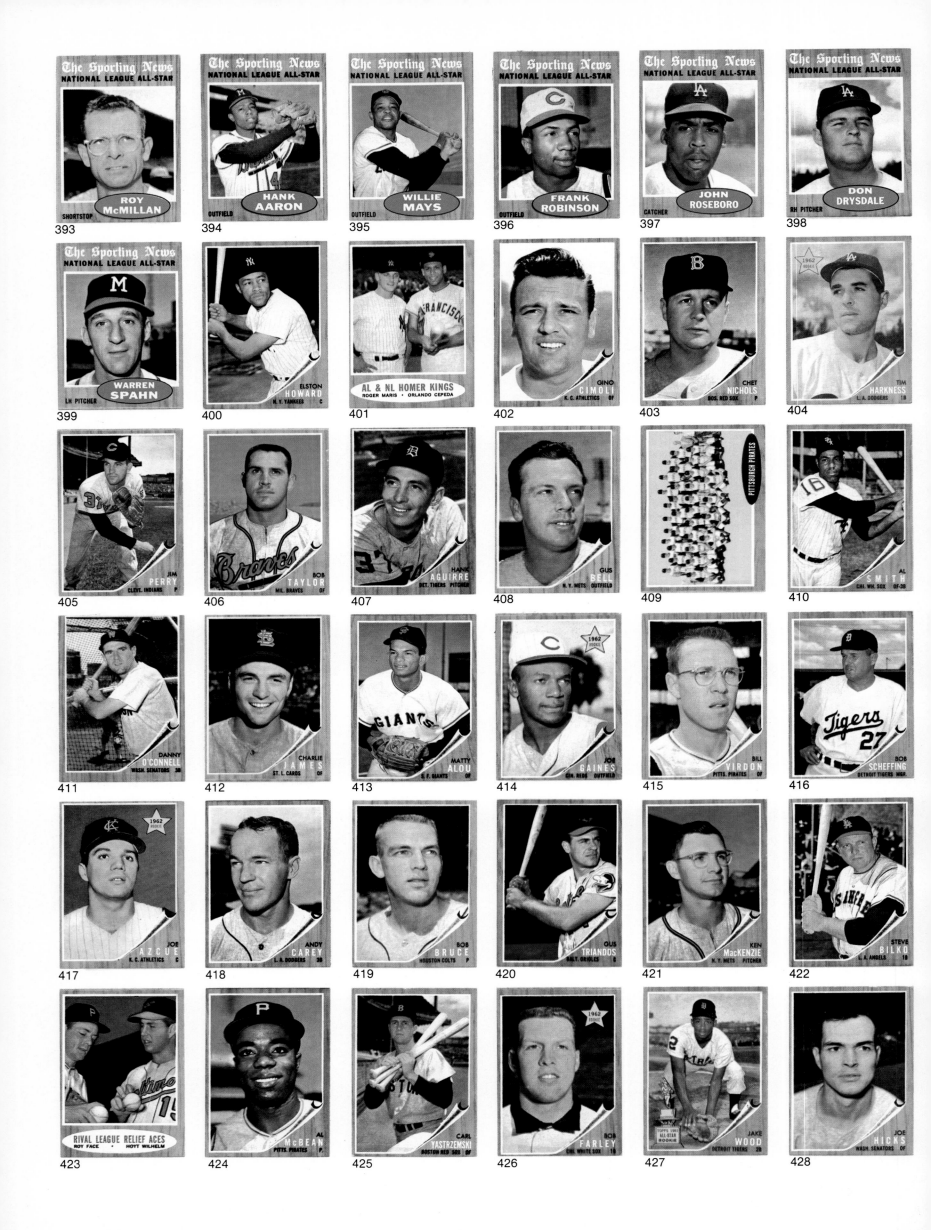

429 BILLY O'DELL — S. F. GIANTS P

430 TONY KUBEK — N. Y. YANKEES SS

431 BOB RODGERS — L. A. ANGELS C

432 JIM PENDLETON — HOUS. COLTS INF-OF

433 JIM ARCHER — K. C. ATHLETICS P

434 CLAY DALRYMPLE — PHILA. PHILLIES C

435 LARRY SHERRY — L. A. DODGERS P

436 FELIX MANTILLA — N. Y. METS SS

437 RAY MOORE — MINN. TWINS P

438 DICK BROWN — DET. TIGERS CATCHER

439 JERRY BUCHEK — ST. L. CARDS SS

440 JOE JAY — CIN. REDS PITCHER

441
CHECKLIST
6th SERIES Topps BASEBALL
430 ☐ Tony Kubek
431 ☐ Bob Rodgers
432 ☐ Jim Pendleton
433 ☐ Jim Archer
434 ☐ C. Dalrymple
435 ☐ Larry Sherry
436 ☐ Felix Mantilla
437 ☐ Ray Moore
438 ☐ Dick Brown
439 ☐ Jerry Buchek
440 ☐ Joe Jay
441 ☐ Check List 6
442 ☐ Wes Stock
443 ☐ Del Crandall
444 ☐ Ted Wills
445 ☐ Vic Power
446 ☐ Don Elston
447 ☐ Willie Kirkland
448 ☐ Joe Gibbon
449 ☐ Jerry Adair
450 ☐ Jim O'Toole
451 ☐ Jose Tartabull
452 ☐ Earl Averill
453 ☐ Cal McLish
454 ☐ F. Robinson
455 ☐ Luis Arroyo
456 ☐ J. Amalfitano
457 ☐ Lou Clinton
458 ☐ Bob Buhl
459 ☐ Ed Bailey
460 ☐ Jim Bunning
461 ☐ Ken Hubbs

442 WES STOCK — BALT. ORIOLES P

443 DEL CRANDALL — MIL. BRAVES C

444 TED WILLS — BOS. RED SOX P

445 VIC POWER — MIN. TWINS 1B

446 DON ELSTON — CHI. CUBS P

447 WILLIE KIRKLAND — CLEVE. INDIANS OF

448 JOE GIBBON — PITTS. PIRATES P

449 JERRY ADAIR — BALT. ORIOLES SS

450 JIM O'TOOLE — CIN. REDS PITCHER

451 JOSE TARTABULL — K. C. ATHLETICS OF

452 EARL AVERILL — L. A. ANGELS C

453 CAL McLISH — PHILA. PHILLIES P

454 FLOYD ROBINSON — CHI. WHITE SOX OF

455 LUIS ARROYO — N. Y. YANKEES P

456 JOE AMALFITANO — HOUSTON COLTS 2B

457 LOU CLINTON — BOSTON RED SOX OF

458 BOB BUHL — CHICAGO CUBS P

459 ED BAILEY — S. F. GIANTS C

460 JIM BUNNING — DETROIT TIGERS P

461 KEN HUBBS — CHICAGO CUBS 2B

462 WILLIE TASBY — CLEVE. INDIANS OF

463 HANK BAUER — K. C. ATHLETICS MGR.

464 AL JACKSON — N. Y. METS PITCHER

465

466 NORM CASH — 1 BASE

467 CHUCK SCHILLING — 2 BASE

468 BROOKS ROBINSON — 3 BASE

469 LUIS APARICIO — SHORTSTOP

470 AL KALINE — OUTFIELD

471 MICKEY MANTLE — OUTFIELD

472 ROCKY COLAVITO — OUTFIELD

473 ELSTON HOWARD — CATCHER

474 FRANK LARY — R H PITCHER

475 WHITEY FORD — L H PITCHER

476

477 ANDRE RODGERS — CHICAGO CUBS SS

478 DON ZIMMER — CIN. REDS 3 BASE

479 JOEL HORLEN — CHI. WHITE SOX P

480 HARVEY KUENN — S. F. GIANTS OF

481 VIC WERTZ — DETROIT TIGERS 1B

482 SAM MELE — MIN. TWINS MGR.

483 DON McMAHON — MIL. BRAVES PITCHER

484 DICK SCHOFIELD — PITTS. PIRATES INF

485 PEDRO RAMOS — CLEVE. INDIANS P

486 JIM GILLIAM — L. A. DODGERS 2B-3B

487 JERRY LYNCH — CIN. REDS OUTFIELD

488 HAL BROWN — BALT. ORIOLES P

489 JULIO GOTAY — ST. L. CARDS SS

490 CLETE BOYER — N. Y. YANKEES 3B

491 LEON WAGNER — L. A. ANGELS OF

492 HAL SMITH — HOUSTON COLTS C

493 DANNY McDEVITT — K. C. ATHLETICS P

494 SAMMY WHITE — PHILA. PHILLIES C

495 DON CARDWELL — CHICAGO CUBS P

496 WAYNE CAUSEY — K. C. ATHLETICS 3B

497 ED BOUCHEE — N. Y. METS 1 BASE

498 JIM DONOHUE — L. A. ANGELS P

499 ZOILO VERSALLES — MIN. TWINS SS

500 DUKE SNIDER — L. A. DODGERS OF

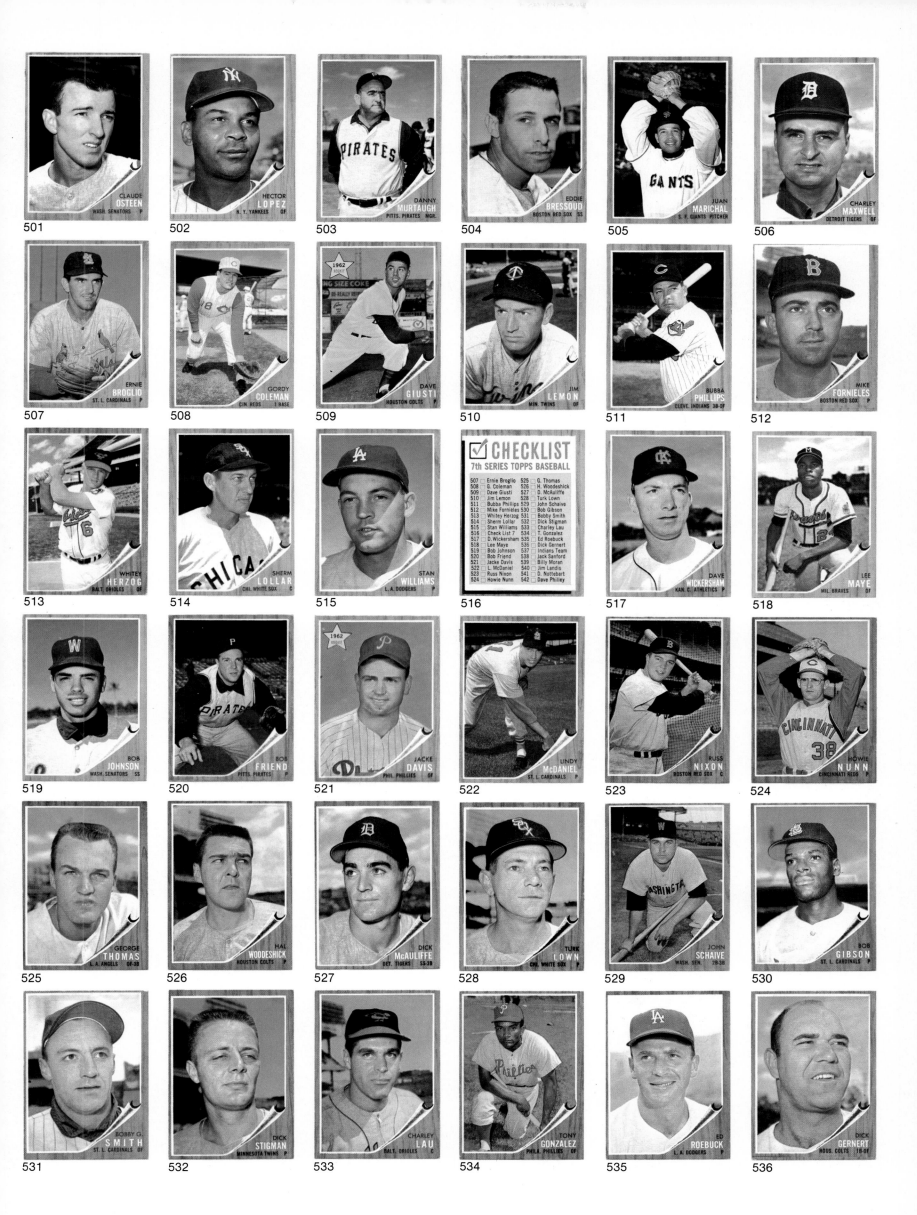

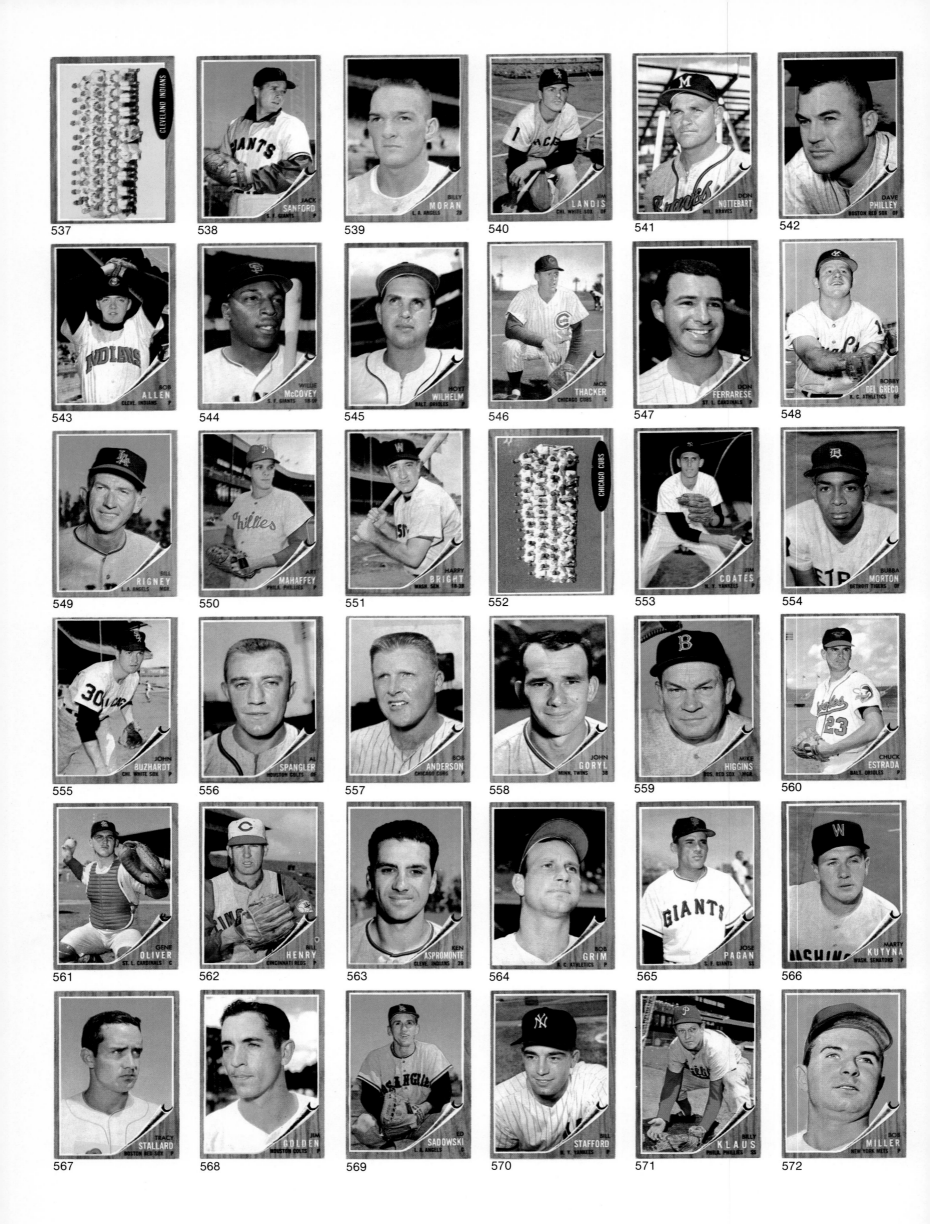

537

538

539

540

541

542

543

544

545

546

547

548

549

550

551

552

553

554

555

556

557

558

559

560

561

562

563

564

565

566

567

568

569

570

571

572

573 JOHNNY LOGAN PITTS. PIRATES SS-3B

574 DEAN STONE HOUSTON COLTS P

575 RED SCHOENDIENST ST. L. CARDINALS 2B

576 RUSS KEMMERER CHI. WHITE SOX P

577 DAVE NICHOLSON BALT. ORIOLES OF

578 HAL DUFFALO S. F. GIANTS

579 JIM SCHAFFER ST. L. CARDINALS C

580 BILL MONBOUQUETTE BOSTON RED SOX P

581 MEL ROACH PHILA. PHILS INF-OF

582 RON PICHE MIL. BRAVES P

583 LARRY OSBORNE DETROIT TIGERS 1B

584 MINNESOTA TWINS

585 GLEN HOBBIE CHICAGO CUBS P

586 SAMMY ESPOSITO CHI. WHITE SOX INF

587 FRANK FUNK CLEVE. INDIANS P

588 BIRDIE TEBBETTS MIL. BRAVES MGR.

589 BOB TURLEY N. Y. YANKEES P

590 CURT FLOOD ST. L. CARDINALS OF

591 ROOKIE PARADE PITCHERS

592 ROOKIE PARADE PITCHERS

593 ROOKIE PARADE PITCHERS

594 ROOKIE PARADE CATCHERS

595 ROOKIE PARADE INFIELDERS

596 ROOKIE PARADE INFIELDERS

597 ROOKIE PARADE INFIELDERS

598 ROOKIE PARADE OUTFIELDERS

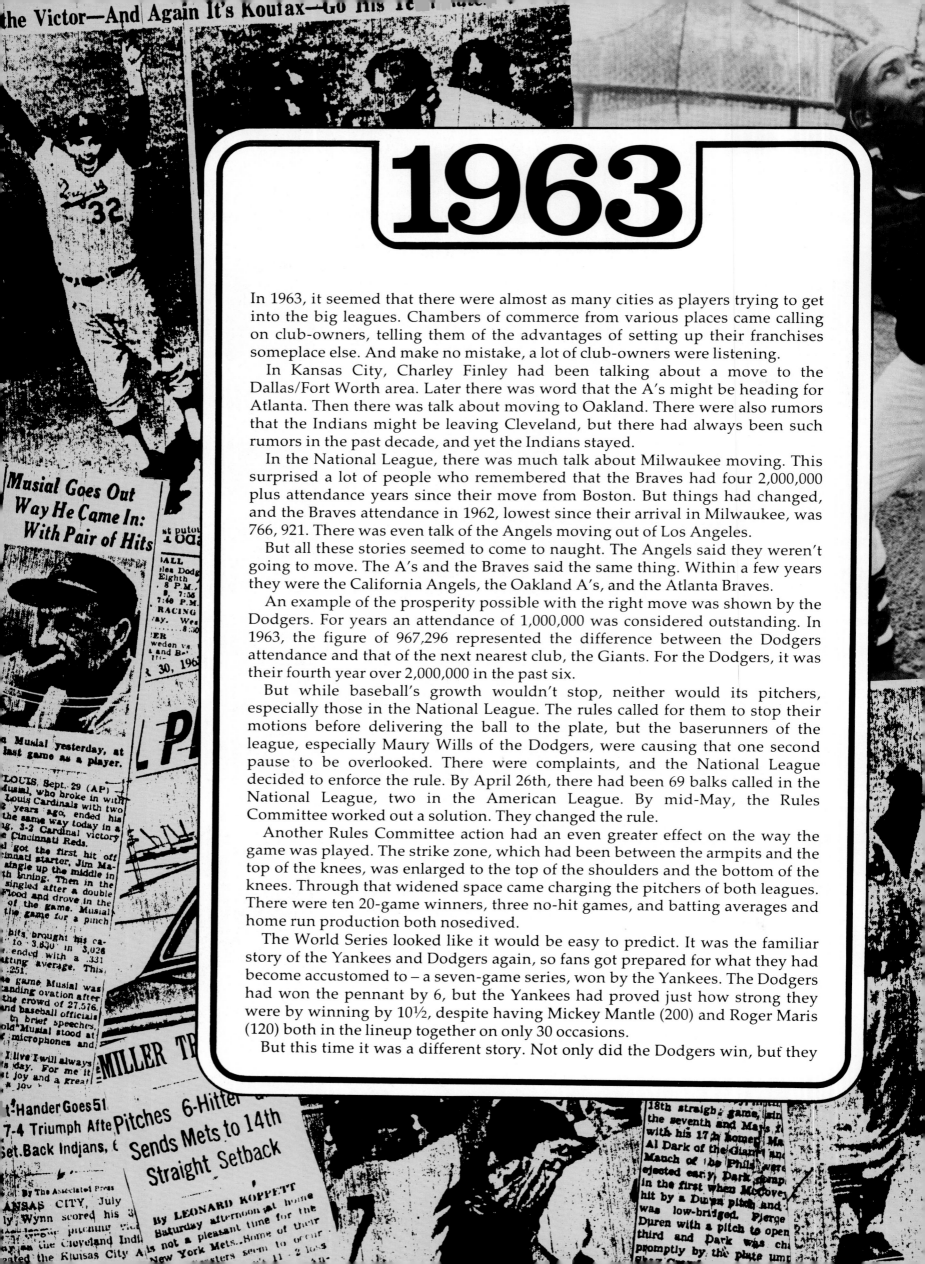

1963

In 1963, it seemed that there were almost as many cities as players trying to get into the big leagues. Chambers of commerce from various places came calling on club-owners, telling them of the advantages of setting up their franchises someplace else. And make no mistake, a lot of club-owners were listening.

In Kansas City, Charley Finley had been talking about a move to the Dallas/Fort Worth area. Later there was word that the A's might be heading for Atlanta. Then there was talk about moving to Oakland. There were also rumors that the Indians might be leaving Cleveland, but there had always been such rumors in the past decade, and yet the Indians stayed.

In the National League, there was much talk about Milwaukee moving. This surprised a lot of people who remembered that the Braves had four 2,000,000 plus attendance years since their move from Boston. But things had changed, and the Braves attendance in 1962, lowest since their arrival in Milwaukee, was 766, 921. There was even talk of the Angels moving out of Los Angeles.

But all these stories seemed to come to naught. The Angels said they weren't going to move. The A's and the Braves said the same thing. Within a few years they were the California Angels, the Oakland A's, and the Atlanta Braves.

An example of the prosperity possible with the right move was shown by the Dodgers. For years an attendance of 1,000,000 was considered outstanding. In 1963, the figure of 967,296 represented the difference between the Dodgers attendance and that of the next nearest club, the Giants. For the Dodgers, it was their fourth year over 2,000,000 in the past six.

But while baseball's growth wouldn't stop, neither would its pitchers, especially those in the National League. The rules called for them to stop their motions before delivering the ball to the plate, but the baserunners of the league, especially Maury Wills of the Dodgers, were causing that one second pause to be overlooked. There were complaints, and the National League decided to enforce the rule. By April 26th, there had been 69 balks called in the National League, two in the American League. By mid-May, the Rules Committee worked out a solution. They changed the rule.

Another Rules Committee action had an even greater effect on the way the game was played. The strike zone, which had been between the armpits and the top of the knees, was enlarged to the top of the shoulders and the bottom of the knees. Through that widened space came charging the pitchers of both leagues. There were ten 20-game winners, three no-hit games, and batting averages and home run production both nosedived.

The World Series looked like it would be easy to predict. It was the familiar story of the Yankees and Dodgers again, so fans got prepared for what they had become accustomed to – a seven-game series, won by the Yankees. The Dodgers had won the pennant by 6, but the Yankees had proved just how strong they were by winning by 10½, despite having Mickey Mantle (200) and Roger Maris (120) both in the lineup together on only 30 occasions.

But this time it was a different story. Not only did the Dodgers win, but they

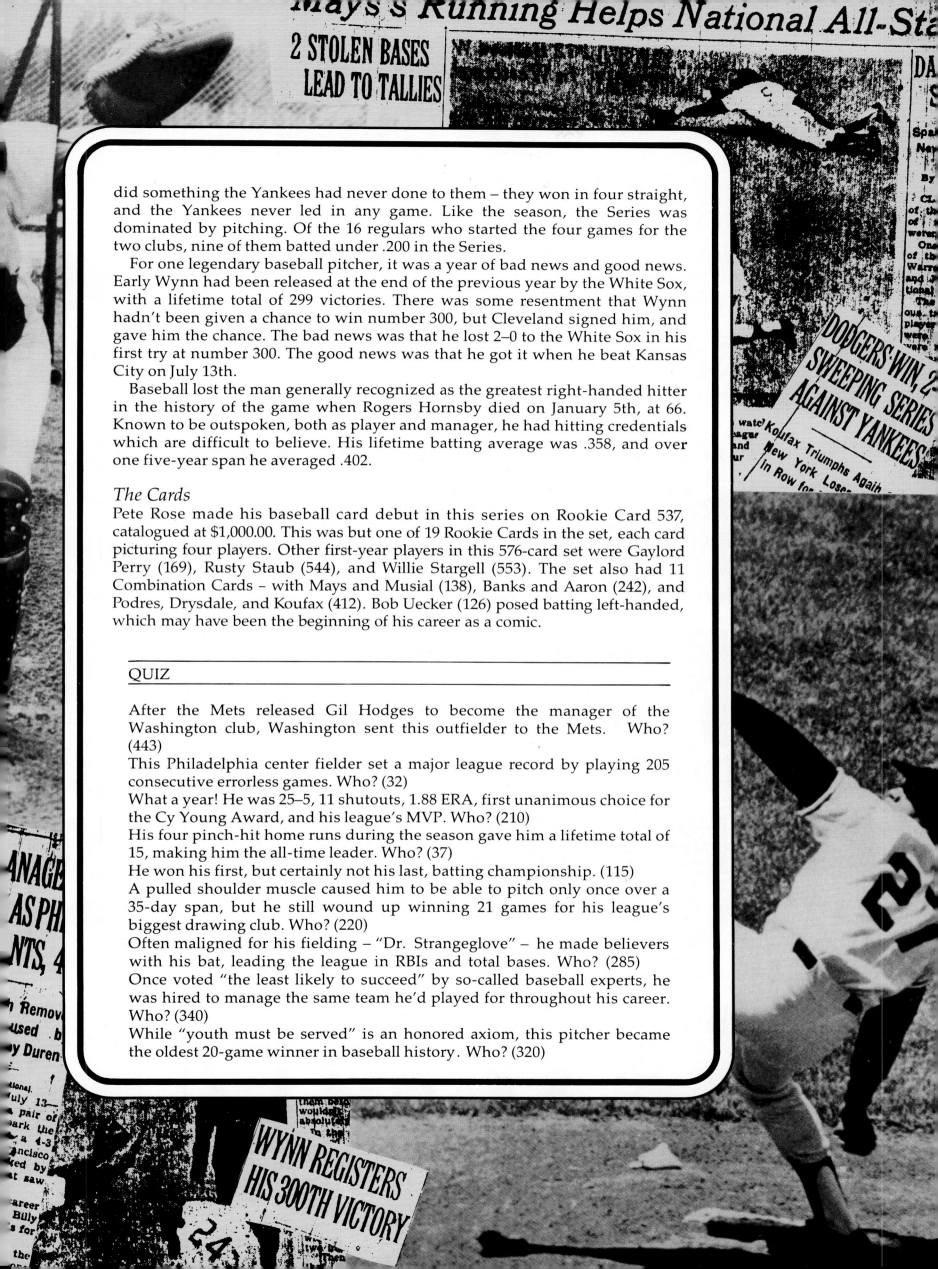

did something the Yankees had never done to them – they won in four straight, and the Yankees never led in any game. Like the season, the Series was dominated by pitching. Of the 16 regulars who started the four games for the two clubs, nine of them batted under .200 in the Series.

For one legendary baseball pitcher, it was a year of bad news and good news. Early Wynn had been released at the end of the previous year by the White Sox, with a lifetime total of 299 victories. There was some resentment that Wynn hadn't been given a chance to win number 300, but Cleveland signed him, and gave him the chance. The bad news was that he lost 2–0 to the White Sox in his first try at number 300. The good news was that he got it when he beat Kansas City on July 13th.

Baseball lost the man generally recognized as the greatest right-handed hitter in the history of the game when Rogers Hornsby died on January 5th, at 66. Known to be outspoken, both as player and manager, he had hitting credentials which are difficult to believe. His lifetime batting average was .358, and over one five-year span he averaged .402.

The Cards
Pete Rose made his baseball card debut in this series on Rookie Card 537, catalogued at $1,000.00. This was but one of 19 Rookie Cards in the set, each card picturing four players. Other first-year players in this 576-card set were Gaylord Perry (169), Rusty Staub (544), and Willie Stargell (553). The set also had 11 Combination Cards – with Mays and Musial (138), Banks and Aaron (242), and Podres, Drysdale, and Koufax (412). Bob Uecker (126) posed batting left-handed, which may have been the beginning of his career as a comic.

QUIZ

After the Mets released Gil Hodges to become the manager of the Washington club, Washington sent this outfielder to the Mets.   Who? (443)

This Philadelphia center fielder set a major league record by playing 205 consecutive errorless games. Who? (32)

What a year! He was 25–5, 11 shutouts, 1.88 ERA, first unanimous choice for the Cy Young Award, and his league's MVP. Who? (210)

His four pinch-hit home runs during the season gave him a lifetime total of 15, making him the all-time leader. Who? (37)

He won his first, but certainly not his last, batting championship. (115)

A pulled shoulder muscle caused him to be able to pitch only once over a 35-day span, but he still wound up winning 21 games for his league's biggest drawing club. Who? (220)

Often maligned for his fielding – "Dr. Strangeglove" – he made believers with his bat, leading the league in RBIs and total bases. Who? (285)

Once voted "the least likely to succeed" by so-called baseball experts, he was hired to manage the same team he'd played for throughout his career. Who? (340)

While "youth must be served" is an honored axiom, this pitcher became the oldest 20-game winner in baseball history. Who? (320)

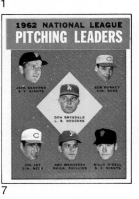

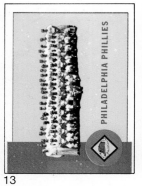
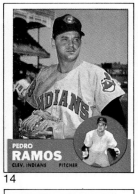
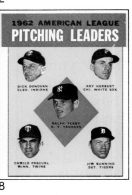
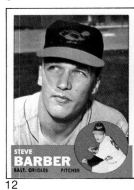

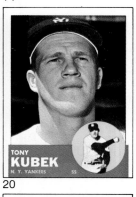
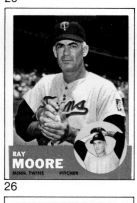

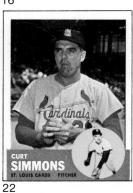

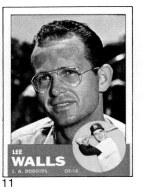
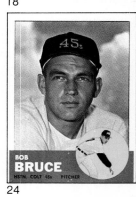
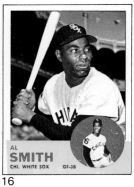
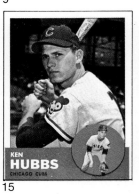
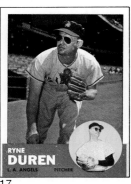
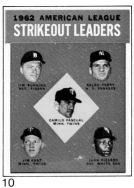
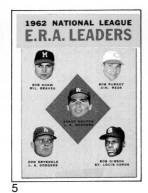

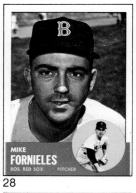
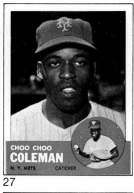
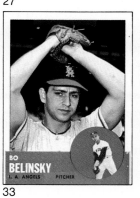

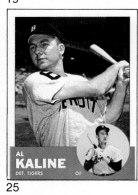
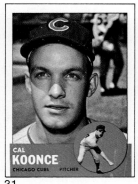
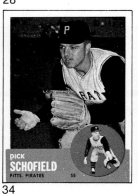

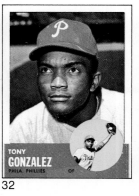
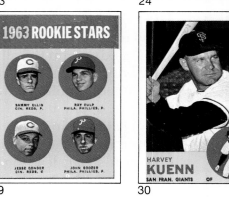

1962 NATIONAL LEAGUE BATTING LEADERS

1962 AMERICAN LEAGUE BATTING LEADERS

1962 NATIONAL LEAGUE HOME RUN LEADERS

1962 AMERICAN LEAGUE HOME RUN LEADERS

1962 NATIONAL LEAGUE E.R.A. LEADERS

1962 AMERICAN LEAGUE E.R.A. LEADERS

1

2

3

4

5

6

1962 NATIONAL LEAGUE PITCHING LEADERS

1962 AMERICAN LEAGUE PITCHING LEADERS

1962 NATIONAL LEAGUE STRIKEOUT LEADERS

1962 AMERICAN LEAGUE STRIKEOUT LEADERS

LEE WALLS — L. A. DODGERS — OF-1B

STEVE BARBER — BALT. ORIOLES — PITCHER

7

8

9

10

11

12

PHILADELPHIA PHILLIES

PEDRO RAMOS — CLEV. INDIANS — PITCHER

KEN HUBBS — CHICAGO CUBS

AL SMITH — CHI. WHITE SOX — OF-3B

RYNE DUREN — L. A. ANGELS — PITCHER

BUC BLASTERS — Smoky Burgess • Dick Stuart • Bob Clemente • Bob Skinner

13

14

15

16

17

18

PETE BURNSIDE — BALT. ORIOLES — PITCHER

TONY KUBEK — N. Y. YANKEES — SS

MARTY KEOUGH — CINCINNATI REDS — OF

CURT SIMMONS — ST. LOUIS CARDS — PITCHER

ED LOPAT — K. C. ATHLETICS — MANAGER

BOB BRUCE — HSTN. COLT .45s — PITCHER

19

20

21

22

23

24

AL KALINE — DET. TIGERS — OF

RAY MOORE — MINN. TWINS — PITCHER

CHOO CHOO COLEMAN — N. Y. METS — CATCHER

MIKE FORNIELES — BOS. RED SOX — PITCHER

1963 ROOKIE STARS — SAMMY ELLIS, CIN. REDS, P • RAY CULP, PHILA. PHILLIES, P • JESSE GONDER, CIN. REDS, C • JOHN BOOZER, PHILA. PHILLIES, P

HARVEY KUENN — SAN FRAN. GIANTS — OF

25

26

27

28

29

30

CAL KOONCE — CHICAGO CUBS — PITCHER

TONY GONZALEZ — PHILA. PHILLIES — OF

BO BELINSKY — L. A. ANGELS — PITCHER

DICK SCHOFIELD — PITTS. PIRATES — SS

JOHN BUZHARDT — CHI. WHITE SOX — PITCHER

JERRY KINDALL — CLEV. INDIANS — 2B

31

32

33

34

35

36

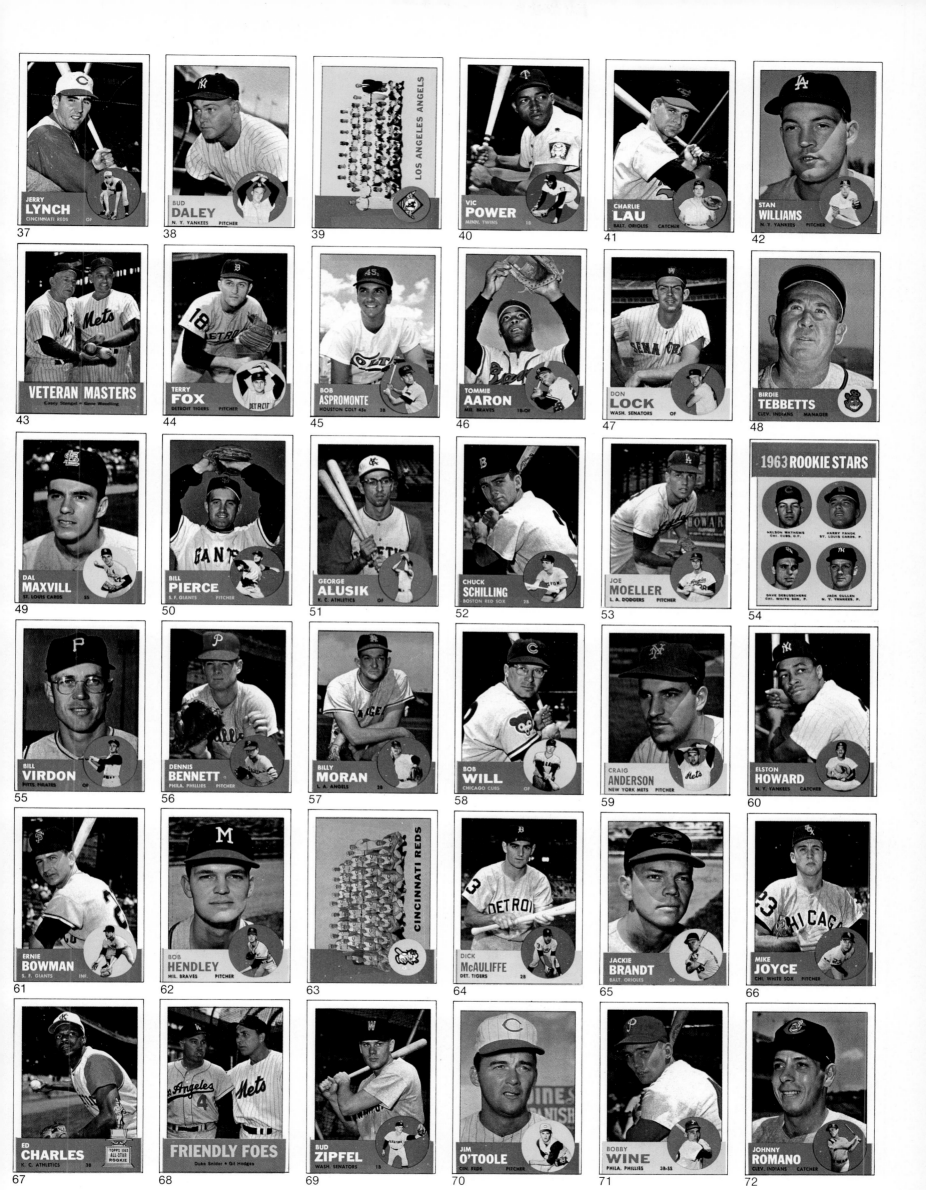

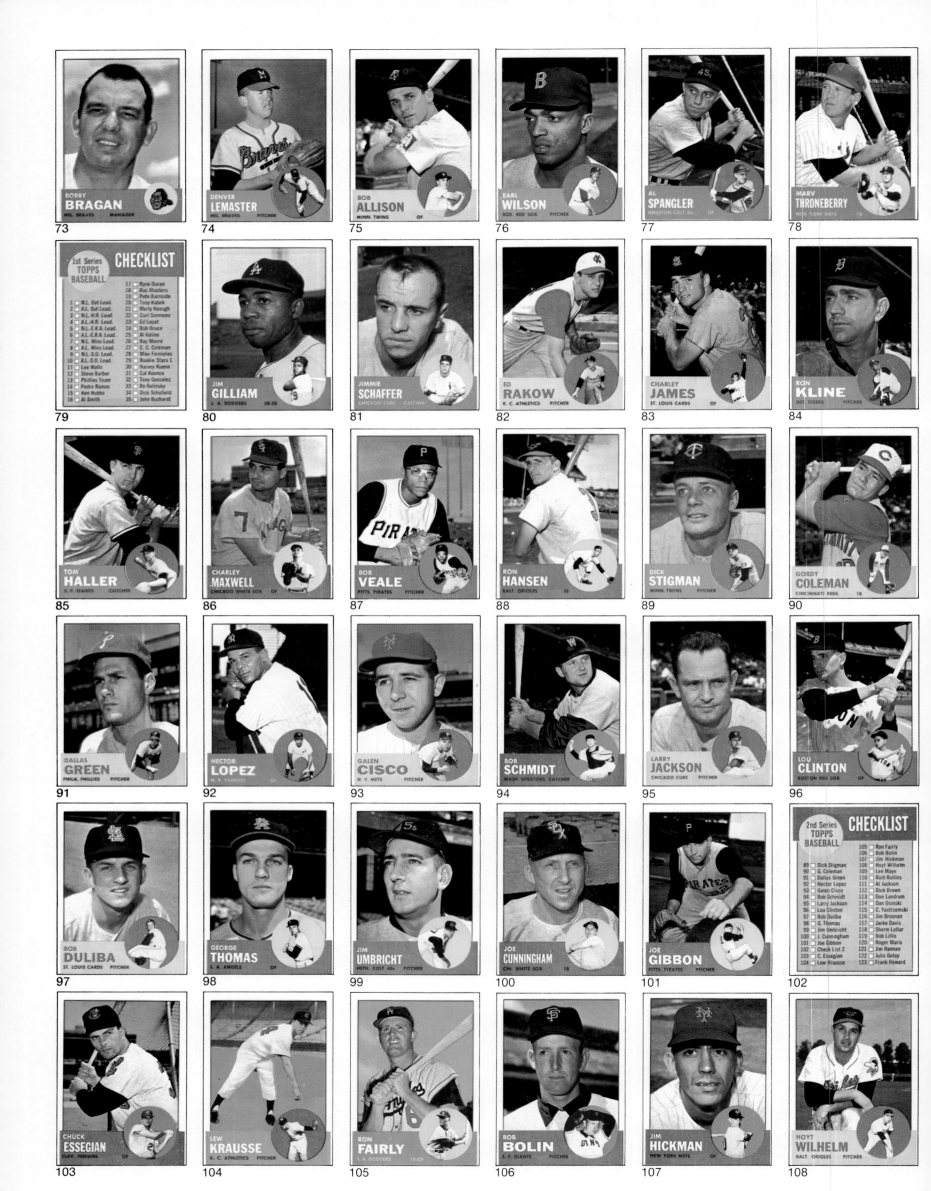

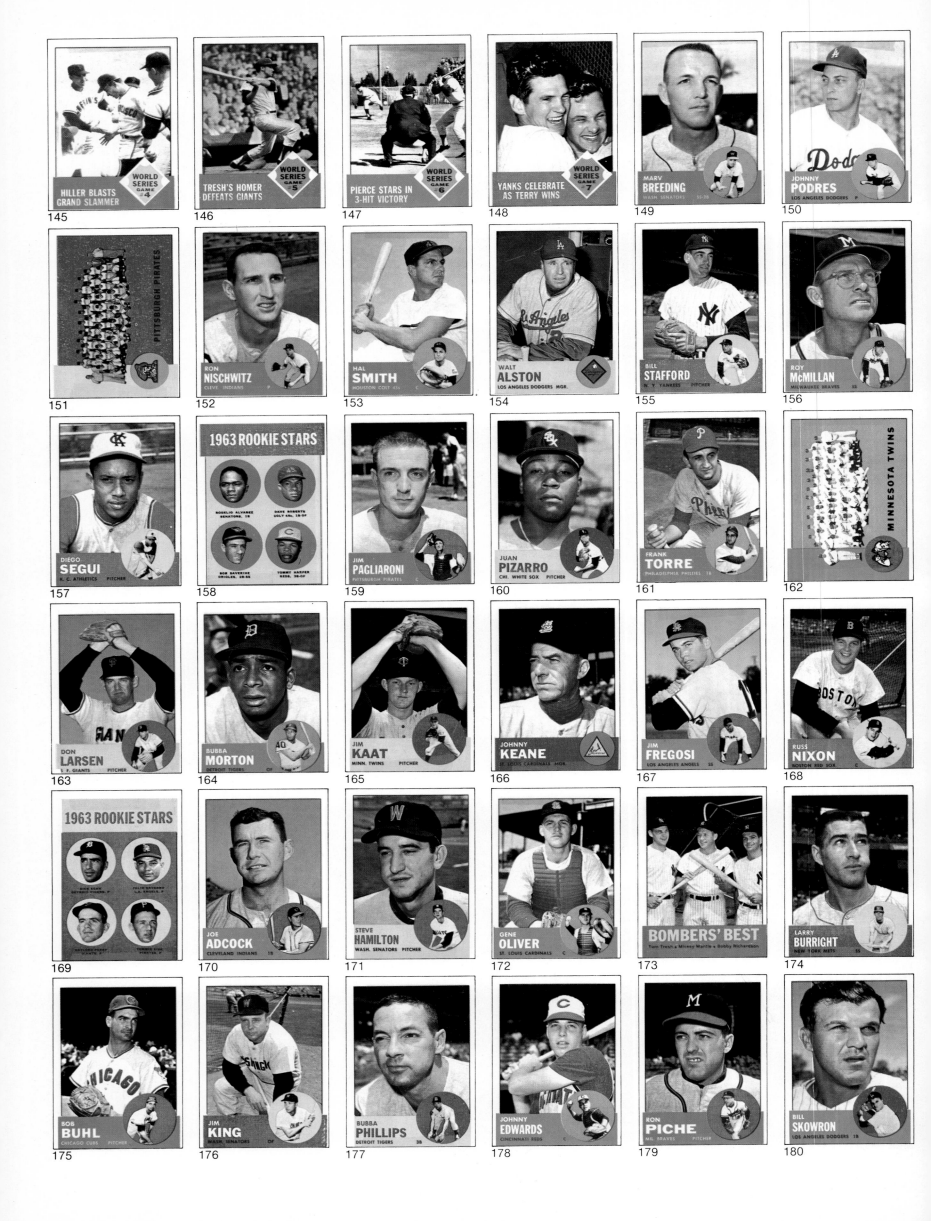

HILLER BLASTS GRAND SLAMMER — WORLD SERIES GAME 4 — 145

TRESH'S HOMER DEFEATS GIANTS — WORLD SERIES GAME 5 — 146

PIERCE STARS IN 3-HIT VICTORY — WORLD SERIES GAME 6 — 147

YANKS CELEBRATE AS TERRY WINS — WORLD SERIES GAME 7 — 148

MARV BREEDING — WASH. SENATORS — SS-2B — 149

JOHNNY PODRES — LOS ANGELES DODGERS — P — 150

PITTSBURGH PIRATES — 151

RON NISCHWITZ — CLEVE. INDIANS — 152

HAL SMITH — HOUSTON COLT 45s — C — 153

WALT ALSTON — LOS ANGELES DODGERS MGR. — 154

BILL STAFFORD — N. Y. YANKEES — PITCHER — 155

ROY McMILLAN — MILWAUKEE BRAVES — SS — 156

DIEGO SEGUI — K. C. ATHLETICS — PITCHER — 157

1963 ROOKIE STARS — ROGELIO ALVAREZ SENATORS, 1B — DAVE ROBERTS COLT 45s, 1B-OF — BOB SAVERINE ORIOLES, 2B-SS — TOMMY HARPER REDS, 3B-OF — 158

JIM PAGLIARONI — PITTSBURGH PIRATES — C — 159

JUAN PIZARRO — CHI. WHITE SOX — PITCHER — 160

FRANK TORRE — PHILADELPHIA PHILLIES — 1B — 161

MINNESOTA TWINS — 162

DON LARSEN — S. F. GIANTS — Pitcher — 163

BUBBA MORTON — DETROIT TIGERS — OF — 164

JIM KAAT — MINN. TWINS — PITCHER — 165

JOHNNY KEANE — ST. LOUIS CARDINALS — MGR. — 166

JIM FREGOSI — LOS ANGELES ANGELS — SS — 167

RUSS NIXON — BOSTON RED SOX — C — 168

1963 ROOKIE STARS — DICK EGAN DETROIT TIGERS, P — JULIO NAVARRO L.A. ANGELS, P — GAYLORD PERRY GIANTS, P — TOMMIE SISK PIRATES, P — 169

JOE ADCOCK — CLEVELAND INDIANS — 1B — 170

STEVE HAMILTON — WASH. SENATORS — PITCHER — 171

GENE OLIVER — ST. LOUIS CARDINALS — C — 172

BOMBERS' BEST — Tom Tresh ● Mickey Mantle ● Bobby Richardson — 173

LARRY BURRIGHT — NEW YORK METS — SS — 174

BOB BUHL — CHICAGO CUBS — PITCHER — 175

JIM KING — WASH. SENATORS — OF — 176

BUBBA PHILLIPS — DETROIT TIGERS — 3B — 177

JOHNNY EDWARDS — CINCINNATI REDS — C — 178

RON PICHE — MIL. BRAVES — PITCHER — 179

BILL SKOWRON — LOS ANGELES DODGERS — 1B — 180

181 SAMMY ESPOSITO — CHICAGO WHITE SOX — INF.
182 ALBIE PEARSON — LOS ANGELES ANGELS — OF
183 JOE PEPITONE — NEW YORK YANKEES — 1B
184 VERN LAW — PITTS. PIRATES — PITCHER
185 CHUCK HILLER — S. F. GIANTS — 2B
186 JERRY ZIMMERMAN — MINNESOTA TWINS — C

187 WILLIE KIRKLAND — CLEVELAND INDIANS — OF
188 EDDIE BRESSOUD — BOSTON RED SOX — SS
189 DAVE GIUSTI — HOUS. COLT 45s — PITCHER
190 MINNIE MINOSO — ST. LOUIS CARDINALS — OF

191
3rd Series TOPPS BASEBALL CHECKLIST
177 Bubba Phillips
178 Johnny Edwards
179 Ron Piche
180 Bill Skowron
181 Sammy Esposito
182 Albie Pearson
183 Joe Pepitone
184 Vern Law
185 Chuck Hiller
186 J. Zimmerman
187 Willie Kirkland
188 Eddie Bressoud
189 Dave Giusti
190 Minnie Minoso
191 Check List 3
192 Clay Dalrymple
193 Andre Rodgers
194 Joe Nuxhall
195 Manny Jimenez
196 Doug Camilli
197 Roger Craig
198 Lenny Green
199 Joe Amalfitano
200 Mickey Mantle
201 Cecil Butler
202 Red Sox Team
203 Chico Cardenas
204 Don Nottebart
205 Luis Aparicio
206 Ray Washburn
207 Ken Hunt
208 Rookie Card 5
209 Hobie Landrith
210 Sandy Koufax
211 Fred Whitfield

192 CLAY DALRYMPLE — PHILADELPHIA PHILLIES — C

193 ANDRE RODGERS — CHICAGO CUBS — SS
194 JOE NUXHALL — CINCINNATI REDS — PITCHER
195 MANNY JIMENEZ — K. C. ATHLETICS — OF — TOPPS 1963 ALL-STAR ROOKIE
196 DOUG CAMILLI — LOS ANGELES DODGERS — C
197 ROGER CRAIG — N. Y. METS — PITCHER
198 LENNY GREEN — MINNESOTA TWINS — OF

199 JOE AMALFITANO — S. F. GIANTS — 2B
200 MICKEY MANTLE — N. Y. YANKEES — OF
201 CECIL BUTLER — MIL. BRAVES — PITCHER
202 BOSTON RED SOX
203 CHICO CARDENAS — CINCINNATI REDS — SS
204 DON NOTTEBART — H. COLT 45s — PITCHER

205 LUIS APARICIO — BALTIMORE ORIOLES — SS
206 RAY WASHBURN — ST. L. CARDS — PITCHER
207 KEN HUNT — L. A. ANGELS — OF
208 1963 ROOKIE STARS — RON HERBEL GIANTS, P. — JOHN MILLER ORIOLES, P. — RON TAYLOR CARDINALS, P. — WALLY WOLF COLT 45s, P.
209 HOBIE LANDRITH — BALTIMORE ORIOLES — C
210 SANDY KOUFAX — L. A. DODGERS — PITCHER

211 FRED WHITFIELD — CLEVELAND INDIANS — 1B — TOPPS 1963 ALL-STAR ROOKIE
212 GLEN HOBBIE — CHICAGO CUBS — PITCHER
213 BILLY HITCHCOCK — BALTIMORE ORIOLES — MGR.
214 ORLANDO PENA — K. C. ATHLETICS — PITCHER
215 BOB SKINNER — PITTS. PIRATES — OF
216 GENE CONLEY — BOS. RED SOX — PITCHER

JOE
CHRISTOPHER
N. Y. METS   OF
217

TIGER TWIRLERS
Frank Lary • Don Mossi • Jim Bunning
218

CHUCK
COTTIER
WASH. SENATORS   2B

219

CAMILO
PASCUAL
MINN. TWINS   PITCHER

220

COOKIE
ROJAS
PHILA. PHILLIES   2B
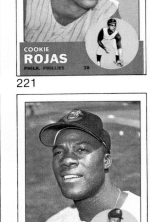
221

CHICAGO CUBS
222

EDDIE
FISHER
CHI. W. SOX   PITCHER
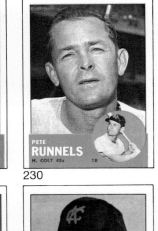
223

MIKE
ROARKE
DETROIT TIGERS   C
224

JOE
JAY
CINN. REDS   PITCHER

225

JULIAN
JAVIER
ST. L. CARDINALS   2B
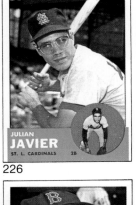
226

JIM
GRANT
CLEVE. INDIANS   PITCHER

227

1963 ROOKIE STARS
MAX ALVIS   ROB BAILEY
INDIANS, 3B   PIRATES, 3B
ED KRANEPOOL   PEDRO OLIVA
N. Y. METS, 1B   TWINS, OF
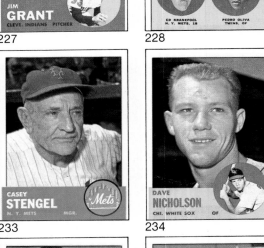
228

WILLIE
DAVIS
L. A. DODGERS   OF
229

PETE
RUNNELS
H. COLT 45s   1B
230

ELI
GRBA
L. A. ANGELS   PITCHER
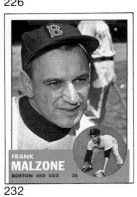
231

FRANK
MALZONE
BOSTON RED SOX   3B

232

CASEY
STENGEL
N. Y. METS   MGR.
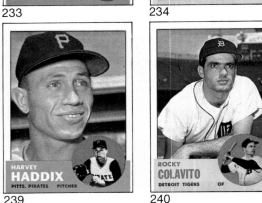
233

DAVE
NICHOLSON
CHI. WHITE SOX   OF
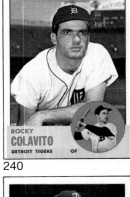
234

BILLY
O'DELL
S. F. GIANTS   PITCHER

235

BILL
BRYAN
K. C. ATHLETICS   C
236

JIM
COATES
N. Y. YANKEES   PITCHER

237

LOU
JOHNSON
MILWAUKEE BRAVES   OF
238

HARVEY
HADDIX
PITTS. PIRATES   PITCHER

239

ROCKY
COLAVITO
DETROIT TIGERS   OF
240

BILLY
SMITH
PHILA. PHILLIES   PITCHER
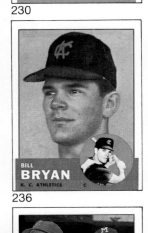
241

POWER PLUS
Ernie Banks • Hank Aaron
242

DON
LEPPERT
WASH. SENATORS   C
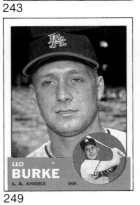
243

JOHN
TSITOURIS
CINN. REDS   PITCHER

244

GIL
HODGES
N. Y. METS   1B

245

LEE
STANGE
MINN. TWINS   PITCHER
246

NEW YORK YANKEES
247

TITO
FRANCONA
CLEVE. INDIANS   OF

248

LEO
BURKE
L. A. ANGELS   INF.

249

STAN
MUSIAL
ST. L. CARDINALS   OF
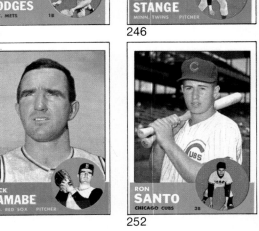
250

JACK
LAMABE
BOS. RED SOX   PITCHER
251

RON
SANTO
CHICAGO CUBS   3B
252

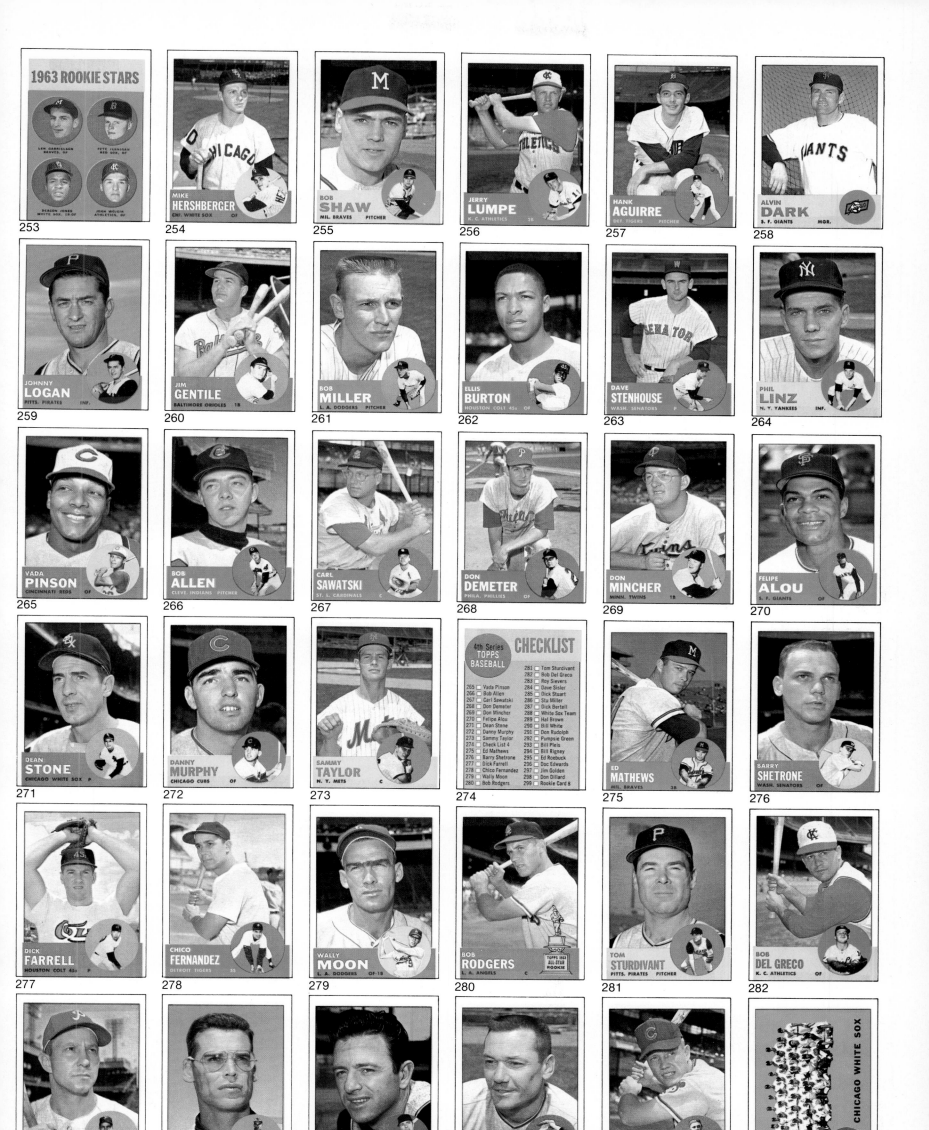

1963 ROOKIE STARS

LEN GABRIELSON BRAVES, OF
PETE JERNIGAN RED SOX, OF
DEACON JONES WHITE SOX, 1B-OF
JOHN WOJCIK ATHLETICS, OF

253

MIKE HERSHBERGER OF
CHI. WHITE SOX
254

BOB SHAW PITCHER
MIL. BRAVES
255

JERRY LUMPE 2B
K. C. ATHLETICS
256

HANK AGUIRRE PITCHER
DET. TIGERS
257

ALVIN DARK MGR.
S. F. GIANTS
258

JOHNNY LOGAN INF.
PITTS. PIRATES
259

JIM GENTILE 1B
BALTIMORE ORIOLES
260

BOB MILLER PITCHER
L. A. DODGERS
261

ELLIS BURTON OF
HOUSTON COLT 45s
262

DAVE STENHOUSE P
WASH. SENATORS
263

PHIL LINZ INF.
N. Y. YANKEES
264

VADA PINSON OF
CINCINNATI REDS
265

BOB ALLEN PITCHER
CLEVE. INDIANS
266

CARL SAWATSKI C
ST. L. CARDINALS
267

DON DEMETER OF
PHILA. PHILLIES
268

DON MINCHER 1B
MINN. TWINS
269

FELIPE ALOU OF
S. F. GIANTS
270

DEAN STONE P
CHICAGO WHITE SOX
271

DANNY MURPHY OF
CHICAGO CUBS
272

SAMMY TAYLOR C
N. Y. METS
273

4th Series TOPPS BASEBALL CHECKLIST

265 ☐ Vada Pinson
266 ☐ Bob Allen
267 ☐ Carl Sawatski
268 ☐ Don Demeter
269 ☐ Don Mincher
270 ☐ Felipe Alou
271 ☐ Dean Stone
272 ☐ Danny Murphy
273 ☐ Sammy Taylor
274 ☐ Check List 4
275 ☐ Ed Mathews
276 ☐ Barry Shetrone
277 ☐ Dick Farrell
278 ☐ Chico Fernandez
279 ☐ Wally Moon
280 ☐ Bob Rodgers

281 ☐ Tom Sturdivant
282 ☐ Bob Del Greco
283 ☐ Roy Sievers
284 ☐ Dave Sisler
285 ☐ Dick Stuart
286 ☐ Stu Miller
287 ☐ Dick Bertell
288 ☐ White Sox Team
289 ☐ Hal Brown
290 ☐ Bill White
291 ☐ Don Rudolph
292 ☐ Pumpsie Green
293 ☐ Bill Pleis
294 ☐ Bill Rigney
295 ☐ Ed Roebuck
296 ☐ Doc Edwards
297 ☐ Jim Golden
298 ☐ Don Dillard
299 ☐ Rookie Card 8

274

ED MATHEWS 3B
MIL. BRAVES
275

BARRY SHETRONE OF
WASH. SENATORS
276

DICK FARRELL P
HOUSTON COLT 45s
277

CHICO FERNANDEZ SS
DETROIT TIGERS
278

WALLY MOON OF-1B
L. A. DODGERS
279

BOB RODGERS C
L. A. ANGELS
280

TOM STURDIVANT PITCHER
PITTS. PIRATES
281

BOB DEL GRECO OF
K. C. ATHLETICS
282

ROY SIEVERS 1B
PHILA. PHILLIES
283

DAVE SISLER P
CINCINNATI REDS
284

DICK STUART 1B
BOSTON RED SOX
285

STU MILLER P
BALTIMORE ORIOLES
286

DICK BERTELL C
CHICAGO CUBS
287

CHICAGO WHITE SOX
288

HAL BROWN
NEW YORK YANKEES P

289

BILL WHITE
ST. LOUIS CARDINALS 1B

290

DON RUDOLPH
WASH. SENATORS P

291

PUMPSIE GREEN
NEW YORK METS SS-2B

292

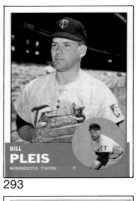

BILL PLEIS
MINNESOTA TWINS P

293

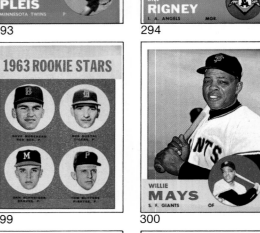

BILL RIGNEY
L. A. ANGELS MGR.

294

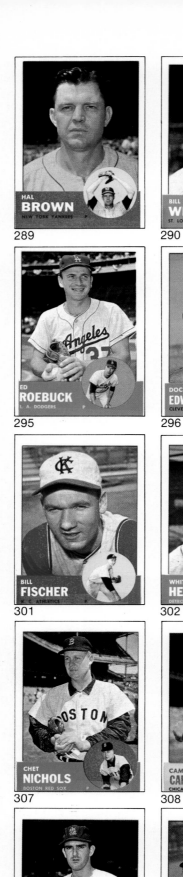

ED ROEBUCK
L. A. DODGERS P

295

DOC EDWARDS
CLEVELAND INDIANS C

296

JIM GOLDEN
HOUSTON COLT 45s P

297

DON DILLARD
MILWAUKEE BRAVES OF

298

1963 ROOKIE STARS

299

WILLIE MAYS
S. F. GIANTS OF

300

BILL FISCHER
K. C. ATHLETICS P

301

WHITEY HERZOG
DETROIT TIGERS OF

302

EARL FRANCIS
PITTSBURGH PIRATES P

303

HARRY BRIGHT
CINCINNATI REDS INF.

304

DON HOAK
PHILADELPHIA PHILLIES 3B

305

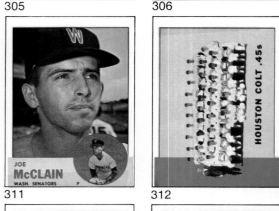

STAR RECEIVERS
Earl Battey • Elston Howard

306

CHET NICHOLS
BOSTON RED SOX P

307

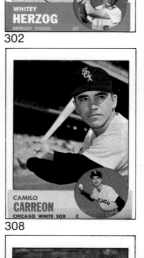

CAMILO CARREON
CHICAGO WHITE SOX C

308

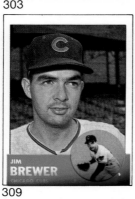

JIM BREWER
CHICAGO CUBS P

309

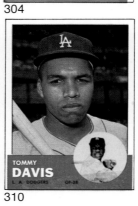

TOMMY DAVIS
L. A. DODGERS OF-3B

310

JOE McCLAIN
WASH. SENATORS P

311

HOUSTON COLT .45s

312

ERNIE BROGLIO
ST. LOUIS CARDINALS P

313

JOHN GORYL
MINNESOTA TWINS 3B-2B

314

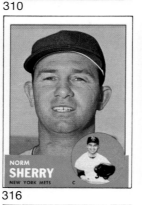

RALPH TERRY
N. Y. YANKEES P

315

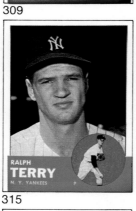

NORM SHERRY
NEW YORK METS C

316

SAM McDOWELL
CLEVELAND INDIANS P

317

GENE MAUCH
PHILA. PHILLIES MGR.

318

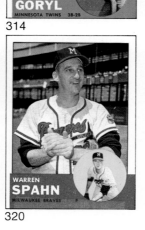

JOE GAINES
BALTIMORE ORIOLES OF

319

WARREN SPAHN
MILWAUKEE BRAVES P

320

GINO CIMOLI
K. C. ATHLETICS OF

321

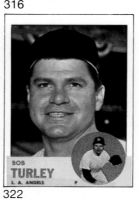

BOB TURLEY
L. A. ANGELS P

322

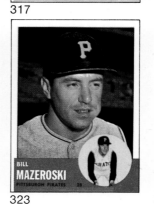

BILL MAZEROSKI
PITTSBURGH PIRATES 2B

323

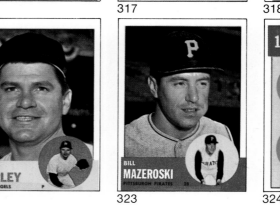

1963 ROOKIE STARS

324

325	326	327	328	329	330
JACK SANFORD S. F. GIANTS P	HANK FOILES CINCINNATI REDS C	PAUL FOYTACK DETROIT TIGERS P	DICK WILLIAMS BOSTON RED SOX INF-OF	LINDY McDANIEL CHICAGO CUBS P	CHUCK HINTON WASH. SENATORS OF

331	332	333	334	335	336
SERIES FOES Bill Stafford • Bill Pierce	JOEL HORLEN CHICAGO WHITE SOX P	CARL WARWICK HOUSTON COLT 45s OF	WYNN HAWKINS NEW YORK METS P	LEON WAGNER L. A. ANGELS OF	ED BAUTA ST. LOUIS CARDINALS P

337	338	339	340	341	342
LOS ANGELES DODGERS	RUSS KEMMERER HOUSTON COLT 45s P	TED BOWSFIELD K. C. ATHLETICS P	YOGI BERRA N. Y. YANKEES C-COACH	JACK BALDSCHUN PHILADELPHIA PHILLIES P	GENE WOODLING NEW YORK METS OF

343	344	345	346	347	348
JOHNNY PESKY BOSTON RED SOX MGR.	DON SCHWALL PITTSBURGH PIRATES P	BROOKS ROBINSON BALTIMORE ORIOLES 3B	BILLY HOEFT S. F. GIANTS P	JOE TORRE MILWAUKEE BRAVES C	VIC WERTZ DETROIT TIGERS 1B

349	350	351	352	353	354
ZOILO VERSALLES MINNESOTA TWINS SS	BOB PURKEY CINCINNATI REDS P	AL LUPLOW CLEVELAND INDIANS OF	KEN JOHNSON HOUSTON COLT 45s P	BILLY WILLIAMS CHICAGO CUBS OF	DOM ZANNI CHICAGO WHITE SOX P

355	356	357	358	359	360
DEAN CHANCE L. A. ANGELS P	JOHN SCHAIVE WASH. SENATORS 2B-3B	GEORGE ALTMAN ST. LOUIS CARDINALS OF	MILT PAPPAS BALTIMORE ORIOLES P	HAYWOOD SULLIVAN K. C. ATHLETICS C	DON DRYSDALE L. A. DODGERS P

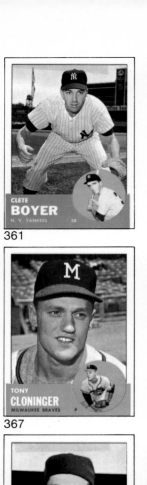

CLETE BOYER N. Y. Yankees 3B
361

5th Series TOPPS BASEBALL **CHECKLIST**

353 □ Billy Williams
354 □ Dom Zanni
355 □ Dean Chance
356 □ John Schaive
357 □ George Altman
358 □ Milt Pappas
359 □ Haywood Sullivan
360 □ Don Drysdale
361 □ Clete Boyer
362 □ Check List 5
363 □ Dick Radatz
364 □ Howie Goss
365 □ Jim Bunning
366 □ Tony Taylor
367 □ Tony Cloninger
368 □ Ed Bailey

369 □ Jim Lemon
370 □ Dick Donovan
371 □ Rod Kanehl
372 □ Don Lee
373 □ Jim Campbell
374 □ Claude Osteen
375 □ Ken Boyer
376 □ Johnnie Wyatt
377 □ Orioles Team
378 □ Bill Henry
379 □ Bob Anderson
380 □ Ernie Banks
381 □ Frank Baumann
382 □ Ralph Houk
383 □ Pete Richert
384 □ Bob Tillman
385 □ Art Mahaffey
386 □ Rookie Card 10
387 □ Al McBean
362

DICK RADATZ BOSTON RED SOX P
363

HOWIE GOSS PITTSBURGH PIRATES OF
364

JIM BUNNING DETROIT TIGERS
365

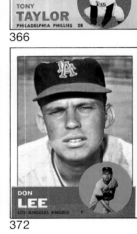

TONY TAYLOR PHILADELPHIA PHILLIES 2B
366

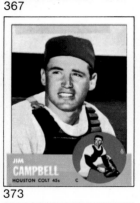

TONY CLONINGER MILWAUKEE BRAVES P
367

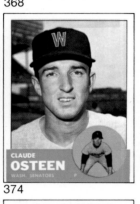

ED BAILEY S. F. GIANTS C
368

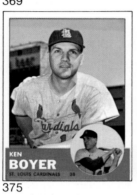

JIM LEMON MINNESOTA TWINS OF
369

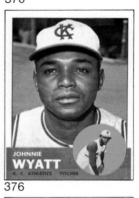

DICK DONOVAN CLEVELAND INDIANS P
370

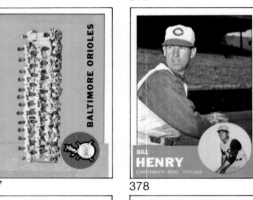

ROD KANEHL NEW YORK METS INF-OF
371

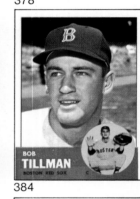

DON LEE LOS ANGELES ANGELS
372

JIM CAMPBELL HOUSTON COLT 45s C
373

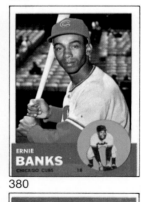

CLAUDE OSTEEN WASH. SENATORS P
374

KEN BOYER ST. LOUIS CARDINALS 3B
375

JOHNNIE WYATT K. C. ATHLETICS PITCHER
376

BALTIMORE ORIOLES
377

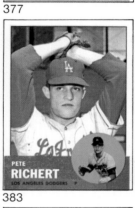

BILL HENRY CINCINNATI REDS PITCHER
378

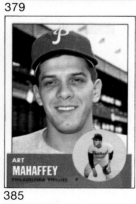

BOB ANDERSON DETROIT TIGERS PITCHER
379

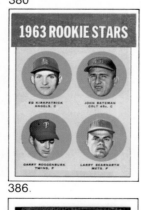

ERNIE BANKS CHICAGO CUBS 1B
380

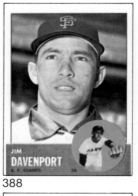

FRANK BAUMANN CHICAGO WHITE SOX P
381

RALPH HOUK NEW YORK YANKEES MGR.
382

PETE RICHERT LOS ANGELES DODGERS P
383

BOB TILLMAN BOSTON RED SOX C
384

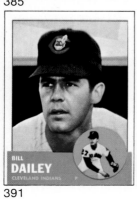

ART MAHAFFEY PHILADELPHIA PHILLIES P
385

1963 ROOKIE STARS

ED KIRKPATRICK ANGELS, C
JOHN BATEMAN COLT 45s, C
GARRY ROGGENBURK TWINS, P
LARRY BEARNARTH METS, P

386.

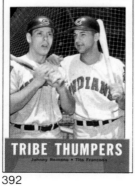

AL McBEAN PITTSBURGH PIRATES P
387

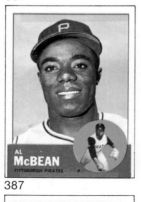

JIM DAVENPORT S. F. GIANTS 3B
388

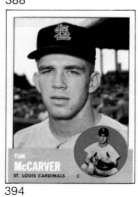

FRANK SULLIVAN MINN. TWINS PITCHER
389

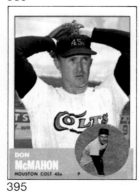

HANK AARON MILWAUKEE BRAVES OF
390

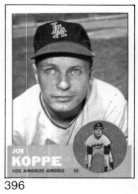

BILL DAILEY CLEVELAND INDIANS
391

TRIBE THUMPERS
Johnny Romano • Tito Francona
392

KEN MacKENZIE NEW YORK METS PITCHER
393

TIM McCARVER ST. LOUIS CARDINALS C
394

DON McMAHON HOUSTON COLT 45s
395

JOE KOPPE LOS ANGELES ANGELS SS
396

397

398 BOOG POWELL BALTIMORE ORIOLES OF

399 DICK ELLSWORTH CHICAGO CUBS PITCHER

400 FRANK ROBINSON CINCINNATI REDS OF

401 JIM BOUTON NEW YORK YANKEES P

402 MICKEY VERNON WASH SENATORS MGR.

403 RON PERRANOSKI LOS ANGELES DODGERS P

404 BOB OLDIS PHILADELPHIA PHILLIES C

405 FLOYD ROBINSON CHICAGO WHITE SOX OF

406 HOWIE KOPLITZ DETROIT TIGERS PITCHER

407 1963 ROOKIE STARS
FRANK KOSTRO TIGERS 3B • CHICO RUIZ REDS 2B • DICK SIMPSON ANGELS OF • LARRY ELLIOT PIRATES OF

408 BILLY GARDNER BOSTON RED SOX 2B

409 ROY FACE PITTSBURGH PIRATES P

410 EARL BATTEY MINNESOTA TWINS C

411 JIM CONSTABLE MILWAUKEE BRAVES P

412 DODGERS' BIG THREE Johnny Podres • Don Drysdale • Sandy Koufax

413 JERRY WALKER CLEVELAND INDIANS P

414 TY CLINE MILWAUKEE BRAVES OF

415 BOB GIBSON ST. LOUIS CARDINALS P

416 ALEX GRAMMAS CHICAGO CUBS SS

417 SAN FRANCISCO GIANTS

418 JOHNNY ORSINO BALTIMORE ORIOLES C

419 TRACY STALLARD NEW YORK METS PITCHER

420 BOBBY RICHARDSON NEW YORK YANKEES 2B

421 TOM MORGAN LOS ANGELES ANGELS P

422 FRED HUTCHINSON CINCINNATI REDS MGR.

423 ED HOBAUGH WASH. SENATORS P

424 CHARLEY SMITH CHICAGO WHITE SOX 3B

425 SMOKY BURGESS PITTSBURGH PIRATES C

426 BARRY LATMAN CLEVELAND INDIANS P

427 BERNIE ALLEN MINNESOTA TWINS 2B

428 CARL BOLES S.F. GIANTS OF

429 LOU BURDETTE MILWAUKEE BRAVES P

430 NORM SIEBERN K.C. ATHLETICS 1B

431 6th Series TOPPS BASEBALL CHECKLIST
430 □ Norm Siebern
431 □ Check List 6
432 □ Roman Mejias
433 □ Denis Menke
434 □ Johnny Callison
435 □ Woody Held
436 □ Tim Harkness
437 □ Bill Bruton
438 □ Wes Stock
439 □ Don Zimmer
440 □ Juan Marichal
441 □ Lee Thomas
442 □ J. C. Hartman
443 □ Jim Piersall
444 □ Jim Maloney
445 □ Norm Cash
446 □ Whitey Ford
447 □ Felix Mantilla
448 □ Jack Kralick
449 □ Jose Tartabull
450 □ Bob Friend
451 □ Indians Team
452 □ Barney Schultz
453 □ Jake Wood
454 □ Art Fowler
455 □ Ruben Amaro
456 □ Jim Coker
457 □ Tex Clevenger
458 □ Al Lopez
459 □ Dick LeMay
460 □ Del Crandall
461 □ Norm Bass
462 □ Wally Post
463 □ Joe Schaffernoth
464 □ Ken Aspromonte

432 ROMAN MEJIAS BOSTON RED SOX OF

DENIS
MENKE
MILWAUKEE BRAVES SS-2B
433

JOHNNY
CALLISON
PHILADELPHIA PHILLIES OF
434

WOODY
HELD
CLEVELAND INDIANS SS
435

TIM
HARKNESS
NEW YORK METS 1B
436

BILL
BRUTON
DETROIT TIGERS OF
437

WES
STOCK
BALTIMORE ORIOLES P
438

DON
ZIMMER
L.A. DODGERS 3B-2B
439

JUAN
MARICHAL
S.F. GIANTS PITCHER
440

LEE
THOMAS
L.A. ANGELS OF-1B
441

J. C.
HARTMAN
HOUSTON COLT 45s SS
442

JIM
PIERSALL
WASH. SENATORS OF
443

JIM
MALONEY
CINCINNATI REDS PITCHER
444

NORM
CASH
DETROIT TIGERS 1B
445

WHITEY
FORD
NEW YORK YANKEES P
446

FELIX
MANTILLA
BOSTON RED SOX INF-OF
447

JACK
KRALICK
MINNESOTA TWINS P
448

JOSE
TARTABULL
ATHLETICS OF
449

BOB
FRIEND
PITTSBURGH PIRATES P
450

CLEVELAND INDIANS
451

BARNEY
SCHULTZ
CHICAGO CUBS PITCHER
452

JAKE
WOOD
DETROIT TIGERS 2B-SS
453

ART
FOWLER
LOS ANGELES ANGELS P
454

RUBEN
AMARO
PHIL. PHILLIES SS
455

JIM
COKER
S.F. GIANTS C
456

TEX
CLEVENGER
NEW YORK YANKEES P
457

AL
LOPEZ
CHICAGO WHITE SOX MGR.
458

DICK
LeMAY
CHICAGO CUBS
459

DEL
CRANDALL
MILWAUKEE BRAVES C
460

NORM
BASS
K. C. ATHLETICS
461

WALLY
POST
CINCINNATI REDS OF
462

JOE
SCHAFFERNOTH
CLEVELAND INDIANS P
463

KEN
ASPROMONTE
CHICAGO CUBS 2B
464

CHUCK
ESTRADA
BALTIMORE ORIOLES P
465

1963 ROOKIE STARS

NATE OLIVER
L. A. DODGERS, 2B

TONY MARTINEZ
CLEVELAND INDIANS, SS

JERRY ROBINSON
S. F. GIANTS, 2B-OF

BILL FREEHAN
DETROIT TIGERS, C

466

PHIL
ORTEGA
LOS ANGELES DODGERS P
467

CARROLL
HARDY
HOUSTON COLT .45s OF
468

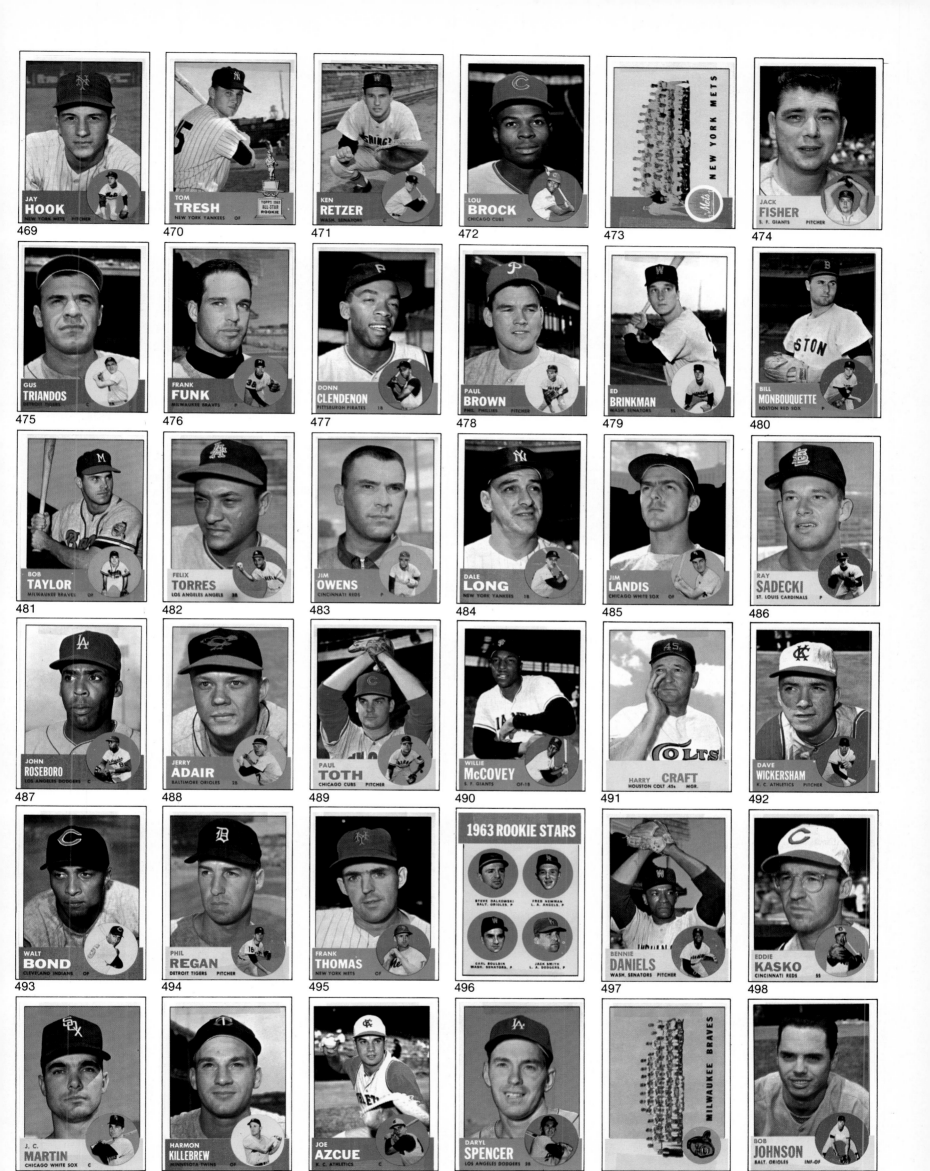

JAY HOOK NEW YORK METS PITCHER
469

TOM TRESH NEW YORK YANKEES OF
470

KEN RETZER WASH. SENATORS C
471

LOU BROCK CHICAGO CUBS OF
472

NEW YORK METS
473

JACK FISHER S. F. GIANTS PITCHER
474

GUS TRIANDOS DETROIT TIGERS C
475

FRANK FUNK MILWAUKEE BRAVES P
476

DONN CLENDENON PITTSBURGH PIRATES 1B
477

PAUL BROWN PHIL. PHILLIES PITCHER
478

ED BRINKMAN WASH. SENATORS SS
479

BILL MONBOUQUETTE BOSTON RED SOX P
480

BOB TAYLOR MILWAUKEE BRAVES OF
481

FELIX TORRES LOS ANGELES ANGELS 3B
482

JIM OWENS CINCINNATI REDS P
483

DALE LONG NEW YORK YANKEES 1B
484

JIM LANDIS CHICAGO WHITE SOX OF
485

RAY SADECKI ST. LOUIS CARDINALS P
486

JOHN ROSEBORO LOS ANGELES DODGERS C
487

JERRY ADAIR BALTIMORE ORIOLES 2B
488

PAUL TOTH CHICAGO CUBS PITCHER
489

WILLIE McCOVEY S. F. GIANTS OF-1B
490

HARRY CRAFT HOUSTON COLT 45s MGR.
491

DAVE WICKERSHAM K. C. ATHLETICS PITCHER
492

WALT BOND CLEVELAND INDIANS OF
493

PHIL REGAN DETROIT TIGERS PITCHER
494

FRANK THOMAS NEW YORK METS OF
495

1963 ROOKIE STARS
STEVE DALKOWSKI BALT. ORIOLES, P
FRED NEWMAN L. A. ANGELS, P
CARL BOULDIN WASH. SENATORS, P
JACK SMITH L. A. DODGERS, P
496

BENNIE DANIELS WASH. SENATORS PITCHER
497

EDDIE KASKO CINCINNATI REDS SS
498

J. C. MARTIN CHICAGO WHITE SOX C
499

HARMON KILLEBREW MINNESOTA TWINS OF
500

JOE AZCUE K. C. ATHLETICS C
501

DARYL SPENCER LOS ANGELES DODGERS 2B
502

MILWAUKEE BRAVES
503

BOB JOHNSON BALT. ORIOLES INF-OF
504

CURT
FLOOD
ST. LOUIS CARDINALS OF
505

GENE
GREEN
CLEVELAND INDIANS OF-C
506

ROLAND
SHELDON
NEW YORK YANKEES P
507

TED
SAVAGE
PITTSBURGH PIRATES OF
508

509

KEN
McBRIDE
LOS ANGELES ANGELS
510

CHARLIE
NEAL
NEW YORK METS 3B-SS
511

CAL
McLISH
PHILA PHILLIES PITCHER
512

GARY
GEIGER
BOSTON RED SOX OF
513

LARRY
OSBORNE
WASH SENATORS 3B-1B
514

DON
ELSTON
CHICAGO CUBS PITCHER
515

PURNAL
GOLDY
DETROIT TIGERS OF
516

HAL
WOODESHICK
HOUSTON COLT 45s P
517

DON
BLASINGAME
CINCINNATI REDS 2B
518

CLAUDE
RAYMOND
MILWAUKEE BRAVES P
519

ORLANDO
CEPEDA
S. F. GIANTS 1B
520

DAN
PFISTER
K. C. ATHLETICS PITCHER
521

1963 ROOKIE STARS

MEL NELSON
L. A. ANGELS P

GARY PETERS
CHI. WHITE SOX P

ART QUIRK
WASH. SENATORS, P

JIM ROLAND
MINNESOTA TWINS, P
522

BILL
KUNKEL
NEW YORK YANKEES P
523

ST. LOUIS CARDINALS
524

NELLIE
FOX
CHI. WHITE SOX 2B
525

DICK
HALL
BALTIMORE ORIOLES P
526

ED
SADOWSKI
L. A. ANGELS C
527

CARL
WILLEY
NEW YORK METS PITCHER
528

WES
COVINGTON
PHILA PHILLIES OF
529

DON
MOSSI
DETROIT TIGERS PITCHER
530

SAM
MELE
MINNESOTA TWINS MGR.
531

STEVE
BOROS
CHICAGO CUBS 3B
532

BOBBY
SHANTZ
ST. LOUIS CARDS PITCHER
533

KEN
WALTERS
CINCINNATI REDS OF
534

JIM
PERRY
MINNESOTA TWINS P
535

NORM
LARKER
MILWAUKEE BRAVES 1B
536

1963 ROOKIE STARS

PEDRO GONZALEZ
N. Y. YANKEES, 2B

KEN McMULLEN
L. A. DODGERS, 3B

PETE ROSE
CINCINNATI REDS, 2B

AL WEIS
CHI. WHITE SOX, SS
537

GEORGE
BRUNET
HOUSTON COLT 45s P
538

WAYNE
CAUSEY
K. C. ATHLETICS SS-3B
539

BOB
CLEMENTE
PITTSBURGH PIRATES OF
540

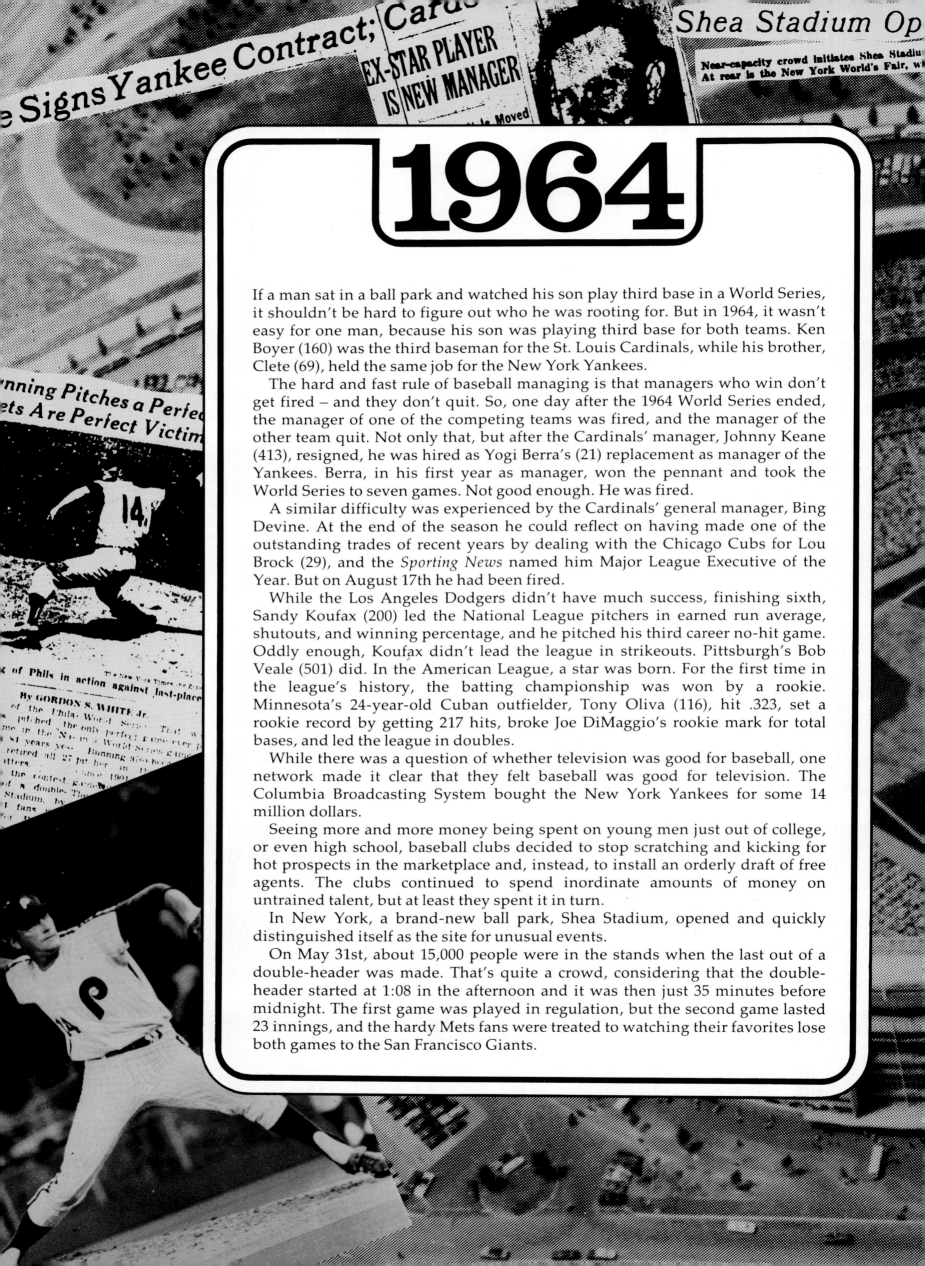

1964

If a man sat in a ball park and watched his son play third base in a World Series, it shouldn't be hard to figure out who he was rooting for. But in 1964, it wasn't easy for one man, because his son was playing third base for both teams. Ken Boyer (160) was the third baseman for the St. Louis Cardinals, while his brother, Clete (69), held the same job for the New York Yankees.

The hard and fast rule of baseball managing is that managers who win don't get fired – and they don't quit. So, one day after the 1964 World Series ended, the manager of one of the competing teams was fired, and the manager of the other team quit. Not only that, but after the Cardinals' manager, Johnny Keane (413), resigned, he was hired as Yogi Berra's (21) replacement as manager of the Yankees. Berra, in his first year as manager, won the pennant and took the World Series to seven games. Not good enough. He was fired.

A similar difficulty was experienced by the Cardinals' general manager, Bing Devine. At the end of the season he could reflect on having made one of the outstanding trades of recent years by dealing with the Chicago Cubs for Lou Brock (29), and the *Sporting News* named him Major League Executive of the Year. But on August 17th he had been fired.

While the Los Angeles Dodgers didn't have much success, finishing sixth, Sandy Koufax (200) led the National League pitchers in earned run average, shutouts, and winning percentage, and he pitched his third career no-hit game. Oddly enough, Koufax didn't lead the league in strikeouts. Pittsburgh's Bob Veale (501) did. In the American League, a star was born. For the first time in the league's history, the batting championship was won by a rookie. Minnesota's 24-year-old Cuban outfielder, Tony Oliva (116), hit .323, set a rookie record by getting 217 hits, broke Joe DiMaggio's rookie mark for total bases, and led the league in doubles.

While there was a question of whether television was good for baseball, one network made it clear that they felt baseball was good for television. The Columbia Broadcasting System bought the New York Yankees for some 14 million dollars.

Seeing more and more money being spent on young men just out of college, or even high school, baseball clubs decided to stop scratching and kicking for hot prospects in the marketplace and, instead, to install an orderly draft of free agents. The clubs continued to spend inordinate amounts of money on untrained talent, but at least they spent it in turn.

In New York, a brand-new ball park, Shea Stadium, opened and quickly distinguished itself as the site for unusual events.

On May 31st, about 15,000 people were in the stands when the last out of a double-header was made. That's quite a crowd, considering that the double-header started at 1:08 in the afternoon and it was then just 35 minutes before midnight. The first game was played in regulation, but the second game lasted 23 innings, and the hardy Mets fans were treated to watching their favorites lose both games to the San Francisco Giants.

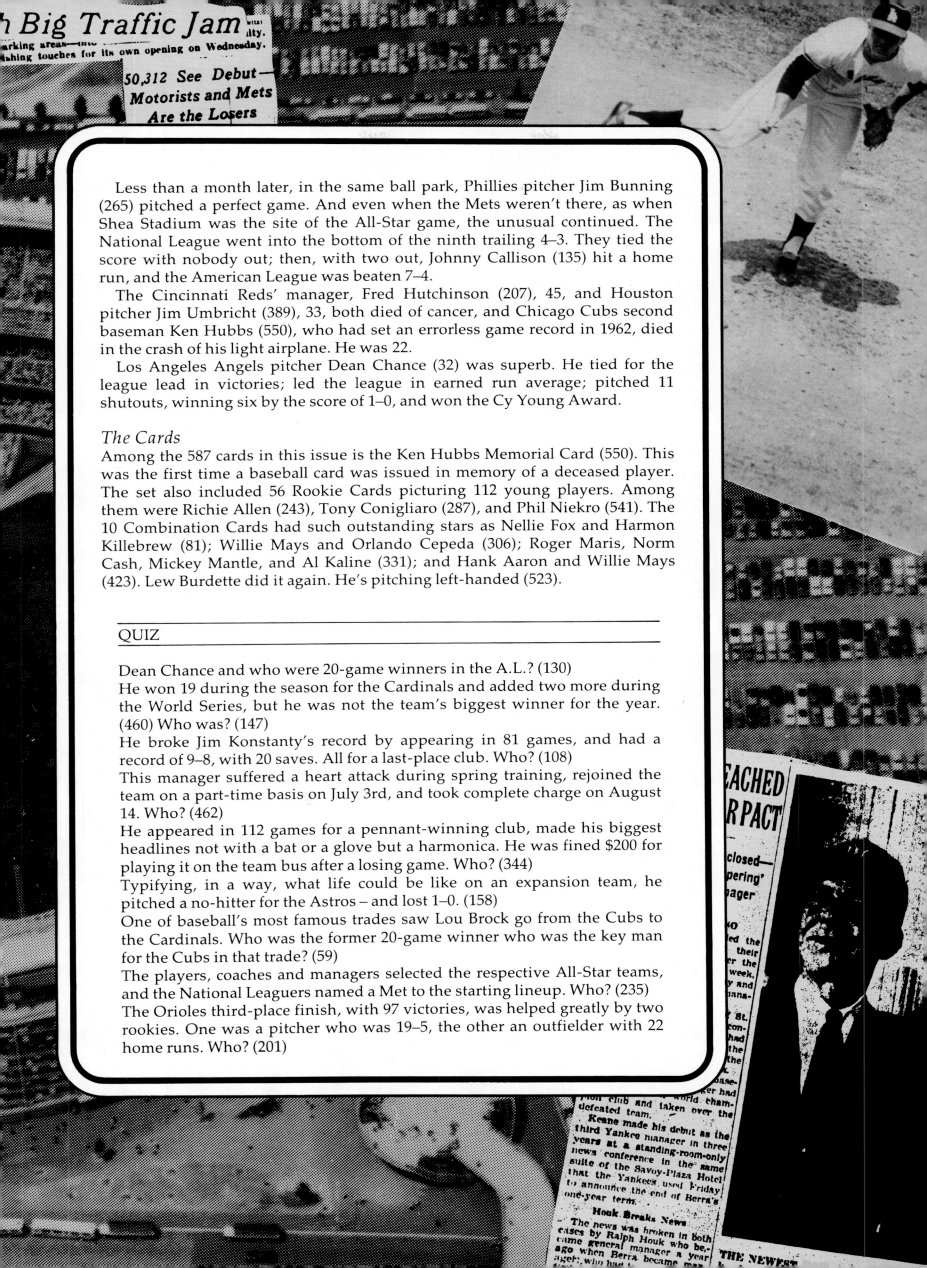

h Big Traffic Jam

arking areas—into
shing touches for its own opening on Wednesday.

**50,312 See Debut—
Motorists and Mets
Are the Losers**

Less than a month later, in the same ball park, Phillies pitcher Jim Bunning (265) pitched a perfect game. And even when the Mets weren't there, as when Shea Stadium was the site of the All-Star game, the unusual continued. The National League went into the bottom of the ninth trailing 4–3. They tied the score with nobody out; then, with two out, Johnny Callison (135) hit a home run, and the American League was beaten 7–4.

The Cincinnati Reds' manager, Fred Hutchinson (207), 45, and Houston pitcher Jim Umbricht (389), 33, both died of cancer, and Chicago Cubs second baseman Ken Hubbs (550), who had set an errorless game record in 1962, died in the crash of his light airplane. He was 22.

Los Angeles Angels pitcher Dean Chance (32) was superb. He tied for the league lead in victories; led the league in earned run average; pitched 11 shutouts, winning six by the score of 1–0, and won the Cy Young Award.

The Cards

Among the 587 cards in this issue is the Ken Hubbs Memorial Card (550). This was the first time a baseball card was issued in memory of a deceased player. The set also included 56 Rookie Cards picturing 112 young players. Among them were Richie Allen (243), Tony Conigliaro (287), and Phil Niekro (541). The 10 Combination Cards had such outstanding stars as Nellie Fox and Harmon Killebrew (81); Willie Mays and Orlando Cepeda (306); Roger Maris, Norm Cash, Mickey Mantle, and Al Kaline (331); and Hank Aaron and Willie Mays (423). Lew Burdette did it again. He's pitching left-handed (523).

QUIZ

Dean Chance and who were 20-game winners in the A.L.? (130)

He won 19 during the season for the Cardinals and added two more during the World Series, but he was not the team's biggest winner for the year. (460) Who was? (147)

He broke Jim Konstanty's record by appearing in 81 games, and had a record of 9–8, with 20 saves. All for a last-place club. Who? (108)

This manager suffered a heart attack during spring training, rejoined the team on a part-time basis on July 3rd, and took complete charge on August 14. Who? (462)

He appeared in 112 games for a pennant-winning club, made his biggest headlines not with a bat or a glove but a harmonica. He was fined $200 for playing it on the team bus after a losing game. Who? (344)

Typifying, in a way, what life could be like on an expansion team, he pitched a no-hitter for the Astros – and lost 1–0. (158)

One of baseball's most famous trades saw Lou Brock go from the Cubs to the Cardinals. Who was the former 20-game winner who was the key man for the Cubs in that trade? (59)

The players, coaches and managers selected the respective All-Star teams, and the National Leaguers named a Met to the starting lineup. Who? (235)

The Orioles third-place finish, with 97 victories, was helped greatly by two rookies. One was a pitcher who was 19–5, the other an outfielder with 22 home runs. Who? (201)

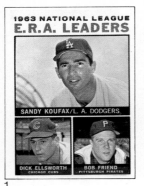

1963 NATIONAL LEAGUE E.R.A. LEADERS
SANDY KOUFAX/L. A. DODGERS
DICK ELLSWORTH CHICAGO CUBS
BOB FRIEND PITTSBURGH PIRATES

1

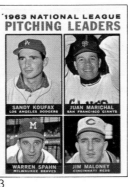

1963 AMERICAN LEAGUE E.R.A. LEADERS
GARY PETERS/CHIC. WHITE SOX
JUAN PIZARRO CHICAGO WHITE SOX
CAMILO PASCUAL MINNESOTA TWINS

2

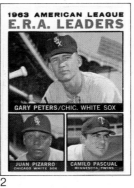

1963 NATIONAL LEAGUE PITCHING LEADERS
SANDY KOUFAX LOS ANGELES DODGERS
JUAN MARICHAL SAN FRANCISCO GIANTS
WARREN SPAHN MILWAUKEE BRAVES
JIM MALONEY CINCINNATI REDS

3

1963 AMERICAN LEAGUE PITCHING LEADERS
WHITEY FORD/N. Y. YANKEES
CAMILO PASCUAL MINNESOTA TWINS
JIM BOUTON NEW YORK YANKEES

4

1963 NATIONAL LEAGUE STRIKEOUT LEADERS
SANDY KOUFAX/L. A. DODGERS
JIM MALONEY CINCINNATI REDS
DON DRYSDALE LOS ANGELES DODGERS

5

1963 AMERICAN LEAGUE STRIKEOUT LEADERS
CAMILO PASCUAL/MINN. TWINS
JIM BUNNING DETROIT TIGERS
DICK STIGMAN MINNESOTA TWINS

6

1963 NATIONAL LEAGUE BATTING LEADERS
TOMMY DAVIS/L. A. DODGERS
BOB CLEMENTE PITTS. PIRATES
DICK GROAT ST. L. CARDS
HANK AARON MIL. BRAVES

7

1963 AMERICAN LEAGUE BATTING LEADERS
CARL YASTRZEMSKI/RED SOX
AL KALINE DETROIT TIGERS
RICH ROLLINS MINNESOTA TWINS

8

1963 NATIONAL LEAGUE HOME RUN LEADERS
HANK AARON MILWAUKEE BRAVES
WILLIE McCOVEY SAN FRANCISCO GIANTS
WILLIE MAYS SAN FRANCISCO GIANTS
ORLANDO CEPEDA SAN FRANCISCO GIANTS

9

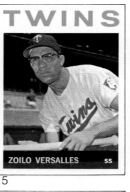

1963 AMERICAN LEAGUE HOME RUN LEADERS
HARMON KILLEBREW/M. TWINS
DICK STUART BOSTON RED SOX
BOB ALLISON MINNESOTA TWINS

10

1963 NATIONAL LEAGUE R.B.I. LEADERS
HANK AARON/MILW. BRAVES
KEN BOYER ST. LOUIS CARDINALS
BILL WHITE ST. LOUIS CARDINALS

11

1963 AMERICAN LEAGUE R.B.I. LEADERS
DICK STUART/BOSTON RED SOX
AL KALINE DETROIT TIGERS
HARMON KILLEBREW MINNESOTA TWINS

12

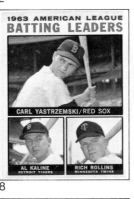

WHITE SOX
HOYT WILHELM pitcher

13

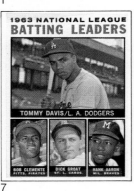

1964 ROOKIE STARS DODGERS
DICK NEN FIRST BASE
NICK WILLHITE PITCHER

14

TWINS
ZOILO VERSALLES ss

15

PHILLIES
JOHN BOOZER pitcher

16

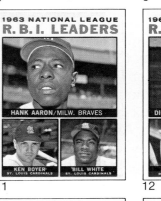

ORIOLES
WILLIE KIRKLAND outfield

17

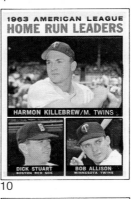

GIANTS
BILLY O'DELL pitcher

18

TIGERS
DON WERT 3rd base

19

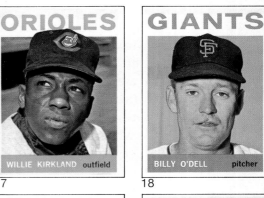

PIRATES
BOB FRIEND pitcher

20

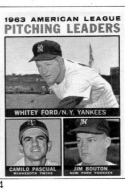

YANKEES
YOGI BERRA manager

21

ORIOLES
JERRY ADAIR 2nd base

22

COLTS
CHRIS ZACHARY pitcher

23

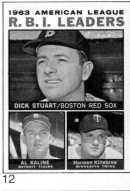

CARDINALS
CARL SAWATSKI catcher

24

RED SOX
BILL MONBOUQUETTE p

25

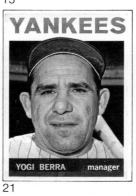

ATHLETICS
GINO CIMOLI outfield

26

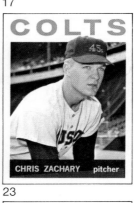

NEW YORK METS

27

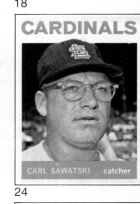

SENATORS
CLAUDE OSTEEN pitcher

28

CUBS
LOU BROCK outfield

29

DODGERS
RON PERRANOSKI pitcher

30

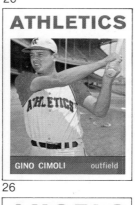

WHITE SOX
DAVE NICHOLSON outfield

31

ANGELS
DEAN CHANCE pitcher

32

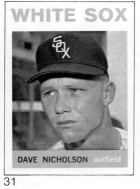

1964 ROOKIE STARS REDS
SAMMY ELLIS PITCHER
MEL QUEEN OUTFIELD

33

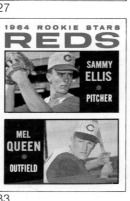

TWINS
JIM PERRY pitcher

34

BRAVES
ED MATHEWS 3b-of

35

YANKEES
HAL RENIFF pitcher

36

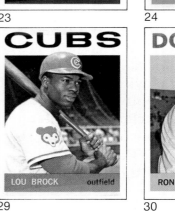
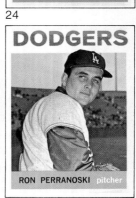

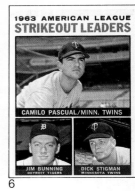

PIRATES	COLTS	TIGERS	CARDINALS	FRIENDLY FOES	ATHLETICS
	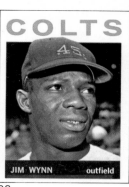				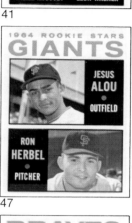
SMOKY BURGESS catcher	JIM WYNN outfield	HANK AGUIRRE pitcher	DICK GROAT shortstop	WILLIE McCOVEY • LEON WAGNER	MOE DRABOWSKY pitcher
37	38	39	40	41	42

PHILLIES	METS	ORIOLES	SENATORS	1964 ROOKIE STARS GIANTS	ANGELS
		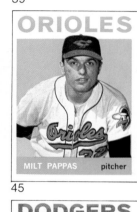	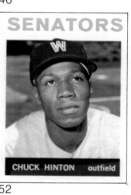	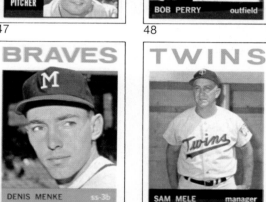	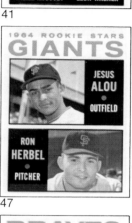
ROY SIEVERS 1st base	DUKE CARMEL of-1b	MILT PAPPAS pitcher	ED BRINKMAN shortstop	JESUS ALOU OUTFIELD / RON HERBEL PITCHER	BOB PERRY outfield
43	44	45	46	47	48

REDS	YANKEES	DODGERS	SENATORS	BRAVES	TWINS
		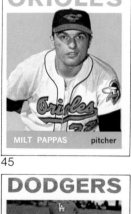		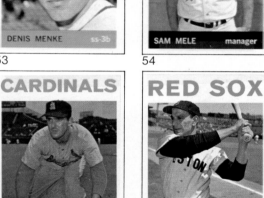	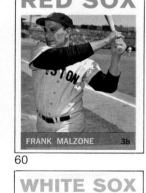
BILL HENRY pitcher	MICKEY MANTLE outfield	PETE RICHERT pitcher	CHUCK HINTON outfield	DENIS MENKE ss-3b	SAM MELE manager
49	50	51	52	53	54

CUBS	COLTS	METS	TIGERS	CARDINALS	RED SOX
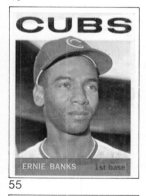			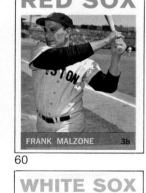		
ERNIE BANKS 1st base	HAL BROWN pitcher	TIM HARKNESS 1st base	DON DEMETER outfield	ERNIE BROGLIO pitcher	FRANK MALZONE 3b
55	56	57	58	59	60

ANGEL BACKSTOPS	PIRATES	ORIOLES	INDIANS	BRAVES	WHITE SOX
 BOB RODGERS • ED SADOWSKI	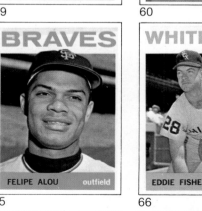				
	TED SAVAGE outfield	JOHNNY ORSINO catcher	TED ABERNATHY pitcher	FELIPE ALOU outfield	EDDIE FISHER pitcher
61	62	63	64	65	66

DETROIT TIGERS	DODGERS	YANKEES	BRAVES	ANGELS	REDS
		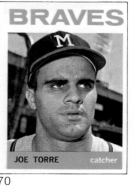			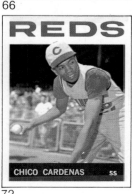
	WILLIE DAVIS outfield	CLETE BOYER 3rd base	JOE TORRE catcher	JACK SPRING pitcher	CHICO CARDENAS ss
67	68	69	70	71	72

TWINS  JIMMIE HALL outfield	**1964 ROOKIE STARS PIRATES** BOB PRIDDY PITCHER TOM BUTTERS PITCHER 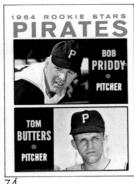	**ATHLETICS**  WAYNE CAUSEY shortstop	**TOPPS BASEBALL CHECKLIST 1ST SERIES** 	**INDIANS**  JERRY WALKER pitcher	**CUBS**  MERRITT RANEW c-1b
73	74	75	76	77	78

RED SOX  BOB HEFFNER pitcher	**REDS**  VADA PINSON outfield	**ALL-STAR VETS**  NELLIE FOX • HARMON KILLEBREW	**GIANTS**  JIM DAVENPORT 3b-2b	**PHILLIES** 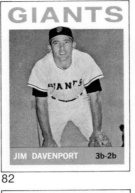 GUS TRIANDOS catcher	**METS** 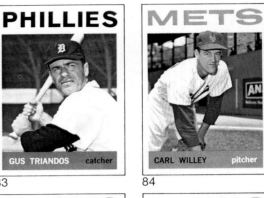 CARL WILLEY pitcher
79	80	81	82	83	84

WHITE SOX 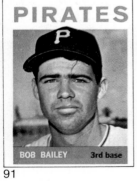 PETE WARD 3rd base	**YANKEES**  AL DOWNING pitcher	**ST. LOUIS CARDINALS** 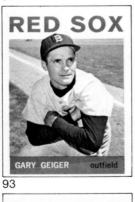	**DODGERS** 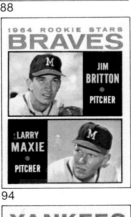 JOHN ROSEBORO catcher	**ORIOLES**  BOOG POWELL outfield	**TWINS** 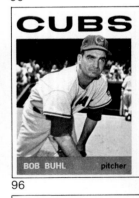 EARL BATTEY catcher
85	86	87	88	89	90

PIRATES  BOB BAILEY 3rd base	**SENATORS** 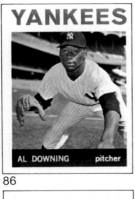 STEVE RIDZIK pitcher	**RED SOX** 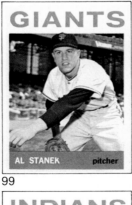 GARY GEIGER outfield	**1964 ROOKIE STARS BRAVES** JIM BRITTON PITCHER LARRY MAXIE PITCHER 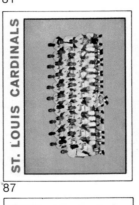	**METS** 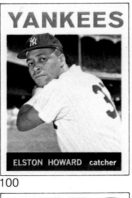 GEORGE ALTMAN outfield	**CUBS** 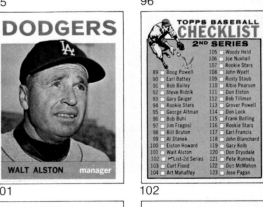 BOB BUHL pitcher
91	92	93	94	95	96

ANGELS  JIM FREGOSI shortstop	**TIGERS** 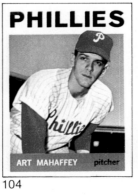 BILL BRUTON outfield	**GIANTS**  AL STANEK pitcher	**YANKEES**  ELSTON HOWARD catcher	**DODGERS**  WALT ALSTON manager	**TOPPS BASEBALL CHECKLIST 2ND SERIES** 
97	98	99	100	101	102

CARDINALS  CURT FLOOD outfield	**PHILLIES** ART MAHAFFEY pitcher	**INDIANS** WOODY HELD of-2b	**REDS** JOE NUXHALL pitcher	**1964 ROOKIE STARS WHITE SOX** BRUCE HOWARD PITCHER FRANK KREUTZER PITCHER	**ATHLETICS** JOHN WYATT pitcher
103	104	105	106	107	108

COLTS	ANGELS	CUBS	RED SOX	METS	SENATORS
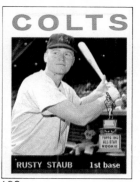		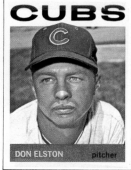			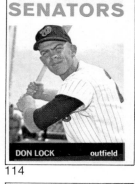
RUSTY STAUB 1st base	ALBIE PEARSON outfield	DON ELSTON pitcher	BOB TILLMAN catcher	GROVER POWELL pitcher	DON LOCK outfield
109	110	111	112	113	114

BRAVES	1964 ROOKIE STARS TWINS	PIRATES	YANKEES	CARDINALS	DODGERS
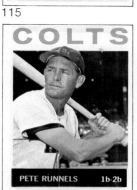	JAY WARD 3B-OF / TONY OLIVA OUTFIELD				
FRANK BOLLING 2nd base		EARL FRANCIS pitcher	JOHN BLANCHARD c-of	GARY KOLB outfield	DON DRYSDALE pitcher
115	116	117	118	119	120

COLTS	INDIANS	GIANTS	ATHLETICS	REDS	ORIOLES
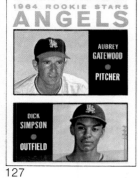		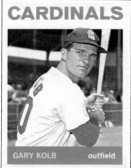	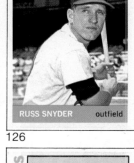		
PETE RUNNELS 1b-2b	DON McMAHON pitcher	JOSE PAGAN shortstop	ORLANDO PENA pitcher	PETE ROSE 2nd base	RUSS SNYDER outfield
121	122	123	124	125	126

1964 ROOKIE STARS ANGELS	TIGERS	METS	WHITE SOX	CUBS	MILWAUKEE BRAVES
AUBREY GATEWOOD PITCHER / DICK SIMPSON OUTFIELD		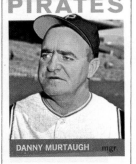	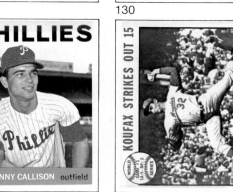		
	MICKEY LOLICH pitcher	AMADO SAMUEL shortstop	GARY PETERS pitcher	STEVE BOROS 3rd base	
127	128	129	130	131	132

INDIANS	SENATORS	PHILLIES	KOUFAX STRIKES OUT 15	DAVIS SPARKS RALLY	L.A. TAKES 3RD STRAIGHT

JIM GRANT pitcher	DON ZIMMER 3rd base	JOHNNY CALLISON outfield			
133	134	135	136	137	138

SEALING YANKS' DOOM	THE DODGERS CELEBRATE	PIRATES	COLTS	TIGERS	REDS

		DANNY MURTAUGH mgr.	JOHN BATEMAN catcher	BUBBA PHILLIPS 3b-of	AL WORTHINGTON pitcher
139	140	141	142	143	144

ORIOLES 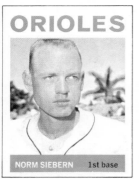 NORM SIEBERN 1st base	1964 ROOKIE STARS INDIANS  TOMMY JOHN PITCHER BOB CHANCE OUTFIELD	CARDINALS  RAY SADECKI pitcher	WHITE SOX  J. C. MARTIN catcher	ANGELS 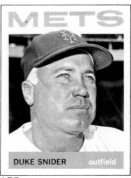 PAUL FOYTACK pitcher	GIANTS 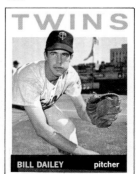 WILLIE MAYS outfield
145	146	147	148	149	150
K. C. ATHLETICS 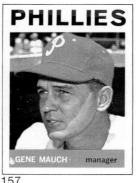	BRAVES  DENVER LEMASTER pitcher	RED SOX  DICK WILLIAMS of-1b	DODGERS  DICK TRACEWSKI ss-2b	METS  DUKE SNIDER outfield	TWINS  BILL DAILEY pitcher
151	152	153	154	155	156
PHILLIES 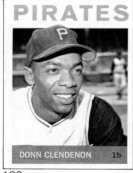 GENE MAUCH · manager	COLTS  KEN JOHNSON pitcher	ANGELS  CHARLIE DEES 1st base	CARDINALS 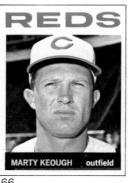 KEN BOYER 3rd base	ORIOLES 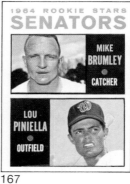 DAVE McNALLY pitcher	HITTING AREA 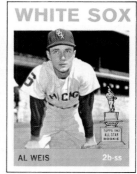 DICK SISLER · VADA PINSON
157	158	159	160	161	162
PIRATES  DONN CLENDENON 1b	YANKEES 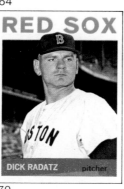 BUD DALEY pitcher	TIGERS  JERRY LUMPE 2nd base	REDS  MARTY KEOUGH outfield	1964 ROOKIE STARS SENATORS  MIKE BRUMLEY CATCHER LOU PINIELLA OUTFIELD	WHITE SOX 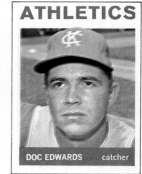 AL WEIS 2b-ss
163	164	165	166	167	168
GIANTS 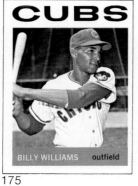 DEL CRANDALL catcher	RED SOX  DICK RADATZ pitcher	BRAVES TY CLINE outfield	CLEVELAND INDIANS 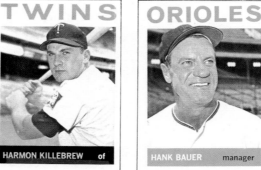	PHILLIES 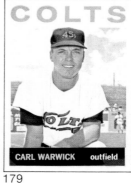 RYNE DUREN pitcher	ATHLETICS  DOC EDWARDS catcher
169	170	171	172	173	174
CUBS BILLY WILLIAMS outfield	METS TRACY STALLARD pitcher	TWINS HARMON KILLEBREW of	ORIOLES HANK BAUER manager	COLTS CARL WARWICK outfield	DODGERS TOMMY DAVIS outfield
175	176	177	178	179	180

TIGERS

DAVE WICKERSHAM   pitcher
181

SOX SOCKERS

YASTRZEMSKI • SCHILLING
182

CARDINALS
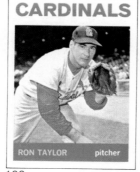
RON TAYLOR   pitcher
183

INDIANS

AL LUPLOW   outfield
184

REDS

JIM O'TOOLE   pitcher
185

RED SOX
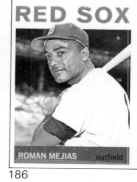
ROMAN MEJIAS   outfield
186

SENATORS
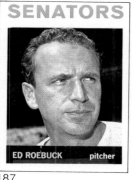
ED ROEBUCK   pitcher
187

TOPPS BASEBALL
CHECKLIST
3RD SERIES
193 ☐ Jerry Lynch
194 ☐ John Goryl
195 ☐ Floyd Robinson
177 ☐ Harmon Killebrew 196 ☐ Jim Gentile
178 ☐ Hank Bauer   197 ☐ Frank Lary
179 ☐ Carl Warwick   198 ☐ Len Gabrielson
180 ☐ Tommy Davis   199 ☐ Joe Azcue
181 ☐ Dave Wickersham   200 ☐ Sandy Koufax
182 ☐ Sox Sockers   201 ☐ Rookie Stars
183 ☐ Ron Taylor   202 ☐ Galen Cisco
184 ☐ Al Luplow   203 ☐ John Kennedy
185 ☐ Jim O'Toole   204 ☐ Matty Alou
186 ☐ Roman Mejias   205 ☐ Nellie Fox
187 ☐ Ed Roebuck   206 ☐ Steve Hamilton
188 ☐ List-3rd Series   207 ☐ Fred Hutchinson
189 ☐ Bob Hendley   208 ☐ Wes Covington
190 ☐ B. Richardson   209 ☐ Bob Allen
191 ☐ Clay Dalrymple   210 ☐ Carl Yastrzemski
192 ☐ Rookie Stars   211 ☐ Jim Coker
188

GIANTS

BOB HENDLEY   pitcher
189

YANKEES

BOBBY RICHARDSON   2b
190

PHILLIES

CLAY DALRYMPLE   catcher
191

1964 ROOKIE STARS
CUBS
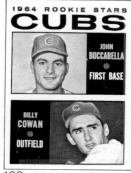
JOHN BOCCABELLA   FIRST BASE

BILLY COWAN   OUTFIELD
192

PIRATES
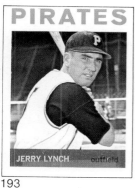
JERRY LYNCH   outfield
193

TWINS

JOHN GORYL   3b-2b
194

WHITE SOX
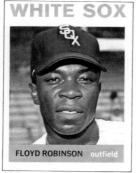
FLOYD ROBINSON   outfield
195

ATHLETICS
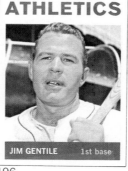
JIM GENTILE   1st base
196

TIGERS

FRANK LARY   pitcher
197

BRAVES

LEN GABRIELSON   of
198

INDIANS
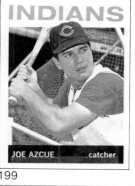
JOE AZCUE   catcher
199

DODGERS

SANDY KOUFAX   pitcher
200

1964 ROOKIE STARS
ORIOLES
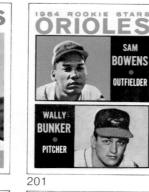
SAM BOWENS   OUTFIELDER

WALLY BUNKER   PITCHER
201

METS

GALEN CISCO   pitcher
202

SENATORS
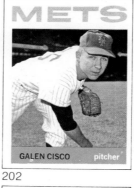
JOHN KENNEDY   shortstop
203

GIANTS
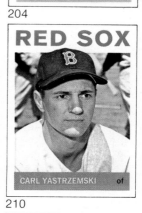
MATTY ALOU   outfielder
204

COLTS

NELLIE FOX   2nd base
205

YANKEES
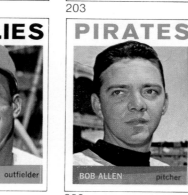
STEVE HAMILTON   pitcher
206

REDS

FRED HUTCHINSON   mgr.
207

PHILLIES

WES COVINGTON   outfield
208

PIRATES

BOB ALLEN   pitcher
209

RED SOX

CARL YASTRZEMSKI   of
210

CARDINALS

JIM COKER   catcher
211

ATHLETICS

PETE LOVRICH   pitcher
212

LOS ANGELES ANGELS
213

DODGERS

KEN McMULLEN   3rd base
214

WHITE SOX
RAY HERBERT   pitcher
215

INDIANS
MIKE DE LA HOZ   2nd base
216

SENATORS	BRAVES	YOUNG ACES	CUBS	ORIOLES	GIANTS
				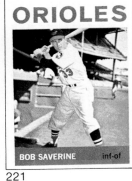	
JIM KING outfielder	HANK FISCHER pitcher	AL DOWNING • JIM BOUTON	DICK ELLSWORTH pitcher	BOB SAVERINE inf-of	BILL PIERCE pitcher
217	218	219	220	221	222

TWINS	PIRATES	YANKEES	1964 ROOKIE STARS COLTS	ANGELS	RED SOX
		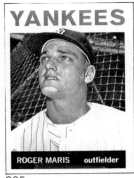	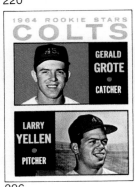		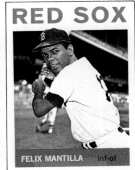
GEORGE BANKS 3b-of	TOMMIE SISK pitcher	ROGER MARIS outfielder	GERALD GROTE CATCHER / LARRY YELLEN PITCHER	BARRY LATMAN pitcher	FELIX MANTILLA inf-of
223	224	225	226	227	228

ATHLETICS	ORIOLES	DODGERS	WHITE SOX	REDS	INDIANS
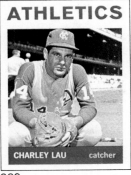				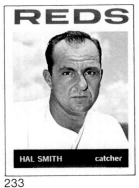	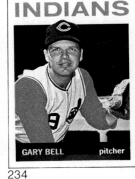
CHARLEY LAU catcher	BROOKS ROBINSON 3b	DICK CALMUS pitcher	AL LOPEZ Manager	HAL SMITH catcher	GARY BELL pitcher
229	230	231	232	233	234

METS	TIGERS	CHICAGO CUBS	BRAVES	ORIOLES	CARDINALS
			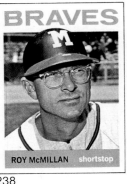		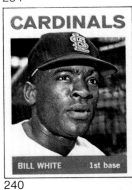
RON HUNT 2nd base	BILL FAUL pitcher		ROY McMILLAN shortstop	HERM STARRETTE pitcher	BILL WHITE 1st base
235	236	237	238	239	240

COLTS	GIANTS	1964 ROOKIE STARS PHILLIES	ATHLETICS	TWINS	PIRATES
		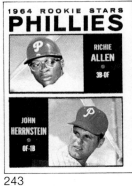	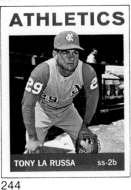		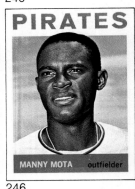
JIM OWENS pitcher	HARVEY KUENN of-3b	RICHIE ALLEN 3B-OF / JOHN HERRNSTEIN OF-1B	TONY LA RUSSA ss-2b	DICK STIGMAN pitcher	MANNY MOTA outfielder
241	242	243	244	245	246

WHITE SOX	RED SOX	DODGERS	TIGERS	METS	CUBS
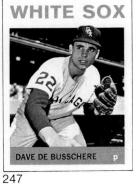	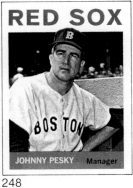	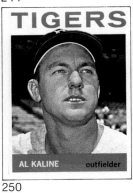		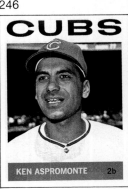	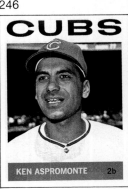
DAVE DE BUSSCHERE p	JOHNNY PESKY Manager	DOUG CAMILLI catcher	AL KALINE outfielder	CHOO CHOO COLEMAN c	KEN ASPROMONTE 2b
247	248	249	250	251	252

INDIANS  WALLY POST outfielder 253	**PHILLIES** 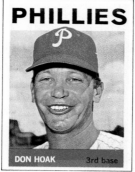 DON HOAK 3rd base 254	**ANGELS**  LEE THOMAS 1b-of 255	**COLTS**  JOHNNY WEEKLY outfielder 256	**SAN FRANCISCO GIANTS**  257	**TWINS** 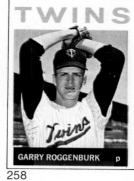 GARRY ROGGENBURK p 258

YANKEES  HARRY BRIGHT inf-of 259

REDS 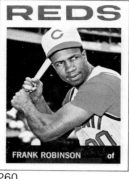 FRANK ROBINSON of 260

SENATORS 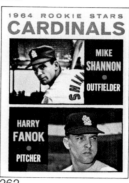 JIM HANNAN pitcher 261

1964 ROOKIE STARS CARDINALS  MIKE SHANNON OUTFIELDER HARRY FANOK PITCHER 262

ORIOLES 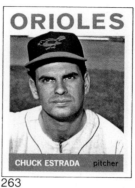 CHUCK ESTRADA pitcher 263

WHITE SOX 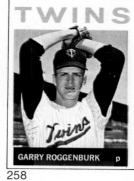 JIM LANDIS outfielder 264

PHILLIES  JIM BUNNING pitcher 265

PIRATES  GENE FREESE 3rd base 266

RED SOX 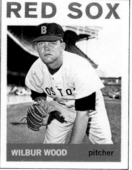 WILBUR WOOD pitcher 267

BILL'S GOT IT  DANNY MURTAUGH • BILL VIRDON 268

CUBS  ELLIS BURTON outfielder 269

TWINS 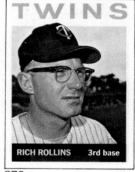 RICH ROLLINS 3rd base 270

BRAVES 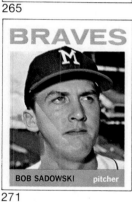 BOB SADOWSKI pitcher 271

TIGERS  JAKE WOOD 3b-of 272

ANGELS  MEL NELSON pitcher 273

TOPPS BASEBALL CHECKLIST 4TH SERIES
265 ☐ Jim Bunning
266 ☐ Gene Freese
267 ☐ Wilbur Wood
268 ☐ Bill's Got It
269 ☐ Ellis Burton
270 ☐ Rich Rollins
271 ☐ Bob Sadowski
272 ☐ Jake Wood
273 ☐ Mel Nelson
274 ☐ List-4th Series
275 ☐ John Tsitouris
276 ☐ Jose Tartabull
277 ☐ Ken Retzer
278 ☐ Bobby Shantz
279 ☐ Joe Koppe
280 ☐ Juan Marichal
281 ☐ Rookie Stars
282 ☐ Bob Bruce
283 ☐ Tommy McCraw
284 ☐ Dick Schofield
285 ☐ Robin Roberts
286 ☐ Don Landrum
287 ☐ Rookie Stars
288 ☐ Al Moran
289 ☐ Frank Funk
290 ☐ Bob Allison
291 ☐ Phil Ortega
292 ☐ Mike Roarke
293 ☐ Phillies Team
294 ☐ Ken Hunt
295 ☐ Roger Craig
296 ☐ Ed Kirkpatrick
297 ☐ Ken MacKenzie
298 ☐ Harry Craft
299 ☐ Bill Stafford
274

REDS  JOHN TSITOURIS pitcher 275

ATHLETICS 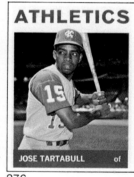 JOSE TARTABULL of 276

SENATORS  KEN RETZER catcher 277

CARDINALS 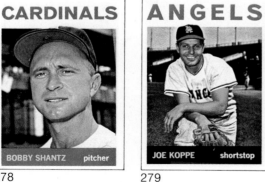 BOBBY SHANTZ pitcher 278

ANGELS  JOE KOPPE shortstop 279

GIANTS  JUAN MARICHAL pitcher 280

1964 ROOKIE STARS YANKEES 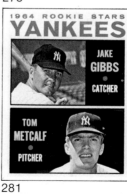 JAKE GIBBS CATCHER TOM METCALF PITCHER 281

COLTS  BOB BRUCE pitcher 282

WHITE SOX  TOMMY McCRAW 1st base 283

PIRATES  DICK SCHOFIELD ss 284

ORIOLES ROBIN ROBERTS pitcher 285

CUBS  DON LANDRUM outfield 286

1964 ROOKIE STARS RED SOX TONY CONIGLIARO OUTFIELD BILL SPANSWICK PITCHER 287

METS  AL MORAN shortstop 288

BRAVES	TWINS	DODGERS	TIGERS	PHILLIES TEAM	SENATORS
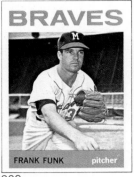	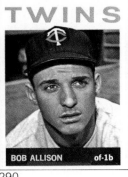	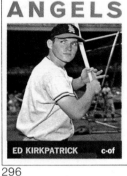	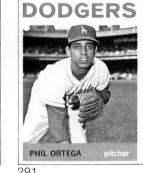	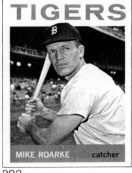	
FRANK FUNK pitcher	BOB ALLISON of-1b	PHIL ORTEGA pitcher	MIKE ROARKE catcher		KEN HUNT outfield
289	290	291	292	293	294

CARDINALS	ANGELS	GIANTS	COLTS	YANKEES	BRAVES
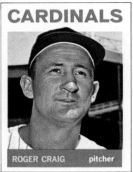	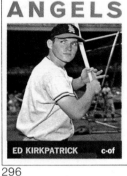	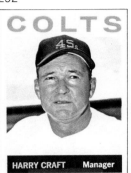		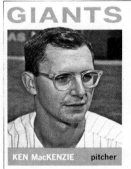	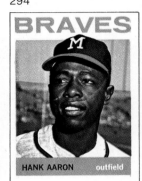
ROGER CRAIG pitcher	ED KIRKPATRICK c-of	KEN MacKENZIE pitcher	HARRY CRAFT Manager	BILL STAFFORD pitcher	HANK AARON outfield
295	296	297	298	299	300

INDIANS	ATHLETICS	REDS	ORIOLES	RED SOX	GIANT GUNNERS
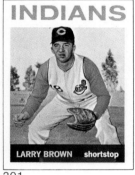	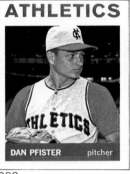	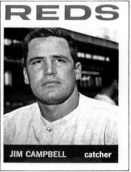			
LARRY BROWN shortstop	DAN PFISTER pitcher	JIM CAMPBELL catcher	BOB JOHNSON inf-of	JACK LAMABE pitcher	WILLIE MAYS • ORLANDO CEPEDA
301	302	303	304	305	306

PIRATES	WHITE SOX	CUBS	DODGERS	SENATORS	1964 ROOKIE STARS TIGERS
				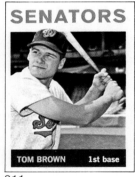	
JOE GIBBON pitcher	GENE STEPHENS outfield	PAUL TOTH pitcher	JIM GILLIAM 2b-3b	TOM BROWN 1st base	FRITZ FISHER PITCHER / FRED GLADDING PITCHER
307	308	309	310	311	312

GIANTS	CARDINALS	ANGELS	BRAVES	INDIANS	TWINS TEAM
	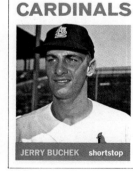	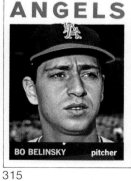			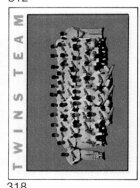
CHUCK HILLER 2d base	JERRY BUCHEK shortstop	BO BELINSKY pitcher	GENE OLIVER c-1b	AL SMITH outfield	
313	314	315	316	317	318

PHILLIES	ATHLETICS	COLTS	ORIOLES	WHITE SOX	METS
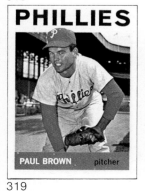	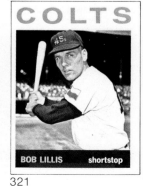	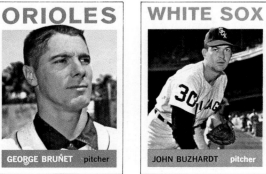			
PAUL BROWN pitcher	ROCKY COLAVITO outfield	BOB LILLIS shortstop	GEORGE BRUNET pitcher	JOHN BUZHARDT pitcher	CASEY STENGEL Manager
319	320	321	322	323	324

YANKEES

HECTOR LOPEZ   outfield
325

PIRATES
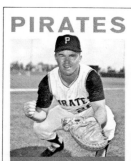
RON BRAND   catcher
326

SENATORS

DON BLASINGAME   2d base
327

GIANTS
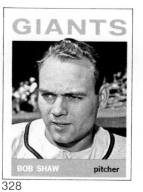
BOB SHAW   pitcher
328

RED SOX

RUSS NIXON   catcher
329

REDS

TOMMY HARPER   outfield
330

A. L. BOMBERS

MARIS • CASH • MANTLE • KALINE
331

CARDINALS

RAY WASHBURN   pitcher
332

ANGELS
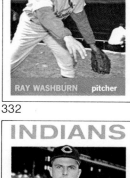
BILLY MORAN   2b-3b
333

ATHLETICS
LEW KRAUSSE   pitcher
334

TIGERS
DON MOSSI   pitcher
335

CUBS
ANDRE RODGERS   ss
336

DODGERS
1964 ROOKIE STARS
AL FERRARA OUTFIELD
JEFF TORBORG CATCHER
337

INDIANS
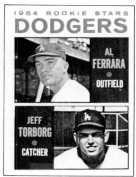
JACK KRALICK   pitcher
338

COLTS
WALT BOND   outfield
339

WHITE SOX

JOE CUNNINGHAM   1b
340

TWINS
JIM ROLAND   pitcher
341

PIRATES
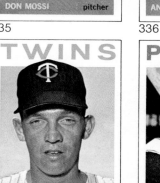
WILLIE STARGELL   of-1b
342

SENATORS TEAM

343

YANKEES
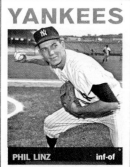
PHIL LINZ   inf-of
344

METS
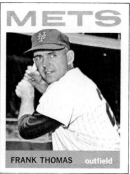
FRANK THOMAS   outfield
345

REDS

JOE JAY   pitcher
346

PHILLIES

BOBBY WINE   shortstop
347

ATHLETICS
ED LOPAT   Manager
348

ANGELS

ART FOWLER   pitcher
349

GIANTS
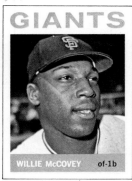
WILLIE McCOVEY   of-1b
350

BRAVES

DAN SCHNEIDER   pitcher
351

RED SOX
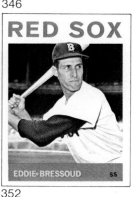
EDDIE BRESSOUD   ss
352

DODGERS

WALLY MOON   outfield
353

COLTS
DAVE GIUSTI   pitcher
354

TWINS
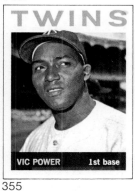
VIC POWER   1st base
355

REDS
1964 ROOKIE STARS
BILL McCOOL PITCHER
CHICO RUIZ 3B-SS
356

CARDINALS
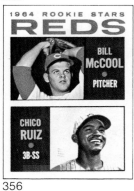
CHARLEY JAMES   outfield
357

SENATORS
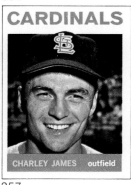
RON KLINE   pitcher
358

CUBS

JIM SCHAFFER   catcher
359

YANKEES

JOE PEPITONE   1st base
360

METS
JAY HOOK pitcher
361

TOPPS BASEBALL
CHECKLIST
5TH SERIES
369 □ Jerry Zimmerman
370 □ Hal Woodeshick
371 □ Frank Howard
372 □ Howie Koplitz
353 □ Wally Moon   373 □ Pirates Team
354 □ Dave Giusti   374 □ Bobby Bolin
355 □ Vic Power   375 □ Ron Santo
356 □ Rookie Stars   376 □ Dave Morehead
357 □ Charley James   377 □ Bob Skinner
358 □ Ron Kline   378 □ Rookie Stars
359 □ Jim Schaffer   379 □ Tony Gonzalez
360 □ Joe Pepitone   380 □ Whitey Ford
361 □ Jay Hook   381 □ Bob Taylor
362 □ List, 5thSeries 382 □ Wes Stock
363 □ Dick McAuliffe   383 □ Bill Rigney
364 □ Joe Gaines   384 □ Ron Hansen
365 □ Cal McLish   385 □ Curt Simmons
366 □ Nelson Mathews   386 □ Lenny Green
367 □ Fred Whitfield   387 □ Terry Fox
368 □ Rookie Stars
362

TIGERS
DICK McAULIFFE ss
363

ORIOLES
JOE GAINES outfield
364

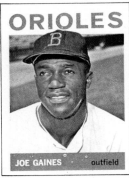
PHILLIES
CAL McLISH pitcher
365

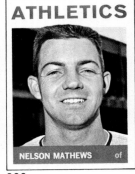
ATHLETICS
NELSON MATHEWS of
366

INDIANS
FRED WHITFIELD 1st base
367

1964 ROOKIE STARS
WHITE SOX
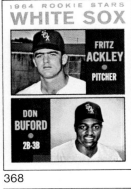
FRITZ ACKLEY PITCHER
DON BUFORD 2B-3B
368

TWINS
JERRY ZIMMERMAN c
369

COLTS
HAL WOODESHICK pitcher
370

DODGERS
FRANK HOWARD outfield
371

SENATORS
HOWIE KOPLITZ pitcher
372

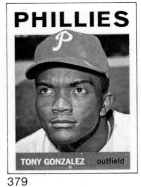
PITTSBURGH PIRATES
373

GIANTS
BOBBY BOLIN pitcher
374

CUBS
RON SANTO 3rd base
375

RED SOX
DAVE MOREHEAD pitcher
376

REDS
BOB SKINNER outfield
377

1964 ROOKIE STARS
BRAVES
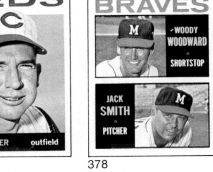
WOODY WOODWARD SHORTSTOP
JACK SMITH PITCHER
378

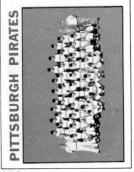
PHILLIES
TONY GONZALEZ outfield
379

YANKEES
WHITEY FORD p-Coach
380

METS
BOB TAYLOR c-of
381

ORIOLES
WES STOCK pitcher
382

ANGELS
BILL RIGNEY manager
383

WHITE SOX
RON HANSEN shortstop
384

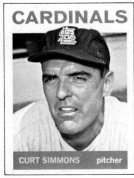
CARDINALS
CURT SIMMONS pitcher
385

TWINS
LENNY GREEN outfield
386

TIGERS
TERRY FOX pitcher
387

1964 ROOKIE STARS
ATHLETICS
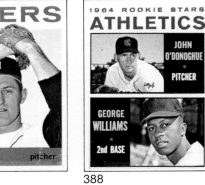
JOHN O'DONOGHUE PITCHER
GEORGE WILLIAMS 2nd BASE
388

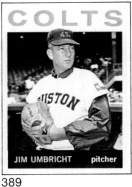
COLTS
JIM UMBRICHT pitcher
389

GIANTS
ORLANDO CEPEDA 1b
390

INDIANS
SAM McDOWELL pitcher
391

PIRATES
JIM PAGLIARONI catcher
392

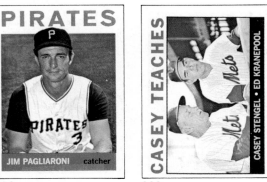
CASEY TEACHES
CASEY STENGEL • ED KRANEPOOL
393

DODGERS
BOB MILLER pitcher
394

YANKEES
TOM TRESH outfield
395

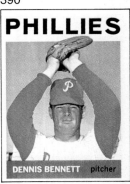
PHILLIES
DENNIS BENNETT pitcher
396

SENATORS  CHUCK COTTIER 2d base 397	**1964 ROOKIE STARS** **METS**  BILL HAAS 1st BASE DICK SMITH 1st BASE-OF 398	**ORIOLES** 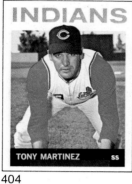 JACKIE BRANDT outfield 399	**BRAVES** 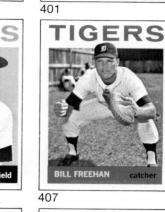 WARREN SPAHN pitcher 400	**WHITE SOX** 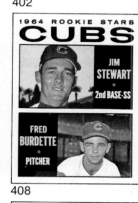 CHARLIE MAXWELL of 401	**ATHLETICS** 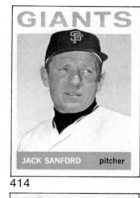 TOM STURDIVANT pitcher 402
CINCINNATI REDS  403	**INDIANS** 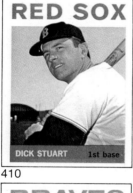 TONY MARTINEZ ss 404	**ANGELS** 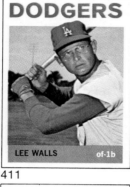 KEN McBRIDE pitcher 405	**COLTS** 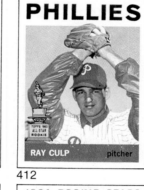 AL SPANGLER outfield 406	**TIGERS**  BILL FREEHAN catcher 407	**1964 ROOKIE STARS** **CUBS** 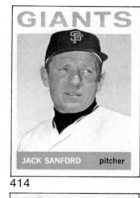 JIM STEWART 2nd BASE-SS FRED BURDETTE PITCHER 408
TWINS 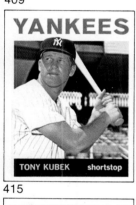 BILL FISCHER pitcher 409	**RED SOX** 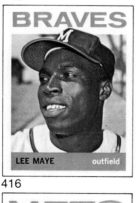 DICK STUART 1st base 410	**DODGERS**  LEE WALLS of-1b 411	**PHILLIES** 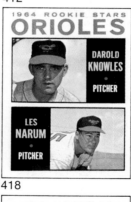 RAY CULP pitcher 412	**CARDINALS**  JOHNNY KEANE manager 413	**GIANTS**  JACK SANFORD pitcher 414
YANKEES 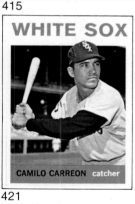 TONY KUBEK shortstop 415	**BRAVES** 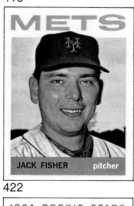 LEE MAYE outfield 416	**PIRATES**  DON CARDWELL pitcher 417	**ORIOLES**  DAROLD KNOWLES PITCHER LES NARUM PITCHER 418	**ATHLETICS**  KEN HARRELSON 1b-of 419	**REDS**  JIM MALONEY pitcher 420
WHITE SOX  CAMILO CARREON catcher 421	**METS** 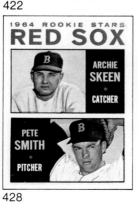 JACK FISHER pitcher 422	**TOPS IN NL**  HANK AARON • WILLIE MAYS 423	**CUBS** 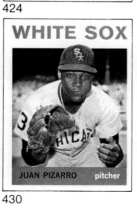 DICK BERTELL catcher 424	**TIGERS**  NORM CASH 1st base 425	**ANGELS**  BOB RODGERS catcher 426

SENATORS DON RUDOLPH pitcher 427	**1964 ROOKIE STARS** **RED SOX** ARCHIE SKEEN CATCHER PETE SMITH PITCHER 428	**CARDINALS** TIM McCARVER catcher 429	**WHITE SOX** JUAN PIZARRO pitcher 430	**ATHLETICS** GEORGE ALUSIK outfield 431	**PHILLIES** RUBEN AMARO shortstop 432

NEW YORK YANKEES

433

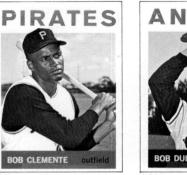

COLTS

DON NOTTEBART   pitcher

434

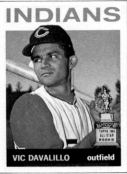

INDIANS

VIC DAVALILLO   outfield

435

REDS

CHARLIE NEAL   inf

436

BRAVES

ED BAILEY   catcher

437

TOPPS BASEBALL CHECKLIST 6TH SERIES

430	Juan Pizarro	446	Julian Javier
431	George Alusik	447	Ted Bowsfield
432	Ruben Amaro	448	Cookie Rojas
433	Yankees Team	449	Deron Johnson
434	Don Nottebart	450	Steve Barber
435	Vic Davalillo	451	Joe Amalfitano
436	Charlie Neal	452	Rookie Stars
437	Ed Bailey	453	Frank Baumann
438	List, 6th Series	454	Tommie Aaron
439	Harvey Haddix	455	Bernie Allen
440	Bob Clemente	456	Rookie Stars
441	Bob Duliba	457	Jesse Gonder
442	Pumpsie Green	458	Ralph Terry
443	Chuck Dressen	459	Bob Gibson
444	Larry Jackson	460	George Thomas
445	Bill Skowron	461	Birdie Tebbetts
		462	Dallas Green
		463	Don Leppert
		464	Dallas Green

438

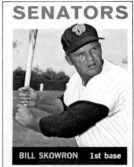

ORIOLES

HARVEY HADDIX   pitcher

439

PIRATES

BOB CLEMENTE   outfield

440

ANGELS

BOB DULIBA   pitcher

441

METS

PUMPSIE GREEN   3b-ss

442

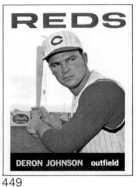

TIGERS

CHUCK DRESSEN   manager

443

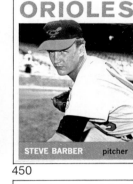

CUBS

LARRY JACKSON   pitcher

444

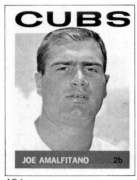

SENATORS

BILL SKOWRON   1st base

445

CARDINALS

JULIAN JAVIER   2nd base

446

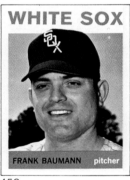

ATHLETICS

TED BOWSFIELD   pitcher

447

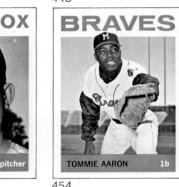

PHILLIES

COOKIE ROJAS   infield

448

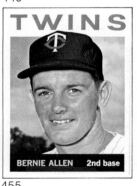

REDS

DERON JOHNSON   outfield

449

ORIOLES

STEVE BARBER   pitcher

450

CUBS

JOE AMALFITANO   2b

451

1964 ROOKIE STARS

GIANTS

GIL GARRIDO   SHORTSTOP

JIM HART   3rd BASE

452

WHITE SOX

FRANK BAUMANN   pitcher

453

BRAVES

TOMMIE AARON   1b

454

TWINS

BERNIE ALLEN   2nd base

455

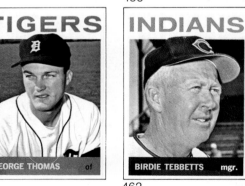

1964 ROOKIE STARS

DODGERS

WES PARKER   1st B-OF

JOHN WERHAS   3rd BASE

456

METS

JESSE GONDER   catcher

457

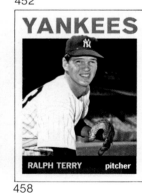

YANKEES

RALPH TERRY   pitcher

458

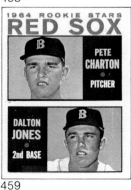

1964 ROOKIE STARS

RED SOX

PETE CHARTON   PITCHER

DALTON JONES   2nd BASE

459

CARDINALS

BOB GIBSON   pitcher

460

TIGERS

GEORGE THOMAS   of

461

INDIANS

BIRDIE TEBBETTS   mgr.

462

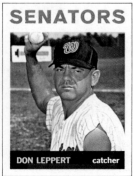

SENATORS

DON LEPPERT   catcher

463

PHILLIES

DALLAS GREEN   pitcher

464

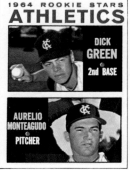

WHITE SOX

MIKE HERSHBERGER   of

465

1964 ROOKIE STARS

ATHLETICS

DICK GREEN   2nd BASE

AURELIO MONTEAGUDO   PITCHER

466

COLTS

BOB ASPROMONTE   3b

467

GIANTS

GAYLORD PERRY   pitcher

468

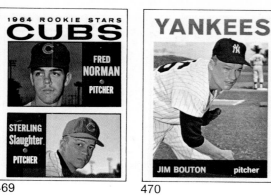

1964 ROOKIE STARS CUBS
FRED NORMAN · PITCHER
STERLING Slaughter · PITCHER
469

YANKEES
JIM BOUTON · pitcher
470

TIGERS
GATES BROWN · outfield
471

PIRATES
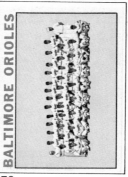
VERN LAW · pitcher
472

BALTIMORE ORIOLES
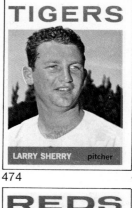
473

TIGERS
LARRY SHERRY · pitcher
474

ATHLETICS

ED CHARLES · 3rd base
475

1964 ROOKIE STARS BRAVES
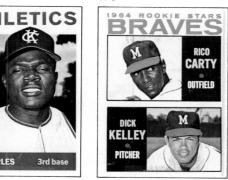
RICO CARTY · OUTFIELD
DICK KELLEY · PITCHER
476

METS

MIKE JOYCE · pitcher
477

INDIANS

DICK HOWSER · ss
478

1964 ROOKIE STARS CARDINALS
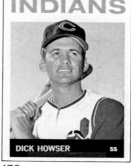
DAVE Bakenhaster · PITCHER
JOHNNY LEWIS · OUTFIELD
479

REDS
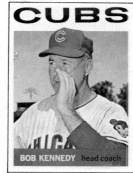
BOB PURKEY · pitcher
480

RED SOX

CHUCK SCHILLING · 2b
481

1964 ROOKIE STARS PHILLIES
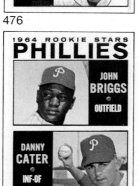
JOHN BRIGGS · OUTFIELD
DANNY CATER · INF-OF
482

SENATORS

FRED VALENTINE · of
483

TWINS

BILL PLEIS · pitcher
484

GIANTS
TOM HALLER · catcher
485

CUBS

BOB KENNEDY · head coach
486

ORIOLES

MIKE McCORMICK · pitcher
487

1964 ROOKIE STARS YANKEES
PETE Mikkelsen · PITCHER
BOB MEYER · PITCHER
488

TIGERS

JULIO NAVARRO · pitcher
489

DODGERS

RON FAIRLY · of-1b
490

TIGERS

ED RAKOW · pitcher
491

1964 ROOKIE STARS COLTS

JIM Beauchamp · OUTFIELD
MIKE WHITE · 2nd BASE
492

ANGELS
DON LEE · pitcher
493

METS

AL JACKSON · pitcher
494

PIRATES

BILL VIRDON · outfield
495

CHICAGO WHITE SOX
496

CARDINALS

JEOFF LONG · 1st base
497

SENATORS

DAVE STENHOUSE · pitcher
498

1964 ROOKIE STARS INDIANS
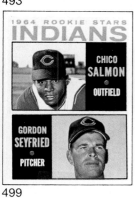
CHICO SALMON · OUTFIELD
GORDON SEYFRIED · PITCHER
499

TWINS

CAMILO PASCUAL · pitcher
500

PIRATES
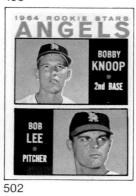
BOB VEALE · pitcher
501

1964 ROOKIE STARS ANGELS

BOBBY KNOOP · 2nd BASE
BOB LEE · PITCHER
502

RED SOX

EARL WILSON · pitcher
503

COLTS
CLAUDE RAYMOND · pitcher
504

YANKEES
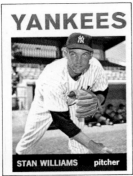
STAN WILLIAMS pitcher
505

BRAVES

BOBBY BRAGAN mgr.
506

REDS

JOHN EDWARDS catcher
507

ATHLETICS

DIEGO SEGUI pitcher
508

1964 ROOKIE STARS PIRATES
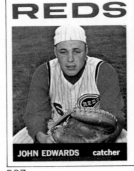
GENE ALLEY SS-3rd B
ORLANDO McFARLANE C-3rd B
509

CUBS

LINDY McDANIEL pitcher
510

ORIOLES
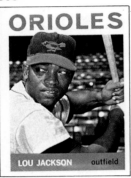
LOU JACKSON outfield
511

1964 ROOKIE STARS TIGERS

WILLIE HORTON OUTFIELD
JOE SPARMA PITCHER
512

GIANTS

DON LARSEN pitcher
513

METS

JIM HICKMAN outfield
514

INDIANS

JOHNNY ROMANO catcher
515

1964 ROOKIE STARS TWINS

JERRY ARRIGO PITCHER
DWIGHT SIEBLER PITCHER
516

TOPPS BASEBALL CHECKLIST 7TH SERIES

507 ☐ John Edwards	523 ☐ Lou Burdette
508 ☐ Diego Segui	524 ☐ Rookie Stars
509 ☐ Rookie Stars	525 ☐ Al McBean
510 ☐ Lindy McDaniel	526 ☐ Lou Clinton
511 ☐ Lou Jackson	527 ☐ Larry Bearnarth
512 ☐ Rookie Stars	528 ☐ Rookie Stars
513 ☐ Don Larsen	529 ☐ Al Dark
514 ☐ Jim Hickman	530 ☐ Leon Wagner
515 ☐ Johnny Romano	531 ☐ Dodgers Team
516 ☐ Rookie Stars	532 ☐ Rookie Stars
517 ☐ List-7th Series	533 ☐ J. Klippstein
	534 ☐ Gus Bell
518 ☐ Carl Bouldin	535 ☐ Phil Regan
519 ☐ Charlie Smith	536 ☐ Rookie Stars
520 ☐ Jack Baldschun	537 ☐ Dan Osinski
521 ☐ Tom Satriano	538 ☐ Minnie Minoso
522 ☐ Bobby Tiefenauer	539 ☐ Roy Face
	540 ☐ Luis Aparicio
	541 ☐ Rookie Stars
517

SENATORS

CARL BOULDIN pitcher
518

METS

CHARLIE SMITH 3b
519

PHILLIES

JACK BALDSCHUN pitcher
520

ANGELS

TOM SATRIANO inf-c
521

BRAVES
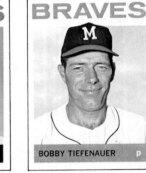
BOBBY TIEFENAUER P
522

CARDINALS

LOU BURDETTE pitcher
523

1964 ROOKIE STARS REDS
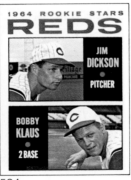
JIM DICKSON PITCHER
BOBBY KLAUS 2 BASE
524

PIRATES

AL McBEAN pitcher
525

RED SOX

LOU CLINTON outfield
526

METS
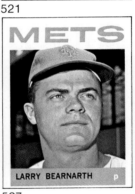
LARRY BEARNARTH p
527

1964 ROOKIE STARS ATHLETICS
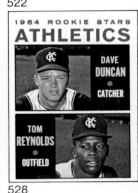
DAVE DUNCAN CATCHER
TOM REYNOLDS OUTFIELD
528

GIANTS

AL DARK manager
529

INDIANS

LEON WAGNER outfield
530

L. A. DODGERS
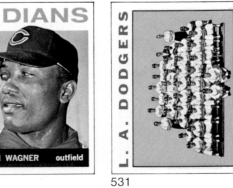
531

1964 ROOKIE STARS TWINS
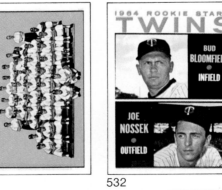
BUD BLOOMFIELD INFIELD
JOE NOSSEK OUTFIELD
532

PHILLIES

JOHNNY KLIPPSTEIN p
533

BRAVES
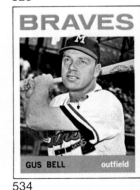
GUS BELL outfield
534

TIGERS

PHIL REGAN pitcher
535

1964 ROOKIE STARS METS

LARRY ELLIOT OUTFIELD
JOHN STEPHENSON CATCHER
536

ANGELS

DAN OSINSKI pitcher
537

WHITE SOX

MINNIE MINOSO of
538

PIRATES
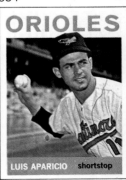
ROY FACE pitcher
539

ORIOLES

LUIS APARICIO shortstop
540

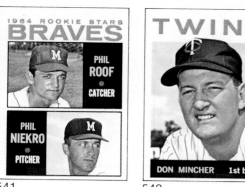
1964 ROOKIE STARS
BRAVES
PHIL ROOF — CATCHER
PHIL NIEKRO — PITCHER
541

TWINS
DON MINCHER — 1st base
542

CARDINALS
BOB UECKER — catcher
543

1964 ROOKIE STARS
COLTS
STEVE HERTZ — INFIELD
JOE HOERNER — PITCHER
544

INDIANS
MAX ALVIS — 3rd base
545

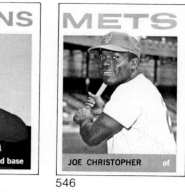
METS
JOE CHRISTOPHER — of
546

SENATORS
GIL HODGES — manager
547

1964 ROOKIE STARS
N. LEAGUE
WAYNE SCHURR — PITCHER
PAUL SPECKENBACH — PITCHER
548

DODGERS
JOE MOELLER — pitcher
549

IN MEMORIAM
KEN HUBBS
550

BRAVES
BILLY HOEFT — pitcher
551

1964 ROOKIE STARS
INDIANS
TOM KELLEY — PITCHER
SONNY SIEBERT — PITCHER
552

DODGERS
JIM BREWER — pitcher
553

ANGELS
HANK FOILES — catcher
554

TWINS
LEE STANGE — pitcher
555

1964 ROOKIE STARS
METS
STEVE DILLON — PITCHER
RON LOCKE — PITCHER
556

CUBS
LEO BURKE — infield
557

PIRATES
DON SCHWALL — pitcher
558

SENATORS
DICK PHILLIPS — 1b-of
559

COLTS
DICK FARRELL — pitcher
560

PHILLIES
DAVE BENNETT — PITCHER
RICK WISE — PITCHER
561

INDIANS
PEDRO RAMOS — pitcher
562

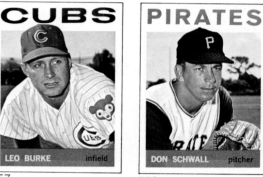
CARDINALS
DAL MAXVILL — shortstop
563

1964 ROOKIE STARS
A. LEAGUE
JOE McCABE — CATCHER
JERRY McNERTNEY — CATCHER
564

ORIOLES
STU MILLER — pitcher
565

METS
ED KRANEPOOL — 1b-of
566

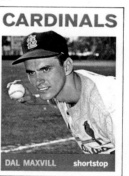
TWINS
JIM KAAT — pitcher
567

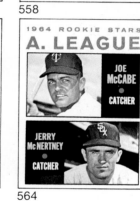
1964 ROOKIE STARS
N. LEAGUE
PHIL GAGLIANO — INFIELD
CAP PETERSON — INF-OF
568

ANGELS
FRED NEWMAN — pitcher
569

PIRATES
BILL MAZEROSKI — 2b
570

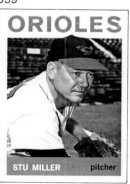
INDIANS
GENE CONLEY — pitcher
571

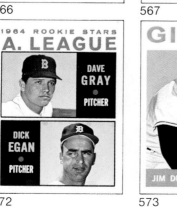
1964 ROOKIE STARS
A. LEAGUE
DAVE GRAY — PITCHER
DICK EGAN — PITCHER
572

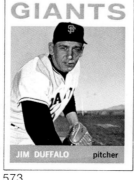
GIANTS
JIM DUFFALO — pitcher
573

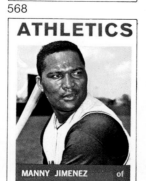
ATHLETICS
MANNY JIMENEZ — of
574

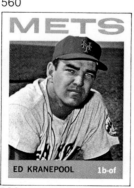
BRAVES
TONY CLONINGER — pitcher
575

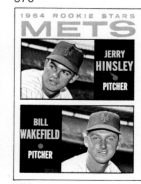
1964 ROOKIE STARS
METS
JERRY HINSLEY — PITCHER
BILL WAKEFIELD — PITCHER
576

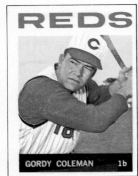
REDS
GORDY COLEMAN   1b
577

CUBS
GLEN HOBBIE   pitcher
578

BOSTON RED SOX
579

DODGERS
JOHNNY PODRES   pitcher
580

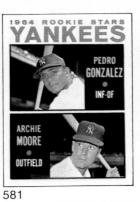
1964 ROOKIE STARS
YANKEES
PEDRO GONZALEZ   INF-OF
ARCHIE MOORE   OUTFIELD
581

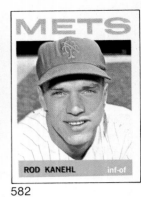
METS
ROD KANEHL   inf-of
582

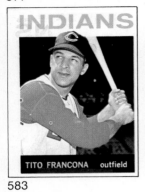
INDIANS
TITO FRANCONA   outfield
583

WHITE SOX
JOEL HORLEN   pitcher
584

PHILLIES
TONY TAYLOR   2nd base
585

ANGELS
JIM PIERSALL   outfield
586

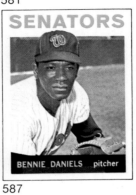
SENATORS
BENNIE DANIELS   pitcher
587

1965

Nineteen sixty-five brought baseball a new commissioner, a new ball park with a roof on it, a World Series between two clubs which had finished in the second division the previous year, a free-agent draft, and a rash of players hitting, not baseballs, but other players – with bats. There were also beginning to be serious doubts about whether or not a certain left-handed pitcher was a mere mortal.

All Sandy Koufax (300), of the Dodgers, managed to accomplish during the year was leading the league in earned run average, winning percentage, victories, and strikeouts. The strikeout total, incidentally, was a new major league record. He became the first pitcher in the 10-year history of the Cy Young Award to win it a second time. As in the first selection, he was a unanimous choice. No one else had been unanimously chosen. He also pitched his fourth career no-hitter, this one a perfect game. He won two decisions in the World Series, including the seventh game. He was even the winning pitcher in the All-Star game. There were rumors that he put on his uniform in a telephone booth.

William D. Eckert, a 56-year-old former three-star general in the air force, was chosen to succeed Fork Frick as commissioner of baseball. It was a choice that came as a complete surprise to the public, and to most baseball people as well. Eckert became the game's fourth commissioner.

In Houston, a ball park modestly described as "the eighth wonder of the world" opened for business. It had a roof, air-conditioning, a scoreboard that put on a light show, and 44,500 padded seats. There was everything a fan could want, except a winning ball club. The tenants, the Astros, lost 97 games and finished ninth, 32 games out of first place. But if the ball club wasn't an attraction, the ball park was, and the club almost tripled its attendance of the previous year, drawing 2,151,470.

But in another city that once drew two million a year, the story was different. The Braves opened the season with the knowledge that next year they would move from Milwaukee to Atlanta. The trouble is that it was no secret to the people of Milwaukee. The Braves tried to buy out of their commitments, so they wouldn't have to go through a "lame duck" season, but to no avail. The team didn't have a bad year on the field, finishing ten games over .500, and in late August they actually were in first place for a brief time. Even so, local apathy produced an attendance of a little over half a million, their lowest since the club moved there and 355,000 under the previous year.

The free-agent draft finally became a reality. Instead of scrambling to sign young players, the clubs drafted the right to negotiate with them. The very first player selected was a 19-year-old outfielder from Arizona State University, Rick Monday, selected by Kansas City. The economic advantages of the free-agent draft were still questionable, since the A's reportedly gave Monday over $100,000 to sign.

The so-called "turbulent sixties" flowed over into the fun and games world of baseball. A Giants pitcher hit a Dodgers catcher over the head with a bat. A

Cleveland infielder charged the mound after a Detroit pitcher and, according to the umpires, swung the bat he should have left at home plate at the pitcher. Two Philadelphia players got into a disagreement during batting practice, and one of them hit his teammate on the shoulder with a bat. By the next day, they were no longer teammates.

The Chicago Cubs' plan to substitute a rotating coaching staff for a full-time manager breathed its last when the club announced they had signed Leo Durocher to take over the reins of the team. Leo had not managed since 1955, but it was doubtful if there would be any question about who was in charge in the Chicago clubhouse and dugout.

But if this was to be the year that "the Lip" came back, it was also to be the year that "the Ol' Perfesser" stepped down. Casey Stengel (187) fell, broke a hip, and was hospitalized for about three weeks. Shortly afterward, the 75-year-old Mets manager announced he was, on advice of doctors, retiring.

At the end of the season, White Sox manager, Al Lopez (414), also announced that he would retire. It was ironic that both decisions came in the same year because not only had Lopez been a catcher for Stengel early in Casey's managerial career, but they were close personal friends – and the only two years that Stengel didn't win the pennant when he was with the Yankees, Lopez won, first with Cleveland and later with the White Sox.

Two second-division clubs from the previous year met in the World Series, and the Yankees, after five straight pennants, finished sixth, 25 games out of first.

The Minnesota Twins, despite a rash of injuries, managed to win the American League pennant by seven games. The Dodgers, boasting the first infield in major league history composed entirely of switch-hitters (Wes Parker (344), Jim Lefebvre (561), Maury Wills, and Jim Gilliam), didn't lock the pennant up until the next-to-last day of the season, on season victory number 26 for Koufax.

The World Series looked, until the very end, like a strong case for home field advantages. The Twins won the first two in Minnesota, and the Dodgers won the next three in Los Angeles. When the clubs returned to Minnesota, the Twins won the sixth game there to tie it up. To keep the progression going and win the Series, all the Twins had to do was get by Koufax. He threw a three-hit shutout, struck out ten, and the Dodgers were World Champions.

In July, the National League won the All-Star game for the seventh time in the last eight years, and for the first time since Babe Ruth won the very first All-Star game in 1933, the National Leaguers led the series, 18–17. (There was one tie.)

One of the game's great hitters, Paul Waner; one of the game's great managers, Bill McKechnie; and one of the game's great minds, Branch Rickey, all died in 1965. Rickey's contributions to baseball included establishing the farm system, which allowed poorer clubs to compete with the rich ones; the breaking of the color barrier, when he signed Jackie Robinson to a Brooklyn contract; and service as president of the Continental League, which brought about major league expansion.

The Cards

Similar to 1964, this series was heavy with rookies. It contained 55 Rookie Cards picturing 126 young players. Among them were Joe Morgan (16); Phil Niekro

(461), who appeared on a Rookie Card for the second time; Dave Johnson (473); Steve Carlton (477); Jim Hunter (526); Jim Lonborg (573); and Tony Perez (581). The card on which Carlton was pictured is, at $450, the second most valued card in the series. [Mantle (350) is listed at $550.] In this set there were World Series and Leader Cards, but Combination Cards were not to be found.

QUIZ

It had to take some kind of year for anybody to beat out Koufax for the Most Valuable Player honor in the National League. Who did it? (250)

Only five men in major league history had pitched ten or more no-hit innings in a game. In 1965, one man did it twice, winning one and losing one. Who? (530)

After five years with other clubs, he returned to his first major league team, and the fans who loved him, and led the league in RBIs. Who? (380)

It was the only year he played only one position, third base, and he also found another position he liked. On top in the National League RBI race. Who? (75)

Who hit the very first home run in the Astrodome? It was in an exhibition game. (350)

Another American League manager suffered a heart attack during spring training, but was back with the team on May 31st. Who? (538)

He got 20 pinch-hits during the year, bringing his lifetime total to a record 115. Who? (198)

Who led the American League in strikeouts and earned run average? (76)

Who was elected the American League Most Valuable Player in 1965? (157)

Traded from the Dodgers during the winter, he led the Washington Senators in batting average, hits, doubles, home runs, runs batted in, height, and weight. Who? (40)

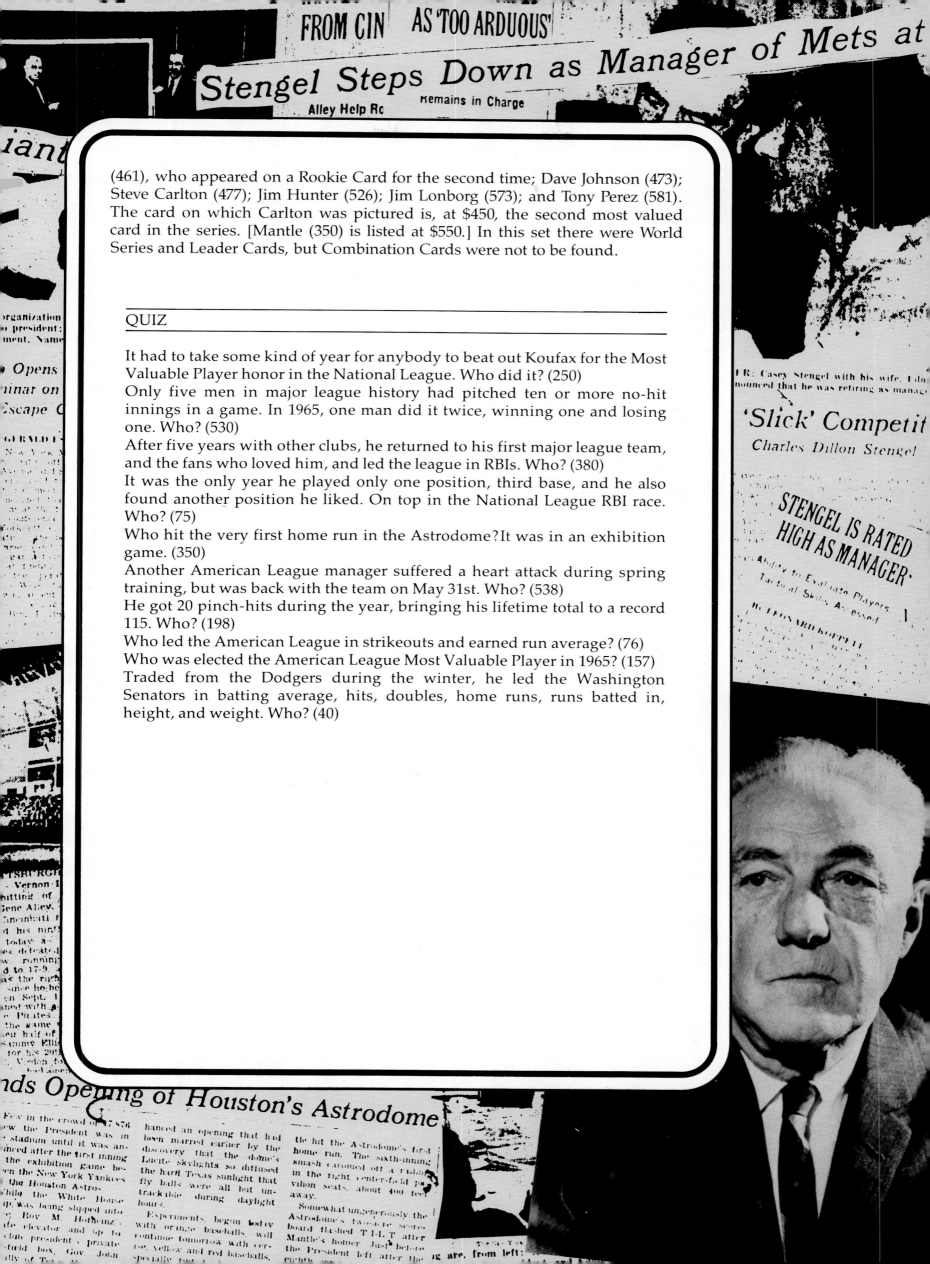

37 FRED GLADDING — TIGERS — PITCHER

38 JIM KING — SENATORS — OUTFIELD

39 GERRY ARRIGO — TWINS — PITCHER

40 FRANK HOWARD — DODGERS — OUTFIELD

41 1965 ROOKIE STARS — MARV STAEHLE 2nd base — BRUCE HOWARD pitcher — WHITE SOX

42 EARL WILSON — RED SOX — PITCHER

43 MIKE SHANNON — CARDS — OUTFIELD

44 WADE BLASINGAME — BRAVES — PITCHER

45 ROY McMILLAN — METS — SHORTSTOP

46 BOB LEE — ANGELS — PITCHER

47 TOMMY HARPER — REDS — OUTFIELD

48 CLAUDE RAYMOND — HOUSTON — PITCHER

49 1965 ROOKIE STARS — JOHN MILLER pitcher — CURT BLEFARY 1st b-of — ORIOLES

50 JUAN MARICHAL — GIANTS — PITCHER

51 BILLY BRYAN — ATHLETICS — CATCHER

52 ED ROEBUCK — PHILLIES — PITCHER

53 DICK McAULIFFE — TIGERS — SHORTSTOP

54 JOE GIBBON — PIRATES — PITCHER

55 TONY CONIGLIARO — RED SOX — OUTFIELD

56 RON KLINE — SENATORS — PITCHER

57 CARDS — 1ST PLACE · NATIONAL LEAGUE

58 FRED TALBOT — WHITE SOX — PITCHER

59 NATE OLIVER — DODGERS — 2nd BASE

60 JIM O'TOOLE — REDS — PITCHER

61 CHRIS CANNIZZARO — METS — CATCHER

62 JIM KATT — TWINS — PITCHER

63 TY CLINE — BRAVES — OUTFIELD

64 LOU BURDETTE — CUBS — PITCHER

65 TONY KUBEK — YANKEES — SHORTSTOP

66 BILL RIGNEY — ANGELS — MANAGER

67 HARVEY HADDIX — ORIOLES — PITCHER

68 DEL CRANDALL — GIANTS — CATCHER

69 BILL VIRDON — PIRATES — OUTFIELD

70 BILL SKOWRON — WHITE SOX — 1st BASE

71 JOHN O'DONOGHUE — ATHLETICS — PITCHER

72 TONY GONZALEZ — PHILLIES — OUTFIELD

73 DENNIS RIBANT — PITCHER — METS

74 1965 ROOKIE STARS — RICO PETROCELLI / JERRY STEPHENSON — RED SOX

75 DERON JOHNSON — 1st BASE — REDS

76 SAM McDOWELL — PITCHER — INDIANS

77 DOUG CAMILLI — CATCHER — DODGERS

78 DAL MAXVILL — 2nd BASE — CARDS

79 TOPPS BASEBALL CHECKLIST — 1ST SERIES

80 TURK FARRELL — PITCHER — HOUSTON

81 DON BUFORD — 2nd BASE — WHITE SOX

82 1965 ROOKIE STARS — JOHN BRAUN / SANTOS ALOMAR — BRAVES

83 GEORGE THOMAS — OUTFIELD — TIGERS

84 RON HERBEL — PITCHER — GIANTS

85 WILLIE SMITH — OUTFIELD — ANGELS

86 LES NARUM — PITCHER — SENATORS

87 NELSON MATHEWS — OUTFIELD — ATHLETICS

88 JACK LAMABE — PITCHER — RED SOX

89 MIKE HERSHBERGER — OUTFIELD — WHITE SOX

90 RICH ROLLINS — 3rd BASE — TWINS

91 CUBS — 8TH PLACE · NATIONAL LEAGUE

92 DICK HOWSER — SHORTSTOP — INDIANS

93 JACK FISHER — PITCHER — METS

94 CHARLIE LAU — CATCHER — ORIOLES

95 BILL MAZEROSKI — 2nd BASE — PIRATES

96 SONNY SIEBERT — PITCHER — INDIANS

97 PEDRO GONZALEZ — INFIELD-OF — YANKEES

98 BOB MILLER — PITCHER — DODGERS

99 GIL HODGES — MANAGER — SENATORS

100 KEN BOYER — 3rd BASE — CARDS

101 FRED NEWMAN — PITCHER — ANGELS

102 STEVE BOROS — 3rd BASE — REDS

103 HARVEY KUENN — OUTFIELD — GIANTS

104 TOPPS BASEBALL CHECKLIST — 2ND SERIES

105 CHICO SALMON — OUTFIELD — INDIANS

106 GENE OLIVER — 1st BASE-C — BRAVES

107 1965 ROOKIE STARS — COSTEN SHOCKLEY / PAT CORRALES — PHILLIES

108 DON MINCHER — 1st BASE — TWINS

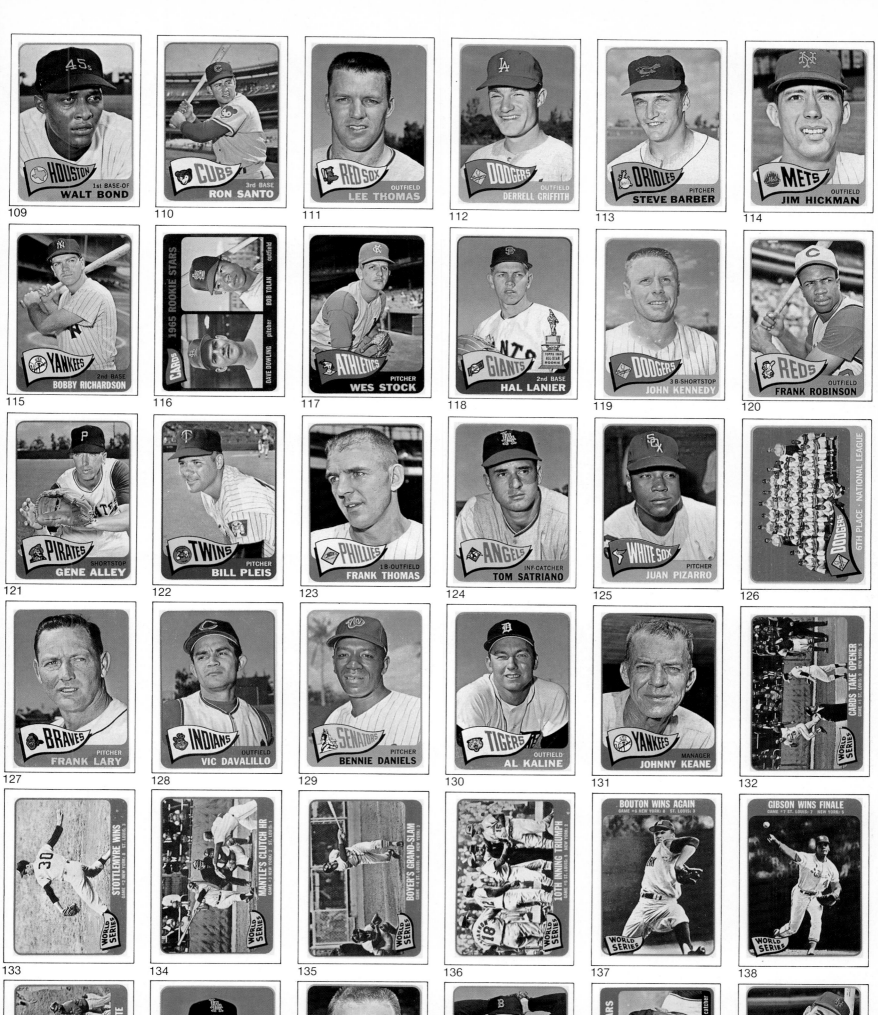

HOUSTON 1st BASE-OF **WALT BOND** 109	CUBS 3rd BASE **RON SANTO** 110	RED SOX OUTFIELD **LEE THOMAS** 111	DODGERS OUTFIELD **DERRELL GRIFFITH** 112	ORIOLES PITCHER **STEVE BARBER** 113	METS OUTFIELD **JIM HICKMAN** 114
YANKEES 2nd BASE **BOBBY RICHARDSON** 115	1965 ROOKIE STARS BOB TOLAN outfield DAVE DOWLING pitcher CARDS **DAVE DOWLING** 116	ATHLETICS PITCHER **WES STOCK** 117	GIANTS 2nd BASE **HAL LANIER** 118	DODGERS 3 B-SHORTSTOP **JOHN KENNEDY** 119	REDS OUTFIELD **FRANK ROBINSON** 120
PIRATES SHORTSTOP **GENE ALLEY** 121	TWINS PITCHER **BILL PLEIS** 122	PHILLIES 1 B-OUTFIELD **FRANK THOMAS** 123	ANGELS INF-CATCHER **TOM SATRIANO** 124	WHITE SOX PITCHER **JUAN PIZARRO** 125	DODGERS 6TH PLACE - NATIONAL LEAGUE 126
BRAVES PITCHER **FRANK LARY** 127	INDIANS OUTFIELD **VIC DAVALILLO** 128	SENATORS PITCHER **BENNIE DANIELS** 129	TIGERS OUTFIELD **AL KALINE** 130	YANKEES MANAGER **JOHNNY KEANE** 131	CARDS TAKE OPENER GAME #1 ST. LOUIS; 9 NEW YORK; 5 WORLD SERIES 132
STOTTLEMYRE WINS GAME #2 NEW YORK; 8 ST. LOUIS; 3 WORLD SERIES 133	MANTLE'S CLUTCH HR GAME #3 NEW YORK; 2 ST. LOUIS; 1 WORLD SERIES 134	BOYER'S GRAND-SLAM GAME #4 ST. LOUIS; 4 NEW YORK; 3 WORLD SERIES 135	10TH INNING TRIUMPH GAME #5 ST. LOUIS; 5 NEW YORK; 2 WORLD SERIES 136	BOUTON WINS AGAIN GAME #6 NEW YORK; 8 ST. LOUIS; 3 WORLD SERIES 137	GIBSON WINS FINALE GAME #7 ST. LOUIS; 7 NEW YORK; 5 WORLD SERIES 138
THE CARDS CELEBRATE WORLD SERIES 139	ANGELS PITCHER **DEAN CHANCE** 140	REDS OUTFIELD **CHARLIE JAMES** 141	RED SOX PITCHER **BILL MONBOUQUETTE** 142	1965 ROOKIE STARS JERRY MAY catcher JOHN GELNAR pitcher PIRATES 143	METS 1st BASE **ED KRANEPOOL** 144

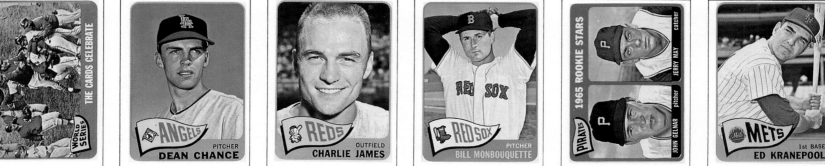

145

146

147

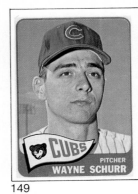

148

149

150

151

152

153

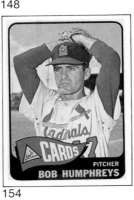

154

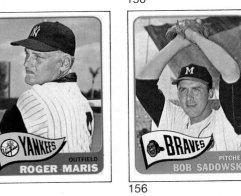

155

156

157

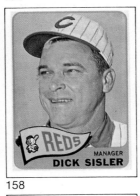

158

159

160

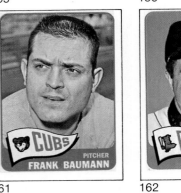

161

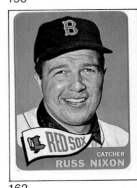

162

163

164

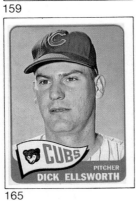

165

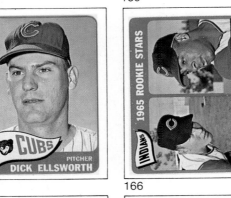

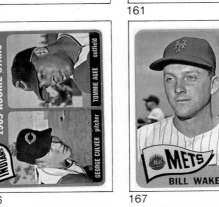

166

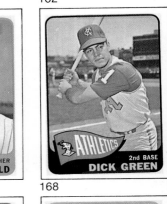

167

168

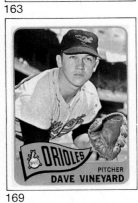

169

170

171

172

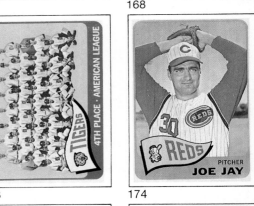

173

174

175

176

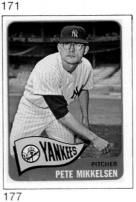

177

178

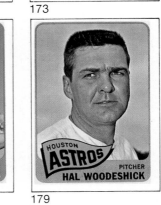

179

180

 MIKE DE LA HOZ — BRAVES — INFIELD

182

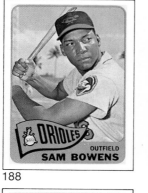 DAVE NICHOLSON — WHITE SOX — OUTFIELD

183

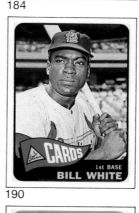 JOHN BOOZER — PHILLIES

184

 MAX ALVIS — INDIANS — 3rd BASE

185

 BILLY COWAN — CUBS — OUTFIELD

186

181

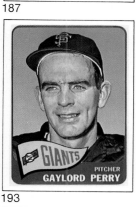 CASEY STENGEL — METS — MANAGER

187

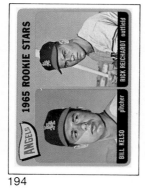 SAM BOWENS — ORIOLES — OUTFIELD

188

TOPPS BASEBALL
CHECKLIST
3rd SERIES

177 □ Pete Mikkelsen
178 □ Dalton Jones
179 □ Hal Woodeshick
180 □ Bob Allison
181 □ Senators Rookies
182 □ Mike de la Hoz
183 □ Dave Nicholson
184 □ John Boozer
185 □ Max Alvis
186 □ Billy Cowan
187 □ Casey Stengel
188 □ Sam Bowens
189 □ List-3rd Series
190 □ Bill White
191 □ Phil Regan
192 □ Jim Coker
193 □ Gaylord Perry

194 □ Angels Rookies
195 □ Bob Veale
196 □ Ron Fairly
197 □ Diego Segui
198 □ Smoky Burgess
199 □ Bob Heffner
200 □ Joe Torre
201 □ Twins Rookies
202 □ Leo Burke
203 □ Dallas Green
204 □ Russ Snyder
205 □ Warren Spahn
206 □ Willie Horton
207 □ Pete Rose
208 □ Tommy John
209 □ Pirates Team
210 □ Jim Fregosi

189

 BILL WHITE — CARDS — 1st BASE

190

 PHIL REGAN — TIGERS — PITCHER

191

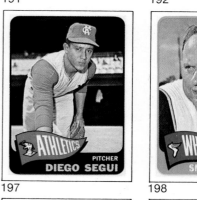 JIM COKER — REDS — CATCHER

192

 GAYLORD PERRY — GIANTS — PITCHER

193

 1965 ROOKIE STARS — ANGELS — RICK REICHARDT outfield — BILL KELSO pitcher

194

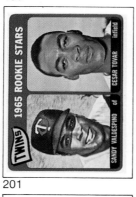 BOB VEALE — PIRATES — PITCHER

195

 RON FAIRLY — DODGERS — 1 B-OUTFIELD

196

 DIEGO SEGUI — ATHLETICS — PITCHER

197

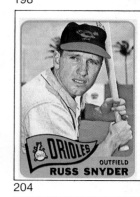 SMOKY BURGESS — WHITE SOX — CATCHER

198

 BOB HEFFNER — RED SOX — PITCHER

199

 JOE TORRE — BRAVES — CATCHER-1B

200

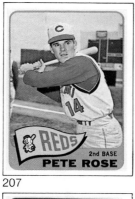 1965 ROOKIE STARS — TWINS — CESAR TOVAR infield — SANDY VALDESPINO of

201

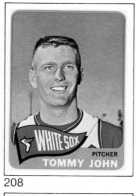 LEO BURKE — CUBS — INF-OF

202

 DALLAS GREEN — PHILLIES — PITCHER

203

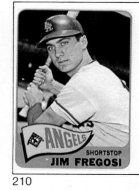 RUSS SNYDER — ORIOLES — OUTFIELD

204

 WARREN SPAHN — METS — P-COACH

205

 WILLIE HORTON — TIGERS — OUTFIELD

206

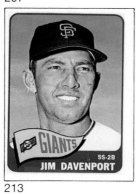 PETE ROSE — REDS — 2nd BASE

207

 TOMMY JOHN — WHITE SOX — PITCHER

208

 PIRATES — 6TH PLACE · NATIONAL LEAGUE

209

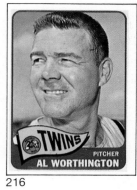 JIM FREGOSI — ANGELS — SHORTSTOP

210

STEVE RIDZIK — SENATORS — PITCHER

211

RON BRAND — HOUSTON ASTROS — CATCHER

212

JIM DAVENPORT — GIANTS — SS-2B

213

BOB PURKEY — CARDS — PITCHER

214

PETE WARD — WHITE SOX — 3rd BASE

215

AL WORTHINGTON — TWINS — PITCHER

216

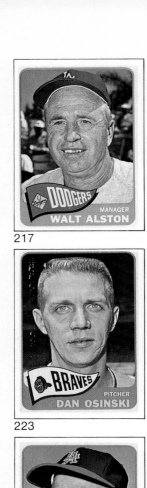  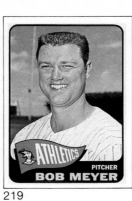  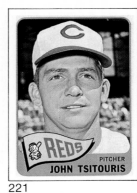 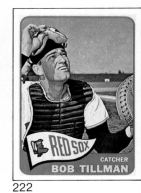

217	218	219	220	221	222
WALT ALSTON	DICK SCHOFIELD	BOB MEYER	BILLY WILLIAMS	JOHN TSITOURIS	BOB TILLMAN

   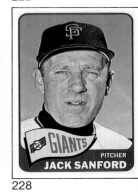

223	224	225	226	227	228
DAN OSINSKI	BOB CHANCE	BO BELINSKY		BOBBY KLAUS	JACK SANFORD

229	230	231	232	233	234
LOU CLINTON	RAY SADECKI	JERRY ADAIR	STEVE BLASS	DON ZIMMER	

   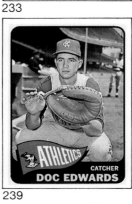 

235	236	237	238	239	240
CHUCK HINTON	DENNIS McLAIN	BERNIE ALLEN	JOE MOELLER	DOC EDWARDS	BOB BRUCE

  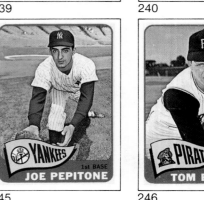 

241	242	243	244	245	246
MACK JONES	GEORGE BRUNET		LINDY McDANIEL	JOE PEPITONE	TOM BUTTERS

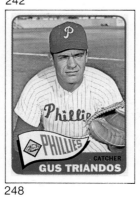    

247	248	249	250	251	252
WALLY MOON	GUS TRIANDOS	DAVE McNALLY	WILLIE MAYS	BILLY HERMAN	PETE RICHERT

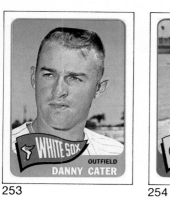
253 DANNY CATER — WHITE SOX OUTFIELD

254 ROLAND SHELDON — YANKEES PITCHER

255 CAMILO PASCUAL — TWINS PITCHER

256 TITO FRANCONA — CARDS OF-1B

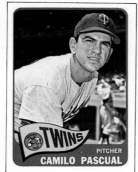
257 JIM WYNN — HOUSTON ASTROS OUTFIELD

258 LARRY BEARNARTH — METS PITCHER

259 1965 ROOKIE STARS — RAY OYLER shortstop / JIM NORTHRUP outfield — TIGERS

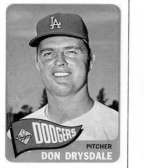
260 DON DRYSDALE — DODGERS PITCHER

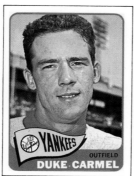
261 DUKE CARMEL — YANKEES OUTFIELD

262 BUD DALEY — INDIANS PITCHER

263 MARTY KEOUGH — REDS OUTFIELD

264 BOB BUHL — CUBS PITCHER

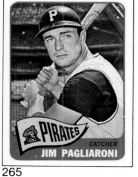
265 JIM PAGLIARONI — PIRATES CATCHER

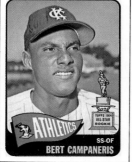
266 BERT CAMPANERIS — ATHLETICS SS-OF

267 SENATORS — 9TH PLACE AMERICAN LEAGUE

268 KEN McBRIDE — ANGELS PITCHER

269 FRANK BOLLING — BRAVES 2nd BASE

270 MILT PAPPAS — BALTIMORE ORIOLES PITCHER

271 DON WERT — TIGERS 3rd BASE

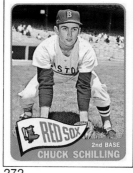
272 CHUCK SCHILLING — RED SOX 2nd BASE

273
TOPPS BASEBALL CHECKLIST 4th SERIES

265 ☐ Jim Pagliaroni	282 ☐ Giants Rookies
266 ☐ Bert Campaneris	283 ☐ Fred Whitfield
267 ☐ Senators Team	284 ☐ Nick Willhite
268 ☐ Ken McBride	285 ☐ Ron Hunt
269 ☐ Frank Bolling	286 ☐ Ath. Rookies
270 ☐ Milt Pappas	287 ☐ Gary Kolb
271 ☐ Don Wert	288 ☐ Jack Hamilton
272 ☐ Chuck Schilling	289 ☐ Gordy Coleman
273 ☑ List—4th Series	290 ☐ Wally Bunker
274 ☐ Lum Harris	291 ☐ Jerry Lynch
275 ☐ Dick Groat	292 ☐ Larry Yellen
276 ☐ Hoyt Wilhelm	293 ☐ Angels Team
277 ☐ Johnny Lewis	294 ☐ Tim McCarver
278 ☐ Ken Retzer	295 ☐ Dick Radatz
279 ☐ Dick Tracewski	296 ☐ Tony Taylor
280 ☐ Dick Stuart	297 ☐ D. DeBusschere
281 ☐ Bill Stafford	298 ☐ Jim Stewart

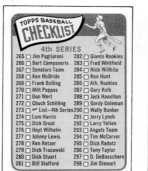
274 LUM HARRIS — HOUSTON ASTROS MANAGER

275 DICK GROAT — CARDS SHORTSTOP

276 HOYT WILHELM — WHITE SOX PITCHER

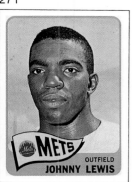
277 JOHNNY LEWIS — METS OUTFIELD

278 KEN RETZER — TWINS CATCHER

279 DICK TRACEWSKI — DODGERS 2B-SS

280 DICK STUART — PHILLIES 1st BASE

281 BILL STAFFORD — YANKEES PITCHER

282 1965 ROOKIE STARS — MASANORI MURAKAMI p / DICK ESTELLE pitcher — GIANTS

283 FRED WHITFIELD — INDIANS 1st BASE

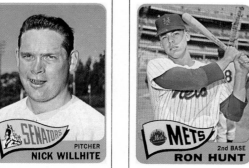
284 NICK WILLHITE — SENATORS PITCHER

285 RON HUNT — METS 2nd BASE

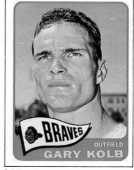
286 1965 ROOKIE STARS — AURELIO MONTEAGUDO p / JIM DICKSON pitcher — ATHLETICS

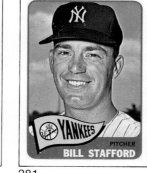
287 GARY KOLB — BRAVES OUTFIELD

288 JACK HAMILTON — TIGERS PITCHER

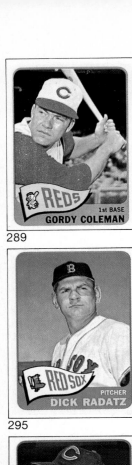
289 GORDY COLEMAN — 1st BASE — REDS

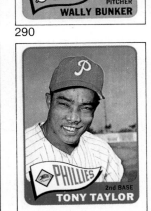
290 WALLY BUNKER — PITCHER — ORIOLES

291 JERRY LYNCH — OUTFIELD — PIRATES

292 LARRY YELLEN — PITCHER — HOUSTON ASTROS

293 ANGELS — 5TH PLACE · AMERICAN LEAGUE

294 TIM McCARVER — CATCHER — CARDS

295 DICK RADATZ — PITCHER — RED SOX

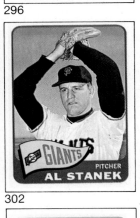
296 TONY TAYLOR — 2nd BASE — PHILLIES

297 DAVE DeBUSSCHERE — PITCHER — WHITE SOX

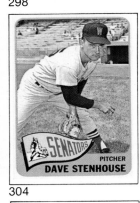
298 JIM STEWART — SS-2nd BASE — CUBS

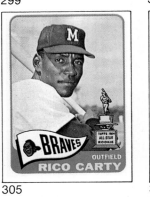
299 JERRY ZIMMERMAN — CATCHER — TWINS

300 SANDY KOUFAX — PITCHER — DODGERS

301 BIRDIE TEBBETTS — MANAGER — INDIANS

302 AL STANEK — PITCHER — GIANTS

303 JOHNNY ORSINO — CATCHER — ORIOLES

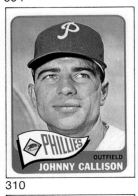
304 DAVE STENHOUSE — PITCHER — SENATORS

305 RICO CARTY — OUTFIELD — BRAVES

306 BUBBA PHILLIPS — OF-3rd BASE — TIGERS

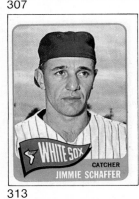
307 BARRY LATMAN — PITCHER — ANGELS

308 1965 ROOKIE STARS — TOM PARSONS pitcher / CLEON JONES outfield — METS

309 STEVE HAMILTON — PITCHER — YANKEES

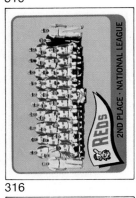
310 JOHNNY CALLISON — OUTFIELD — PHILLIES

311 ORLANDO PENA — PITCHER — ATHLETICS

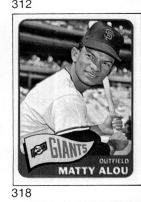
312 JOE NUXHALL — PITCHER — REDS

313 JIMMIE SCHAFFER — CATCHER — WHITE SOX

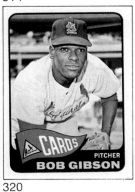
314 STERLING SLAUGHTER — PITCHER — CUBS

315 FRANK MALZONE — 3rd BASE — RED SOX

316 REDS — 2ND PLACE · NATIONAL LEAGUE

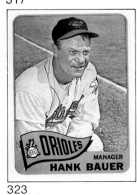
317 DON McMAHON — PITCHER — INDIANS

318 MATTY ALOU — OUTFIELD — GIANTS

319 KEN McMULLEN — 3rd BASE — SENATORS

320 BOB GIBSON — PITCHER — CARDS

321 RUSTY STAUB — OUTFIELD — HOUSTON ASTROS

322 RICK WISE — PITCHER — PHILLIES

323 HANK BAUER — MANAGER — ORIOLES

324 BOBBY LOCKE — PITCHER — ANGELS

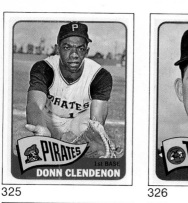 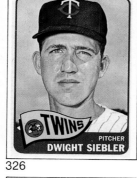  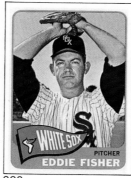 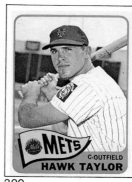 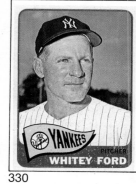

325 DONN CLENDENON   326 DWIGHT SIEBLER   327 DENIS MENKE   328 EDDIE FISHER   329 HAWK TAYLOR   330 WHITEY FORD

331   332 TED ABERNATHY   333 TOMMIE REYNOLDS   334 VIC ROZNOVSKY   335 MICKEY LOLICH   336 WOODY HELD

  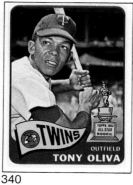  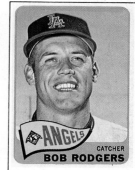

337 MIKE CUELLAR   338   339 RYNE DUREN   340 TONY OLIVA   341 BOBBY BOLIN   342 BOB RODGERS

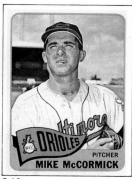  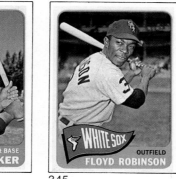 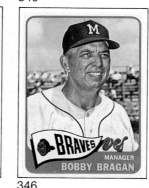  

343 MIKE McCORMICK   344 WES PARKER   345 FLOYD ROBINSON   346 BOBBY BRAGAN   347 ROY FACE   348 GEORGE BANKS

 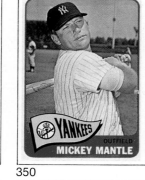 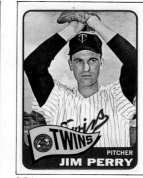   

349 LARRY MILLER   350 MICKEY MANTLE   351 JIM PERRY   352 ALEX JOHNSON   353 JERRY LUMPE   354

 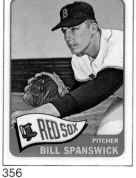 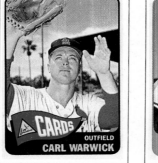  

355 VADA PINSON   356 BILL SPANSWICK   357 CARL WARWICK   358 ALBIE PEARSON   359 KEN JOHNSON   360 ORLANDO CEPEDA

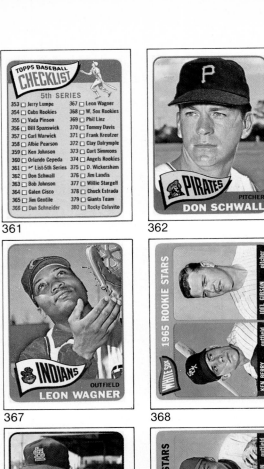

TOPPS BASEBALL
CHECKLIST
5th SERIES

353 ☐ Jerry Lumpe	367 ☐ Leon Wagner
354 ☐ Cubs Rookies	368 ☐ W. Sox Rookies
355 ☐ Vada Pinson	369 ☐ Phil Linz
356 ☐ Bill Spanswick	370 ☐ Tommy Davis
357 ☐ Carl Warwick	371 ☐ Frank Kreutzer
358 ☐ Albie Pearson	372 ☐ Clay Dalrymple
359 ☐ Ken Johnson	373 ☐ Curt Simmons
360 ☐ Orlando Cepeda	374 ☐ Angels Rookies
361 ☑ List-5th Series	375 ☐ D. Wickersham
362 ☐ Don Schwall	376 ☐ Jim Landis
363 ☐ Bob Johnson	377 ☐ Willie Stargell
364 ☐ Galen Cisco	378 ☐ Chuck Estrada
365 ☐ Jim Gentile	379 ☐ Giants Team
366 ☐ Dan Schneider	380 ☐ Rocky Colavito

361

DON SCHWALL — PIRATES — PITCHER
362

BOB JOHNSON — ORIOLES — INF-OUTFIELD
363

GALEN CISCO — METS — PITCHER
364

JIM GENTILE — ATHLETICS — 1st BASE
365

DAN SCHNEIDER — BRAVES — PITCHER
366

LEON WAGNER — INDIANS — OUTFIELD
367

1965 ROOKIE STARS — WHITE SOX — JOEL GIBSON pitcher / KEN BERRY outfield
368

PHIL LINZ — YANKEES — INF-OUTFIELD
369

TOMMY DAVIS — DODGERS — OUTFIELD
370

FRANK KREUTZER — SENATORS — PITCHER
371

CLAY DALRYMPLE — PHILLIES — CATCHER
372

CURT SIMMONS — CARDS — PITCHER
373

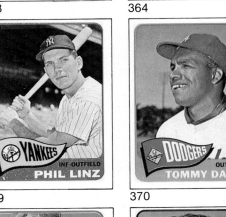

1965 ROOKIE STARS — ANGELS — DICK SIMPSON outfield / JOSE CARDENAL outfield
374

DAVE WICKERSHAM — TIGERS — PITCHER
375

JIM LANDIS — ATHLETICS — OUTFIELD
376

WILLIE STARGELL — PIRATES — OUTFIELD
377

CHUCK ESTRADA — ORIOLES — PITCHER
378

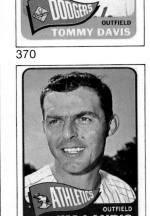

4TH PLACE : NATIONAL LEAGUE — GIANTS
379

ROCKY COLAVITO — INDIANS — OUTFIELD
380

AL JACKSON — METS — PITCHER
381

J. C. MARTIN — WHITE SOX — CATCHER
382

FELIPE ALOU — BRAVES — 1B-OF
383

JOHNNY KLIPPSTEIN — TWINS — PITCHER
384

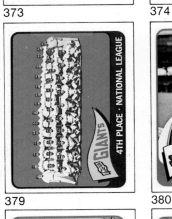

CARL YASTRZEMSKI — RED SOX — OUTFIELD
385

1965 ROOKIE STARS — CUBS — FRED NORMAN pitcher / PAUL JAECKEL pitcher
386

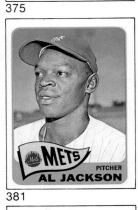

JOHNNY PODRES — DODGERS — PITCHER
387

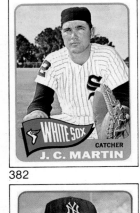

JOHN BLANCHARD — YANKEES — CATCHER
388

DON LARSEN — HOUSTON ASTROS — PITCHER
389

BILL FREEHAN — TIGERS — CATCHER
390

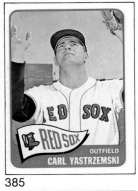

MEL McGAHA — ATHLETICS — MANAGER
391

BOB FRIEND — PIRATES — PITCHER
392

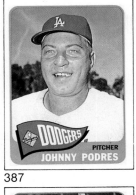

ED KIRKPATRICK — ANGELS — OUTFIELD
393

JIM HANNAN — SENATORS — PITCHER
394

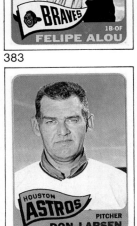

JIM HART — GIANTS — 3RD BASE
395

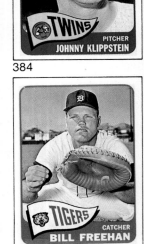

FRANK BERTAINA — ORIOLES — PITCHER
396

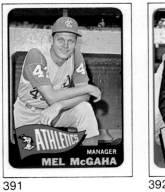

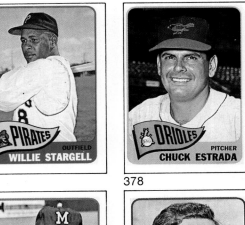

397 JERRY BUCHEK — SHORTSTOP — CARDS

398 1965 ROOKIE STARS — REDS — ART SHAMSKY outfield / DAN NEVILLE pitcher

399 RAY HERBERT — PITCHER — PHILLIES

400 HARMON KILLEBREW — OUTFIELD — TWINS

401 CARL WILLEY — PITCHER — METS

402 JOE AMALFITANO — 2ND BASE — CUBS

403 RED SOX — 8TH PLACE · AMERICAN LEAGUE

404 STAN WILLIAMS — PITCHER — INDIANS

405 JOHN ROSEBORO — CATCHER — DODGERS

406 RALPH TERRY — PITCHER — INDIANS

407 LEE MAYE — OUTFIELD — BRAVES

408 LARRY SHERRY — PITCHER — TIGERS

409 1965 ROOKIE STARS — ASTROS — LARRY DIERKER pitcher / JIM BEAUCHAMP outfield

410 LUIS APARICIO — SHORTSTOP — ORIOLES

411 ROGER CRAIG — PITCHER — REDS

412 BOB BAILEY — 3RD BASE — PIRATES

413 HAL RENIFF — PITCHER — YANKEES

414 AL LOPEZ — MANAGER — WHITE SOX

415 CURT FLOOD — OUTFIELD — CARDS

416 JIM BREWER — PITCHER — DODGERS

417 ED BRINKMAN — SHORTSTOP — SENATORS

418 JOHNNY EDWARDS — CATCHER — REDS

419 RUBEN AMARO — SHORTSTOP — PHILLIES

420 LARRY JACKSON — PITCHER — CUBS

421 1965 ROOKIE STARS — TWINS — JAY WARD 3b-of / GARY DOTTER pitcher

422 AUBREY GATEWOOD — PITCHER — ANGELS

423 JESSE GONDER — CATCHER — METS

424 GARY BELL — PITCHER — INDIANS

425 WAYNE CAUSEY — SHORTSTOP — ATHLETICS

426 BRAVES — 5TH PLACE · NATIONAL LEAGUE

427 BOB SAVERINE — INF-OF — ORIOLES

428 BOB SHAW — PITCHER — GIANTS

429 DON DEMETER — OUTFIELD — TIGERS

430 GARY PETERS — PITCHER — WHITE SOX

431 1965 ROOKIE STARS — CARDS — WAYNE SPIEZIO infield / NELSON BRILES pitcher

432 JIM GRANT — PITCHER — TWINS

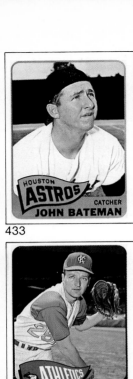

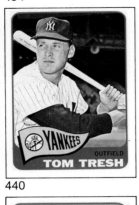
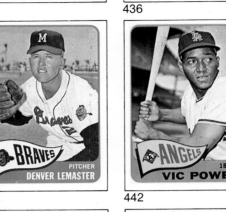

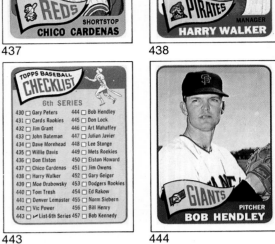

HOUSTON ASTROS — CATCHER — JOHN BATEMAN — 433

RED SOX — PITCHER — DAVE MOREHEAD — 434

DODGERS — OUTFIELD — WILLIE DAVIS — 435

CUBS — PITCHER — DON ELSTON — 436

REDS — SHORTSTOP — CHICO CARDENAS — 437

PIRATES — MANAGER — HARRY WALKER — 438

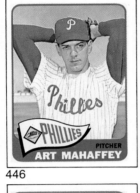

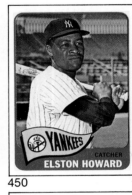

ATHLETICS — PITCHER — MOE DRABOWSKY — 439

YANKEES — OUTFIELD — TOM TRESH — 440

BRAVES — PITCHER — DENVER LEMASTER — 441

ANGELS — 1B-INF — VIC POWER — 442

TOPPS BASEBALL CHECKLIST — 6th Series

430 ☐ Gary Peters		444 ☐ Bob Hendley	
431 ☐ Cards Rookies		445 ☐ Don Lock	
432 ☐ Jim Grant		446 ☐ Art Mahaffey	
433 ☐ John Bateman		447 ☐ Julian Javier	
434 ☐ Dave Morehead		448 ☐ Lee Stange	
435 ☐ Willie Davis		449 ☐ Mets Rookies	
436 ☐ Don Elston		450 ☐ Elston Howard	
437 ☐ Chico Cardenas		451 ☐ Jim Owens	
438 ☐ Harry Walker		452 ☐ Gary Geiger	
439 ☐ Moe Drabowsky		453 ☐ Dodgers Rookies	
440 ☐ Tom Tresh		454 ☐ Ed Rakow	
441 ☐ Denver Lemaster		455 ☐ Norm Siebern	
442 ☐ Vic Power		456 ☐ Bill Henry	
443 ☐ List-6th Series		457 ☐ Bob Kennedy	

443

GIANTS — PITCHER — BOB HENDLEY — 444

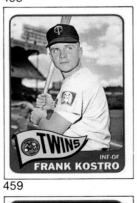
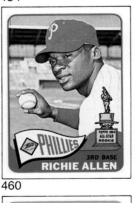

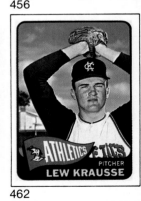

SENATORS — OUTFIELD — DON LOCK — 445

PHILLIES — PITCHER — ART MAHAFFEY — 446

CARDS — 2ND BASE — JULIAN JAVIER — 447

INDIANS — PITCHER — LEE STANGE — 448

METS / 1965 ROOKIE STARS — GARY KROLL pitcher / JERRY HINSLEY pitcher — 449

YANKEES — CATCHER — ELSTON HOWARD — 450

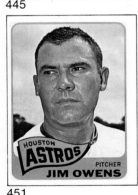
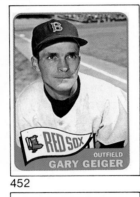

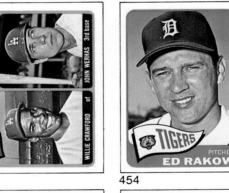

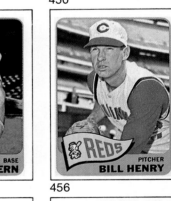

HOUSTON ASTROS — PITCHER — JIM OWENS — 451

RED SOX — OUTFIELD — GARY GEIGER — 452

1965 ROOKIE STARS — JOHN WERHAS 3rd base / WILLIE CRAWFORD of — DODGERS — 453

TIGERS — PITCHER — ED RAKOW — 454

ORIOLES — 1ST BASE — NORM SIEBERN — 455

REDS — PITCHER — BILL HENRY — 456

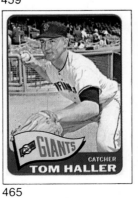

CUBS — HEAD COACH — BOB KENNEDY — 457

WHITE SOX — PITCHER — JOHN BUZHARDT — 458

TWINS — INF-OF — FRANK KOSTRO — 459

PHILLIES — 3RD BASE — RICHIE ALLEN — 460

1965 ROOKIE STARS — PHIL NIEKRO pitcher / CLAY CARROLL pitcher — BRAVES — 461

ATHLETICS — PITCHER — LEW KRAUSSE — 462

PIRATES — OUTFIELD — MANNY MOTA — 463

ANGELS — PITCHER — RON PICHE — 464

GIANTS — CATCHER — TOM HALLER — 465

1965 ROOKIE STARS — DICK NEN 1st base / PETE CRAIG pitcher — SENATORS — 466

CARDS — PITCHER — RAY WASHBURN — 467

INDIANS — 2ND BASE — LARRY BROWN — 468

469 DON NOTTEBART
470 YOGI BERRA
471 BILLY HOEFT
472 DON PAVLETICH
473 DAVE JOHNSON / PAUL BLAIR
474 COOKIE ROJAS

475 CLETE BOYER
476 BILLY O'DELL
477 STEVE CARLTON / FRITZ ACKLEY
478 WILBUR WOOD
479 KEN HARRELSON
480 JOEL HORLEN

481 INDIANS 7TH PLACE · AMERICAN LEAGUE
482 BOB PRIDDY
483 GEORGE SMITH
484 RON PERRANOSKI
485 NELLIE FOX
486 PAT ROGAN / TOM EGAN

487 WOODY WOODWARD
488 TED WILLS
489 GENE MAUCH
490 EARL BATTEY
491 TRACY STALLARD
492 GENE FREESE

493 BRUCE BRUBAKER / BILL ROMAN
494 JAY RITCHIE
495 JOE CHRISTOPHER
496 JOE CUNNINGHAM
497 JACK HIATT / KEN HENDERSON
498 GENE STEPHENS

499 STU MILLER
500 ED MATHEWS
501 JIM RITTWAGE / RALPH GAGLIANO
502 DON CARDWELL
503 PHIL GAGLIANO
504 JERRY GROTE

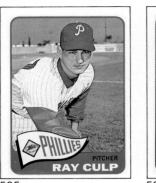
RAY CULP — PHILLIES — PITCHER
505

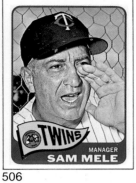
SAM MELE — TWINS — MANAGER
506

SAMMY ELLIS — REDS — PITCHER
507

TOPPS BASEBALL CHECKLIST 7th SERIES

507 Sammy Ellis	528 Jeff Torborg
508 List-7th Series	529 George Altman
509 Red Sox Rookies	530 Jerry Fosnow
510 Ernie Banks	531 Jim Maloney
511 Ron Locke	532 Chuck Hiller
512 Cap Peterson	533 Hector Lopez
513 Yankee Team	534 Mets Rookies
514 Joe Azcue	535 John Herrnstein
515 Vern Law	536 Jack Kralick
516 Al Weis	537 Andre Rodgers
517 Angels Rookies	538 Chuck Dressen
518 Ken Rowe	539 Herm Starrette
519 Bob Uecker	540 Lou Brock
520 Tony Cloninger	541 W. Sox Rookies
521 Phillies Rookies	542 Lou Klimchock
522 Hank Aguirre	543 Ed Connolly
523 Mike Brumley	544 Howie Reed
524 Dave Giusti	545 Jesus Alou
525 Eddie Bressoud	546 Indians Rookies
526 Athletics Rookies	

508

1965 ROOKIE STARS — RED SOX — GERRY VEZENDY pitcher / BOB GUINDON 1st base
509

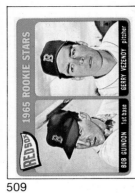
ERNIE BANKS — CUBS — 1ST BASE
510

RON LOCKE — METS — PITCHER
511

CAP PETERSON — GIANTS — OUTFIELD
512

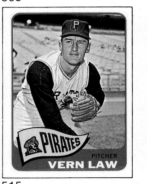
1ST PLACE - AMERICAN LEAGUE — YANKEES
513

JOE AZCUE — INDIANS — CATCHER
514

VERN LAW — PIRATES — PITCHER
515

AL WEIS — WHITE SOX — 2ND BASE
516

1965 ROOKIE STARS — ANGELS — PAUL SCHAAL 3rd base / JACK WARNER outfield
517

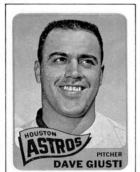
KEN ROWE — ORIOLES — PITCHER
518

BOB UECKER — CARDS — CATCHER
519

TONY CLONINGER — BRAVES — PITCHER
520

1965 ROOKIE STARS — PHILLIES — MORRIE STEVENS p / DAVE BENNETT pitcher
521

HANK AGUIRRE — TIGERS — PITCHER
522

MIKE BRUMLEY — SENATORS — CATCHER
523

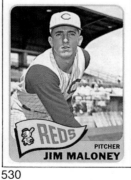
DAVE GIUSTI — HOUSTON ASTROS — PITCHER
524

EDDIE BRESSOUD — RED SOX — SHORTSTOP
525

ATHLETICS 1965 ROOKIE STARS — R. LACHEMANN catcher / JOHNNY ODOM pitcher / SKIP LOCKWOOD infield / JIM HUNTER pitcher
526

JEFF TORBORG — DODGERS — CATCHER
527

GEORGE ALTMAN — CUBS — OUTFIELD
528

JERRY FOSNOW — TWINS — PITCHER
529

JIM MALONEY — REDS — PITCHER
530

CHUCK HILLER — GIANTS — 2nd BASE
531

HECTOR LOPEZ — YANKEES — OUTFIELD
532

METS 1965 ROOKIE STARS — D. NAPOLEON outfield / R. SWOBODA outfield / JIM BETHKE pitcher / TUG McGRAW pitcher
533

JOHN HERRNSTEIN — PHILLIES — OF-1B
534

JACK KRALICK — INDIANS — PITCHER
535

ANDRE RODGERS — PIRATES — SHORTSTOP
536

ANGELS 1965 ROOKIE STARS — MARCELINO LOPEZ PITCHER / RUDY MAY pitcher / PHIL ROOF catcher
537

CHUCK DRESSEN — TIGERS — MANAGER
538

HERM STARRETTE — ORIOLES — PITCHER
539

LOU BROCK — CARDS — OUTFIELD
540

541

LOU KLIMCHOCK · BRAVES · INFIELD

542

ED CONNOLLY · RED SOX · PITCHER

543

HOWIE REED · DODGERS · PITCHER

544

JESUS ALOU · GIANTS · OUTFIELD

545

546

JAKE WOOD · TIGERS · 2B-OF

547

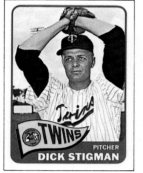

DICK STIGMAN · TWINS · PITCHER

548

549

MEL STOTTLEMYRE · YANKEES · PITCHER

550

METS · 10TH PLACE · NATIONAL LEAGUE

551

JULIO GOTAY · ANGELS · 3B-SS

552

553

CHICO RUIZ · REDS · INFIELD

554

JACK BALDSCHUN · PHILLIES · PITCHER

555

RED SCHOENDIENST · CARDS · MANAGER

556

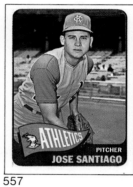

JOSE SANTIAGO · ATHLETICS · PITCHER

557

TOMMIE SISK · PIRATES · PITCHER

558

ED BAILEY · GIANTS · CATCHER

559

BOOG POWELL · ORIOLES · OUTFIELD

560

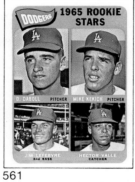

561

BILLY MORAN · INDIANS · 2ND BASE

562

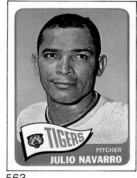

JULIO NAVARRO · TIGERS · PITCHER

563

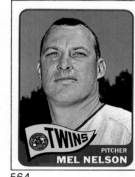

MEL NELSON · TWINS · PITCHER

564

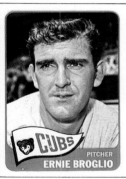

ERNIE BROGLIO · CUBS · PITCHER

565

566

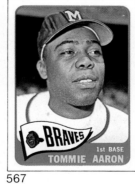

TOMMIE AARON · BRAVES · 1st BASE

567

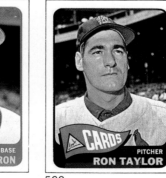

RON TAYLOR · CARDS · PITCHER

568

GINO CIMOLI · ANGELS · OUTFIELD

569

CLAUDE OSTEEN · DODGERS · PITCHER

570

OSSIE VIRGIL · PIRATES · C-INF.

571

ORIOLES · 3RD PLACE · AMERICAN LEAGUE

572

573

ROY SIEVERS · SENATORS · 1st BASE

574

JOSE PAGAN · GIANTS · SHORTSTOP

575

TERRY FOX · TIGERS · PITCHER

576

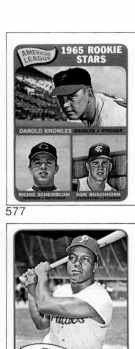

577

578 CAMILO CARREON

579 DICK SMITH

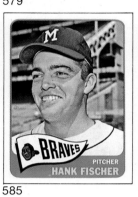
580 JIMMIE HALL

581

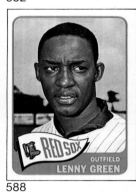
582 BOB SCHMIDT

583 WES COVINGTON

584 HARRY BRIGHT

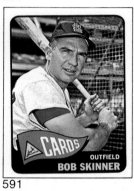
585 HANK FISCHER

586 TOMMY McCRAW

587 JOE SPARMA

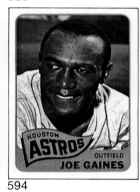
588 LENNY GREEN

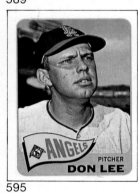
589

590 JOHNNIE WYATT

591 BOB SKINNER

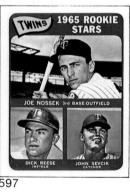
592 FRANK BORK

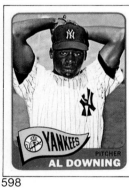
593

594 JOE GAINES

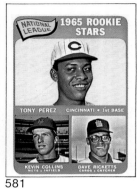
595 DON LEE

596 DON LANDRUM

597

598 AL DOWNING

1966

In 1966, major league baseball was introduced to Atlanta, Anaheim, and artificial grass. A man known for his directness and a master of indirection were inducted together into the Hall of Fame. A pitcher and a hitter dominated their respective leagues, and both added drama to their big years. The Yankees not only didn't win the pennant, they finished dead last in the American League.

The Braves finally set up their teepee in Atlanta, although the Milwaukee ball park was fully prepared in the event that the courts sent the Braves back. But they didn't, and a quarter of a million turned out for a welcoming parade.

Anaheim welcomed the Angels, who moved from Los Angeles without any of the rancor that marked the Milwaukee move. Los Angeles still had the Dodgers.

"What did he mean by that?" was a question frequently asked about Casey Stengel and seldom asked about Ted Williams. But if their approach to the language was different, their affection for baseball and respect for each other were very similar. So it was somehow fitting that Stengel and Williams should be inducted into the Baseball Hall of Fame together on July 25th.

Two players, one in each league, added a touch of drama to the truly outstanding years they had on the field. One was Frank Robinson, who had been regarded as a fixture for the Cincinnati Reds, where he had been a consistent leader in National League offensive departments and had even been chosen the league's Most Valuable Player in 1961. Over the winter, the Reds traded Robinson to Baltimore, and the Cincinnati fans, and Robinson, made no secret of the fact that they thought the deal was a mistake.

It was obvious from his remarks that Robinson felt he had something to prove. It was obvious from his statistics, that he proved it. He not only captured the triple crown, something he had never accomplished in Cincinnati, he also won the Most Valuable Player award again, thus becoming the first man in baseball history to win the award in both leagues. If there was room on Robinson's cake for any more icing, it came when the Orioles won the American League pennant by nine games, and the World Series in four straight.

In the National League, the question of when the invincibility of Sandy Koufax (100) would end was answered. Before that, however, the stylish left-hander had some more headlines to make. Before the club went to Spring training, Koufax and right-hander Don Drysdale (430) announced that they were holding out for a joint contract, believed to be a three-year, $1,000,000 deal, divided equally. No deal was made, and they signed separately on March 30th.

Koufax led the majors in victories, complete games, innings pitched, strikeouts and earned run average. It marked the fifth straight year he led N.L. pitchers in ERA, a record. Also, with two days rest, he pitched the final day of the season to win the pennant. The bombshell was to come after the Series, when Koufax, 30, announced that because he feared permanent damage to his arthritic left arm, he was retiring.

The National League pennant race was close. The Dodgers had a double-header on the last day of the season, and the Giants had a single game. The

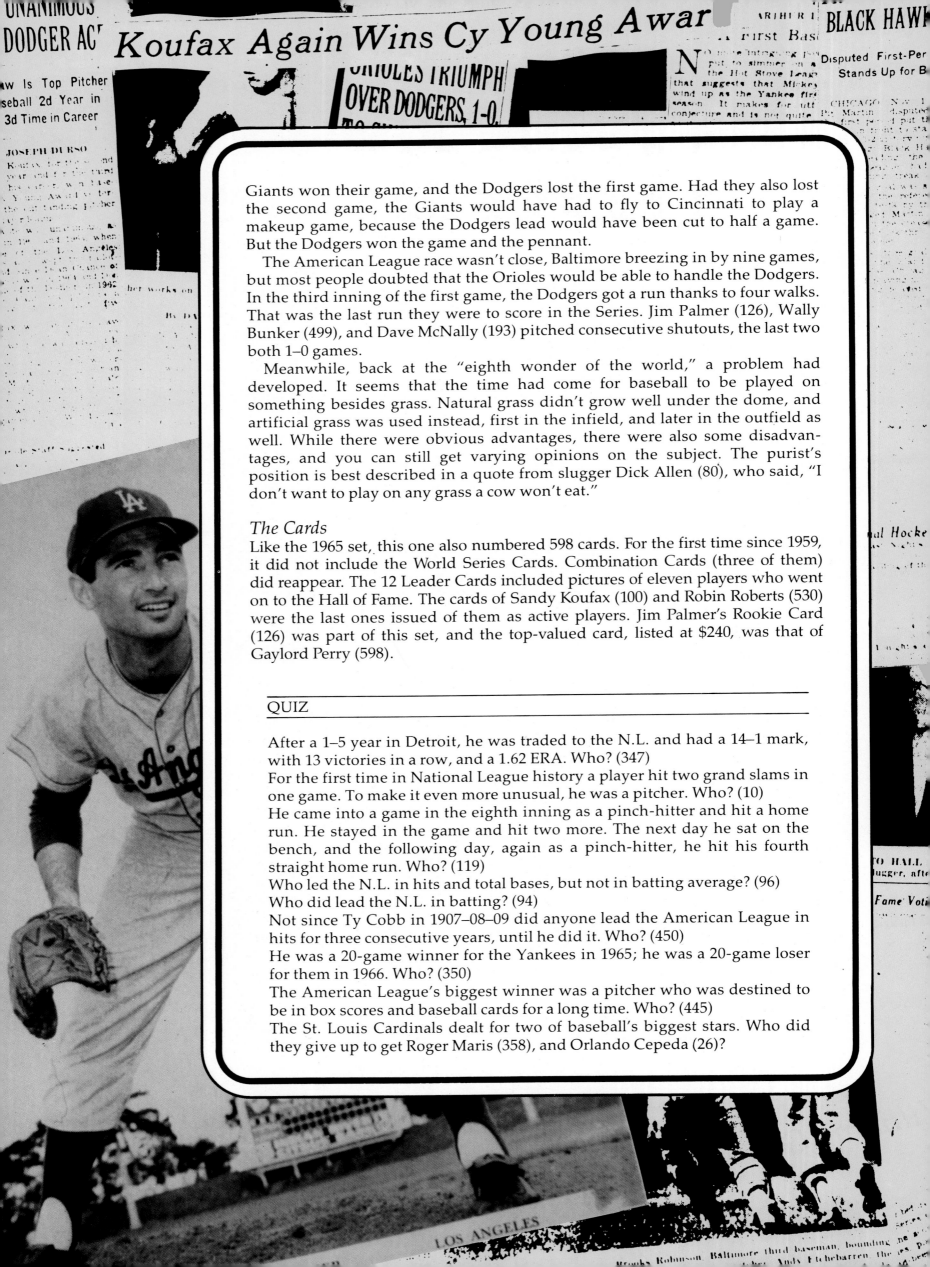

Giants won their game, and the Dodgers lost the first game. Had they also lost the second game, the Giants would have had to fly to Cincinnati to play a makeup game, because the Dodgers lead would have been cut to half a game. But the Dodgers won the game and the pennant.

The American League race wasn't close, Baltimore breezing in by nine games, but most people doubted that the Orioles would be able to handle the Dodgers. In the third inning of the first game, the Dodgers got a run thanks to four walks. That was the last run they were to score in the Series. Jim Palmer (126), Wally Bunker (499), and Dave McNally (193) pitched consecutive shutouts, the last two both 1–0 games.

Meanwhile, back at the "eighth wonder of the world," a problem had developed. It seems that the time had come for baseball to be played on something besides grass. Natural grass didn't grow well under the dome, and artificial grass was used instead, first in the infield, and later in the outfield as well. While there were obvious advantages, there were also some disadvantages, and you can still get varying opinions on the subject. The purist's position is best described in a quote from slugger Dick Allen (80), who said, "I don't want to play on any grass a cow won't eat."

The Cards

Like the 1965 set, this one also numbered 598 cards. For the first time since 1959, it did not include the World Series Cards. Combination Cards (three of them) did reappear. The 12 Leader Cards included pictures of eleven players who went on to the Hall of Fame. The cards of Sandy Koufax (100) and Robin Roberts (530) were the last ones issued of them as active players. Jim Palmer's Rookie Card (126) was part of this set, and the top-valued card, listed at $240, was that of Gaylord Perry (598).

QUIZ

After a 1–5 year in Detroit, he was traded to the N.L. and had a 14–1 mark, with 13 victories in a row, and a 1.62 ERA. Who? (347)

For the first time in National League history a player hit two grand slams in one game. To make it even more unusual, he was a pitcher. Who? (10)

He came into a game in the eighth inning as a pinch-hitter and hit a home run. He stayed in the game and hit two more. The next day he sat on the bench, and the following day, again as a pinch-hitter, he hit his fourth straight home run. Who? (119)

Who led the N.L. in hits and total bases, but not in batting average? (96)

Who did lead the N.L. in batting? (94)

Not since Ty Cobb in 1907–08–09 did anyone lead the American League in hits for three consecutive years, until he did it. Who? (450)

He was a 20-game winner for the Yankees in 1965; he was a 20-game loser for them in 1966. Who? (350)

The American League's biggest winner was a pitcher who was destined to be in box scores and baseball cards for a long time. Who? (445)

The St. Louis Cardinals dealt for two of baseball's biggest stars. Who did they give up to get Roger Maris (358), and Orlando Cepeda (26)?

RED SOX — BILLY HERMAN manager — 37	TIGERS — RON NISCHWITZ pitcher — 38	GIANTS — KEN HENDERSON outfield — 39	TWINS — JIM GRANT pitcher — 40	DODGERS — DON LE JOHN 3rd base — 41	ANGELS — AUBREY GATEWOOD pitcher — 42
CUBS — DON LANDRUM outfield — 43	1966 ROOKIE STARS — TOM KELLEY pitcher / BILL DAVIS 1st base — INDIANS — 44	ASTROS — JIM GENTILE 1st base — 45	SENATORS — HOWIE KOPLITZ pitcher — 46	WHITE SOX — J. C. MARTIN catcher — 47	ORIOLES — PAUL BLAIR outfield — 48
BRAVES — WOODY WOODWARD shortstop — 49	YANKEES — MICKEY MANTLE outfield — 50	METS — GORDON RICHARDSON pitcher — 51	POWER PLUS — WES COVINGTON · JOHNNY CALLISON — 52	RED SOX — BOB DULIBA pitcher — 53	PIRATES — JOSE PAGAN shortstop — 54
ATHLETICS — KEN HARRELSON 1st base — 55	TWINS — SANDY VALDESPINO outfield — 56	DODGERS — JIM LEFEBVRE 2nd base — 57	TIGERS — DAVE WICKERSHAM ...cher — 58	REDS — 4TH PLACE · NATIONAL LEAGUE — 59	CARDS — CURT FLOOD outfield — 60
GIANTS — BOB BOLIN pitcher — 61	ANGELS — MERRITT RANEW catcher — 62	CUBS — JIM STEWART inf-of — 63	ASTROS — BOB BRUCE pitcher — 64	INDIANS — LEON WAGNER outfield — 65	WHITE SOX — AL WEIS 2b-ss — 66
1966 ROOKIE STARS — DICK SELMA pitcher / CLEON JONES outfield — METS — 67	YANKEES — HAL RENIFF pitcher — 68	SENATORS — KEN HAMLIN 2b-ss — 69	RED SOX — CARL YASTRZEMSKI outfield — 70	PIRATES — FRANK CARPIN pitcher — 71	REDS — TONY PEREZ 1st base — 72

73 JERRY ZIMMERMAN catcher — TWINS
74 DON MOSSI pitcher — ATHLETICS
75 TOMMY DAVIS outfield — DODGERS
76 RED SCHOENDIENST manager — CARDS
77 JOHNNY ORSINO catcher — SENATORS
78 FRANK LINZY pitcher — GIANTS

79 JOE PEPITONE 1st base — YANKEES
80 RICHIE ALLEN 3rd base — PHILLIES
81 RAY OYLER shortstop — TIGERS
82 BOB HENDLEY pitcher — CUBS
83 ALBIE PEARSON outfield — ANGELS
84 1966 ROOKIE STARS JIM BEAUCHAMP of DICK KELLEY pitcher — BRAVES

85 EDDIE FISHER pitcher — WHITE SOX
86 JOHN BATEMAN catcher — ASTROS
87 DAN NAPOLEON outfield — METS
88 FRED WHITFIELD 1st base — INDIANS
89 TED DAVIDSON pitcher — REDS
90 LUIS APARICIO shortstop — ORIOLES

91 BOB UECKER catcher — CARDS
92 YANKEES 6TH PLACE · AMERICAN LEAGUE
93 JIM LONBORG pitcher — RED SOX
94 MATTY ALOU outfield — GIANTS
95 PETE RICHERT pitcher — SENATORS
96 FELIPE ALOU outfield — BRAVES

97 JIM MERRITT pitcher — TWINS
98 DON DEMETER outfield — TIGERS
99 BUC BELTERS WILLIE STARGELL · DONN CLENDENON
100 SANDY KOUFAX pitcher — DODGERS
101 TOPPS BASEBALL CHECKLIST 2ND SERIES
102 ED KIRKPATRICK outfield — ANGELS

101 CHECKLIST 2ND SERIES

89 ☐ Ted Davidson	106 ☐ Rusty Staub
90 ☐ Luis Aparicio	107 ☐ A's Rookies
91 ☐ Bob Uecker	108 ☐ Bobby Klaus
92 ☐ Yankees Team	109 ☐ Ralph Terry
93 ☐ Jim Lonborg	110 ☐ Ernie Banks
94 ☐ Matty Alou	111 ☐ Gary Peters
95 ☐ Pete Richert	112 ☐ Manny Mota
96 ☐ Felipe Alou	113 ☐ Hank Aguirre
97 ☐ Jim Merritt	114 ☐ Jim Gosger
98 ☐ Don Demeter	115 ☐ Warren Spahn
99 ☐ Buc Belters	116 ☐ Walt Alston
100 ☐ Sandy Koufax	117 ☐ Jake Gibbs
101 ✔ List-2nd Series	118 ☐ Mike McCormick
102 ☐ Ed Kirkpatrick	119 ☐ Art Shamsky
103 ☐ Dick Groat	120 ☐ H. Killebrew
104 ☐ Alex Johnson	121 ☐ Ray Herbert
105 ☐ Milt Pappas	122 ☐ Joe Gaines

103 DICK GROAT shortstop — CARDS
104 ALEX JOHNSON outfield — PHILLIES
105 MILT PAPPAS pitcher — ORIOLES
106 RUSTY STAUB outfield — ASTROS
107 1966 ROOKIE STARS LARRY STAHL outfield RON TOMPKINS pitcher — ATHLETICS
108 BOBBY KLAUS infield — METS

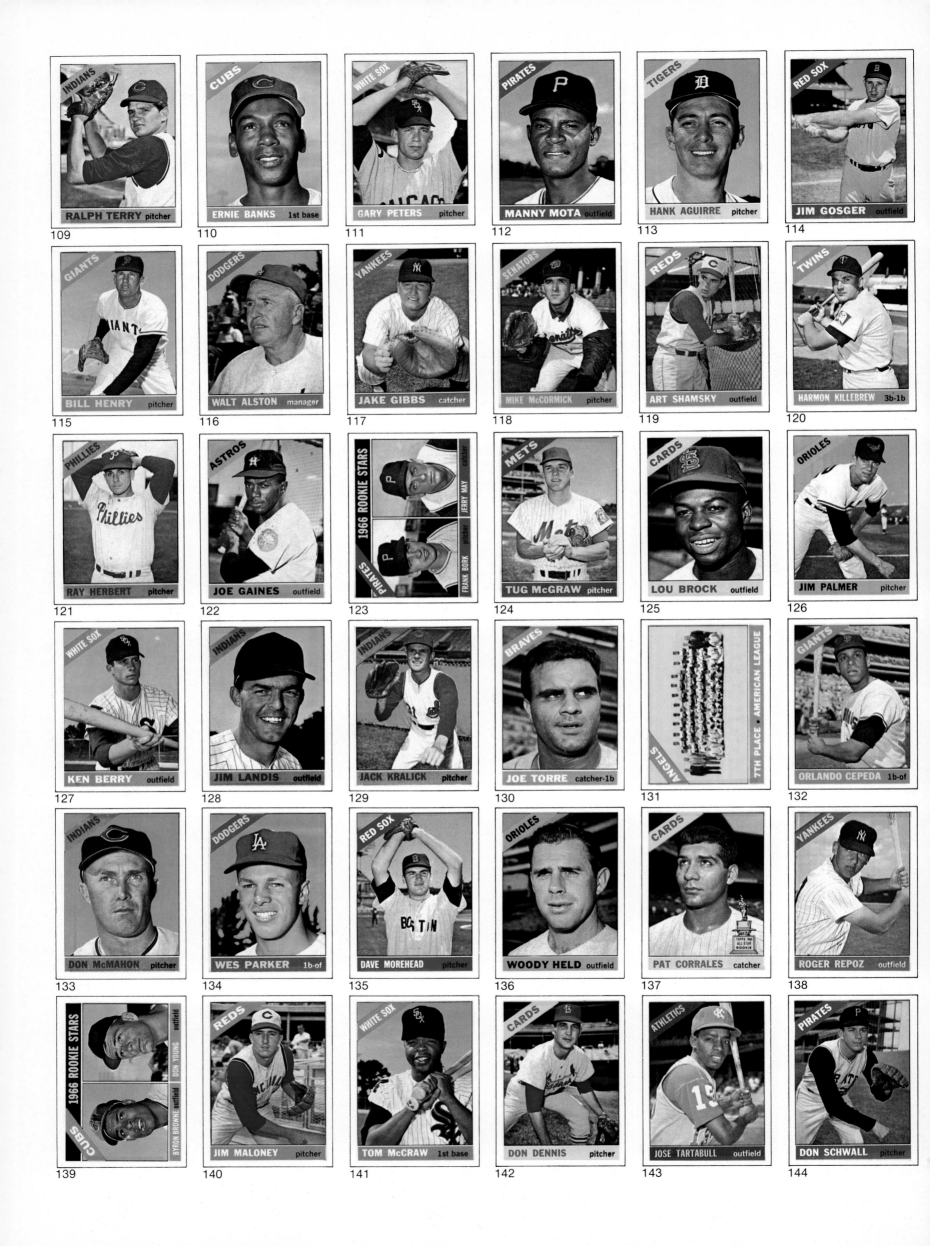

INDIANS RALPH TERRY pitcher 109	CUBS ERNIE BANKS 1st base 110	WHITE SOX GARY PETERS pitcher 111	PIRATES MANNY MOTA outfield 112	TIGERS HANK AGUIRRE pitcher 113	RED SOX JIM GOSGER outfield 114
GIANTS BILL HENRY pitcher 115	DODGERS WALT ALSTON manager 116	YANKEES JAKE GIBBS catcher 117	SENATORS MIKE McCORMICK pitcher 118	REDS ART SHAMSKY outfield 119	TWINS HARMON KILLEBREW 3b-1b 120
PHILLIES RAY HERBERT pitcher 121	ASTROS JOE GAINES outfield 122	1966 ROOKIE STARS JERRY MAY catcher FRANK BORK pitcher PIRATES 123	METS TUG McGRAW pitcher 124	CARDS LOU BROCK outfield 125	ORIOLES JIM PALMER pitcher 126
WHITE SOX KEN BERRY outfield 127	INDIANS JIM LANDIS outfield 128	INDIANS JACK KRALICK pitcher 129	BRAVES JOE TORRE catcher-1b 130	ANGELS 7TH PLACE · AMERICAN LEAGUE 131	GIANTS ORLANDO CEPEDA 1b-of 132
INDIANS DON McMAHON pitcher 133	DODGERS WES PARKER 1b-of 134	RED SOX DAVE MOREHEAD pitcher 135	ORIOLES WOODY HELD outfield 136	CARDS PAT CORRALES catcher 137	YANKEES ROGER REPOZ outfield 138
1966 ROOKIE STARS DON YOUNG outfield BYRON BROWNE outfield CUBS 139	REDS JIM MALONEY pitcher 140	WHITE SOX TOM McCRAW 1st base 141	CARDS DON DENNIS pitcher 142	ATHLETICS JOSE TARTABULL outfield 143	PIRATES DON SCHWALL pitcher 144

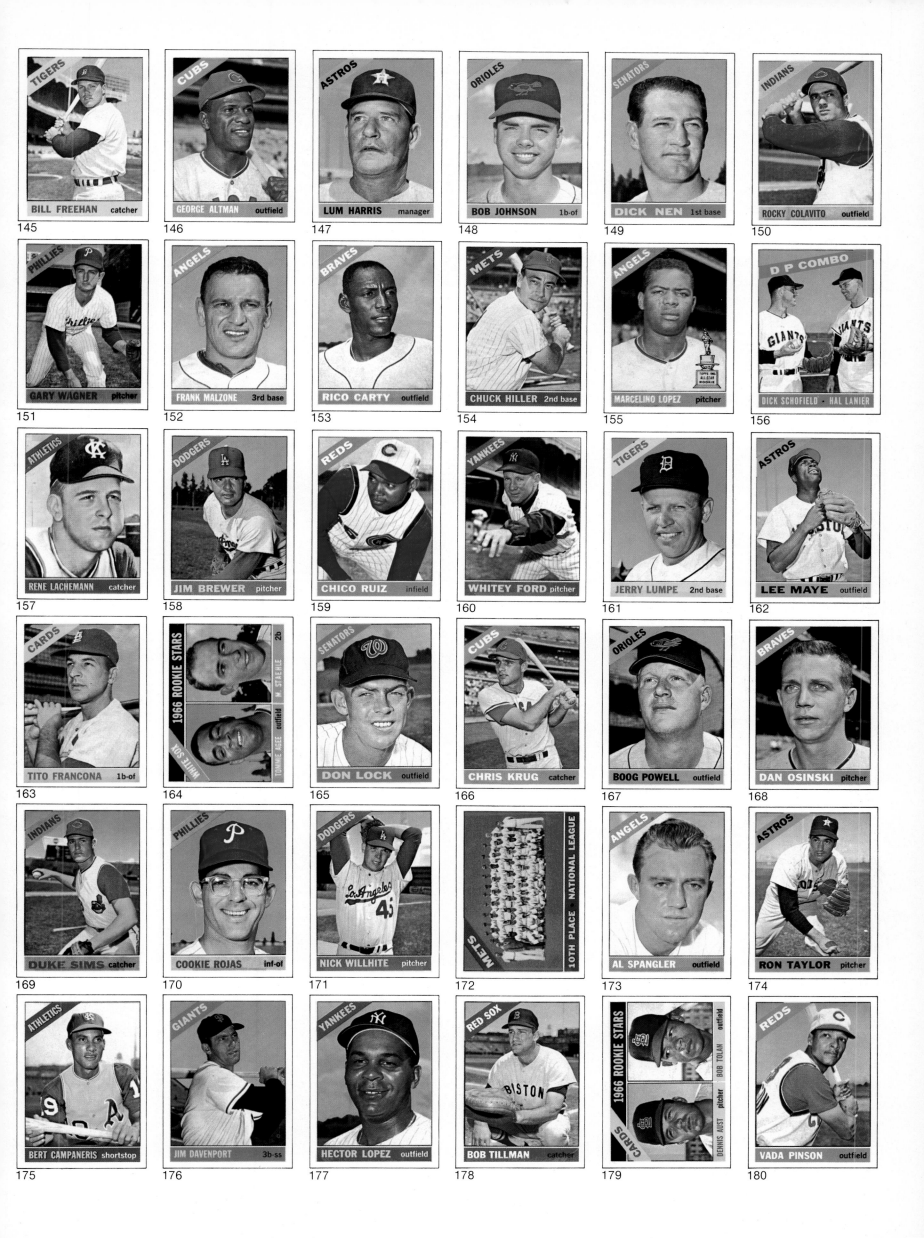

BILL FREEHAN catcher
145

GEORGE ALTMAN outfield
146

LUM HARRIS manager
147

BOB JOHNSON 1b-of
148

DICK NEN 1st base
149

ROCKY COLAVITO outfield
150

GARY WAGNER pitcher
151

FRANK MALZONE 3rd base
152

RICO CARTY outfield
153

CHUCK HILLER 2nd base
154

MARCELINO LOPEZ pitcher
155

DICK SCHOFIELD · HAL LANIER
156

RENE LACHEMANN catcher
157

JIM BREWER pitcher
158

CHICO RUIZ infield
159

WHITEY FORD pitcher
160

JERRY LUMPE 2nd base
161

LEE MAYE outfield
162

TITO FRANCONA 1b-of
163

1966 ROOKIE STARS M. STAEHLE 2b TOMMIE AGEE outfield WHITE SOX
164

DON LOCK outfield
165

CHRIS KRUG catcher
166

BOOG POWELL outfield
167

DAN OSINSKI pitcher
168

DUKE SIMS catcher
169

COOKIE ROJAS inf-of
170

NICK WILLHITE pitcher
171

10TH PLACE · NATIONAL LEAGUE METS
172

AL SPANGLER outfield
173

RON TAYLOR pitcher
174

BERT CAMPANERIS shortstop
175

JIM DAVENPORT 3b-ss
176

HECTOR LOPEZ outfield
177

BOB TILLMAN catcher
178

1966 ROOKIE STARS BOB TOLAN outfield DENNIS AUST pitcher CARDS
179

VADA PINSON outfield
180

TWINS — AL WORTHINGTON — pitcher — 181

PIRATES — JERRY LYNCH — outfield — 182

TOPPS BASEBALL
CHECKLIST
3RD SERIES

☐ 177 Hector Lopez	☐ 194 Senators Team
☐ 178 Bob Tillman	☐ 195 Joe Morgan
☐ 179 Cards Rookies	☐ 196 Don Pavletich
☐ 180 Vada Pinson	☐ 197 Sonny Siebert
☐ 181 Al Worthington	☐ 198 Mickey Stanley
☐ 182 Jerry Lynch	☐ 199 Chisox Clubbers
☐ 183 1st-3rd Series	☐ 200 Ed Mathews
☐ 184 Denis Menke	☐ 201 Jim Dickson
☐ 185 Bob Buhl	☐ 202 Clay Dalrymple
☐ 186 Ruben Amaro	☐ 203 Jose Santiago
☐ 187 Chuck Dressen	☐ 204 Cubs Team
☐ 188 Al Luplow	☐ 205 Tom Tresh
☐ 189 John Roseboro	☐ 206 Alvin Jackson
☐ 190 Jimmie Hall	☐ 207 Frank Quilici
☐ 191 Darrell Sutherland	☐ 208 Bob Miller
☐ 192 Vic Power	☐ 209 Tigers Rookies
☐ 193 Dave McNally	☐ 210 Bill Mazeroski

183

BRAVES — DENIS MENKE — shortstop — 184

CUBS — BOB BUHL — pitcher — 185

YANKEES — RUBEN AMARO — infield — 186

TIGERS — CHUCK DRESSEN — manager — 187

METS — AL LUPLOW — outfield — 188

DODGERS — JOHN ROSEBORO — catcher — 189

TWINS — JIMMIE HALL — outfield — 190

METS — DARRELL SUTHERLAND — pitcher — 191

ANGELS — VIC POWER — 1b-inf — 192

ORIOLES — DAVE McNALLY — pitcher — 193

SENATORS — 8TH PLACE • AMERICAN LEAGUE — 194

ASTROS — JOE MORGAN — 2nd base — 195

REDS — DON PAVLETICH — catcher — 196

INDIANS — SONNY SIEBERT — pitcher — 197

TIGERS — MICKEY STANLEY — outfield — 198

CHISOX CLUBBERS — 199

BRAVES — ED MATHEWS — 3b — 200

ATHLETICS — JIM DICKSON — pitcher — 201

PHILLIES — CLAY DALRYMPLE — catcher — 202

RED SOX — JOSE SANTIAGO — pitcher — 203

CUBS — 8TH PLACE • NATIONAL LEAGUE — 204

YANKEES — TOM TRESH — outfield — 205

CARDS — ALVIN JACKSON — pitcher — 206

TWINS — FRANK QUILICI — 2b — 207

DODGERS — BOB MILLER — pitcher — 208

TIGERS — 1966 ROOKIE STARS — JOHN HILLER pitcher — FRITZ FISHER pitcher — 209

PIRATES — BILL MAZEROSKI — 2b — 210

SENATORS — FRANK KREUTZER — pitcher — 211

METS — ED KRANEPOOL — 1b — 212

ANGELS — FRED NEWMAN — pitcher — 213

REDS — TOMMY HARPER — outfield — 214

1965 BATTING LEADERS — N. LEAGUE — WILLIE MAYS, HANK AARON, BOB CLEMENTE — 215

1965 BATTING LEADERS — A. LEAGUE — VIC DAVALILLO, CARL YASTRZEMSKI, TONY OLIVA — 216

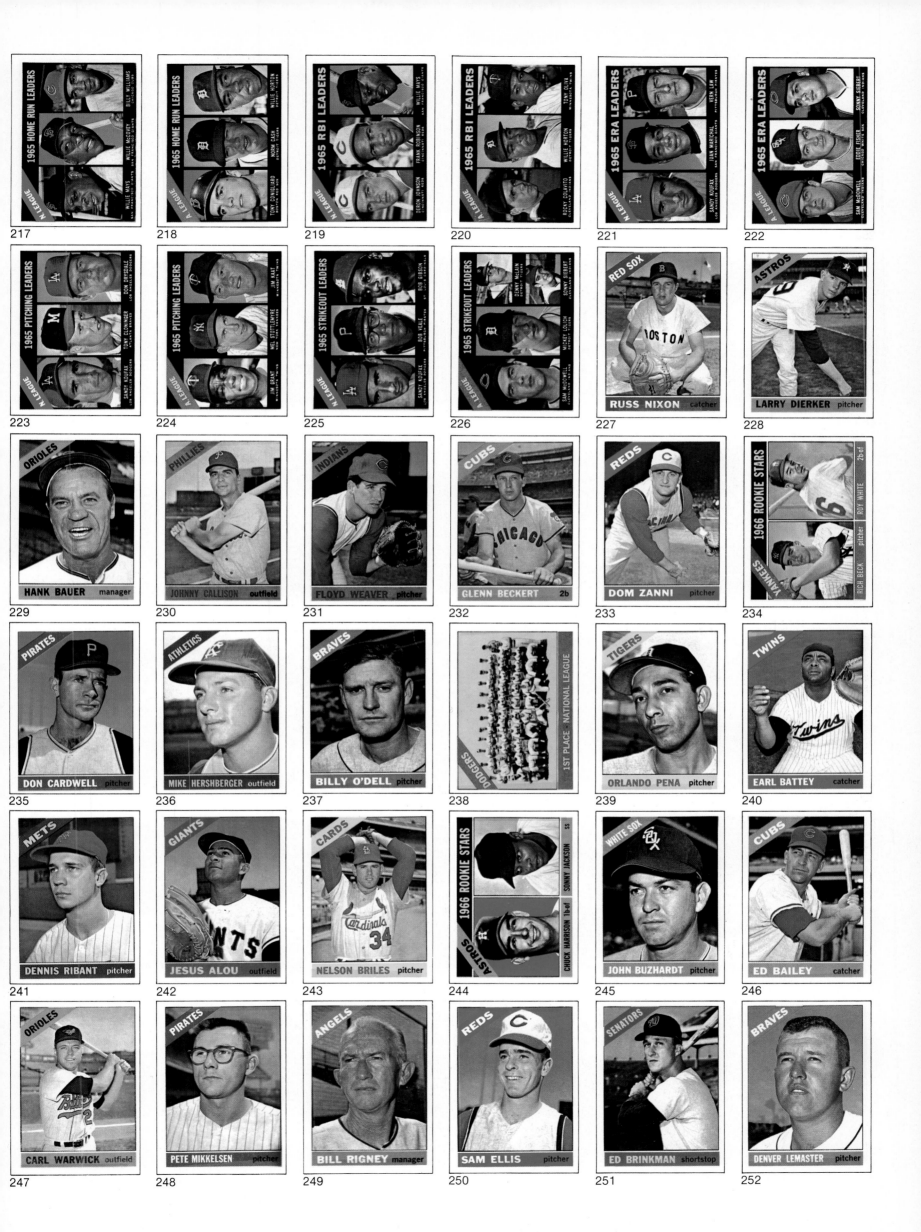

217

218

219

220

221

222

223

224

225

226

227 RUSS NIXON catcher

228 LARRY DIERKER pitcher

229 HANK BAUER manager

230 JOHNNY CALLISON outfield

231 FLOYD WEAVER pitcher

232 GLENN BECKERT 2b

233 DOM ZANNI pitcher

234

235 DON CARDWELL pitcher

236 MIKE HERSHBERGER outfield

237 BILLY O'DELL pitcher

238

239 ORLANDO PENA pitcher

240 EARL BATTEY catcher

241 DENNIS RIBANT pitcher

242 JESUS ALOU outfield

243 NELSON BRILES pitcher

244

245 JOHN BUZHARDT pitcher

246 ED BAILEY catcher

247 CARL WARWICK outfield

248 PETE MIKKELSEN pitcher

249 BILL RIGNEY manager

250 SAM ELLIS pitcher

251 ED BRINKMAN shortstop

252 DENVER LEMASTER pitcher

253 DON WERT 3b

254 1966 ROOKIE STARS — BILL SORRELL 1b-of / FERGUSON JENKINS p — PHILLIES

255 WILLIE STARGELL outfield — PIRATES

256 LEW KRAUSSE pitcher — ATHLETICS

257 JEFF TORBORG catcher — DODGERS

258 DAVE GIUSTI pitcher — ASTROS

259 RED SOX 9TH PLACE AMERICAN LEAGUE

260 BOB SHAW pitcher — GIANTS

261 RON HANSEN shortstop — WHITE SOX

262 JACK HAMILTON pitcher — METS

263 TOM EGAN catcher — ANGELS

264 1966 ROOKIE STARS — TED UHLAENDER of / ANDY KOSCO of — TWINS

265 STU MILLER pitcher — ORIOLES

266 PEDRO GONZALEZ 2b — INDIANS

267 JOE SPARMA pitcher — TIGERS

268 JOHN BLANCHARD catcher — BRAVES

269 DON HEFFNER manager — REDS

270 CLAUDE OSTEEN pitcher — DODGERS

271 HAL LANIER 2b — GIANTS

272 JACK BALDSCHUN pitcher — REDS

273 ASTRO ACES — BOB ASPROMONTE • RUSTY STAUB

274 BUSTER NARUM pitcher — SENATORS

275 TIM McCARVER catcher — CARDS

276 JIM BOUTON pitcher — YANKEES

277 GEORGE THOMAS outfield — RED SOX

278 CALVIN KOONCE pitcher — CUBS

279 TOPPS BASEBALL CHECKLIST 4TH SERIES
265 ☐ Stu Miller
266 ☐ Pedro Gonzalez
267 ☐ Joe Sparma
268 ☐ John Blanchard
269 ☐ Don Heffner
270 ☐ Claude Osteen
271 ☐ Hal Lanier
272 ☐ Jack Baldschun
273 ☐ Astro Aces
274 ☐ Buster Narum
275 ☐ Tim McCarver
276 ☐ Jim Bouton
277 ☐ George Thomas
278 ☐ Calvin Koonce
279 ☑ List 4th Series
280 ☐ Bobby Knoop
281 ☐ Bruce Howard
282 ☐ Johnny Lewis
283 ☐ Jim Perry
284 ☐ Bobby Wine
285 ☐ Luis Tiant
286 ☐ Gary Geiger
287 ☐ Jack Aker
288 ☐ Dodgers Rookies
289 ☐ Larry Sherry
290 ☐ Ron Santo
291 ☐ Moe Drabowsky
292 ☐ Jim Coker
293 ☐ Mike Shannon
294 ☐ Steve Ridzik
295 ☐ Jim Hart
296 ☐ Johnny Keane
297 ☐ Jim Owens
298 ☐ Rico Petrocelli

280 BOBBY KNOOP 2b — ANGELS

281 BRUCE HOWARD pitcher — WHITE SOX

282 JOHNNY LEWIS outfield — METS

283 JIM PERRY pitcher — TWINS

284 BOBBY WINE shortstop — PHILLIES

285 LUIS TIANT pitcher — INDIANS

286 GARY GEIGER outfield — BRAVES

287 JACK AKER pitcher — ATHLETICS

288 1966 ROOKIE STARS — DON SUTTON pitcher / BILL SINGER pitcher — DODGERS

TIGERS — LARRY SHERRY pitcher	CUBS — RON SANTO 3rd base	ORIOLES — MOE DRABOWSKY pitcher	REDS — JIM COKER catcher	CARDS — MIKE SHANNON outfield	SENATORS — STEVE RIDZIK pitcher
289	290	291	292	293	294
GIANTS — JIM HART 3b-of	YANKEES — JOHNNY KEANE manager	ASTROS — JIM OWENS pitcher	RED SOX — RICO PETROCELLI shortstop	ANGELS — LOU BURDETTE pitcher	PIRATES — BOB CLEMENTE outfield
295	296	297	298	299	300
WHITE SOX — GREG BOLLO pitcher	METS — ERNIE BOWMAN infield	INDIANS — 5TH PLACE AMERICAN LEAGUE	PHILLIES — JOHN HERRNSTEIN of-1b	TWINS — CAMILO PASCUAL pitcher	CUBS — TY CLINE outfield
301	302	303	304	305	306
BRAVES — CLAY CARROLL pitcher	GIANTS — TOM HALLER catcher	ATHLETICS — DIEGO SEGUI pitcher	ORIOLES — FRANK ROBINSON outfield	REDS 1966 ROOKIE STARS — DICK SIMPSON of / TOMMY HELMS inf	SENATORS — BOB SAVERINE infield
307	308	309	310	311	312
ASTROS — CHRIS ZACHARY pitcher	DODGERS — HECTOR VALLE catcher	TIGERS — NORM CASH 1st base	METS — JACK FISHER pitcher	RED SOX — DALTON JONES 2b-3b	PIRATES — HARRY WALKER manager
313	314	315	316	317	318
WHITE SOX — GENE FREESE 3rd base	CARDS — BOB GIBSON pitcher	ANGELS — RICK REICHARDT outfield	CUBS — BILL FAUL pitcher	YANKEES — RAY BARKER 1st base	PHILLIES — JOHN BOOZER pitcher
319	320	321	322	323	324

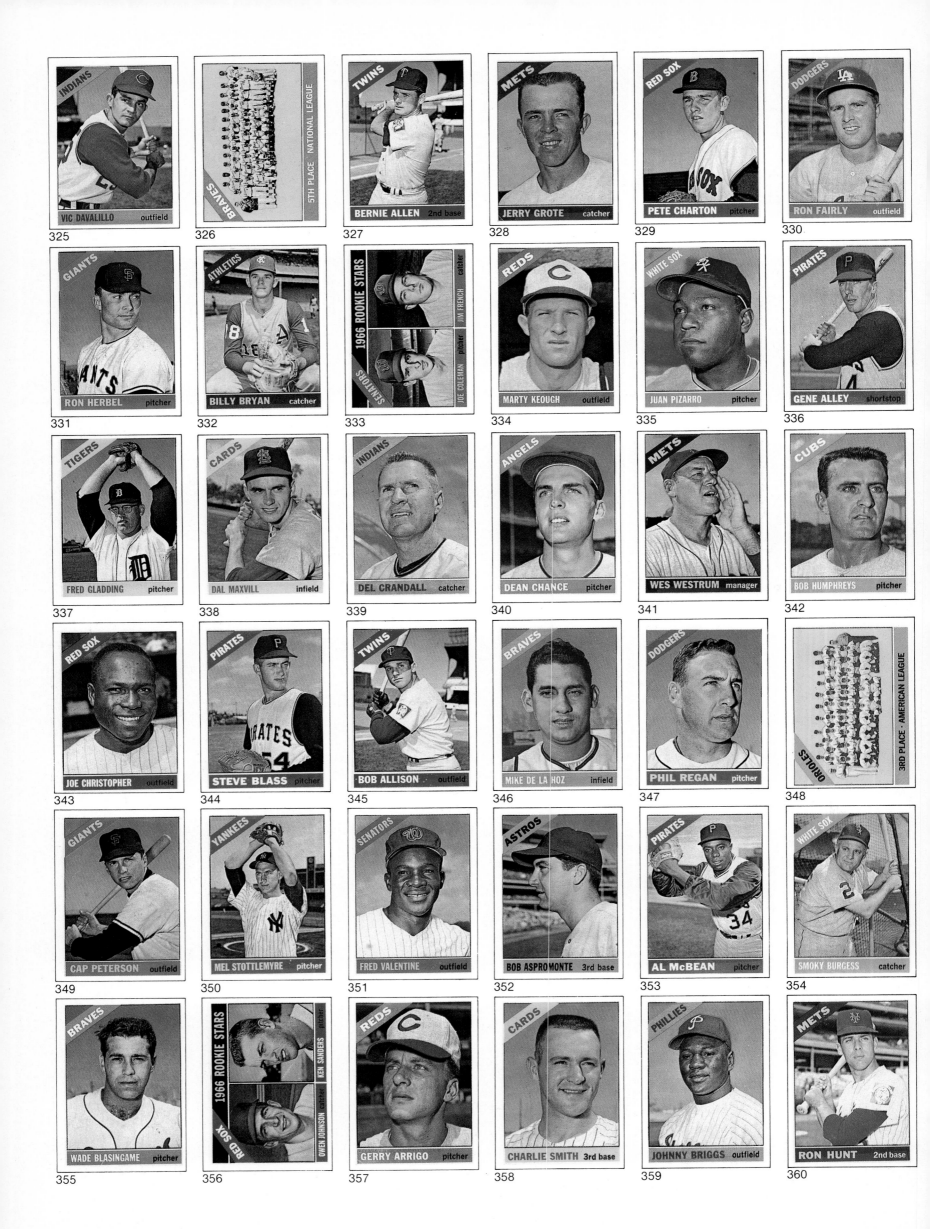

VIC DAVALILLO — INDIANS — outfield — 325

BRAVES — 5TH PLACE · NATIONAL LEAGUE — 326

BERNIE ALLEN — TWINS — 2nd base — 327

JERRY GROTE — METS — catcher — 328

PETE CHARTON — RED SOX — pitcher — 329

RON FAIRLY — DODGERS — outfield — 330

RON HERBEL — GIANTS — pitcher — 331

BILLY BRYAN — ATHLETICS — catcher — 332

1966 ROOKIE STARS — SENATORS — JIM FRENCH catcher — JOE COLEMAN pitcher — 333

MARTY KEOUGH — REDS — outfield — 334

JUAN PIZARRO — WHITE SOX — pitcher — 335

GENE ALLEY — PIRATES — shortstop — 336

FRED GLADDING — TIGERS — pitcher — 337

DAL MAXVILL — CARDS — infield — 338

DEL CRANDALL — INDIANS — catcher — 339

DEAN CHANCE — ANGELS — pitcher — 340

WES WESTRUM — METS — manager — 341

BOB HUMPHREYS — CUBS — pitcher — 342

JOE CHRISTOPHER — RED SOX — outfield — 343

STEVE BLASS — PIRATES — pitcher — 344

BOB ALLISON — TWINS — outfield — 345

MIKE DE LA HOZ — BRAVES — infield — 346

PHIL REGAN — DODGERS — pitcher — 347

ORIOLES — 3RD PLACE · AMERICAN LEAGUE — 348

CAP PETERSON — GIANTS — outfield — 349

MEL STOTTLEMYRE — YANKEES — pitcher — 350

FRED VALENTINE — SENATORS — outfield — 351

BOB ASPROMONTE — ASTROS — 3rd base — 352

AL McBEAN — PIRATES — pitcher — 353

SMOKY BURGESS — WHITE SOX — catcher — 354

WADE BLASINGAME — BRAVES — pitcher — 355

1966 ROOKIE STARS — RED SOX — KEN SANDERS pitcher — OWEN JOHNSON catcher — 356

GERRY ARRIGO — REDS — pitcher — 357

CHARLIE SMITH — CARDS — 3rd base — 358

JOHNNY BRIGGS — PHILLIES — outfield — 359

RON HUNT — METS — 2nd base — 360

ANGELS — TOM SATRIANO catcher
361

TIGERS — GATES BROWN outfield
362

TOPPS BASEBALL CHECKLIST
5th SERIES

353 ☐ Al McBean	370 ☐ Chico Cardenas
354 ☐ Smoky Burgess	371 ☐ Lee Stange
355 ☐ Wade Blasingame	372 ☐ Harvey Kuenn
356 ☐ Red Sox Rookies	373 ☐ Giants Rookies
357 ☐ Gerry Arrigo	374 ☐ Bob Locker
358 ☐ Charlie Smith	375 ☐ Donn Clendenon
359 ☐ Johnny Briggs	376 ☐ Paul Schaal
360 ☐ Ron Hunt	377 ☐ Turk Farrell
361 ☐ Tom Satriano	378 ☐ Dick Tracewski
362 ☐ Gates Brown	379 ☐ Cardinals Team
363 ☑ List-5th Series	380 ☐ Tony Conigliaro
364 ☐ Nate Oliver	381 ☐ Hank Fischer
365 ☐ Roger Maris	382 ☐ Phil Roof
366 ☐ Wayne Causey	383 ☐ Jackie Brandt
367 ☐ Mel Nelson	384 ☐ Al Downing
368 ☐ Charlie Lau	385 ☐ Ken Boyer
369 ☐ Jim King	386 ☐ Gil Hodges

363

DODGERS — NATE OLIVER 2nd base
364

YANKEES — ROGER MARIS outfield
365

ATHLETICS — WAYNE CAUSEY infield
366

TWINS — MEL NELSON pitcher
367

ORIOLES — CHARLIE LAU catcher
368

SENATORS — JIM KING outfield
369

REDS — CHICO CARDENAS shortstop
370

INDIANS — LEE STANGE pitcher
371

CUBS — HARVEY KUENN outfield
372

1966 ROOKIE STARS — DICK ESTELLE pitcher / JACK HIATT catcher — GIANTS
373

WHITE SOX — BOB LOCKER pitcher
374

PIRATES — DONN CLENDENON 1st base
375

ANGELS — PAUL SCHAAL 3rd base
376

ASTROS — TURK FARRELL pitcher
377

TIGERS — DICK TRACEWSKI infield
378

CARDS — 7TH PLACE · NATIONAL LEAGUE
379

RED SOX — TONY CONIGLIARO outfield
380

BRAVES — HANK FISCHER pitcher
381

ATHLETICS — PHIL ROOF catcher
382

PHILLIES — JACKIE BRANDT outfield
383

YANKEES — AL DOWNING pitcher
384

METS — KEN BOYER 3rd base
385

SENATORS — GIL HODGES Manager
386

DODGERS — HOWIE REED pitcher
387

TWINS — DON MINCHER 1st base
388

REDS — JIM O'TOOLE pitcher
389

ORIOLES — BROOKS ROBINSON 3rd base
390

INDIANS — CHUCK HINTON outfield
391

1966 ROOKIE STARS — RANDY HUNDLEY catcher / BILL HANDS pitcher — CUBS
392

ANGELS — GEORGE BRUNET pitcher
393

ASTROS — RON BRAND catcher
394

GIANTS — LEN GABRIELSON outfield
395

RED SOX — JERRY STEPHENSON pitcher
396

PHILLIES — BILL WHITE 1st base 397	WHITE SOX — DANNY CATER outfield 398	CARDS — RAY WASHBURN pitcher 399	TWINS — ZOILO VERSALLES shortstop 400	SENATORS — KEN McMULLEN 3rd base 401	METS — JIM HICKMAN outfield 402
ATHLETICS — FRED TALBOT pitcher 403	PIRATES 3RD PLACE NATIONAL LEAGUE 404	YANKEES — ELSTON HOWARD catcher 405	REDS — JOE JAY pitcher 406	DODGERS — JOHN KENNEDY 3rd base 407	BRAVES — LEE THOMAS 1st base 408
CUBS — BILLY HOEFT pitcher 409	TIGERS — AL KALINE outfield 410	PHILLIES — GENE MAUCH Manager 411	ORIOLES — SAM BOWENS outfield 412	WHITE SOX — JOHN ROMANO catcher 413	ASTROS — DAN COOMBS pitcher 414
INDIANS — MAX ALVIS 3rd base 415	SENATORS — PHIL ORTEGA pitcher 416	1966 ROOKIE STARS — ED SUKLA p / JIM McGLOTHLIN ANGELS 417	CARDS — PHIL GAGLIANO infield 418	RED SOX — MIKE RYAN catcher 419	GIANTS — JUAN MARICHAL pitcher 420
METS — ROY McMILLAN shortstop 421	ATHLETICS — ED CHARLES 3rd base 422	CUBS — ERNIE BROGLIO pitcher 423	1966 ROOKIE STARS — DARRELL OSTEEN p / LEE MAY 1st base REDS 424	PIRATES — BOB VEALE pitcher 425	WHITE SOX 2ND PLACE - AMERICAN LEAGUE 426
ORIOLES — JOHN MILLER pitcher 427	BRAVES — SANDY ALOMAR infield 428	TIGERS — BILL MONBOUQUETTE pitcher 429	DODGERS — DON DRYSDALE pitcher 430	ASTROS — WALT BOND of-1st base 431	INDIANS — BOB HEFFNER pitcher 432

ATHLETICS
ALVIN DARK   Manager
433

SENATORS
WILLIE KIRKLAND   outfield
434

PHILLIES
JIM BUNNING   pitcher
435

CARDS
JULIAN JAVIER   2nd base
436

GIANTS
AL STANEK   pitcher
437

ANGELS
WILLIE SMITH   outfield
438

YANKEES
PEDRO RAMOS   pitcher
439

REDS
DERON JOHNSON   3rd base
440

PIRATES
TOMMIE SISK   pitcher
441

1966 ROOKIE STARS
EDDIE WATT   pitcher
ED BARNOWSKI
ORIOLES
442

METS
BILL WAKEFIELD   pitcher
443

TOPPS BASEBALL
CHECKLIST
6th SERIES
430 ☐ Don Drysdale   447 ☐ Dick Ellsworth
431 ☐ Walt Bond   448 ☐ Eddie Stanky
432 ☐ Bob Heffner   449 ☐ Joe Moeller
433 ☐ Alvin Dark   450 ☐ Tony Oliva
434 ☐ Willie Kirkland   451 ☐ Barry Latman
435 ☐ Jim Bunning   452 ☐ Joe Azcue
436 ☐ Julian Javier   453 ☐ Ron Kline
437 ☐ Al Stanek   454 ☐ Jerry Buchek
438 ☐ Willie Smith   455 ☐ Mickey Lolich
439 ☐ Pedro Ramos   456 ☐ Red Sox Rookies
440 ☐ Deron Johnson   457 ☐ Joe Gibbon
441 ☐ Tommie Sisk   458 ☐ Manny Jiminez
442 ☐ Orioles Rookies   459 ☐ Bill McCool
443 ☐ Bill Wakefield   460 ☐ Curt Blefary
444 ☐ List—6th Series   461 ☐ Roy Face
445 ☐ Jim Kaat   462 ☐ Bob Rodgers
446 ☐ Mack Jones   463 ☐ Phillies Team
444

TWINS
JIM KAAT   pitcher
445

BRAVES
MACK JONES   outfield
446

CUBS
DICK ELLSWORTH   pitcher
447

WHITE SOX
EDDIE STANKY   mgr.
448

DODGERS
JOE MOELLER   pitcher
449

TWINS
TONY OLIVA   outfield
450

ASTROS
BARRY LATMAN   pitcher
451

INDIANS
JOE AZCUE   catcher
452

SENATORS
RON KLINE   pitcher
453

CARDS
JERRY BUCHEK   shortstop
454

TIGERS
MICKEY LOLICH   pitcher
455

1966 ROOKIE STARS
JOE FOY   3rd base
DARRELL BRANDON   p
RED SOX
456

GIANTS
JOE GIBBON   pitcher
457

ATHLETICS
MANNY JIMINEZ   outfield
458

REDS
BILL McCOOL   pitcher
459

ORIOLES
CURT BLEFARY   outfield
460

PIRATES
ROY FACE   pitcher
461

ANGELS
BOB RODGERS   catcher
462

PHILLIES · 6TH PLACE · NATIONAL LEAGUE
463

METS
LARRY BEARNARTH   pitcher
464

WHITE SOX
DON BUFORD   2nd base
465

BRAVES
KEN JOHNSON   pitcher
466

ORIOLES
VIC ROZNOVSKY   catcher
467

DODGERS
JOHNNY PODRES   pitcher
468

469

1966 ROOKIE STARS — BOBBY MURCER ss / DOOLEY WOMACK p — YANKEES

470 SAM McDOWELL pitcher — INDIANS

471 BOB SKINNER outfield — CARDS

472 TERRY FOX pitcher — TIGERS

473 RICH ROLLINS infield — TWINS

474 DICK SCHOFIELD shortstop — GIANTS

475 DICK RADATZ pitcher — RED SOX

476 BOBBY BRAGAN mgr. — BRAVES

477 STEVE BARBER pitcher — ORIOLES

478 TONY GONZALEZ outfield — PHILLIES

479 JIM HANNAN pitcher — SENATORS

480 DICK STUART 1st base — METS

481 BOB LEE pitcher — ANGELS

482 1966 ROOKIE STARS — DAVE DOWLING pitcher / JOHN BOCCABELLA 1b — CUBS

483 JOE NUXHALL pitcher — REDS

484 WES COVINGTON outfield — CUBS

485 BOB BAILEY 3rd base — PIRATES

486 TOMMY JOHN pitcher — WHITE SOX

487 AL FERRARA outfield — DODGERS

488 GEORGE BANKS of-3b — INDIANS

489 CURT SIMMONS pitcher — CARDS

490 BOBBY RICHARDSON 2b — YANKEES

491 DENNIS BENNETT pitcher — RED SOX

492 ATHLETICS — 10TH PLACE: AMERICAN LEAGUE

493 JOHNNY KLIPPSTEIN pitcher — TWINS

494 GORDON COLEMAN 1b — REDS

495 DICK McAULIFFE shortstop — TIGERS

496 LINDY McDANIEL pitcher — GIANTS

497 CHRIS CANNIZZARO catcher — BRAVES

498 1966 ROOKIE STARS — WOODY FRYMAN pitcher / LUKE WALKER pitcher — PIRATES

499 WALLY BUNKER pitcher — ORIOLES

500 HANK AARON outfield — BRAVES

501 JOHN O'DONOGHUE pitcher — INDIANS

502 LENNY GREEN outfield — RED SOX

503 STEVE HAMILTON pitcher — YANKEES

504 GRADY HATTON mgr. — ASTROS

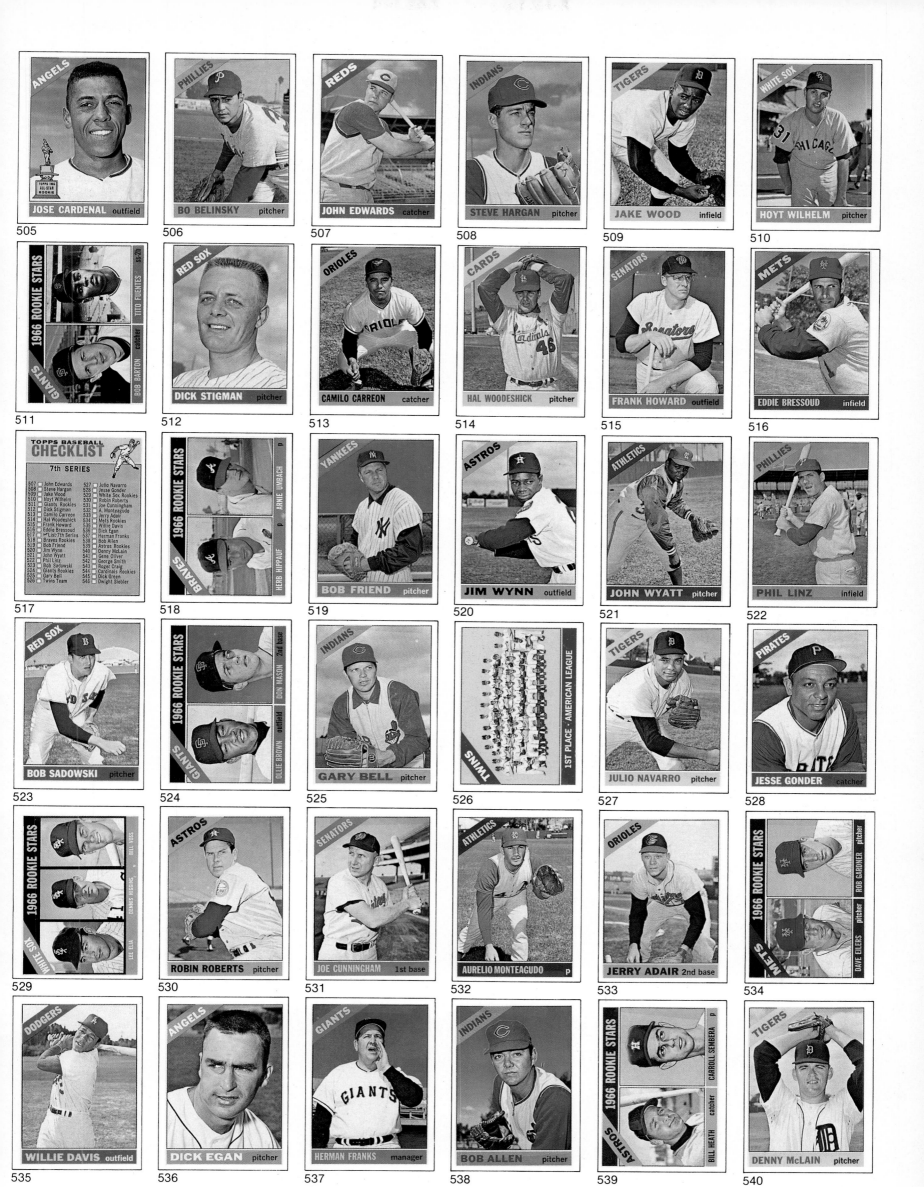

505 JOSE CARDENAL outfield

506 BO BELINSKY pitcher

507 JOHN EDWARDS catcher

508 STEVE HARGAN pitcher

509 JAKE WOOD infield

510 HOYT WILHELM pitcher

511 1966 ROOKIE STARS — TITO FUENTES ss-2b / BOB BARTON catcher

512 DICK STIGMAN pitcher

513 CAMILO CARREON catcher

514 HAL WOODESHICK pitcher

515 FRANK HOWARD outfield

516 EDDIE BRESSOUD infield

517 Topps Baseball CHECKLIST 7th SERIES

518 1966 ROOKIE STARS — HERB HIPPAUF p / ARNIE UMBACH p

519 BOB FRIEND pitcher

520 JIM WYNN outfield

521 JOHN WYATT pitcher

522 PHIL LINZ infield

523 BOB SADOWSKI pitcher

524 1966 ROOKIE STARS — DON MASON 2nd base / OLLIE BROWN outfield

525 GARY BELL pitcher

526 1ST PLACE - AMERICAN LEAGUE TWINS

527 JULIO NAVARRO pitcher

528 JESSE GONDER catcher

529 1966 ROOKIE STARS — BILL VOSS / DENNIS HIGGINS / LEE ELIA

530 ROBIN ROBERTS pitcher

531 JOE CUNNINGHAM 1st base

532 AURELIO MONTEAGUDO p

533 JERRY ADAIR 2nd base

534 1966 ROOKIE STARS — ROB GARDNER pitcher / DAVE EILERS pitcher

535 WILLIE DAVIS outfield

536 DICK EGAN pitcher

537 HERMAN FRANKS manager

538 BOB ALLEN pitcher

539 1966 ROOKIE STARS — CARROLL SEMBERA p / BILL HEATH catcher

540 DENNY McLAIN pitcher

541 GENE OLIVER c-1b — BRAVES

542 GEORGE SMITH 2nd base — RED SOX

543 ROGER CRAIG pitcher — PHILLIES

544 1966 ROOKIE STARS CARDS — JIMMY WILLIAMS, GEORGE KERNEK, JOE HOERNER

545 DICK GREEN 2nd base — ATHLETICS

546 DWIGHT SIEBLER pitcher — TWINS

547 HORACE CLARKE infield — YANKEES

548 GARY KROLL pitcher — ASTROS

549 1966 ROOKIE STARS SENATORS — CASEY COX pitcher, AL CLOSTER pitcher

550 WILLIE McCOVEY 1st base — GIANTS

551 BOB PURKEY pitcher — PIRATES

552 BIRDIE TEBBETTS manager — INDIANS

553 1966 ROOKIE STARS — JACKIE WARNER Angels, PAT GARRETT Braves

554 JIM NORTHRUP outfield — TIGERS

555 RON PERRANOSKI pitcher — DODGERS

556 MEL QUEEN outfield — REDS

557 FELIX MANTILLA 2b-of — ASTROS

558 1966 ROOKIE STARS RED SOX — GEORGE SCOTT, PETE MAGRINI, GUIDO GRILLI

559 ROBERTO PENA ss-2b — CUBS

560 JOEL HORLEN pitcher — WHITE SOX

561 CHOO CHOO COLEMAN catcher — METS

562 RUSS SNYDER outfield — ORIOLES

563 1966 ROOKIE STARS TWINS — CESAR TOVAR outfield, PETE CIMINO pitcher

564 BOB CHANCE of-1b — SENATORS

565 JIMMY PIERSALL outfield — ANGELS

566 MIKE CUELLAR pitcher — ASTROS

567 DICK HOWSER shortstop — INDIANS

568 1966 ROOKIE STARS — RON STONE outfield ATHLETICS, PAUL LINDBLAD pitcher ATHLETICS

569 ORLANDO McFARLANE catcher — TIGERS

570 ART MAHAFFEY pitcher — CARDS

571 DAVE ROBERTS outfield — PIRATES

572 BOB PRIDDY pitcher — GIANTS

573 DERRELL GRIFFITH outfield — DODGERS

574 1966 ROOKIE STARS — BILL MURPHY outfield, BILL HEPLER pitcher METS

575 EARL WILSON pitcher — RED SOX

576 DAVE NICHOLSON outfield — ASTROS

577

578

579

580

581

582

583

584

585

586

587

588

589

590

591

592

593

594

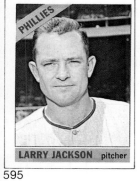

595

596

597

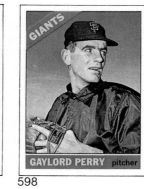

598

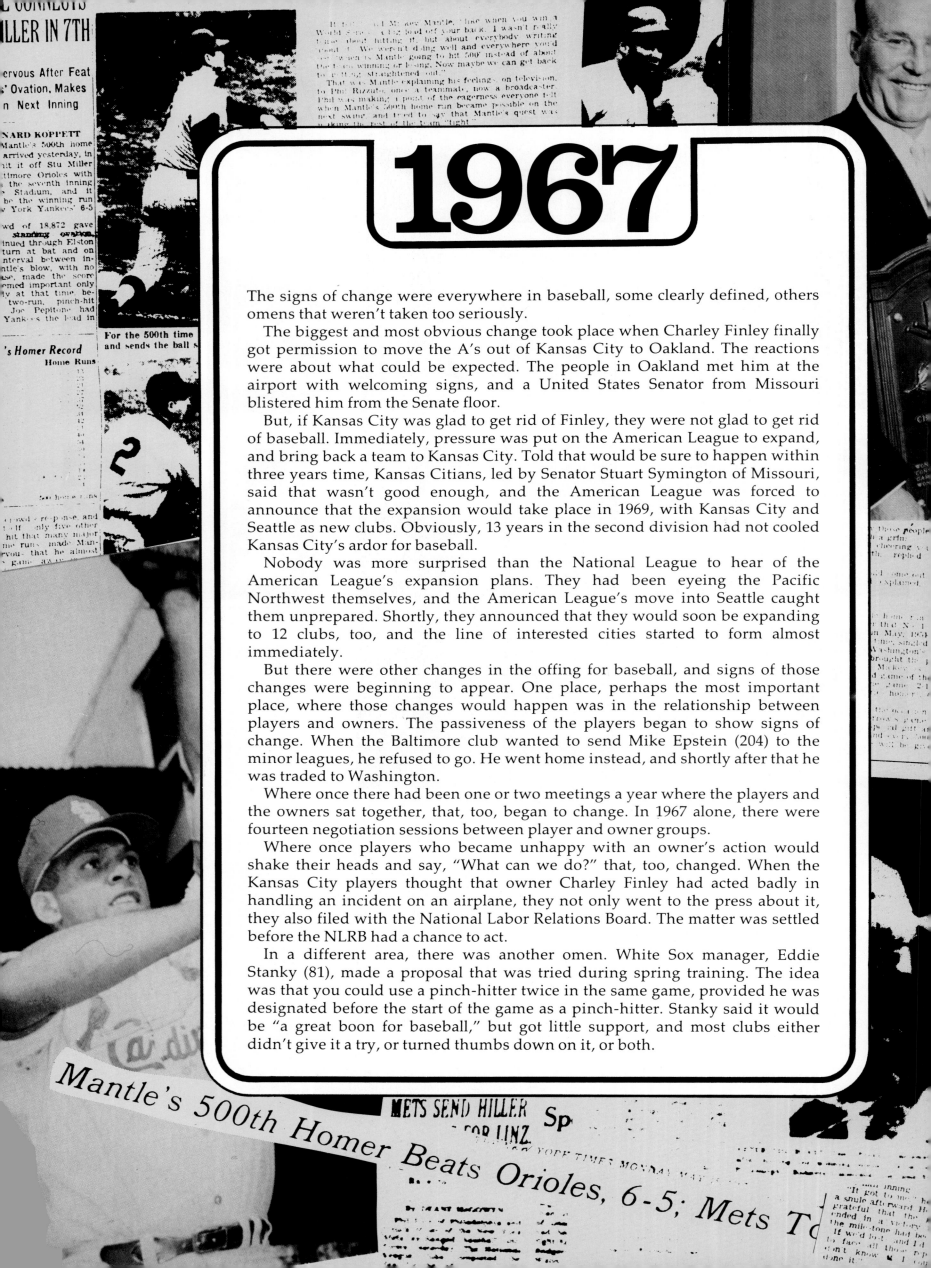

1967

The signs of change were everywhere in baseball, some clearly defined, others omens that weren't taken too seriously.

The biggest and most obvious change took place when Charley Finley finally got permission to move the A's out of Kansas City to Oakland. The reactions were about what could be expected. The people in Oakland met him at the airport with welcoming signs, and a United States Senator from Missouri blistered him from the Senate floor.

But, if Kansas City was glad to get rid of Finley, they were not glad to get rid of baseball. Immediately, pressure was put on the American League to expand, and bring back a team to Kansas City. Told that would be sure to happen within three years time, Kansas Citians, led by Senator Stuart Symington of Missouri, said that wasn't good enough, and the American League was forced to announce that the expansion would take place in 1969, with Kansas City and Seattle as new clubs. Obviously, 13 years in the second division had not cooled Kansas City's ardor for baseball.

Nobody was more surprised than the National League to hear of the American League's expansion plans. They had been eyeing the Pacific Northwest themselves, and the American League's move into Seattle caught them unprepared. Shortly, they announced that they would soon be expanding to 12 clubs, too, and the line of interested cities started to form almost immediately.

But there were other changes in the offing for baseball, and signs of those changes were beginning to appear. One place, perhaps the most important place, where those changes would happen was in the relationship between players and owners. The passiveness of the players began to show signs of change. When the Baltimore club wanted to send Mike Epstein (204) to the minor leagues, he refused to go. He went home instead, and shortly after that he was traded to Washington.

Where once there had been one or two meetings a year where the players and the owners sat together, that, too, began to change. In 1967 alone, there were fourteen negotiation sessions between player and owner groups.

Where once players who became unhappy with an owner's action would shake their heads and say, "What can we do?" that, too, changed. When the Kansas City players thought that owner Charley Finley had acted badly in handling an incident on an airplane, they not only went to the press about it, they also filed with the National Labor Relations Board. The matter was settled before the NLRB had a chance to act.

In a different area, there was another omen. White Sox manager, Eddie Stanky (81), made a proposal that was tried during spring training. The idea was that you could use a pinch-hitter twice in the same game, provided he was designated before the start of the game as a pinch-hitter. Stanky said it would be "a great boon for baseball," but got little support, and most clubs either didn't give it a try, or turned thumbs down on it, or both.

One more omen. The minor league Player of the Year was a young catcher for Buffalo in the International League – John Bench.

After 11 years of being given to the top pitcher in the major leagues, the Cy Young Award was changed to honor one pitcher in each league. The selections were interesting in that each winner had 22 victories for the year, but neither ranked among the leaders in the usual yardstick of pitching effectiveness, the earned run average. Jim Lonborg (371) of the Red Sox was ranked 18th in the American League's ERA standing, and San Francisco left-hander, Mike McCormick (86), was 16th in his league.

Action was taken on a couple of rulebook matters, one involving play on the field and the other the business side of baseball. There were fresh efforts made to enforce the "spitball" rule, which dictated where a pitcher must stand if he puts his fingers in his mouth, etc. Despite the new efforts, spitball rules continued to be as enforcible as "Prohibition" had been 40 years earlier.

The other change meant saying good-bye to one of baseball's most familiar people, "a player to be named later." For years that phrase had been used to indicate that, when they got around to it, one of the clubs in a trade would add another player to the deal. The rules finally were changed to call for all players in the deal to be identified.

On the field, there was again an overpowering person. In 1967, while several players had outstanding years, it was truly "the Year of the Yaz." Red Sox left fielder, Carl Yastrzemski (355), had the kind of year a hitter dreams about. He won the triple crown, he was named the Most Valuable Player, he led the league also in hits, runs, total bases, and slugging percentage. And in a pennant race that was decided on the last day, he got 10 hits in his last 13 times at bat. He tied for the home-run crown with 44, after never having hit more than 20 in a season.

In Boston they called it "the Great Race," which it was. Detroit and Minnesota both finished one game behind Boston, and the fourth-place White Sox were only three games out. The excitement that was felt throughout the league made itself felt at the turnstiles, especially in Boston, where the Red Sox, playing in one of baseball's smallest parks, drew 1,727,832.

In the National League, in their first full season in their new stadium, the St. Louis Cardinals romped to a 10½ game victory over the second-place Giants and were the only club to draw over 2,000,000.

The World Series was again a seven-game thriller. St. Louis won three of the first four, but the Red Sox took the next two, and it all came down to one game. The answer was, again, "too much Gibson." Bob Gibson (210), Cardinals ace, won three games and allowed only fourteen hits in the three route-going performances.

For two clubs, the pennant races put them in some strange places. The Cubs finished third, their first season in 21 in the first division. The Dodgers, for the first time in 62 years, finished eighth.

Also, two more omens of things to come. Neither Mickey Mantle (150) nor Willie Mays (200) got a single mention in the two MVP ballotings.

The Cards

The first baseball-card set to top 600! The excellent color photos in it are applauded by hobbyists. Players' autographs were included for the first time

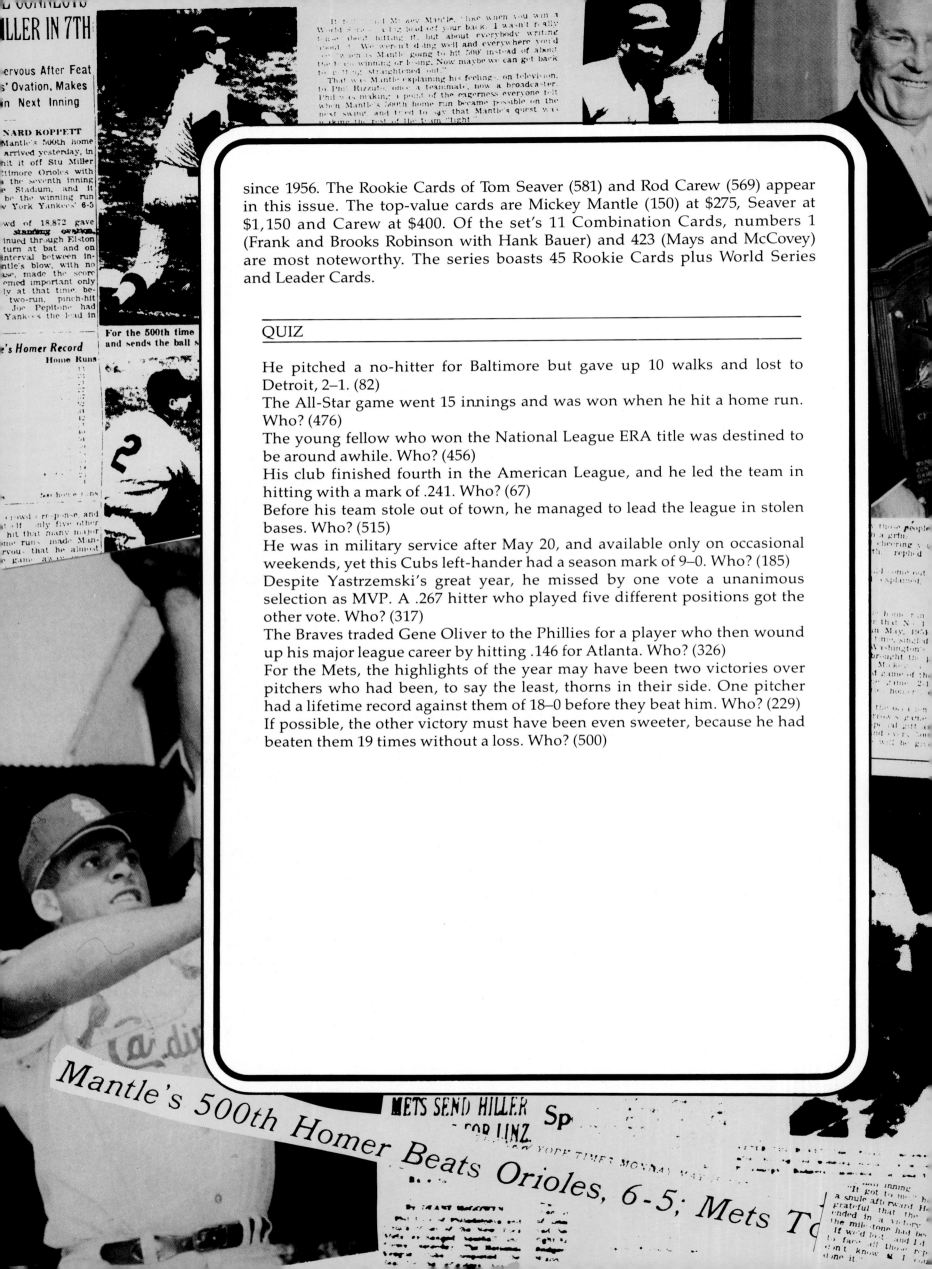

since 1956. The Rookie Cards of Tom Seaver (581) and Rod Carew (569) appear in this issue. The top-value cards are Mickey Mantle (150) at $275, Seaver at $1,150 and Carew at $400. Of the set's 11 Combination Cards, numbers 1 (Frank and Brooks Robinson with Hank Bauer) and 423 (Mays and McCovey) are most noteworthy. The series boasts 45 Rookie Cards plus World Series and Leader Cards.

QUIZ

He pitched a no-hitter for Baltimore but gave up 10 walks and lost to Detroit, 2–1. (82)

The All-Star game went 15 innings and was won when he hit a home run. Who? (476)

The young fellow who won the National League ERA title was destined to be around awhile. Who? (456)

His club finished fourth in the American League, and he led the team in hitting with a mark of .241. Who? (67)

Before his team stole out of town, he managed to lead the league in stolen bases. Who? (515)

He was in military service after May 20, and available only on occasional weekends, yet this Cubs left-hander had a season mark of 9–0. Who? (185)

Despite Yastrzemski's great year, he missed by one vote a unanimous selection as MVP. A .267 hitter who played five different positions got the other vote. Who? (317)

The Braves traded Gene Oliver to the Phillies for a player who then wound up his major league career by hitting .146 for Atlanta. Who? (326)

For the Mets, the highlights of the year may have been two victories over pitchers who had been, to say the least, thorns in their side. One pitcher had a lifetime record against them of 18–0 before they beat him. Who? (229)

If possible, the other victory must have been even sweeter, because he had beaten them 19 times without a loss. Who? (500)

109

JACK AKER · PITCHER
ATHLETICS
110

JOHN KENNEDY · 3B
DODGERS
111

DAVE WICKERSHAM · P
TIGERS
112

DAVE NICHOLSON · OF
BRAVES
113

JACK BALDSCHUN · P
REDS
114

PAUL CASANOVA · C
SENATORS
115

HERMAN FRANKS · MGR.
GIANTS
116

DARRELL BRANDON · P
RED SOX
117

BERNIE ALLEN · 2B
SENATORS
118

WADE BLASINGAME · P
BRAVES
119

FLOYD ROBINSON · OF
REDS
120

ED BRESSOUD · SS
METS
121

GEORGE BRUNET · P
ANGELS
122

1967 ROOKIE STARS
L. WALKER · P
JIM PRICE · C
PIRATES
123

JIM STEWART · INF-OF
CUBS
124

MOE DRABOWSKY · P
ORIOLES
125

TONY TAYLOR · 2B
PHILLIES
126

JOHN O'DONOGHUE · P
INDIANS
127

ED SPIEZIO · 3B
CARDS
128

PHIL ROOF · CATCHER
ATHLETICS
129

PHIL REGAN · PITCHER
DODGERS
130

YANKEES
131

OZZIE VIRGIL · 3B-C
GIANTS
132

RON KLINE · PITCHER
TWINS
133

GATES BROWN · OF
TIGERS
134

DERON JOHNSON · INF-OF
REDS
135

CARROLL SEMBERA · P
ASTROS
136

1967 ROOKIE STARS
JIM OLLOM · P
RON CLARK · INF
TWINS
137

DICK KELLEY · P
BRAVES
138

DALTON JONES · 2B
RED SOX
139

WILLIE STARGELL · OF
PIRATES
140

JOHN MILLER · PITCHER
ORIOLES
141

JACKIE BRANDT · OF
PHILLIES
142

PETE WARD · DON BUFORD
SOX SOCKERS
143

BILL HEPLER · PITCHER
METS
144

TERRY FOX · PITCHER
PHILLIES
181

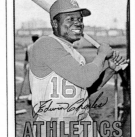
ED CHARLES · 3B
ATHLETICS
182

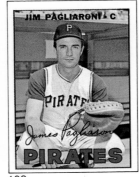
JIM PAGLIARONI · C
PIRATES
183

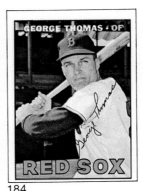
GEORGE THOMAS · OF
RED SOX
184

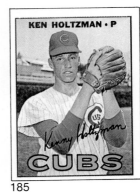
KEN HOLTZMAN · P
CUBS
185

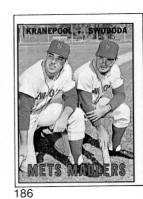
KRANEPOOL · SWOBODA
METS MAULERS
186

PEDRO RAMOS · PITCHER
PHILLIES
187

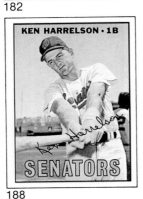
KEN HARRELSON · 1B
SENATORS
188

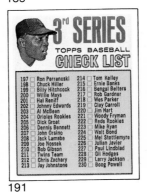
CHUCK HINTON · OF
INDIANS
189

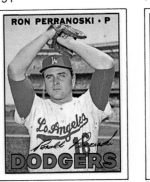
TURK FARRELL · PITCHER
ASTROS
190

3rd SERIES
TOPPS BASEBALL
CHECK LIST

197	Ron Perranoski	214	Tom Kelley
198	Chuck Hiller	215	Ernie Banks
199	Billy Hitchcock	216	Bengal Belters
200	Willie Mays	217	Rob Gardner
201	Hal Reniff	218	Wes Parker
202	Johnny Edwards	219	Clay Carroll
203	Al McBean	220	Jim Hart
204	Orioles Rookies	221	Woody Fryman
205	Dick Groat	222	Reds Rookies
206	Dennis Bennett	223	Mike Ryan
207	John Orsino	224	Walt Bond
208	Jack Lamabe	225	Mel Stottlemyre
209	Joe Nossek	226	Julian Javier
210	Bob Gibson	227	Paul Lindblad
211	Twins Team	228	Gil Hodges
212	Chris Zachary	229	Larry Jackson
213	Jay Johnstone	230	Boog Powell

191

FRED GLADDING · P
TIGERS
192

JOSE CARDENAL · OF
ANGELS
193

BOB ALLISON · OF
TWINS
194

AL JACKSON · PITCHER
CARDS
195

JOHNNY ROMANO · C
CARDS
196

RON PERRANOSKI · P
DODGERS
197

CHUCK HILLER · 2B
METS
198

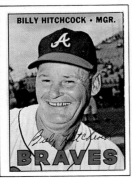
BILLY HITCHCOCK · MGR.
BRAVES
199

WILLIE MAYS · OUTFIELD
GIANTS
200

HAL RENIFF · PITCHER
YANKEES
201

JOHNNY EDWARDS · C
REDS
202

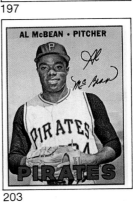
AL McBEAN · PITCHER
PIRATES
203

ORIOLES 1967 ROOKIE STARS
TOM PHOEBUS · P
MIKE EPSTEIN · 1B-OF
204

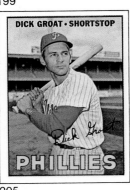
DICK GROAT · SHORTSTOP
PHILLIES
205

DENNIS BENNETT · P
RED SOX
206

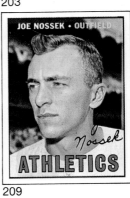
JOHN ORSINO · CATCHER
SENATORS
207

JACK LAMABE · PITCHER
WHITE SOX
208

JOE NOSSEK · OUTFIELD
ATHLETICS
209

BOB GIBSON · PITCHER
CARDS
210

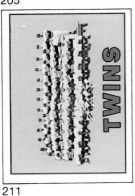
TWINS
211

CHRIS ZACHARY · P
ASTROS
212

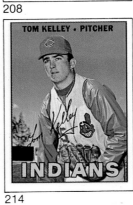
JAY JOHNSTONE · OF
ANGELS
213

TOM KELLEY · PITCHER
INDIANS
214

ERNIE BANKS · 1B
CUBS
215

CASH · KALINE
BENGAL BELTERS
216

ROB GARDNER · P **METS** 217	WES PARKER · 1B-OF **DODGERS** 218	CLAY CARROLL · P **BRAVES** 219	JIM HART · 3B-OF **GIANTS** 220	WOODY FRYMAN · P **PIRATES** 221	REDS 1967 ROOKIE STARS · LEE MAY · 1B-OF · DARRELL OSTEEN · P 222
MIKE RYAN · CATCHER **RED SOX** 223	WALT BOND · OUTFIELD **TWINS** 224	MEL STOTTLEMYRE · P **YANKEES** 225	JULIAN JAVIER · 2B **CARDS** 226	PAUL LINDBLAD · P **ATHLETICS** 227	GIL HODGES · MGR. **SENATORS** 228
LARRY JACKSON · P **PHILLIES** 229	BOOG POWELL · 1B **ORIOLES** 230	JOHN BATEMAN · CATCHER **ASTROS** 231	DON BUFORD · 3B-2B **WHITE SOX** 232	A. LEAGUE 1966 ERA LEADERS 233	N. LEAGUE 1966 ERA LEADERS 234
A. LEAGUE 1966 PITCHING LEADERS 235	N. LEAGUE 1966 PITCHING LEADERS 236	A. LEAGUE 1966 STRIKEOUT LEADERS 237	N. LEAGUE 1966 STRIKEOUT LEADERS 238	A. LEAGUE 1966 BATTING LEADERS 239	N. LEAGUE 1966 BATTING LEADERS 240
A. LEAGUE 1966 RBI LEADERS 241	N. LEAGUE 1966 RBI LEADERS 242	A. LEAGUE 1966 HOME RUN LEADERS 243	N. LEAGUE 1966 HOME RUN LEADERS 244	CURT FLOOD · OUTFIELD **CARDS** 245	JIM PERRY · PITCHER **TWINS** 246
JERRY LUMPE · 2B **TIGERS** 247	GENE MAUCH · MGR. **PHILLIES** 248	NICK WILLHITE · P **ANGELS** 249	HANK AARON · OUTFIELD **BRAVES** 250	WOODY HELD · INF-OF **ORIOLES** 251	BOB BOLIN · PITCHER **GIANTS** 252

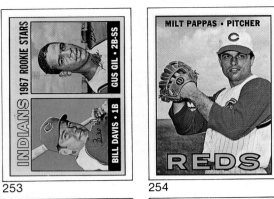
INDIANS 1967 ROOKIE STARS · GUS GIL · 2B-SS · BILL DAVIS · 1B
253

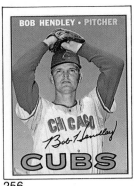
MILT PAPPAS · PITCHER
REDS
254

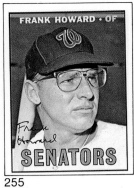
FRANK HOWARD · OF
SENATORS
255

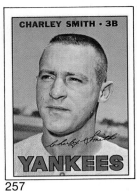
BOB HENDLEY · PITCHER
CUBS
256

CHARLEY SMITH · 3B
YANKEES
257

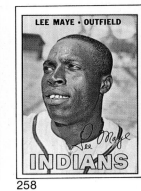
LEE MAYE · OUTFIELD
INDIANS
258

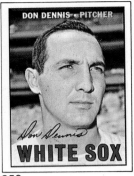
DON DENNIS · PITCHER
WHITE SOX
259

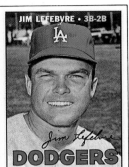
JIM LEFEBVRE · 3B-2B
DODGERS
260

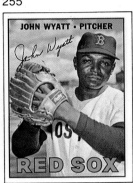
JOHN WYATT · PITCHER
RED SOX
261

ATHLETICS
262

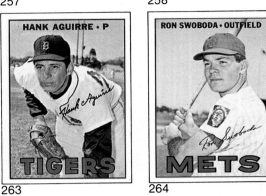
HANK AGUIRRE · P
TIGERS
263

RON SWOBODA · OUTFIELD
METS
264

LOU BURDETTE · PITCHER
ANGELS
265

STARGELL · CLENDENON
PITT POWER
266

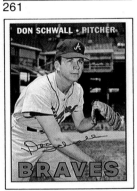
DON SCHWALL · PITCHER
BRAVES
267

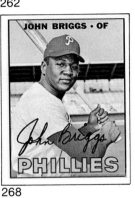
JOHN BRIGGS · OF
PHILLIES
268

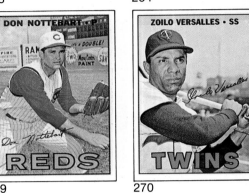
DON NOTTEBART · P
REDS
269

ZOILO VERSALLES · SS
TWINS
270

EDDIE WATT · PITCHER
ORIOLES
271

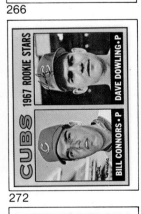
CUBS 1967 ROOKIE STARS · DAVE DOWLING-P · BILL CONNORS-P
272

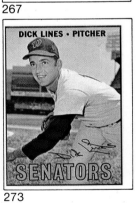
DICK LINES · PITCHER
SENATORS
273

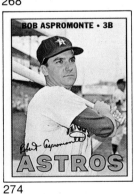
BOB ASPROMONTE · 3B
ASTROS
274

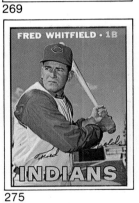
FRED WHITFIELD · 1B
INDIANS
275

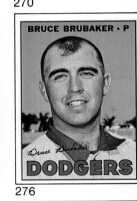
BRUCE BRUBAKER · P
DODGERS
276

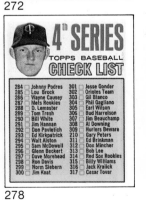
STEVE WHITAKER · OF
YANKEES
277

4ᵗʰ SERIES
TOPPS BASEBALL
CHECK LIST

284	Johnny Podres	301	Jesse Gonder
285	Lou Brock	302	Orioles Team
286	Wayne Causey	303	Gil Blanco
287	Mets Rookies	304	Phil Gagliano
288	D. Lemaster	305	Earl Wilson
289	Tom Tresh	306	Bud Harrelson
290	Bill White	307	Jim Beauchamp
291	Jim Hannan	308	Al Downing
292	Don Pavletich	309	Hurlers Beware
293	Ed Kirkpatrick	310	Gary Peters
294	Walt Alston	311	Ed Brinkman
295	Sam McDowell	312	Don Mincher
296	Glenn Beckert	313	Bob Lee
297	Dave Morehead	314	Red Sox Rookies
298	Ron Davis	315	Billy Williams
299	Norm Siebern	316	Jack Kralick
300	Jim Kaat	317	Cesar Tovar

278

FRANK LINZY · PITCHER
GIANTS
279

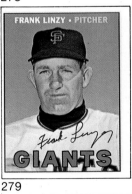
TONY CONIGLIARO · OF
RED SOX
280

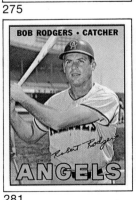
BOB RODGERS · CATCHER
ANGELS
281

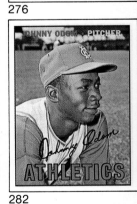
JOHNNY ODOM · PITCHER
ATHLETICS
282

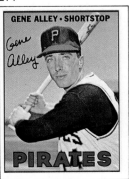
GENE ALLEY · SHORTSTOP
PIRATES
283

JOHNNY PODRES · P
TIGERS
284

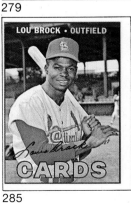
LOU BROCK · OUTFIELD
CARDS
285

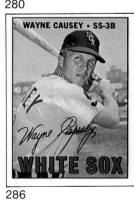
WAYNE CAUSEY · SS-3B
WHITE SOX
286

METS 1967 ROOKIE STARS · BART SHIRLEY · SS · GREG GOOSSEN · C
287

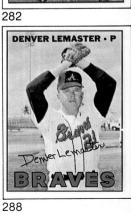
DENVER LEMASTER · P
BRAVES
288

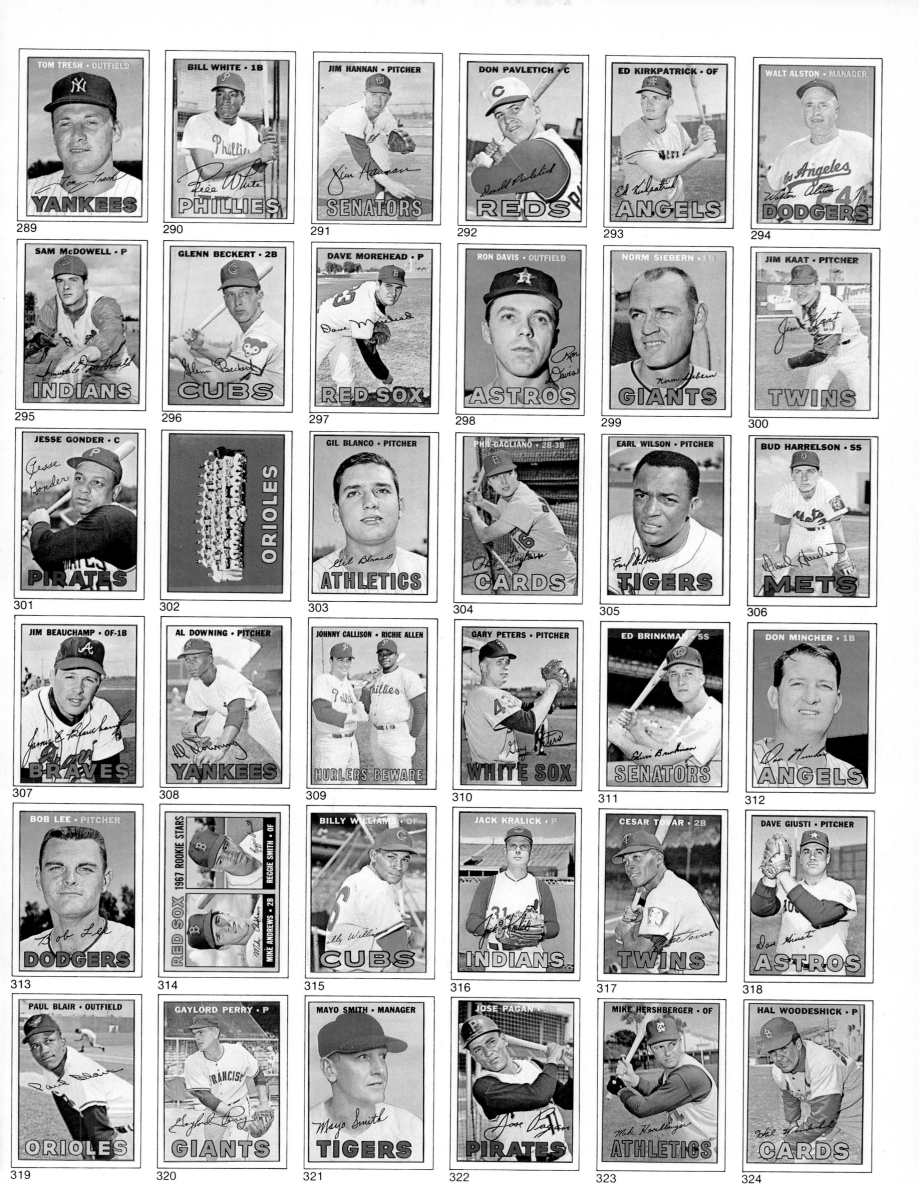

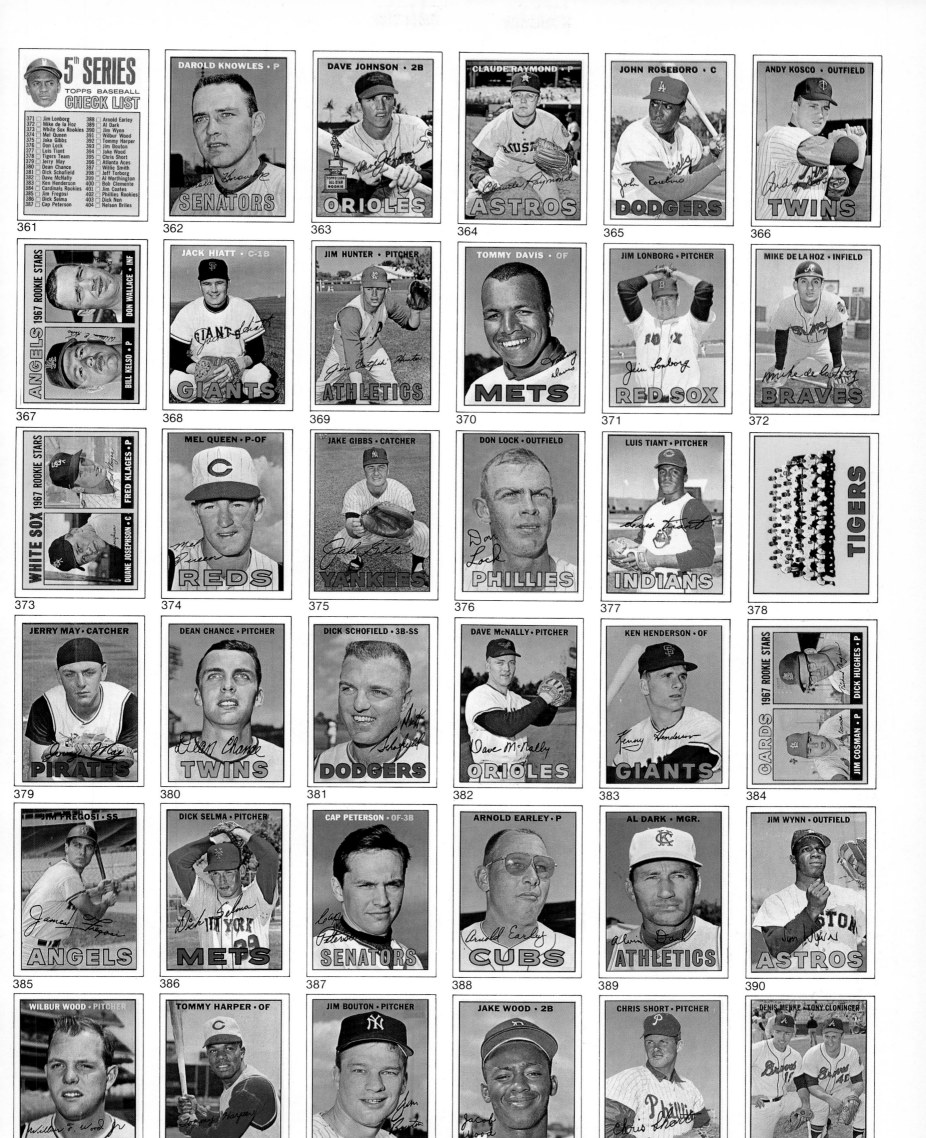

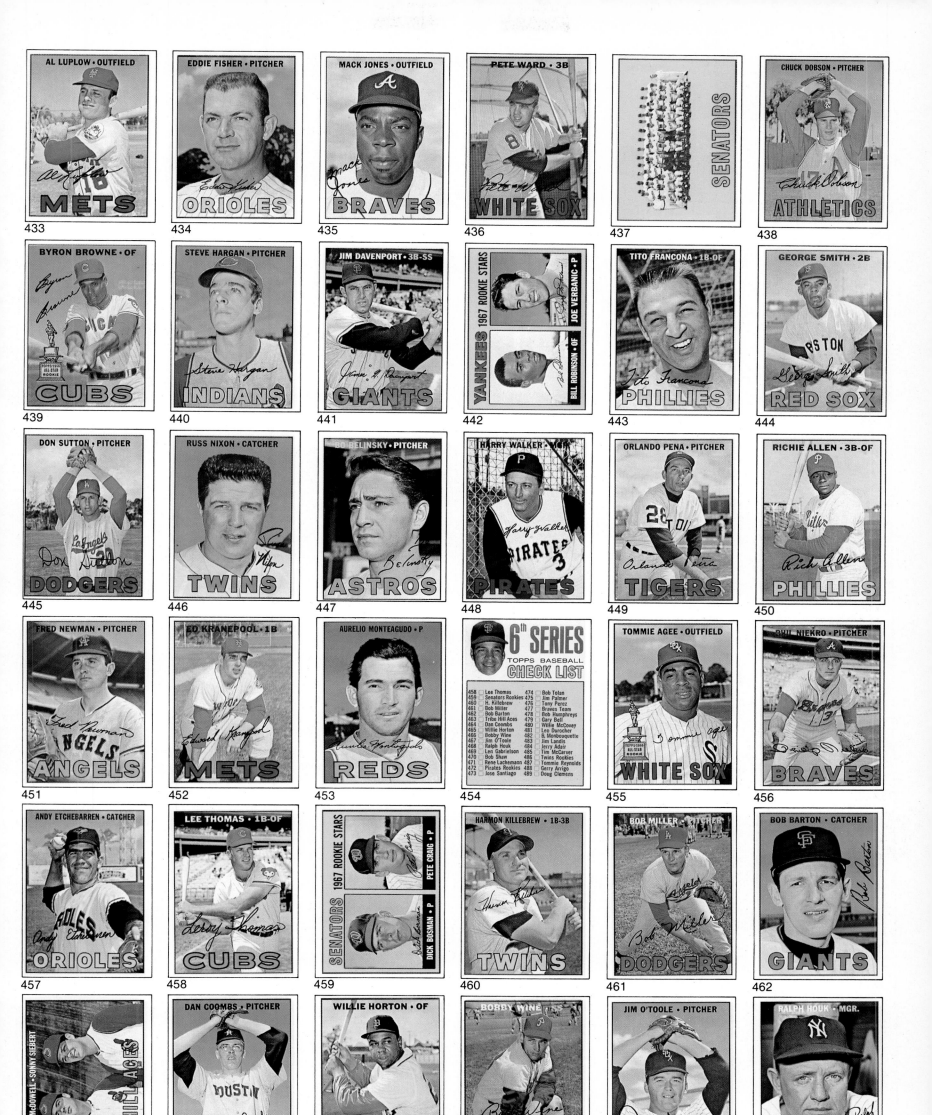

AL LUPLOW · OUTFIELD
METS
433

EDDIE FISHER · PITCHER
ORIOLES
434

MACK JONES · OUTFIELD
BRAVES
435

PETE WARD · 3B
WHITE SOX
436

SENATORS
437

CHUCK DOBSON · PITCHER
ATHLETICS
438

BYRON BROWNE · OF
CUBS
439

STEVE HARGAN · PITCHER
INDIANS
440

JIM DAVENPORT · 3B-SS
GIANTS
441

YANKEES 1967 ROOKIE STARS
JOE VERBANIC · P
BILL ROBINSON · OF
442

TITO FRANCONA · 1B-OF
PHILLIES
443

GEORGE SMITH · 2B
RED SOX
444

DON SUTTON · PITCHER
DODGERS
445

RUSS NIXON · CATCHER
TWINS
446

BO BELINSKY · PITCHER
ASTROS
447

HARRY WALKER · MGR.
PIRATES
448

ORLANDO PENA · PITCHER
TIGERS
449

RICHIE ALLEN · 3B-OF
PHILLIES
450

FRED NEWMAN · PITCHER
ANGELS
451

ED KRANEPOOL · 1B
METS
452

AURELIO MONTEAGUDO · P
REDS
453

6th SERIES
TOPPS BASEBALL
CHECK LIST

458	Lee Thomas	474	Bob Tolan
459	Senators Rookies	475	Jim Palmer
460	H. Killebrew	476	Tony Perez
461	Bob Miller	477	Braves Team
462	Bob Barton	478	Bob Humphreys
463	Tribe Hill Aces	479	Gary Bell
464	Dan Coombs	480	Willie McCovey
465	Willie Horton	481	Leo Durocher
466	Bobby Wine	482	B. Monbouquette
467	Jim O'Toole	483	Jim Landis
468	Len Gabrielson	484	Jerry Adair
469	Len Gabrielson	485	Tim McCarver
470	Bob Shaw	486	Twins Rookies
471	Rene Lachemann	487	Tommie Reynolds
472	Pirates Rookies	488	Gerry Arrigo
473	Jose Santiago	489	Doug Clemens

454

TOMMIE AGEE · OUTFIELD
WHITE SOX
455

PHIL NIEKRO · PITCHER
BRAVES
456

ANDY ETCHEBARREN · CATCHER
ORIOLES
457

LEE THOMAS · 1B-OF
CUBS
458

SENATORS 1967 ROOKIE STARS
PETE CRAIG · P
DICK BOSMAN · P
459

HARMON KILLEBREW · 1B-3B
TWINS
460

BOB MILLER · PITCHER
DODGERS
461

BOB BARTON · CATCHER
GIANTS
462

SAM McDOWELL · SONNY SIEBERT
HILL ACES
463

DAN COOMBS · PITCHER
ASTROS
464

WILLIE HORTON · OF
TIGERS
465

BOBBY WINE
PHILLIES
466

JIM O'TOOLE · PITCHER
WHITE SOX
467

RALPH HOUK · MGR.
YANKEES
468

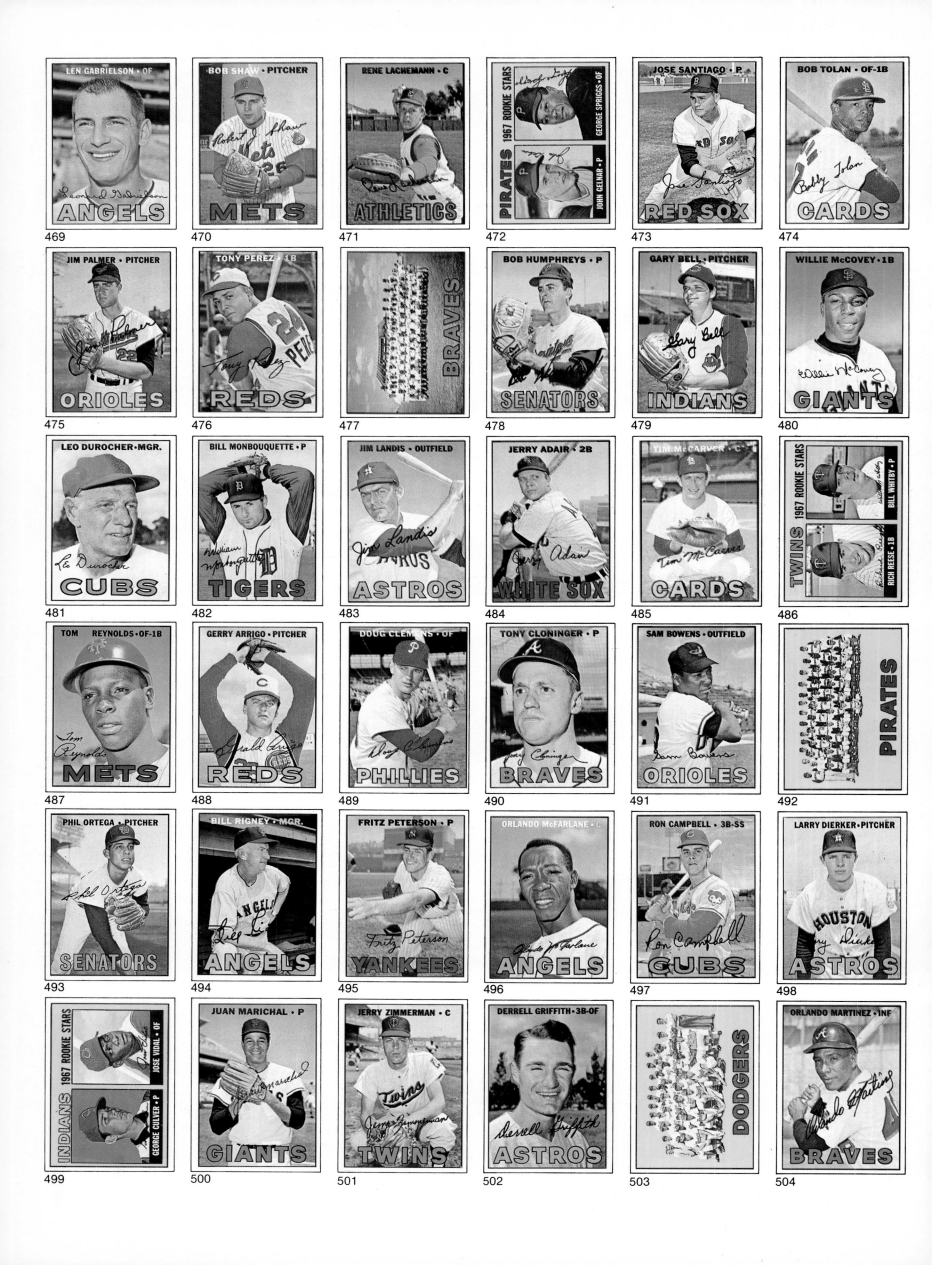

505 TOMMY HELMS · 3B-2B — REDS
506 SMOKY BURGESS — WHITE SOX
507 ORIOLES 1967 ROOKIE STARS — LARRY HANEY · C / ED BARNOWSKI · P
508 DICK HALL · PITCHER — PHILLIES
509 JIM KING · OUTFIELD — SENATORS
510 BILL MAZEROSKI · 2B — PIRATES

511 DON WERT · 3B — TIGERS
512 RED SCHOENDIENST · MGR. — CARDS
513 MARCELINO LOPEZ · P — ANGELS
514 JOHN WERHAS · INFIELD — DODGERS
515 BERT CAMPANERIS · SS — ATHLETICS
516 GIANTS

517 FRED TALBOT · PITCHER — YANKEES
518 DENIS MENKE · SS — BRAVES
519 TED DAVIDSON · PITCHER — REDS
520 MAX ALVIS · 3B — INDIANS
521 BOOG POWELL · CURT BLEFARY — BIRD BOMBERS
522 JOHN STEPHENSON · C — METS

523 JIM MERRITT · PITCHER — TWINS
524 FELIX MANTILLA · OF — CUBS
525 RON HUNT · 2B — DODGERS
526 1967 ROOKIE STARS — GEORGE KORINCE · P / PAT DOBSON · P — TIGERS
527 DENNIS RIBANT · P — PIRATES
528 RICO PETROCELLI · SS — RED SOX

529 GARY WAGNER · PITCHER — PHILLIES
530 FELIPE ALOU · 1B-OF — BRAVES
531 7th SERIES TOPPS BASEBALL CHECK LIST

534	Hank Bauer	550	Vada Pinson
535	Donn Clendenon	551	Doug Camilli
536	Cubs Rookies	552	Ted Savage
537	Chuck Estrada	553	Yankees Rookies
538	J. C. Martin	554	Andre Rodgers
539	Dick Egan	555	Don Cardwell
540	Norm Cash	556	Al Weis
541	Joe Gibbon	557	Al Ferrara
542	Athletics Rookies	558	Orioles Rookies
543	Dan Schneider	559	Dick Tracewski
544	Indians Team	560	Jim Bunning
545	Jim Grant	561	Sandy Alomar
546	Woody Woodward	562	Steve Blass
547	Red Sox Rookies	563	Joe Adcock
548	Tony Gonzalez	564	Astros Rookies
549	Jack Sanford	565	Lew Krausse

532 JIM HICKS · OUTFIELD — WHITE SOX
533 JACK FISHER · PITCHER — METS
534 HANK BAUER · MGR. — ORIOLES

535 DONN CLENDENON · 1B — PIRATES
536 CUBS 1967 ROOKIE STARS — PAUL POPOVICH · INF / JOE NIEKRO · P
537 CHUCK ESTRADA · P — METS
538 J. C. MARTIN · CATCHER — WHITE SOX
539 DICK EGAN · PITCHER — DODGERS
540 NORM CASH · 1B — TIGERS

577 BILL SHORT · PITCHER · PIRATES
578 JOHN BOCCABELLA · 1B · CUBS
579 BILL HENRY · PITCHER · GIANTS
580 ROCKY COLAVITO · OF · INDIANS
581 1967 ROOKIE STARS · METS · TOM SEAVER · P · BILL DENEHY · P
582 JIM OWENS · PITCHER · ASTROS

583 RAY BARKER · 1B · YANKEES
584 JIM PIERSALL · OUTFIELD · ANGELS
585 WALLY BUNKER · PITCHER · ORIOLES
586 MANNY JIMENEZ · OF · PIRATES
587 N. LEAGUE ROOKIE STARS · GARY SUTHERLAND · 2B-SS · PHILADELPHIA PHILLIES · DON SHAW · P · NEW YORK METS
588 JOHNNY KLIPPSTEIN · P · TIGERS

589 DAVE RICKETTS · C · CARDS
590 PETE RICHERT · P · SENATORS
591 TY CLINE · OUTFIELD · BRAVES
592 N. LEAGUE ROOKIE STARS · RON WILLIS · P · ST. LOUIS CARDINALS · JIM SHELLENBACK · P · PITTSBURGH PIRATES
593 WES WESTRUM · MGR. · METS
594 DAN OSINSKI · PITCHER · RED SOX

595 COOKIE ROJAS · 2B-OF · PHILLIES
596 GALEN CISCO · PITCHER · RED SOX
597 TED ABERNATHY · P · REDS
598 1967 ROOKIE STARS · WHITE SOX · ED STROUD · OF · WALT WILLIAMS · OF
599 BOB DULIBA · PITCHER · ATHLETICS
600 BROOKS ROBINSON · 3B · ORIOLES

601 BILL BRYAN · CATCHER · YANKEES
602 JUAN PIZARRO · PITCHER · PIRATES
603 ATHLETICS 1967 ROOKIE STARS · RAMON WEBSTER · 1B-INF · TIM TALTON · C
604 RED SOX
605 MIKE SHANNON · 3B-OF · CARDS
606 RON TAYLOR · PITCHER · METS

607 MICKEY STANLEY · OF · TIGERS
608 1967 ROOKIE STARS · CUBS · JOHN UPHAM · P · RICH NYE · P
609 TOMMY JOHN · PITCHER · WHITE SOX

STRONG EXECUTIVE
SOUGHT FOR POST

1968

The pennant races ended early, and so did the commissioner's term in office. It was a year the big leagues became bigger, a year that hitters left their bats at home, and a year when the natives – both players and umpires – showed definite signs of getting restless.

The two major leagues, which usually confined their big differences to the World Series and the All-Star game, were really having trouble seeing eye-to-eye on the subject of expansion. The American League was getting a jump by putting in a new franchise in Seattle and replacing the one that had moved out of Kansas City. The National League wasn't very happy, feeling that their hand was being forced. Their plan was to expand, perhaps in 1971, but the American League's move caused changes in that timetable. On May 27th, the National League announced that they, too, would expand in 1969, with new clubs in San Diego and Montreal.

While it was generally recognized that franchises were moved for financial rather than artistic reasons, that's not exactly the way things worked out in Oakland. The A's drew only about 110,000 more than they had the previous year in Kansas City, despite the fact that the franchise, for the first time since they were in Philadelphia in 1952, finished with a winning record. Owner Charley Finley reacted in an interesting, if not surprising, way. He fired manager Bob Kennedy (183). In addition to Kennedy, there was somebody else who was not exactly choked up about developments in the Bay Area. Giants owner, Horace Stoneham, who saw the arrival of a franchise in Oakland as a threat to his San Francisco club, was proved right. Although finishing second again, the Giants' gate fell off over 400,000.

These were frenetic times for baseball, and the club-owners decided that their best interests lie in replacing the commissioner. William Eckert's inexperience in baseball matters, which hadn't been an obstacle when he was hired, were recognized as insurmountable. In the third year of a seven-year contract, the commissioner was replaced, although baseball lacked a ready replacement.

The need for that replacement, however, was obvious. The players were making no secret of their disenchantment with the status quo, or of their desire to force changes in the relationship that had existed for years between them and the owners. An excellent indication of that came when the players requested a proportionate rise in their share of the additional monies that would accompany a new television contract.

Suddenly, a new group was heard from. The umpires were up in arms. The National League arbiters had an association, but not those in the American League. But when two American League umpires were dismissed, the two groups joined forces. A meeting held the day after the season closed brought rumblings about a possible strike before the World Series. The decision was made not to walk out.

For pitchers, the theme song for 1968 would have to be, "It Was A Very Good Year." The combined batting average for the two major leagues hit an all-time

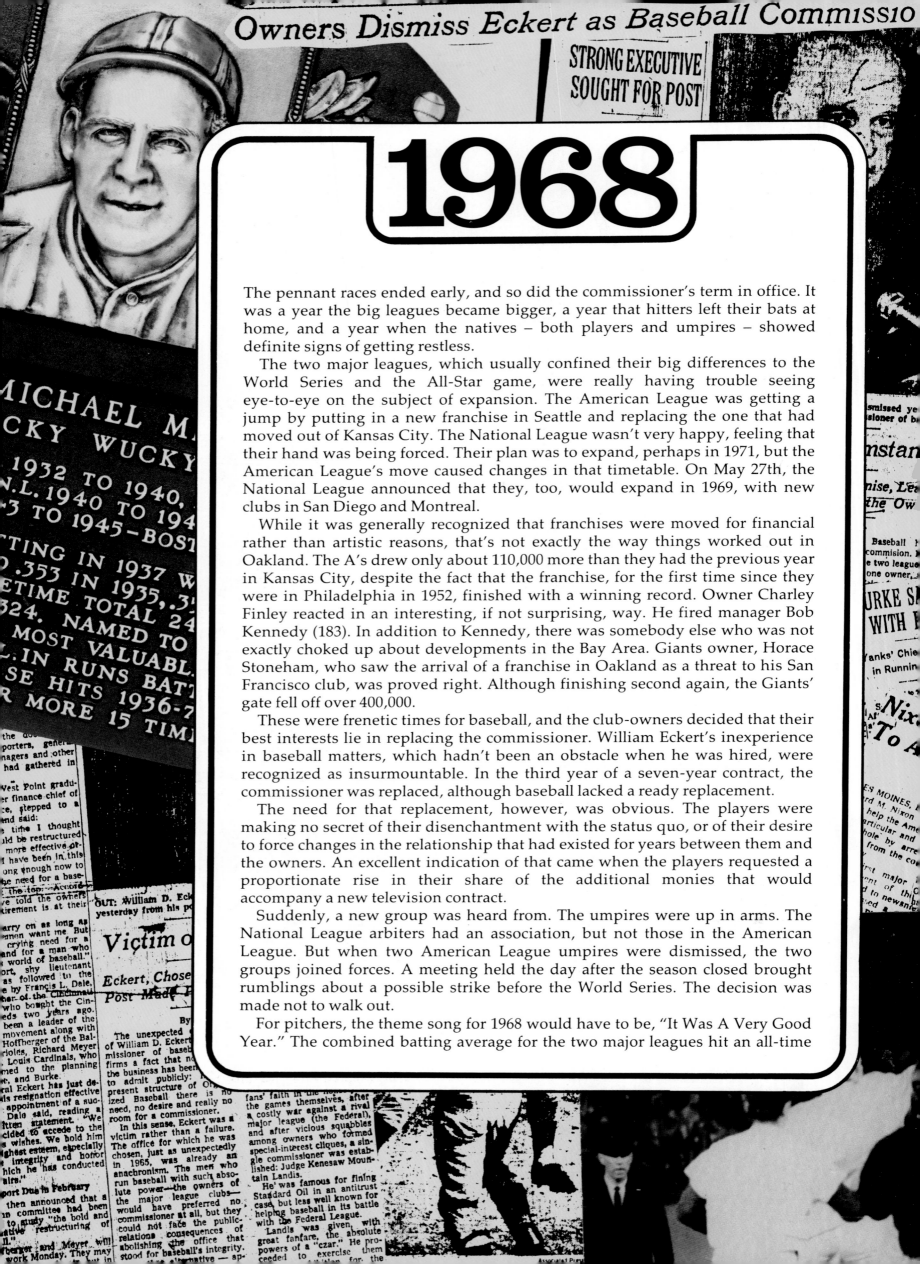

low of .237. There were 339 shutouts in the two leagues, 21 percent of all the games played. And in 82 of those shutouts, the score was 1–0. When the Cy Young Award was split so that each league would have a winner, there was a question of whether that would mitigate against a pitcher's chances to win the Most Valuable Player Award. In 1968, Bob Gibson, (100) and Denny McLain (40) each won both awards, and McLain, who won 31 games for Detroit, won both unanimously.

Both pennant races were over early, the Cardinals locking it up on September 15th and the Tigers clinching it two days later. It was ironic, because it was to be the last time that could possibly happen. Henceforth, pennant winners wouldn't be decided until the winners of the two divisions in each league met in a playoff.

Although both of baseball's dominant pitchers were in the World Series, neither was the pitching "hero." That honor belonged to Detroit's Mickey Lolich (414), a 17-game winner during the season, who won three games in the Series. The seventh game matched Lolich with Gibson, each having won twice. A tie after six innings, Detroit scored three runs in the seventh and won 4–1.

The following is a complete list of A.L. .300 hitters for the year: Carl Yastrzemski (250) hit .301.

The Cards

For the first time since 1962, Topps used All Stars under the banner of the *Sporting News.* This group (361 to 380) boasts 10 players who are now in the Hall of Fame. The 598-card set also features 3 Combination Cards: 480 with Clemente; 490 with Killebrew, Mays, and Mantle; and 530 with Brooks and Frank Robinson. Also included are Leader Cards (1 to 12); 8 World Series (151 to 158), and the last cards published of Mickey Mantle (280) and Eddie Mathews (58) as active players. The top-value card is the Rookie Card of Nolan Ryan (177) at $1,600.

QUIZ

He set a new National League record for strikeouts in a season. Who? (344)

This future Hall of Famer ruptured a hamstring in the All-Star game and was out for two months. Who? (220)

While McLain and Lolich were having big years, so were another pair of pitching teammates. One led the A.L. in strikeouts. Who? (115)

His teammate led the league in shutouts and ERA. Who? (532)

This Cubs righthander won 20 and set a new team record of 236 strikeouts. Who? (410)

This young Pittsburgh pitcher had the best won–lost percentage in the league. Who? (499)

He became the youngest ever to pitch a perfect game. Who? (385)

A top pitcher on a pennant-winning club, he missed most of the 1968 season due to a skiing injury. Who? (460)

Which pitcher set a major league record by appearing in 88 games? (585)

Just in case you still don't think it was an off year for hitters, this one led the National League in runs scored with the lowest total since 1919. Who? (101)

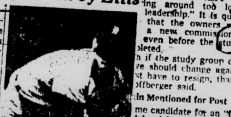

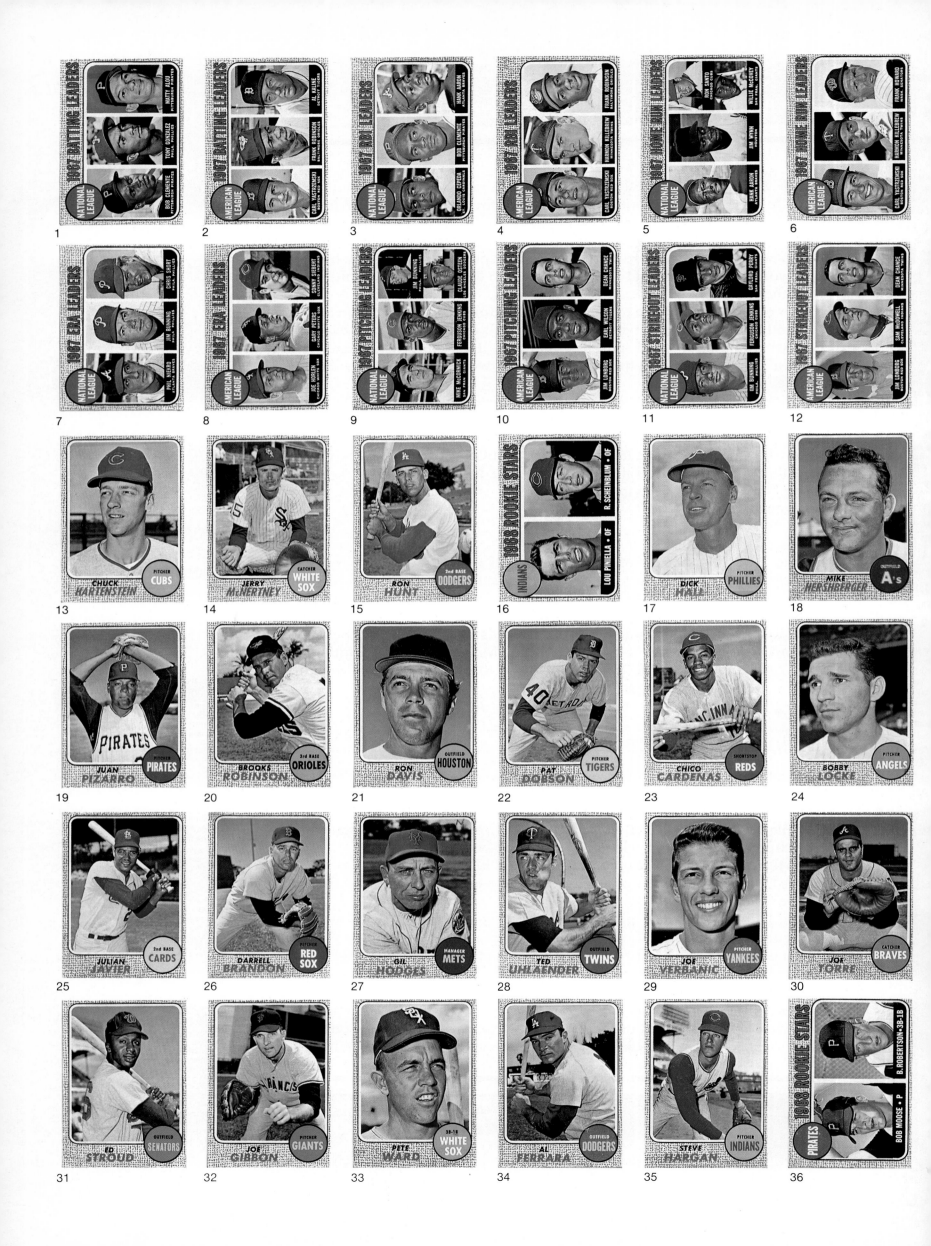

73 JIM HART 3B-OF GIANTS
74 MILT PAPPAS PITCHER REDS
75 DON MINCHER 1st BASE ANGELS
76 1968 ROOKIE STARS RON REED • P JIM BRITTON • P BRAVES
77 DON WILSON PITCHER HOUSTON
78 JIM NORTHRUP OUTFIELD TIGERS

79 TED KUBIAK INFIELD A's
80 ROD CAREW 2nd BASE TWINS
81 LARRY JACKSON PITCHER PHILLIES
82 SAM BOWENS OUTFIELD ORIOLES
83 JOHN STEPHENSON CATCHER CUBS
84 BOB TOLAN OUTFIELD CARDS

85 GAYLORD PERRY PITCHER GIANTS
86 WILLIE STARGELL OUTFIELD PIRATES
87 DICK WILLIAMS MANAGER RED SOX
88 PHIL REGAN PITCHER DODGERS
89 JAKE GIBBS CATCHER YANKEES
90 VADA PINSON OUTFIELD REDS

91 JIM OLLOM PITCHER TWINS
92 ED KRANEPOOL 1st BASE METS
93 TONY CLONINGER PITCHER BRAVES
94 LEE MAYE OUTFIELD INDIANS
95 BOB ASPROMONTE 3rd BASE HOUSTON
96 1968 ROOKIE STARS DICK NOLD • P FRANK COGGINS • 2B SENATORS

97 TOM PHOEBUS PITCHER ORIOLES
98 GARY SUTHERLAND INF-OF PHILLIES
99 ROCKY COLAVITO OUTFIELD WHITE SOX
100 BOB GIBSON PITCHER CARDS
101 GLENN BECKERT 2nd BASE CUBS
102 JOSE CARDENAL OUTFIELD ANGELS

103 DON SUTTON PITCHER DODGERS
104 DICK DIETZ CATCHER GIANTS
105 AL DOWNING PITCHER YANKEES
106 DALTON JONES 2B-3B RED SOX
107 TOPPS BASEBALL 2 SERIES CHECK LIST
108 DON PAVLETICH CATCHER REDS

TOPPS BASEBALL 2 SERIES CHECK LIST

110	Hank Aaron	126	B. Etheridge
111	Rich Reese	127	P. Lindblad
112	Woody Fryman	128	Hous. R'kies
113	Tigers Rookies	129	M. Stanley
114	Ron Swoboda	130	Tony Perez
115	Sam McDowell	131	F. Bertaina
116	Ken McMullen	132	B. Harrelson
117	Larry Jaster	133	F. Whitfield
118	Mark Belanger	134	Pat Jarvis
119	Ted Savage	135	Paul Blair
120	M. Stottlemyre	136	R. Hundley
121	Jimmie Hall	137	Twins Team
122	Gene Mauch	138	R. Amaro
123	Jose Santiago	139	Chris Short
124	Nate Oliver	140	T. Conigliaro
125	Joe Horlen	141	Dal Maxvill

145

146

147

148

149

150

151

152

153

154

155

156

157

158

159

160

161

162

163

164

165

166

167

168

169

170

171

172

173

174

175

176

177

178

179

180

JERRY ZIMMERMAN · CATCHER · TWINS
181

DAVE GIUSTI · PITCHER · HOUSTON
182

BOB KENNEDY · MANAGER · A's
183

LOU JOHNSON · OUTFIELD · CUBS
184

TOM HALLER · CATCHER · GIANTS
185

EDDIE WATT · PITCHER · ORIOLES
186

SONNY JACKSON · SHORTSTOP · BRAVES
187

CAP PETERSON · OUTFIELD · SENATORS
188

BILL LANDIS · PITCHER · RED SOX
189

BILL WHITE · 1st BASE · PHILLIES
190

DAN FRISELLA · PITCHER · METS
191

TOPPS BASEBALL
3rd SERIES CHECK LIST

197 Larry Brown	214 Yanks Rookies
198 Roy Face	215 Jim Bunning
199 A's Rookies	216 Bubba Morton
200 Orlando Cepeda	217 Turk Farrell
201 Mike Marshall	218 Ken Suarez
202 Adolfo Phillips	219 Rob Gardner
203 Dick Kelley	220 H. Killebrew
204 A. Etchebarren	221 Jim Hardin
205 Juan Marichal	222 Braves Team
206 Cal Ermer	223 Ollie Brown
207 Carroll Sembera	224 Jack Aker
208 Willie Davis	225 Richie Allen
209 Tim Cullen	226 Jimmie Price
210 Gary Peters	227 Joe Hoerner
211 J. C. Martin	228 Dodgers Rookies
212 Dave Morehead	229 Fred Klages
213 Chico Ruiz	230 Pete Rose

192

JACK HAMILTON · PITCHER · ANGELS
193

DON BUFORD · 2B-3B · ORIOLES
194

JOE PEPITONE · OUTFIELD · YANKEES
195

GARY NOLAN · PITCHER · REDS
196

LARRY BROWN · SHORTSTOP · INDIANS
197

ROY FACE · PITCHER · PIRATES
198

1968 ROOKIE STARS
DARRELL OSTEEN · P
ROBERTO RODRIGUEZ · P · A's
199

ORLANDO CEPEDA · 1st BASE · CARDS
200

MIKE MARSHALL · PITCHER · TIGERS
201

ADOLFO PHILLIPS · OUTFIELD · CUBS
202

DICK KELLEY · PITCHER · BRAVES
203

ANDY ETCHEBARREN · CATCHER · ORIOLES
204

JUAN MARICHAL · PITCHER · GIANTS
205

CAL ERMER · MANAGER · TWINS
206

CARROLL SEMBERA · PITCHER · HOUSTON
207

WILLIE DAVIS · OUTFIELD · DODGERS
208

TIM CULLEN · 2B-SS · SENATORS
209

GARY PETERS · PITCHER · WHITE SOX
210

J. C. MARTIN · CATCHER · METS
211

DAVE MOREHEAD · PITCHER · RED SOX
212

CHICO RUIZ · INFIELD · REDS
213

1968 ROOKIE STARS
FRANK FERNANDEZ · C
STAN BAHNSEN · P · YANKEES
214

JIM BUNNING · PITCHER · PIRATES
215

BUBBA MORTON · OUTFIELD · ANGELS
216

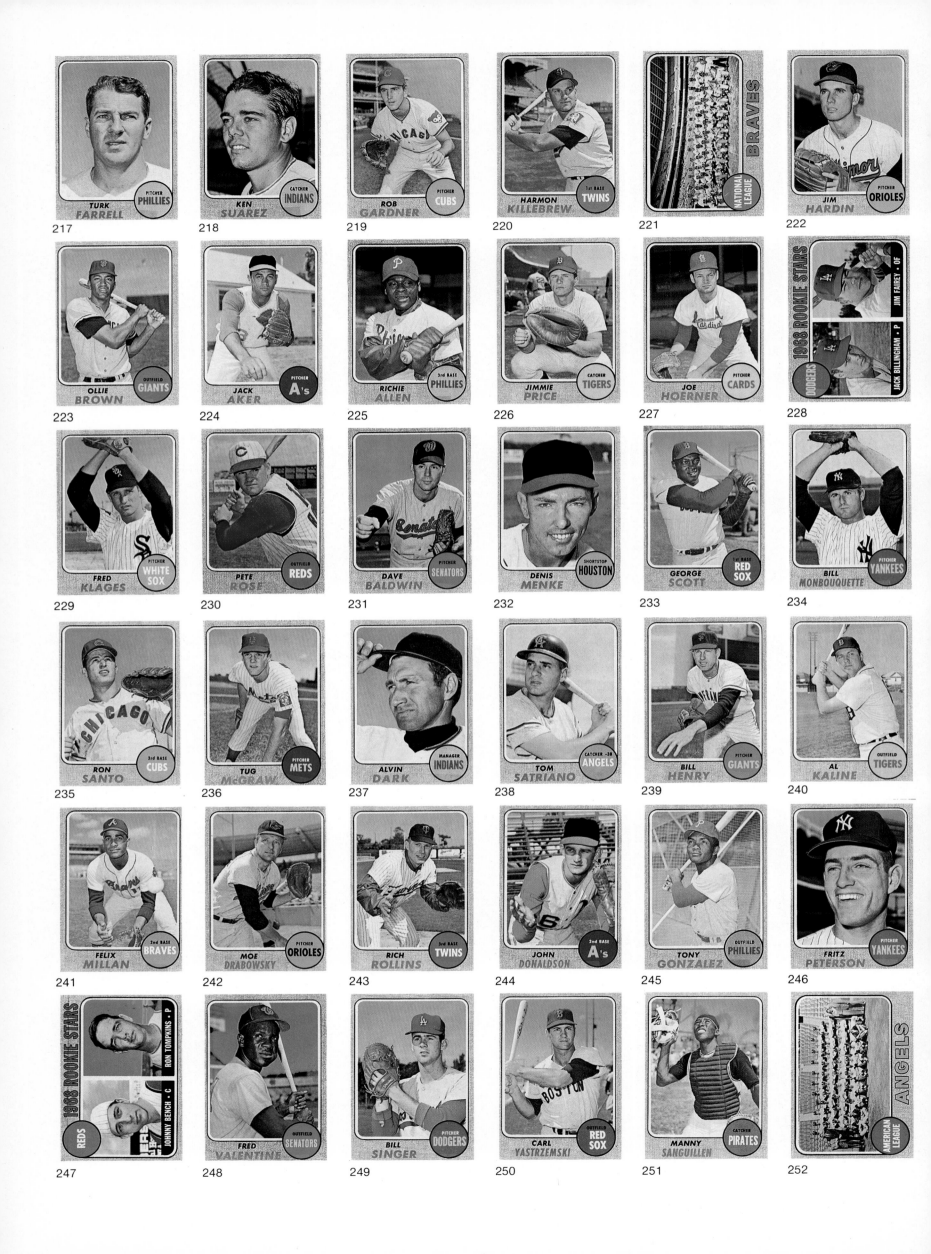

TURK **FARRELL** PITCHER PHILLIES	KEN **SUAREZ** CATCHER INDIANS	ROB **GARDNER** PITCHER CUBS	HARMON **KILLEBREW** 1st BASE TWINS	BRAVES NATIONAL LEAGUE	JIM **HARDIN** PITCHER ORIOLES
217	218	219	220	221	222
OLLIE **BROWN** OUTFIELD GIANTS	JACK **AKER** PITCHER A's	RICHIE **ALLEN** 3rd BASE PHILLIES	JIMMIE **PRICE** CATCHER TIGERS	JOE **HOERNER** PITCHER CARDS	1968 ROOKIE STARS JIM FAIREY • OF JACK BILLINGHAM • P DODGERS
223	224	225	226	227	228
FRED **KLAGES** PITCHER WHITE SOX	PETE **ROSE** OUTFIELD REDS	DAVE **BALDWIN** PITCHER SENATORS	DENIS **MENKE** SHORTSTOP HOUSTON	GEORGE **SCOTT** 1st BASE RED SOX	BILL **MONBOUQUETTE** PITCHER YANKEES
229	230	231	232	233	234
RON **SANTO** 3rd BASE CUBS	TUG **McGRAW** PITCHER METS	ALVIN **DARK** MANAGER INDIANS	TOM **SATRIANO** CATCHER -3B ANGELS	BILL **HENRY** PITCHER GIANTS	AL **KALINE** OUTFIELD TIGERS
235	236	237	238	239	240
FELIX **MILLAN** 2nd BASE BRAVES	MOE **DRABOWSKY** PITCHER ORIOLES	RICH **ROLLINS** 3rd BASE TWINS	JOHN **DONALDSON** 2nd BASE A's	TONY **GONZALEZ** OUTFIELD PHILLIES	FRITZ **PETERSON** PITCHER YANKEES
241	242	243	244	245	246
1968 ROOKIE STARS RON TOMPKINS • P JOHNNY BENCH • C REDS	FRED **VALENTINE** OUTFIELD SENATORS	BILL **SINGER** PITCHER DODGERS	CARL **YASTRZEMSKI** OUTFIELD RED SOX	MANNY **SANGUILLEN** CATCHER PIRATES	ANGELS AMERICAN LEAGUE
247	248	249	250	251	252

DICK HUGHES — PITCHER — CARDS	CLEON JONES — OUTFIELD — METS	DEAN CHANCE — PITCHER — TWINS	NORM CASH — 1st BASE — TIGERS	PHIL NIEKRO — PITCHER — BRAVES	1968 ROOKIE STARS — CUBS — BILL SCHLESINGER · OF — JOSE ARCIA · SS
253	254	255	256	257	258
KEN BOYER — 3rd BASE — WHITE SOX	JIM WYNN — OUTFIELD — HOUSTON	DAVE DUNCAN — CATCHER — A's	RICK WISE — PITCHER — PHILLIES	HORACE CLARKE — 2nd BASE — YANKEES	TED ABERNATHY — PITCHER — REDS
259	260	261	262	263	264
TOMMY DAVIS — OUTFIELD — WHITE SOX	PAUL POPOVICH — INFIELD — DODGERS	HERMAN FRANKS — MANAGER — GIANTS	BOB HUMPHREYS — PITCHER — SENATORS	BOB TIEFENAUER — PITCHER — INDIANS	MATTY ALOU — OUTFIELD — PIRATES
265	266	267	268	269	270
BOBBY KNOOP — 2nd BASE — ANGELS	RAY CULP — PITCHER — RED SOX	DAVE JOHNSON — 2nd BASE — ORIOLES	MIKE CUELLAR — PITCHER — HOUSTON	TIM McCARVER — CATCHER — CARDS	JIM ROLAND — PITCHER — TWINS
271	272	273	274	275	276
JERRY BUCHEK — 2nd BASE — METS	TOPPS BASEBALL 4th SERIES CHECK LIST	BILL HANDS — PITCHER — CUBS	MICKEY MANTLE — 1st BASE — YANKEES	JIM CAMPANIS — CATCHER — DODGERS	RICK MONDAY — OUTFIELD — A's
277	278	279	280	281	282
MEL QUEEN — PITCHER — REDS	JOHN BRIGGS — OUTFIELD — PHILLIES	DICK McAULIFFE — 2nd BASE — TIGERS	CECIL UPSHAW — PITCHER — BRAVES	1968 ROOKIE STARS — WHITE SOX — MICKEY ABARBANEL · P — CISCO CARLOS · P	DAVE WICKERSHAM — PITCHER — PIRATES
283	284	285	286	287	288

TOPPS BASEBALL 4th SERIES CHECK LIST

284	John Briggs	301	Twins Rookies
285	Dick McAuliffe	302	Gerry Arrigo
286	Cecil Upshaw	303	Dick Green
287	W. Sox Rookies	304	S. Valdespino
288	D. Wickersham	305	Minnie Rojas
289	Woody Held	306	Mike Ryan
290	Willie McCovey	307	John Hiller
291	Dick Lines	308	Pirates Team
292	Art Shamsky	309	Ken Henderson
293	Bruce Howard	310	Luis Aparicio
294	R. Schoendienst	311	Jack Lamabe
295	Sonny Siebert	312	Curt Blefary
296	Byron Browne	313	Al Weis
297	Russ Gibson	314	R. Sox Rookies
298	Jim Brewer	315	Zoilo Versalles
299	Gene Michael	316	Steve Barber
300	Rusty Staub	317	Ron Brand

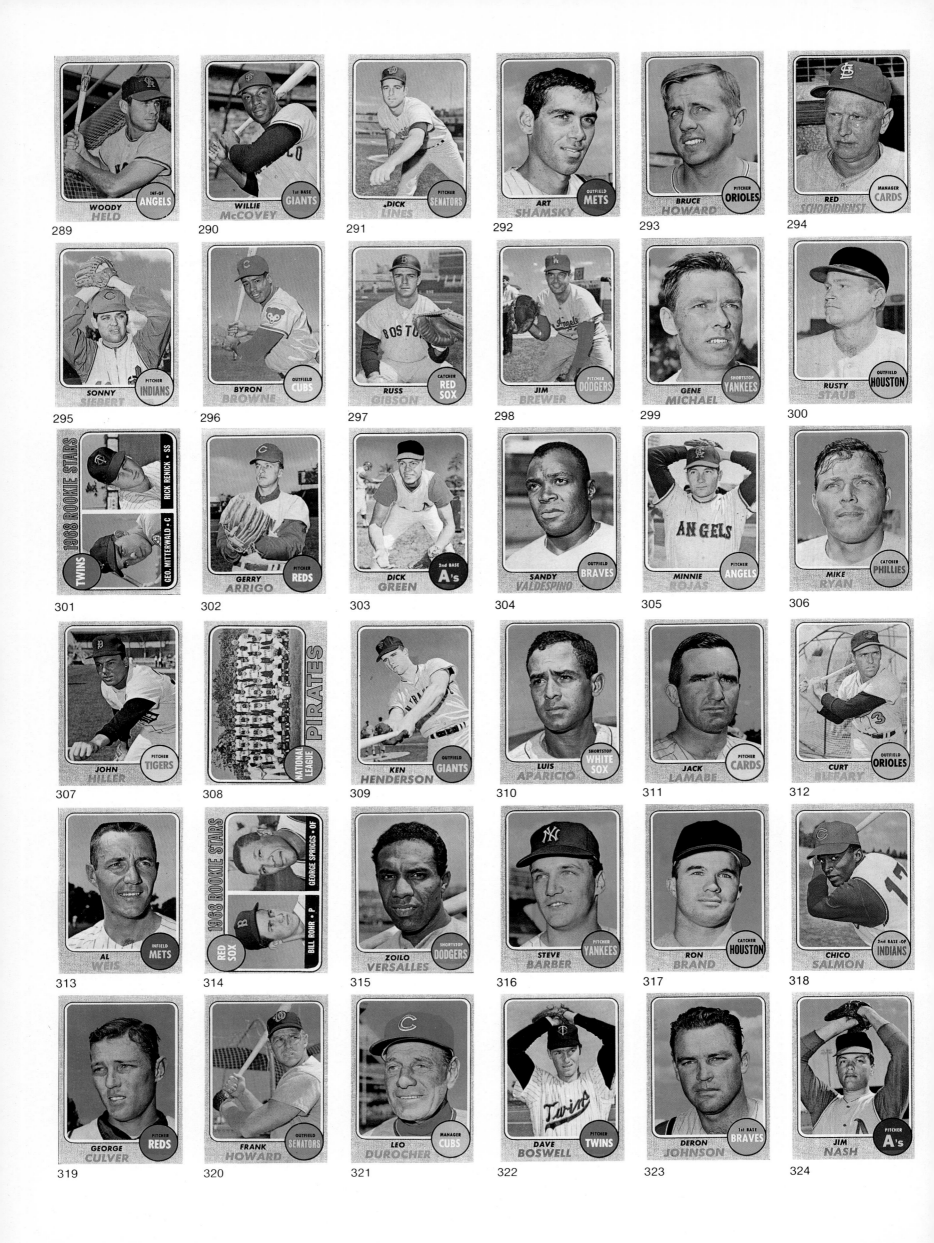

WOODY **HELD** INF-OF ANGELS
289

WILLIE **McCOVEY** 1st BASE GIANTS
290

DICK **LINES** PITCHER SENATORS
291

ART **SHAMSKY** OUTFIELD METS
292

BRUCE **HOWARD** PITCHER ORIOLES
293

RED **SCHOENDIENST** MANAGER CARDS
294

SONNY **SIEBERT** PITCHER INDIANS
295

BYRON **BROWNE** OUTFIELD CUBS
296

RUSS **GIBSON** CATCHER RED SOX
297

JIM **BREWER** PITCHER DODGERS
298

GENE **MICHAEL** SHORTSTOP YANKEES
299

RUSTY **STAUB** OUTFIELD HOUSTON
300

1968 ROOKIE STARS TWINS RICK RENICK · SS GEO. MITTERWALD · C
301

GERRY **ARRIGO** PITCHER REDS
302

DICK **GREEN** 2nd BASE A's
303

SANDY **VALDESPINO** OUTFIELD BRAVES
304

MINNIE **ROJAS** PITCHER ANGELS
305

MIKE **RYAN** CATCHER PHILLIES
306

JOHN **HILLER** PITCHER TIGERS
307

PIRATES NATIONAL LEAGUE
308

KEN **HENDERSON** OUTFIELD GIANTS
309

LUIS **APARICIO** SHORTSTOP WHITE SOX
310

JACK **LAMABE** PITCHER CARDS
311

CURT **BLEFARY** OUTFIELD ORIOLES
312

AL **WEIS** INFIELD METS
313

1968 ROOKIE STARS RED SOX GEORGE SPRIGGS · OF BILL ROHR · P
314

ZOILO **VERSALLES** SHORTSTOP DODGERS
315

STEVE **BARBER** PITCHER YANKEES
316

RON **BRAND** CATCHER HOUSTON
317

CHICO **SALMON** 2nd BASE -OF INDIANS
318

GEORGE **CULVER** PITCHER REDS
319

FRANK **HOWARD** OUTFIELD SENATORS
320

LEO **DUROCHER** MANAGER CUBS
321

DAVE **BOSWELL** PITCHER TWINS
322

DERON **JOHNSON** 1st BASE BRAVES
323

JIM **NASH** PITCHER A's
324

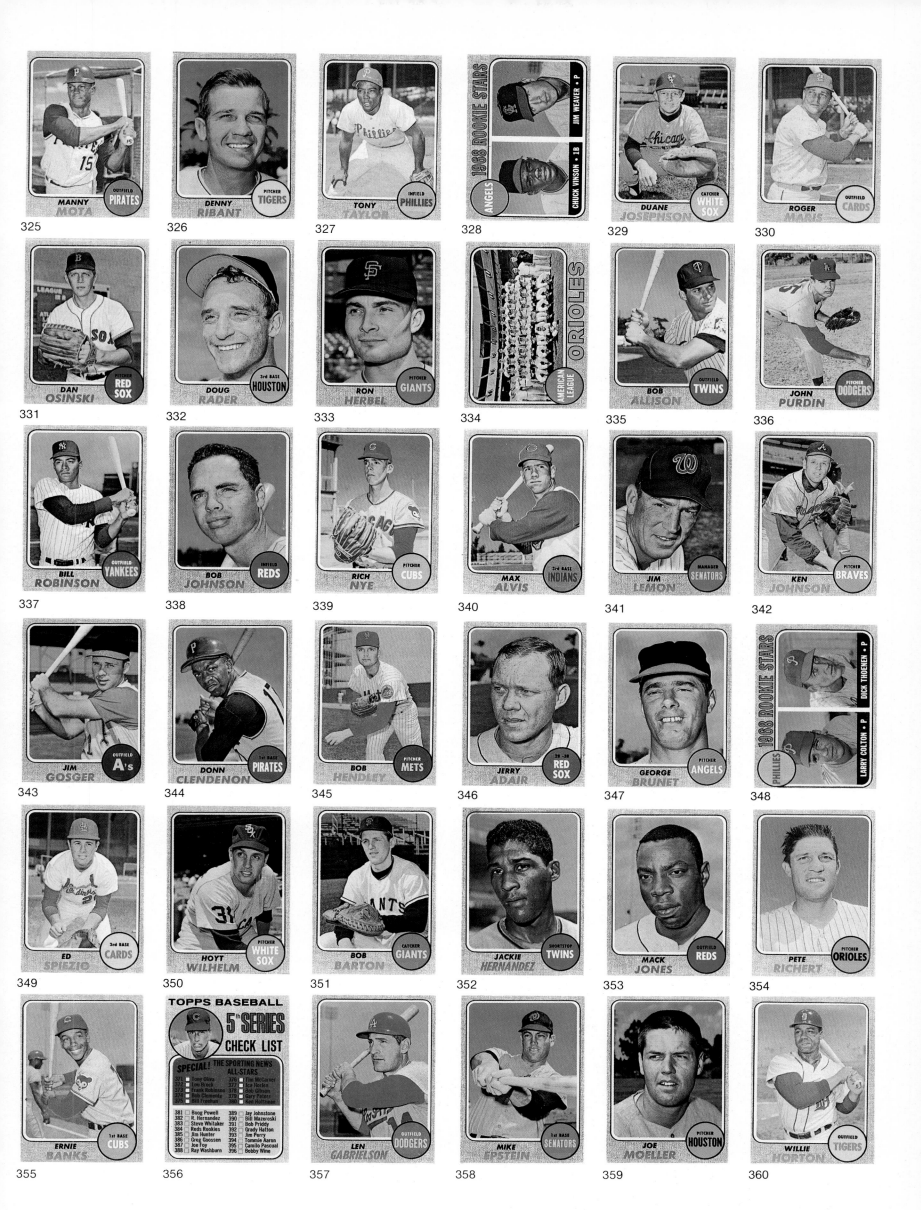

325   326   327   328   329   330

331   332   333   334   335   336

337   338   339   340   341   342

343   344   345   346   347   348

349   350   351   352   353   354

355   356   357   358   359   360

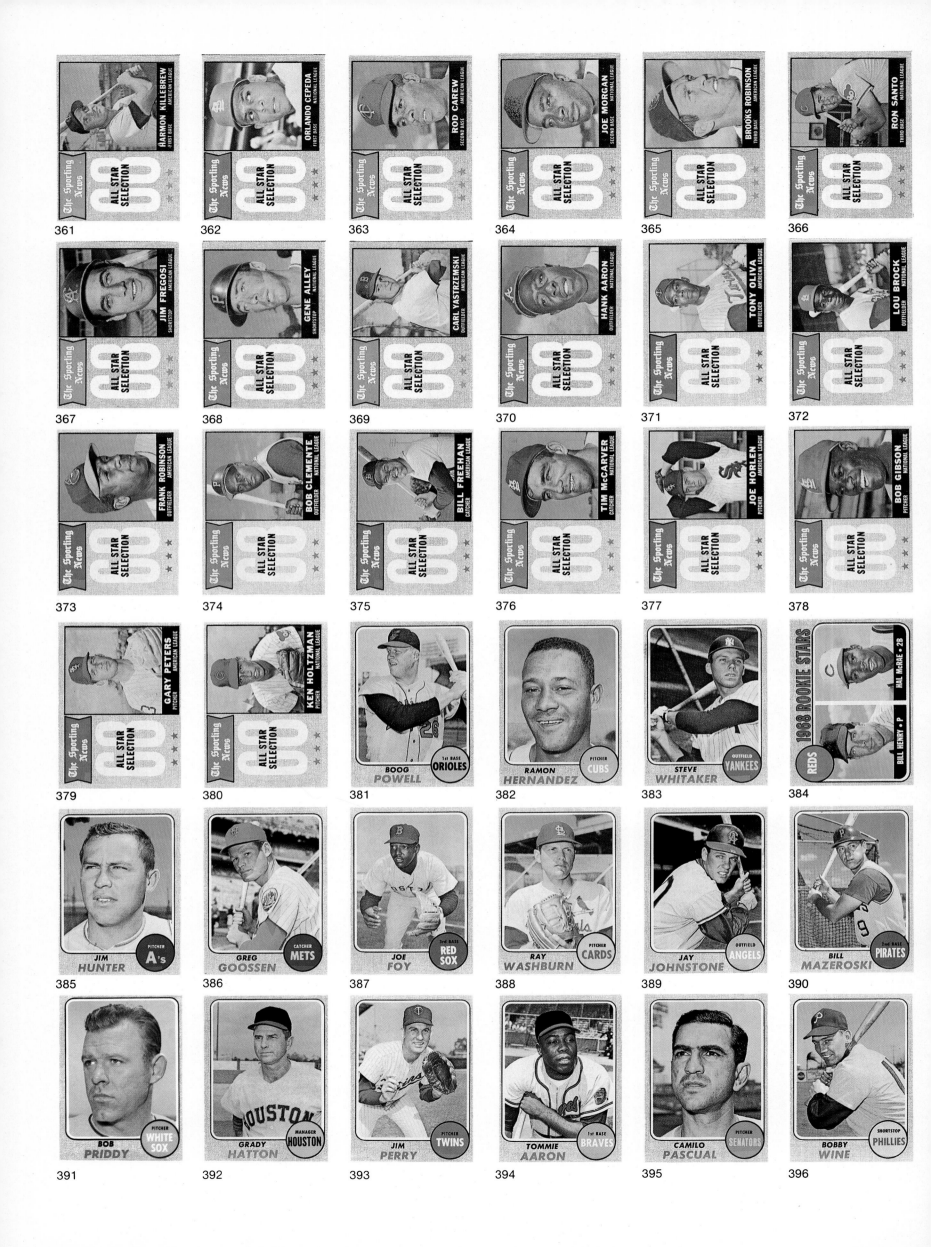

361

362

363

364

365

366

367

368

369

370

371

372

373

374

375

376

377

378

379

380

381

382

383

384

385

386

387

388

389

390

391

392

393

394

395

396

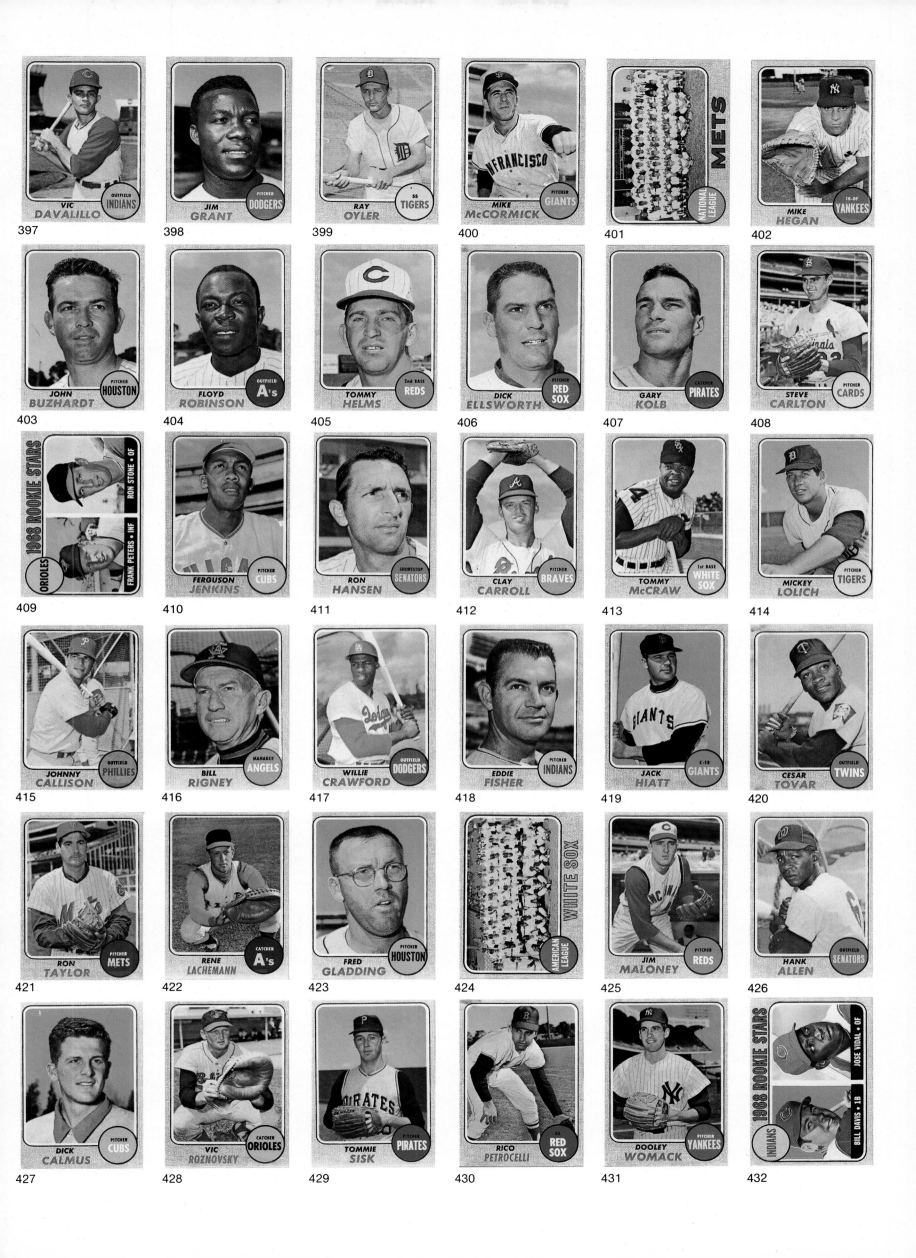

397 VIC DAVALILLO — OUTFIELD INDIANS
398 JIM GRANT — PITCHER DODGERS
399 RAY OYLER — SS TIGERS
400 MIKE McCORMICK — PITCHER GIANTS
401 METS — NATIONAL LEAGUE
402 MIKE HEGAN — 1B-OF YANKEES
403 JOHN BUZHARDT — PITCHER HOUSTON
404 FLOYD ROBINSON — OUTFIELD A's
405 TOMMY HELMS — 2nd BASE REDS
406 DICK ELLSWORTH — PITCHER RED SOX
407 GARY KOLB — CATCHER PIRATES
408 STEVE CARLTON — PITCHER CARDS
409 1968 ROOKIE STARS — RON STONE • OF / FRANK PETERS • INF ORIOLES
410 FERGUSON JENKINS — PITCHER CUBS
411 RON HANSEN — SHORTSTOP SENATORS
412 CLAY CARROLL — PITCHER BRAVES
413 TOMMY McCRAW — 1st BASE WHITE SOX
414 MICKEY LOLICH — PITCHER TIGERS
415 JOHNNY CALLISON — OUTFIELD PHILLIES
416 BILL RIGNEY — MANAGER ANGELS
417 WILLIE CRAWFORD — OUTFIELD DODGERS
418 EDDIE FISHER — PITCHER INDIANS
419 JACK HIATT — C-1B GIANTS
420 CESAR TOVAR — OUTFIELD TWINS
421 RON TAYLOR — PITCHER METS
422 RENE LACHEMANN — CATCHER A's
423 FRED GLADDING — PITCHER HOUSTON
424 WHITE SOX — AMERICAN LEAGUE
425 JIM MALONEY — PITCHER REDS
426 HANK ALLEN — OUTFIELD SENATORS
427 DICK CALMUS — PITCHER CUBS
428 VIC ROZNOVSKY — CATCHER ORIOLES
429 TOMMIE SISK — PITCHER PIRATES
430 RICO PETROCELLI — SS RED SOX
431 DOOLEY WOMACK — PITCHER YANKEES
432 1968 ROOKIE STARS — JOSE VIDAL • OF / BILL DAVIS • 1B INDIANS

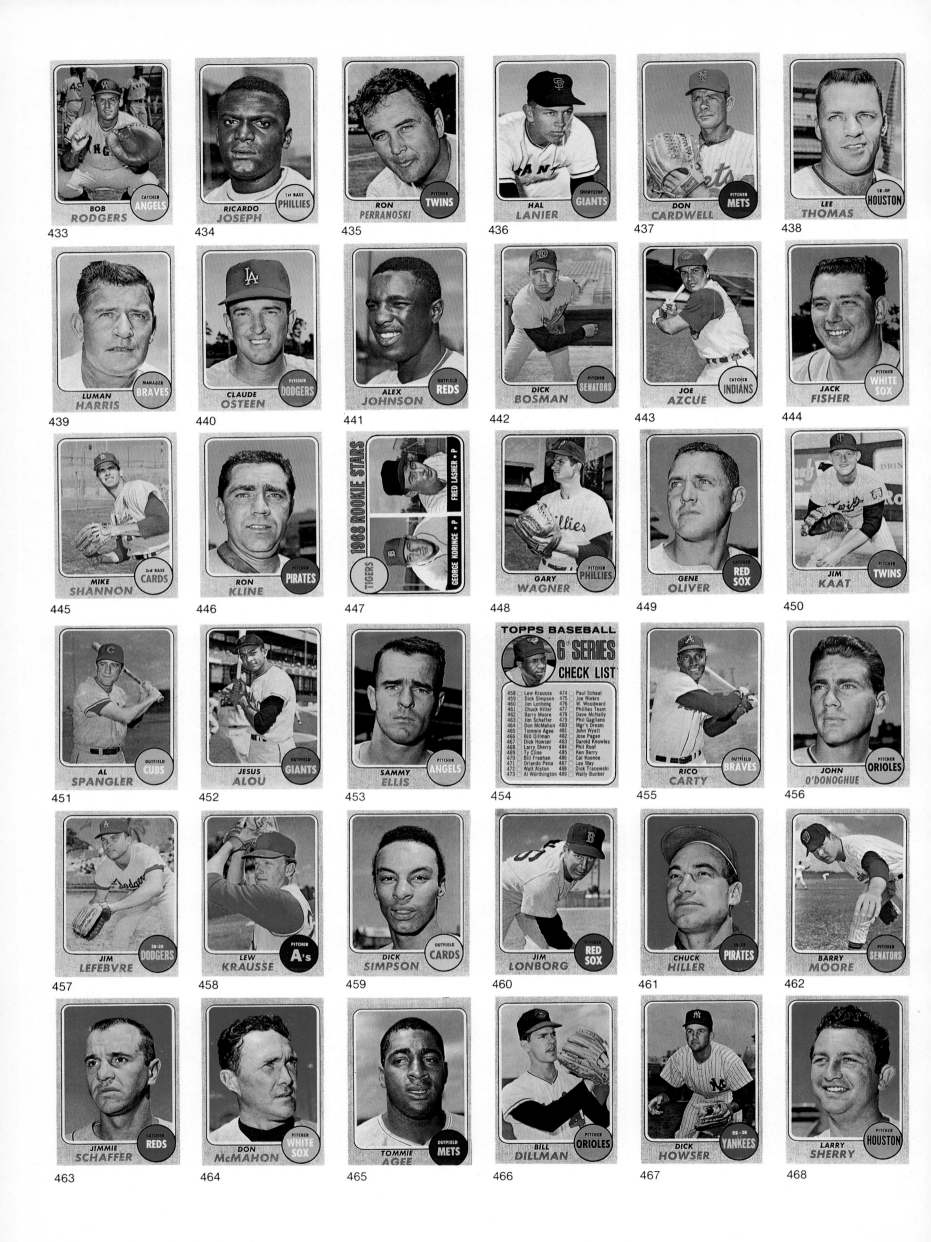

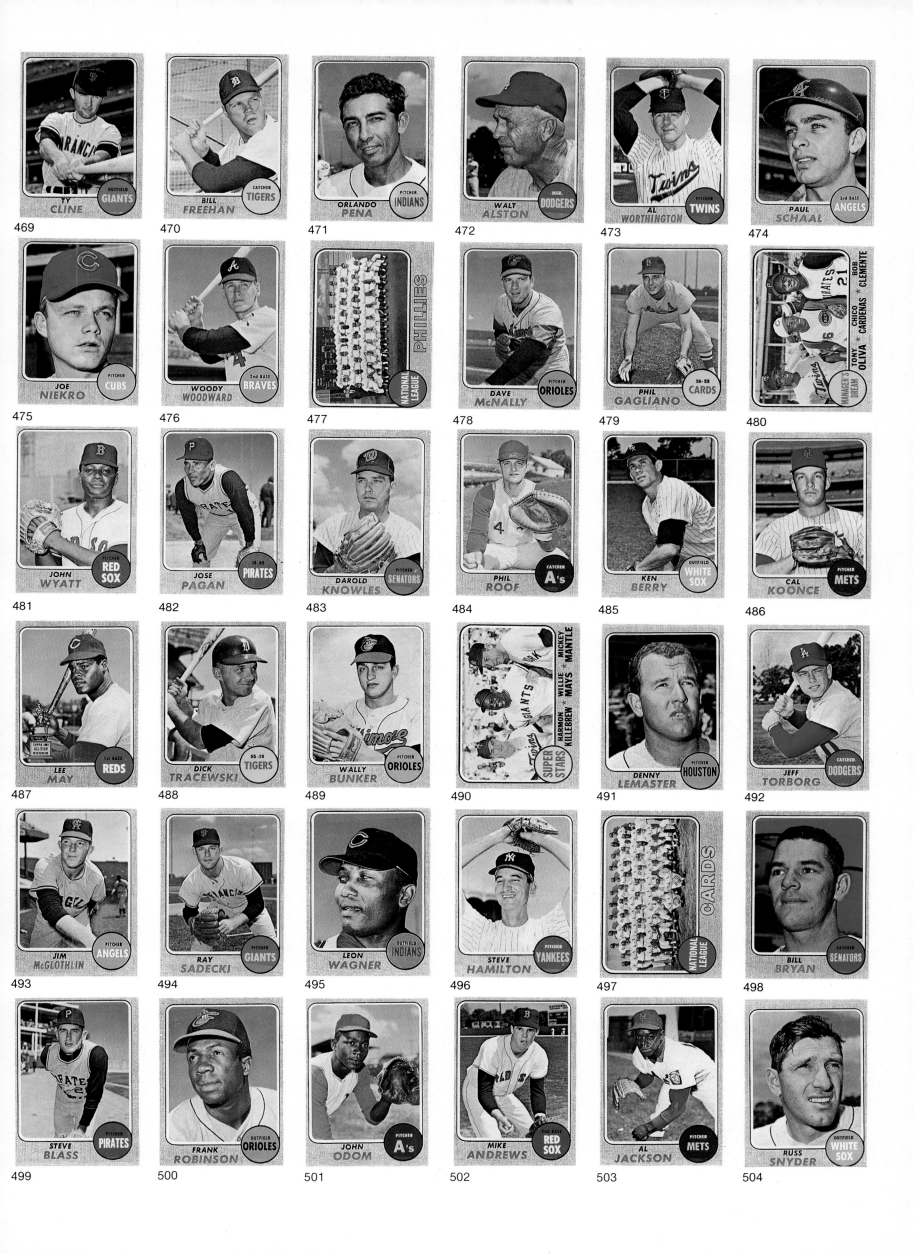

TY
CLINE
OUTFIELD
GIANTS
469

BILL
FREEHAN
CATCHER
TIGERS
470

ORLANDO
PENA
PITCHER
INDIANS
471

WALT
ALSTON
MGR.
DODGERS
472

AL
WORTHINGTON
PITCHER
TWINS
473

PAUL
SCHAAL
3rd BASE
ANGELS
474

JOE
NIEKRO
PITCHER
CUBS
475

WOODY
WOODWARD
2nd BASE
BRAVES
476

PHILLIES
NATIONAL
LEAGUE
477

DAVE
McNALLY
PITCHER
ORIOLES
478

PHIL
GAGLIANO
2B-SS
CARDS
479

TONY OLIVA CHICO CARDENAS BOB CLEMENTE
MANAGER'S DREAM
480

JOHN
WYATT
PITCHER
RED SOX
481

JOSE
PAGAN
2B-SS
PIRATES
482

DAROLD
KNOWLES
PITCHER
SENATORS
483

PHIL
ROOF
CATCHER
A's
484

KEN
BERRY
OUTFIELD
WHITE SOX
485

CAL
KOONCE
PITCHER
METS
486

LEE
MAY
1st BASE
REDS
487

DICK
TRACEWSKI
SS-2B
TIGERS
488

WALLY
BUNKER
PITCHER
ORIOLES
489

HARMON KILLEBREW WILLIE MAYS MICKEY MANTLE
SUPER STARS
490

DENNY
LEMASTER
PITCHER
HOUSTON
491

JEFF
TORBORG
CATCHER
DODGERS
492

JIM
McGLOTHLIN
PITCHER
ANGELS
493

RAY
SADECKI
PITCHER
GIANTS
494

LEON
WAGNER
OUTFIELD
INDIANS
495

STEVE
HAMILTON
PITCHER
YANKEES
496

CARDS
NATIONAL
LEAGUE
497

BILL
BRYAN
CATCHER
SENATORS
498

STEVE
BLASS
PITCHER
PIRATES
499

FRANK
ROBINSON
OUTFIELD
ORIOLES
500

JOHN
ODOM
PITCHER
A's
501

MIKE
ANDREWS
2nd BASE
RED SOX
502

AL
JACKSON
PITCHER
METS
503

RUSS
SNYDER
OUTFIELD
WHITE SOX
504

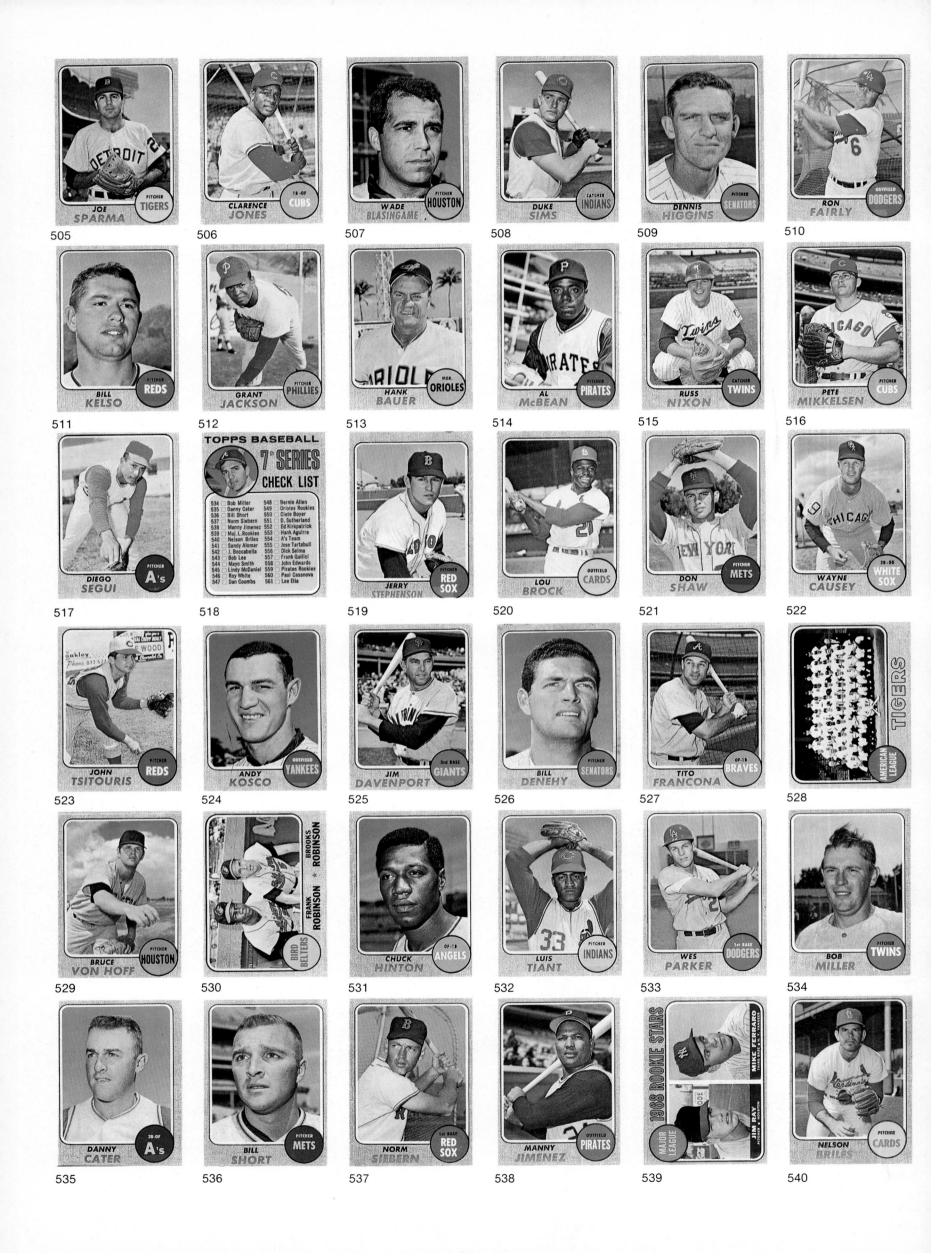

JOE **SPARMA** PITCHER TIGERS
505

CLARENCE **JONES** 1B-OF CUBS
506

WADE **BLASINGAME** HOUSTON
507

DUKE **SIMS** CATCHER INDIANS
508

DENNIS **HIGGINS** PITCHER SENATORS
509

RON **FAIRLY** OUTFIELD DODGERS
510

BILL **KELSO** PITCHER REDS
511

GRANT **JACKSON** PITCHER PHILLIES
512

HANK **BAUER** MGR. ORIOLES
513

AL **McBEAN** PITCHER PIRATES
514

RUSS **NIXON** CATCHER TWINS
515

PETE **MIKKELSEN** PITCHER CUBS
516

DIEGO **SEGUI** PITCHER A's
517

TOPPS BASEBALL 7th SERIES CHECK LIST

534	Bob Miller	548	Bernie Allen
535	Danny Cater	549	Orioles Rookies
536	Bill Short	550	Clete Boyer
537	Norm Siebern	551	D. Sutherland
538	Manny Jimenez	552	Ed Kirkpatrick
539	Maj.L.Rookies	553	Hank Aguirre
540	Nelson Briles	554	A's Team
541	Sandy Alomar	555	Jose Tartabull
542	J. Boccabella	556	Dick Selma
543	Bob Lee	557	Frank Quilici
544	Mayo Smith	558	John Edwards
545	Lindy McDaniel	559	Pirates Rookies
546	Roy White	560	Paul Casanova
547	Dan Coombs	561	Lee Elia

518

JERRY **STEPHENSON** PITCHER RED SOX
519

LOU **BROCK** OUTFIELD CARDS
520

DON **SHAW** PITCHER METS
521

WAYNE **CAUSEY** 2B-SS WHITE SOX
522

JOHN **TSITOURIS** PITCHER REDS
523

ANDY **KOSCO** OUTFIELD YANKEES
524

JIM **DAVENPORT** 3rd BASE GIANTS
525

BILL **DENEHY** PITCHER SENATORS
526

TITO **FRANCONA** OF-1B BRAVES
527

TIGERS AMERICAN LEAGUE
528

BRUCE **VON HOFF** PITCHER HOUSTON
529

BROOKS **ROBINSON** ★ FRANK **ROBINSON** BIRD BELTERS
530

CHUCK **HINTON** OF-1B ANGELS
531

LUIS **TIANT** PITCHER INDIANS
532

WES **PARKER** 1st BASE DODGERS
533

BOB **MILLER** PITCHER TWINS
534

DANNY **CATER** 3B-OF A's
535

BILL **SHORT** PITCHER METS
536

NORM **SIEBERN** 1st BASE RED SOX
537

MANNY **JIMENEZ** OUTFIELD PIRATES
538

1968 ROOKIE STARS MIKE FERRARO THIRD BASE N.Y. YANKEES / JIM RAY PITCHER, HOUSTON MAJOR LEAGUE
539

NELSON **BRILES** PITCHER CARDS
540

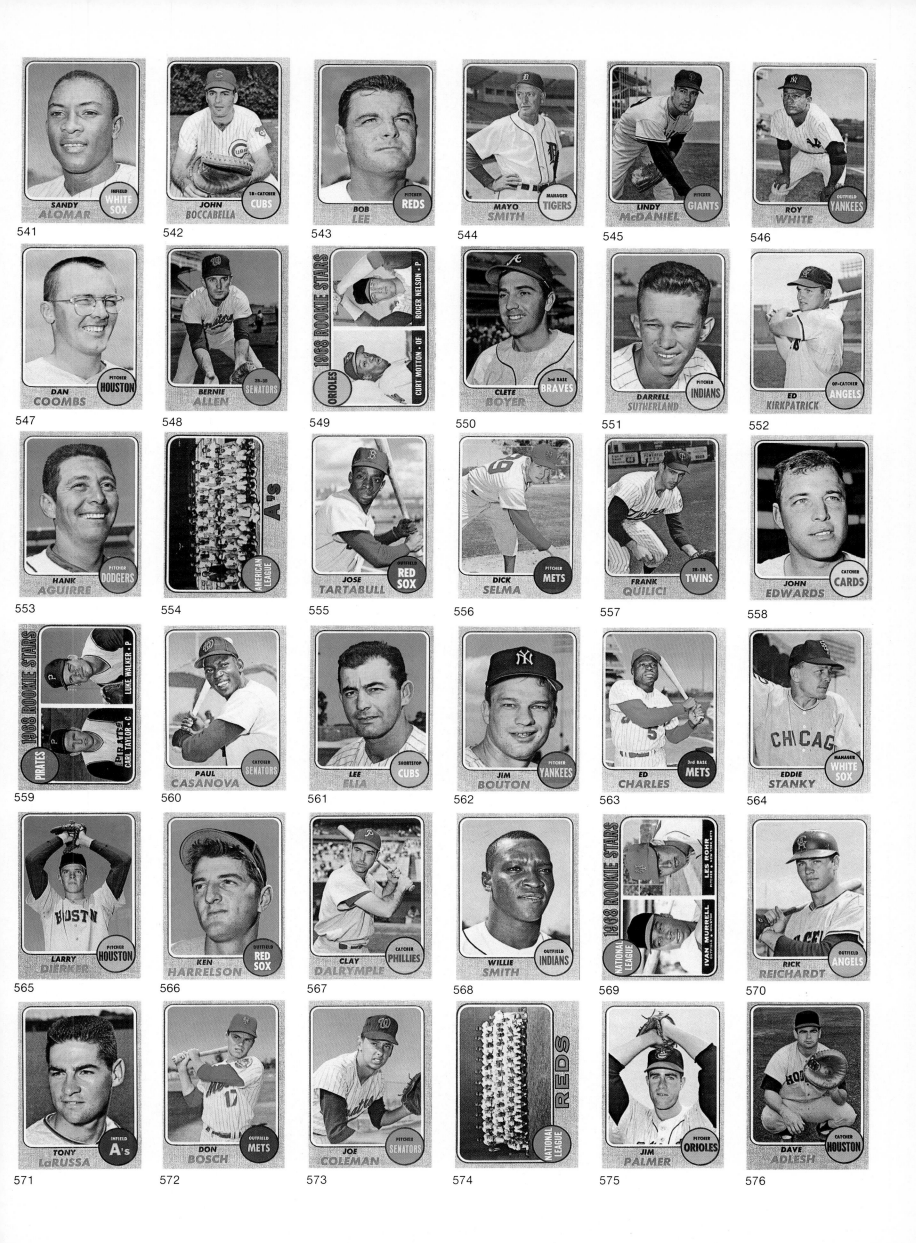

SANDY **ALOMAR** — INFIELD WHITE SOX — 541

JOHN **BOCCABELLA** — 1B-CATCHER CUBS — 542

BOB **LEE** — PITCHER REDS — 543

MAYO **SMITH** — MANAGER TIGERS — 544

LINDY **McDANIEL** — PITCHER GIANTS — 545

ROY **WHITE** — OUTFIELD YANKEES — 546

DAN **COOMBS** — PITCHER HOUSTON — 547

BERNIE **ALLEN** — 2B-3B SENATORS — 548

1968 ROOKIE STARS — ROGER NELSON - P — CURT MOTTON - OF — ORIOLES — 549

CLETE **BOYER** — 3rd BASE BRAVES — 550

DARRELL **SUTHERLAND** — PITCHER INDIANS — 551

ED **KIRKPATRICK** — OF-CATCHER ANGELS — 552

HANK **AGUIRRE** — PITCHER DODGERS — 553

AMERICAN LEAGUE A's — 554

JOSE **TARTABULL** — OUTFIELD RED SOX — 555

DICK **SELMA** — PITCHER METS — 556

FRANK **QUILICI** — 1B-SS TWINS — 557

JOHN **EDWARDS** — CATCHER CARDS — 558

1968 ROOKIE STARS — LUKE WALKER - P — CARL TAYLOR - C — PIRATES — 559

PAUL **CASANOVA** — CATCHER SENATORS — 560

LEE **ELIA** — SHORTSTOP CUBS — 561

JIM **BOUTON** — PITCHER YANKEES — 562

ED **CHARLES** — 3rd BASE METS — 563

EDDIE **STANKY** — MANAGER WHITE SOX — 564

LARRY **DIERKER** — PITCHER HOUSTON — 565

KEN **HARRELSON** — OUTFIELD RED SOX — 566

CLAY **DALRYMPLE** — CATCHER PHILLIES — 567

WILLIE **SMITH** — OUTFIELD INDIANS — 568

1968 ROOKIE STARS — LES ROHR — IVAN MURRELL — NATIONAL LEAGUE — 569

RICK **REICHARDT** — OUTFIELD ANGELS — 570

TONY **LaRUSSA** — INFIELD A's — 571

DON **BOSCH** — OUTFIELD METS — 572

JOE **COLEMAN** — PITCHER SENATORS — 573

NATIONAL LEAGUE REDS — 574

JIM **PALMER** — PITCHER ORIOLES — 575

DAVE **ADLESH** — CATCHER HOUSTON — 576

577 FRED TALBOT — PITCHER YANKEES
578 ORLANDO MARTINEZ — INFIELD BRAVES
579 1968 ROOKIE STARS NATIONAL LEAGUE — MIKE LUM / LARRY HISLE
580 BOB BAILEY — 3rd BASE DODGERS
581 GARRY ROGGENBURK — PITCHER RED SOX
582 JERRY GROTE — CATCHER METS

583 GATES BROWN — OUTFIELD TIGERS
584 LARRY SHEPARD — MANAGER PIRATES
585 WILBUR WOOD — PITCHER WHITE SOX
586 JIM PAGLIARONI — CATCHER A's
587 ROGER REPOZ — OUTFIELD ANGELS
588 DICK SCHOFIELD — INFIELD CARDS

589 1968 ROOKIE STARS TWINS — MOE OGIER • P / RON CLARK • 3B
590 TOMMY HARPER — OUTFIELD INDIANS
591 DICK NEN — 1st BASE CUBS
592 JOHN BATEMAN — CATCHER HOUSTON
593 LEE STANGE — PITCHER RED SOX
594 PHIL LINZ — INFIELD METS

595 PHIL ORTEGA — PITCHER SENATORS
596 CHARLIE SMITH — 3rd BASE YANKEES
597 BILL McCOOL — PITCHER REDS
598 JERRY MAY — CATCHER PIRATES

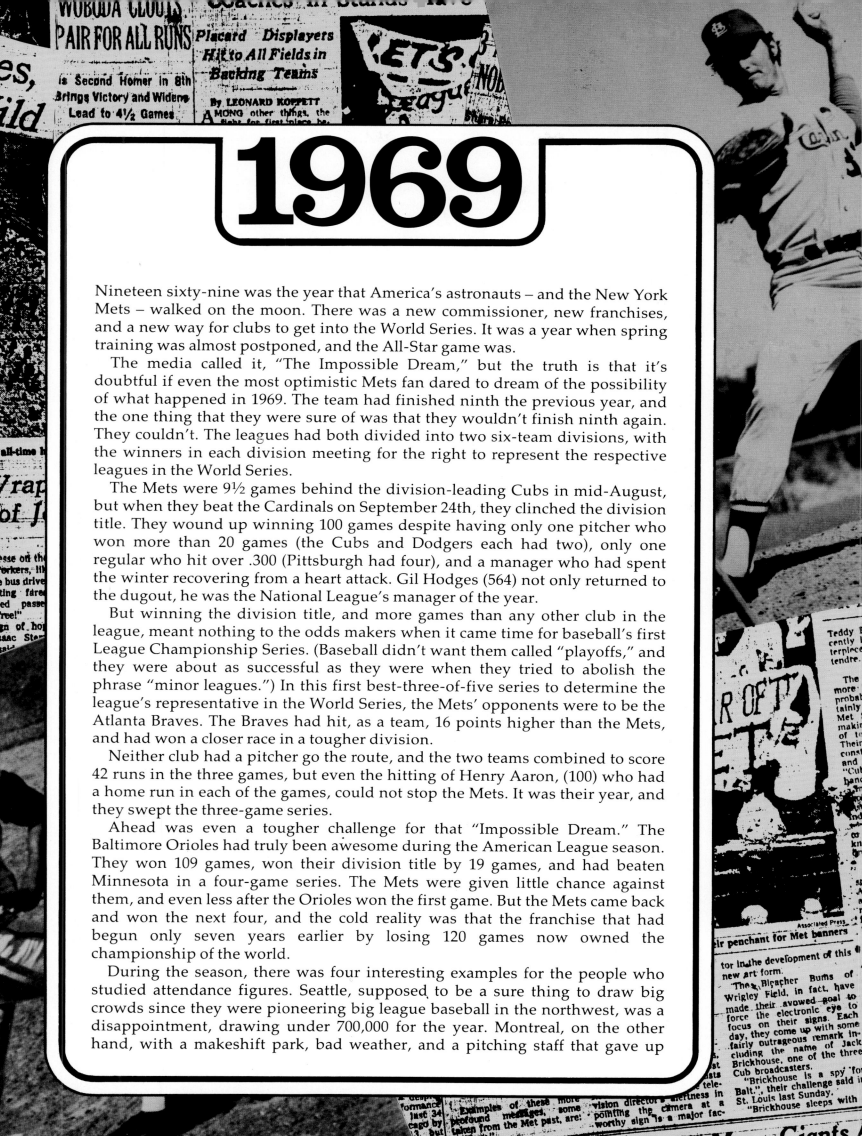

1969

Nineteen sixty-nine was the year that America's astronauts – and the New York Mets – walked on the moon. There was a new commissioner, new franchises, and a new way for clubs to get into the World Series. It was a year when spring training was almost postponed, and the All-Star game was.

The media called it, "The Impossible Dream," but the truth is that it's doubtful if even the most optimistic Mets fan dared to dream of the possibility of what happened in 1969. The team had finished ninth the previous year, and the one thing that they were sure of was that they wouldn't finish ninth again. They couldn't. The leagues had both divided into two six-team divisions, with the winners in each division meeting for the right to represent the respective leagues in the World Series.

The Mets were 9½ games behind the division-leading Cubs in mid-August, but when they beat the Cardinals on September 24th, they clinched the division title. They wound up winning 100 games despite having only one pitcher who won more than 20 games (the Cubs and Dodgers each had two), only one regular who hit over .300 (Pittsburgh had four), and a manager who had spent the winter recovering from a heart attack. Gil Hodges (564) not only returned to the dugout, he was the National League's manager of the year.

But winning the division title, and more games than any other club in the league, meant nothing to the odds makers when it came time for baseball's first League Championship Series. (Baseball didn't want them called "playoffs," and they were about as successful as they were when they tried to abolish the phrase "minor leagues.") In this first best-three-of-five series to determine the league's representative in the World Series, the Mets' opponents were to be the Atlanta Braves. The Braves had hit, as a team, 16 points higher than the Mets, and had won a closer race in a tougher division.

Neither club had a pitcher go the route, and the two teams combined to score 42 runs in the three games, but even the hitting of Henry Aaron, (100) who had a home run in each of the games, could not stop the Mets. It was their year, and they swept the three-game series.

Ahead was even a tougher challenge for that "Impossible Dream." The Baltimore Orioles had truly been awesome during the American League season. They won 109 games, won their division title by 19 games, and had beaten Minnesota in a four-game series. The Mets were given little chance against them, and even less after the Orioles won the first game. But the Mets came back and won the next four, and the cold reality was that the franchise that had begun only seven years earlier by losing 120 games now owned the championship of the world.

During the season, there was four interesting examples for the people who studied attendance figures. Seattle, supposed to be a sure thing to draw big crowds since they were pioneering big league baseball in the northwest, was a disappointment, drawing under 700,000 for the year. Montreal, on the other hand, with a makeshift park, bad weather, and a pitching staff that gave up

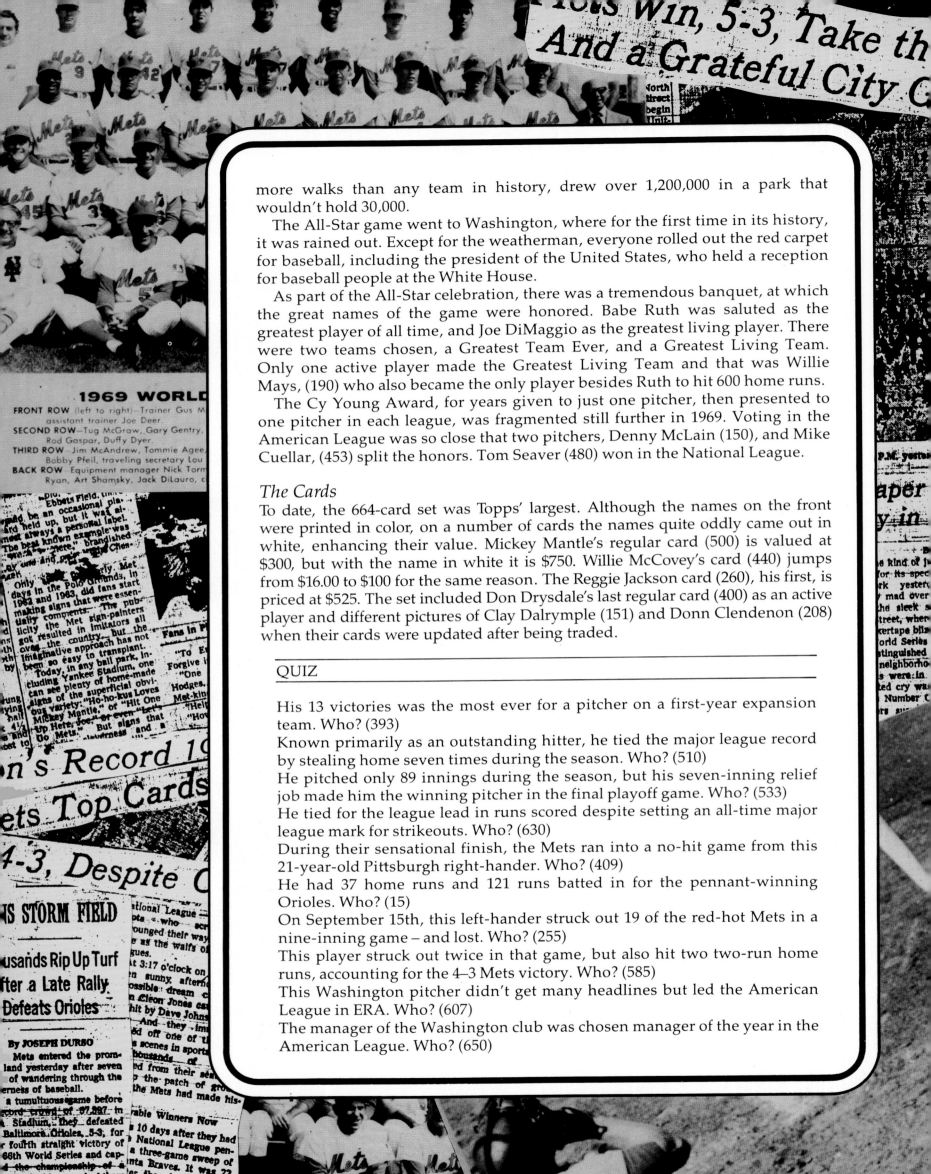

more walks than any team in history, drew over 1,200,000 in a park that wouldn't hold 30,000.

The All-Star game went to Washington, where for the first time in its history, it was rained out. Except for the weatherman, everyone rolled out the red carpet for baseball, including the president of the United States, who held a reception for baseball people at the White House.

As part of the All-Star celebration, there was a tremendous banquet, at which the great names of the game were honored. Babe Ruth was saluted as the greatest player of all time, and Joe DiMaggio as the greatest living player. There were two teams chosen, a Greatest Team Ever, and a Greatest Living Team. Only one active player made the Greatest Living Team and that was Willie Mays, (190) who also became the only player besides Ruth to hit 600 home runs.

The Cy Young Award, for years given to just one pitcher, then presented to one pitcher in each league, was fragmented still further in 1969. Voting in the American League was so close that two pitchers, Denny McLain (150), and Mike Cuellar, (453) split the honors. Tom Seaver (480) won in the National League.

The Cards

To date, the 664-card set was Topps' largest. Although the names on the front were printed in color, on a number of cards the names quite oddly came out in white, enhancing their value. Mickey Mantle's regular card (500) is valued at $300, but with the name in white it is $750. Willie McCovey's card (440) jumps from $16.00 to $100 for the same reason. The Reggie Jackson card (260), his first, is priced at $525. The set included Don Drysdale's last regular card (400) as an active player and different pictures of Clay Dalrymple (151) and Donn Clendenon (208) when their cards were updated after being traded.

QUIZ

His 13 victories was the most ever for a pitcher on a first-year expansion team. Who? (393)

Known primarily as an outstanding hitter, he tied the major league record by stealing home seven times during the season. Who? (510)

He pitched only 89 innings during the season, but his seven-inning relief job made him the winning pitcher in the final playoff game. Who? (533)

He tied for the league lead in runs scored despite setting an all-time major league mark for strikeouts. Who? (630)

During their sensational finish, the Mets ran into a no-hit game from this 21-year-old Pittsburgh right-hander. Who? (409)

He had 37 home runs and 121 runs batted in for the pennant-winning Orioles. Who? (15)

On September 15th, this left-hander struck out 19 of the red-hot Mets in a nine-inning game – and lost. Who? (255)

This player struck out twice in that game, but also hit two two-run home runs, accounting for the 4—3 Mets victory. Who? (585)

This Washington pitcher didn't get many headlines but led the American League in ERA. Who? (607)

The manager of the Washington club was chosen manager of the year in the American League. Who? (650)

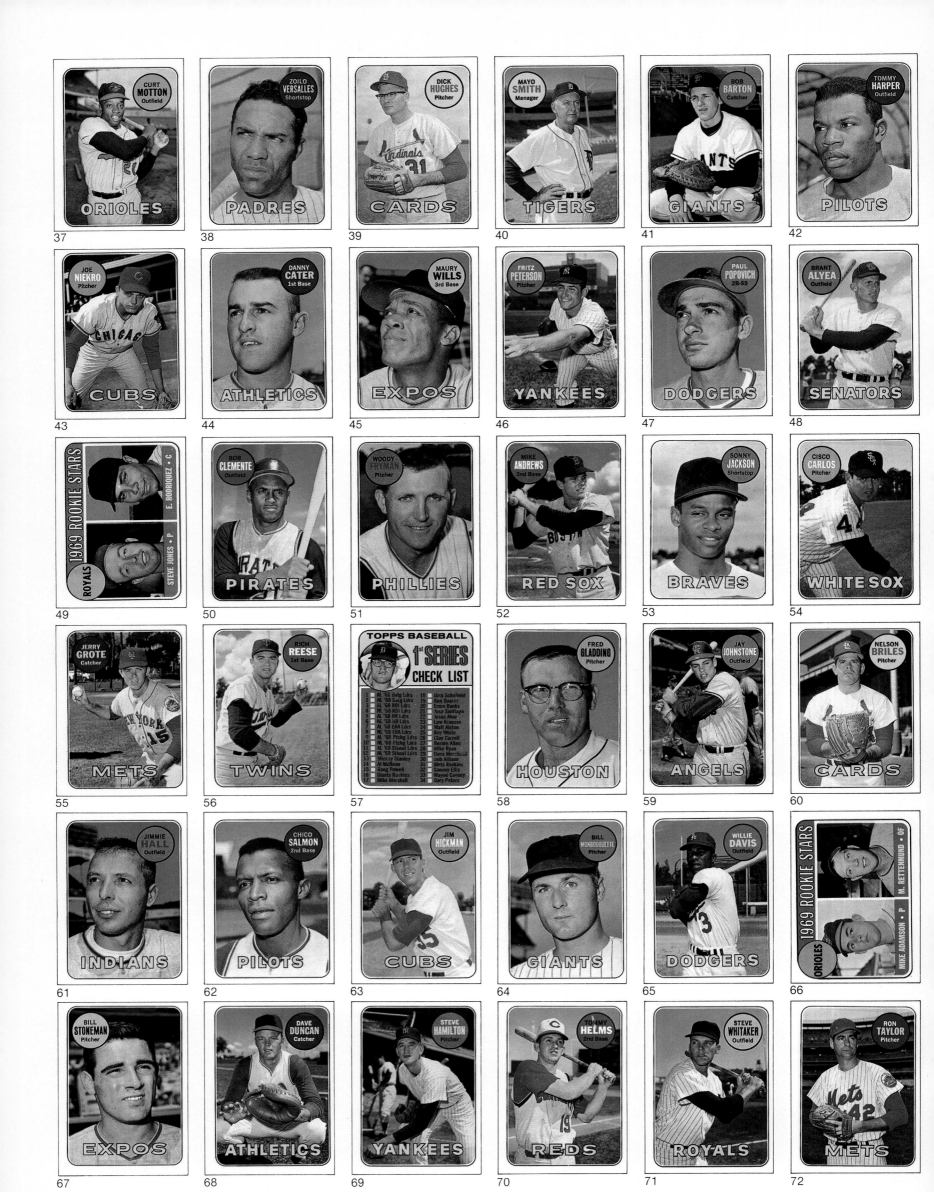

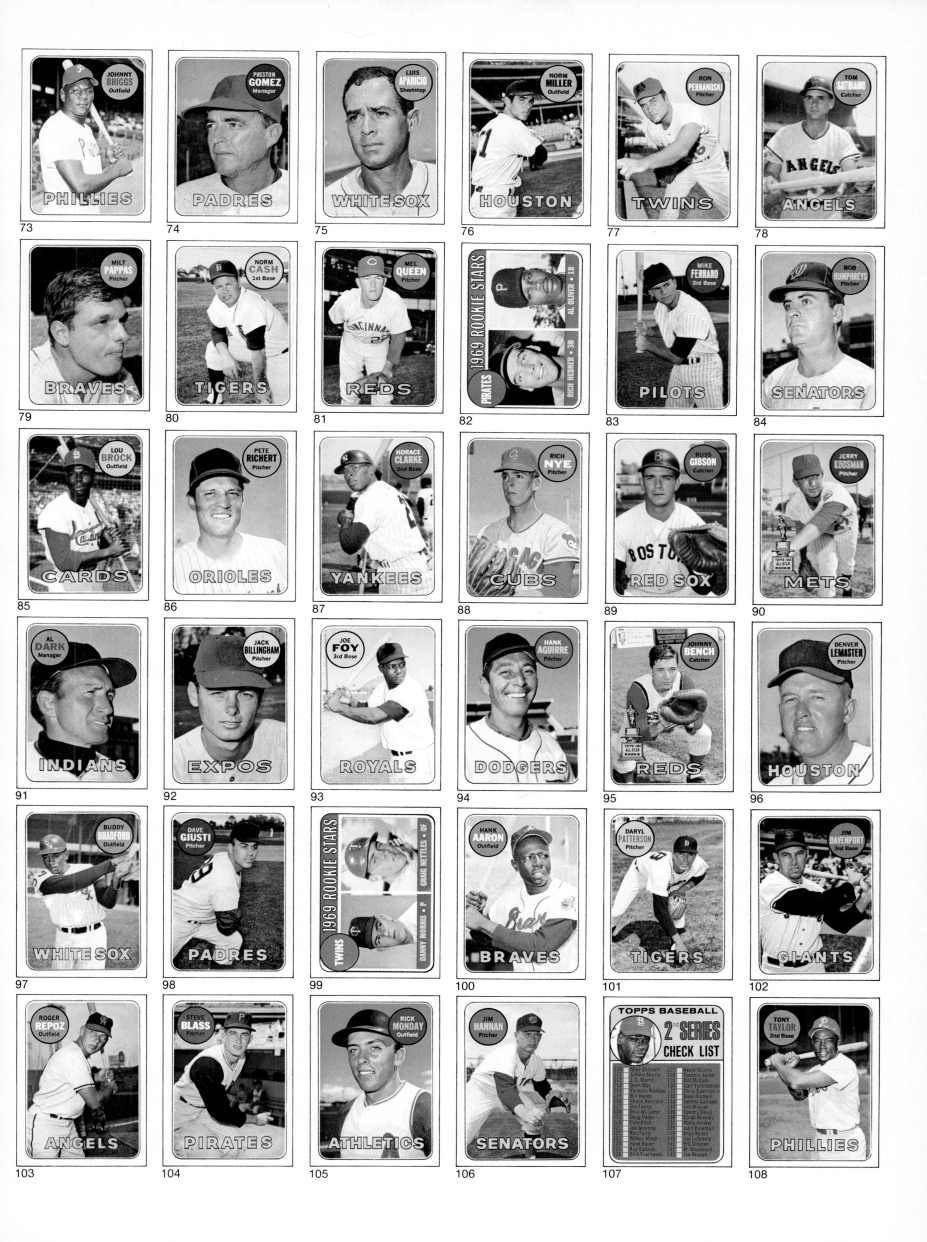

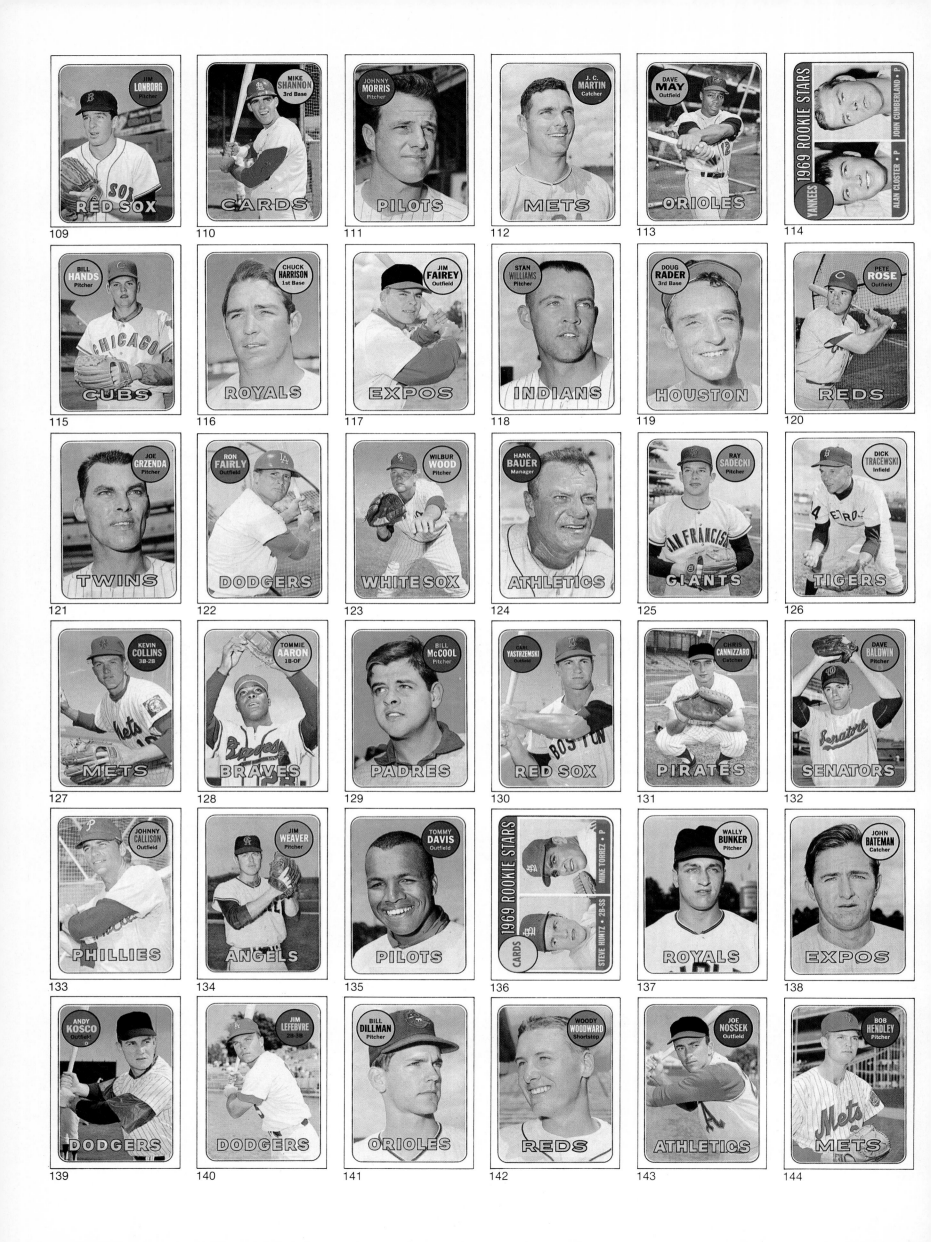

MAX ALVIS
3rd Base
INDIANS
145

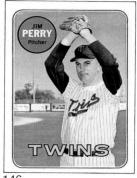
JIM PERRY
Pitcher
TWINS
146

LEO DUROCHER
Manager
CHICAGO
CUBS
147

LEE STANGE
Pitcher
RED SOX
148

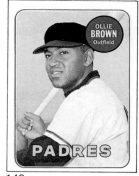
OLLIE BROWN
Outfield
PADRES
149

DENNY McLAIN
Pitcher
TIGERS
150

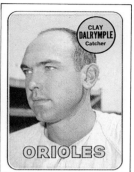
CLAY DALRYMPLE
Catcher
ORIOLES
151

TOMMIE SISK
Pitcher
PIRATES
152

ED BRINKMAN
Shortstop
SENATORS
153

JIM BRITTON
Pitcher
BRAVES
154

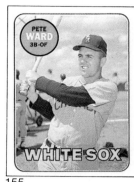
PETE WARD
3B-OF
WHITE SOX
155

1969 ROOKIE STARS
LEON McFADDEN · SS
HAL GILSON · P
HOUSTON
156

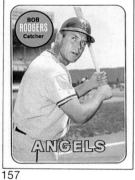
BOB RODGERS
Catcher
ANGELS
157

JOE GIBBON
Pitcher
SAN FRANCISCO
GIANTS
158

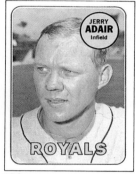
JERRY ADAIR
Infield
ROYALS
159

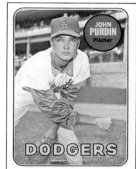
VADA PINSON
Outfield
CARDS
160

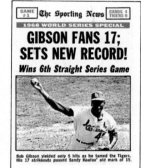
JOHN PURDIN
Pitcher
DODGERS
161

GAME #1 — The Sporting News — CARDS 4 TIGERS 0
1968 WORLD SERIES SPECIAL
GIBSON FANS 17; SETS NEW RECORD!
Wins 6th Straight Series Game
Bob Gibson yielded only 5 hits as he tamed the Tigers. His 17 strikeouts passed Sandy Koufax' old mark of 15.
162

GAME #2 — The Sporting News — TIGERS 8 CARDS 1
1968 WORLD SERIES SPECIAL
TIGER HOMERS DECK THE CARDS
Horton, Cash & Lolich Connect
Willie Horton socked his home run in the 2nd inning. Lolich hit his first homer ever in the next frame.
163

GAME #3 — The Sporting News — CARDS 7 TIGERS 3
1968 WORLD SERIES SPECIAL
McCARVER'S HOMER PUTS ST. LOUIS AHEAD
3-Run Blast Gives Cards Lead
Tim McCarver is greeted by teammates Mike Shannon, Roger Maris and Curt Flood after 5th inning homer.
164

GAME #4 — The Sporting News — CARDS 10 TIGERS 1
1968 WORLD SERIES SPECIAL
BROCK'S LEAD-OFF HR STARTS CARDS' ROMP;
Gibson Wins 7th In A Row
Lou Brock socked Denny McLain's 2nd pitch into seats in first inning, to start a 10-1 St. Louis massacre.
165

GAME #5 — The Sporting News — TIGERS 5 CARDS 3
1968 WORLD SERIES SPECIAL
KALINE'S KEY HIT SPARKS TIGER RALLY
Sends Home Winning Runs In 7th
Al Kaline's single produced the go-ahead runs as Mickey Lolich won his 2nd game of the series for Detroit.
166

GAME #6 — The Sporting News — TIGERS 13 CARDS 1
1968 WORLD SERIES SPECIAL
TIGER 10-RUN INNING TIES MARK
Northrup Hits Grand-Slammer
Jim Northrup's bases loaded home run off Larry Jaster topped 10-run Detroit rally in 3rd inning of Game #6.
167

GAME #7 — The Sporting News — TIGERS 4 CARDS 1
1968 WORLD SERIES SPECIAL
LOLICH SERIES HERO OUTDUELS GIBSON
Mickey Wins His 3rd Game
After six scoreless frames, Mickey and his mates broke through to wrap up the 1968 World Series.
168

★ The Sporting News ★
1968 WORLD SERIES SPECIAL
TIGERS CELEBRATE THEIR VICTORY
Detroit's Heroes Go Wild
Detroit's Dick McAuliffe, Denny McLain and Willie Horton spent happy times after winning 1968 World Series.
169

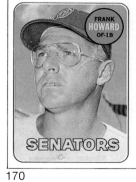
FRANK HOWARD
OF-1B
SENATORS
170

GLENN BECKERT
2nd Base
CUBS
171

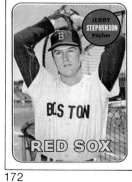
JERRY STEPHENSON
Pitcher
BOSTON
RED SOX
172

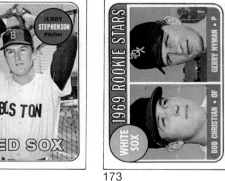
1969 ROOKIE STARS
GERRY NYMAN · P
BOB CHRISTIAN · OF
WHITE SOX
173

GRANT JACKSON
Pitcher
Phillies
PHILLIES
174

JIM BUNNING
Pitcher
PIRATES
175

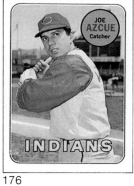
JOE AZCUE
Catcher
INDIANS
176

RON REED
Pitcher
BRAVES
177

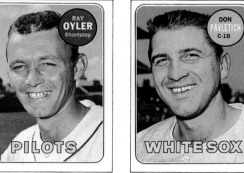
RAY OYLER
Shortstop
PILOTS
178

DON PAVLETICH
C-1B
WHITE SOX
179

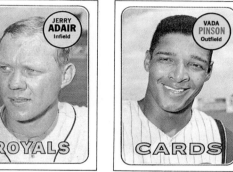
WILLIE HORTON
Outfield
TIGERS
180

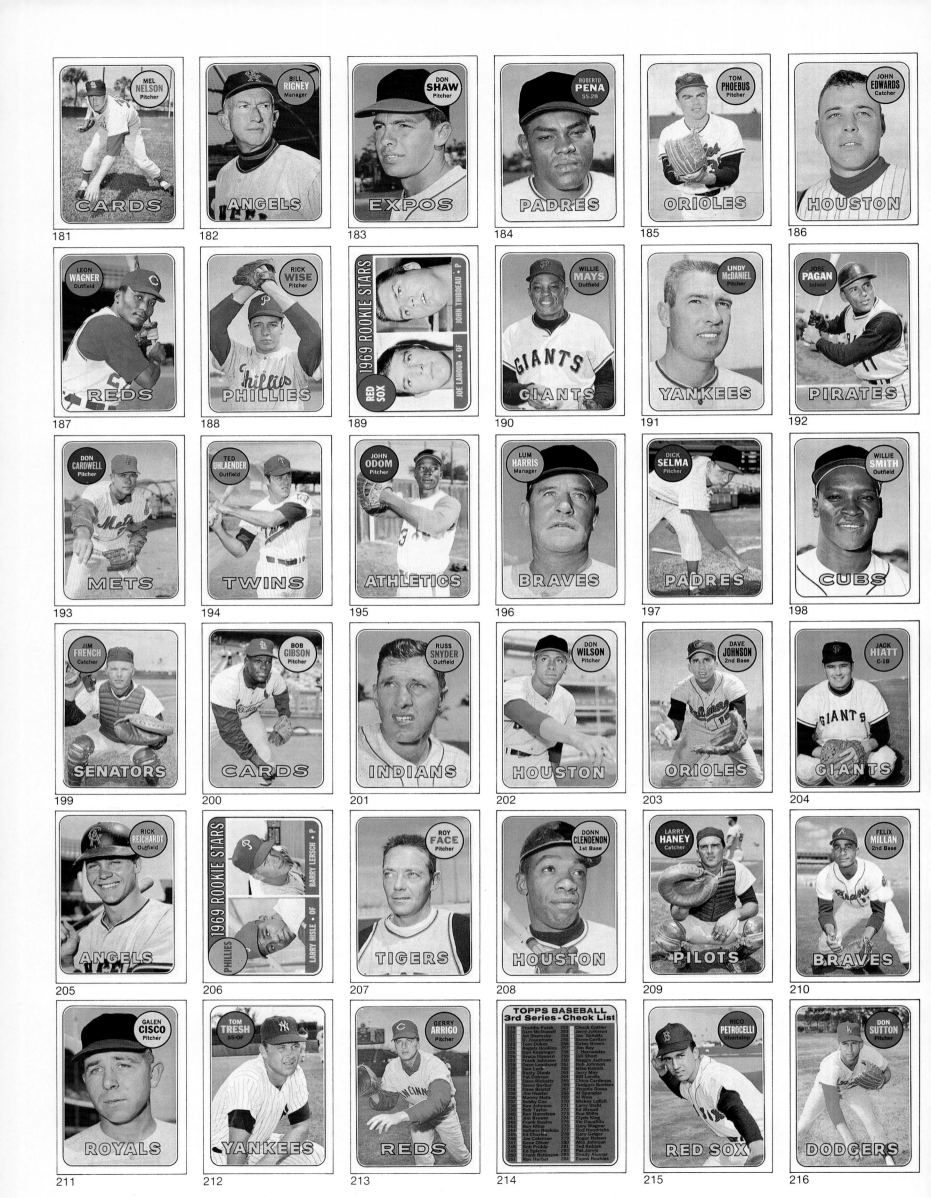

MEL NELSON Pitcher — CARDS — 181

BILL RIGNEY Manager — ANGELS — 182

DON SHAW Pitcher — EXPOS — 183

ROBERTO PENA SS-2B — PADRES — 184

TOM PHOEBUS Pitcher — ORIOLES — 185

JOHN EDWARDS Catcher — HOUSTON — 186

LEON WAGNER Outfield — REDS — 187

RICK WISE Pitcher — PHILLIES — 188

1969 ROOKIE STARS — JOHN THIBDEAU P — JOE LAHOUD OF — RED SOX — 189

WILLIE MAYS Outfield — GIANTS — 190

LINDY McDANIEL Pitcher — YANKEES — 191

JOSE PAGAN Infield — PIRATES — 192

DON CARDWELL Pitcher — METS — 193

TED UHLAENDER Outfield — TWINS — 194

JOHN ODOM Pitcher — ATHLETICS — 195

LUM HARRIS Manager — BRAVES — 196

DICK SELMA Pitcher — PADRES — 197

WILLIE SMITH Outfield — CUBS — 198

JIM FRENCH Catcher — SENATORS — 199

BOB GIBSON Pitcher — CARDS — 200

RUSS SNYDER Outfield — INDIANS — 201

DON WILSON Pitcher — HOUSTON — 202

DAVE JOHNSON 2nd Base — ORIOLES — 203

JACK HIATT C-1B — GIANTS — 204

RICK REICHARDT Outfield — ANGELS — 205

1969 ROOKIE STARS — BARRY LERSCH P — LARRY HISLE OF — PHILLIES — 206

ROY FACE Pitcher — TIGERS — 207

DONN CLENDENON 1st Base — HOUSTON — 208

LARRY HANEY Catcher — PILOTS — 209

FELIX MILLAN 2nd Base — BRAVES — 210

GALEN CISCO Pitcher — ROYALS — 211

TOM TRESH SS-OF — YANKEES — 212

GERRY ARRIGO Pitcher — REDS — 213

TOPPS BASEBALL 3rd Series - Check List — 214

RICO PETROCELLI Shortstop — RED SOX — 215

DON SUTTON Pitcher — DODGERS — 216

217   218   219   220   221   222

223   224   225   226   227   228

229   230   231   232   233   234

235   236   237   238   239   240

241   242   243   244   245   246

247   248   249   250   251   252

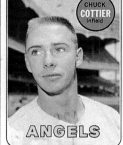

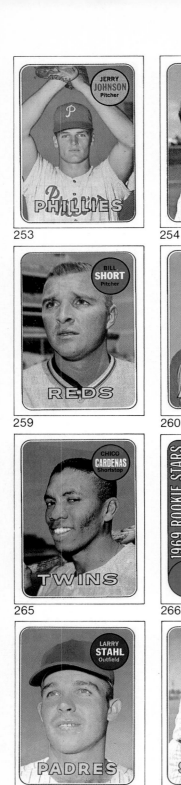

JERRY JOHNSON Pitcher
PHILLIES
253

JOE SCHULTZ Manager
PILOTS
254

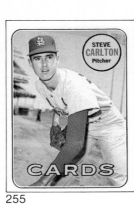
STEVE CARLTON Pitcher
CARDS
255

GATES BROWN Outfield
TIGERS
256

JIM RAY Pitcher
HOUSTON
257

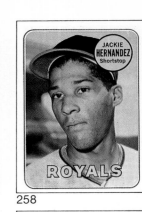
JACKIE HERNANDEZ Shortstop
ROYALS
258

BILL SHORT Pitcher
REDS
259

REGGIE JACKSON Outfield
ATHLETICS
260

BOB JOHNSON Infield
BRAVES
261

MIKE KEKICH Pitcher
YANKEES
262

JERRY MAY Catcher
PIRATES
263

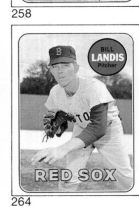
BILL LANDIS Pitcher
RED SOX
264

CHICO CARDENAS Shortstop
TWINS
265

1969 ROOKIE STARS
ALAN FOSTER • P
TOM HUTTON • 1B
DODGERS
266

VICENTE ROMO Pitcher
INDIANS
267

AL SPANGLER Outfield

CUBS
268

AL WEIS 2B-SS
METS
269

MICKEY LOLICH Pitcher
TIGERS
270

LARRY STAHL Outfield
PADRES
271

ED STROUD Outfield

SENATORS
272

RON WILLIS Pitcher

CARDS
273

CLYDE KING Manager
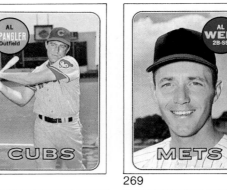
GIANTS
274

VIC DAVALILLO Outfield
ANGELS
275

GARY WAGNER Pitcher

PHILLIES
276

ROD HENDRICKS Catcher
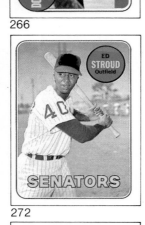
ORIOLES
277

GARY GEIGER Outfield
HOUSTON
278

ROGER NELSON Pitcher

ROYALS
279

ALEX JOHNSON Outfield
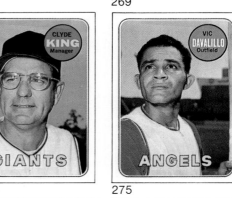
REDS
280

TED KUBIAK Shortstop
ATHLETICS
281

PAT JARVIS Pitcher

BRAVES
282

SANDY ALOMAR 2nd Base

WHITE SOX
283

1969 ROOKIE STARS
MIKE WEGENER • P
JERRY ROBERTSON • P
EXPOS
284

DON MINCHER 1st Base

PILOTS
285

DOCK ELLIS Pitcher
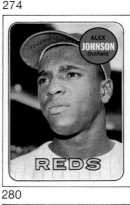
PIRATES
286

JOSE TARTABULL Outfield
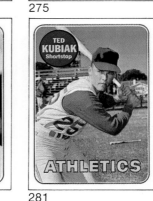
RED SOX
287

KEN HOLTZMAN Pitcher

CUBS
288

325   326   327   328   329   330

331   332   333   334   335   336

337   338   339   340   341   342

343   344   345   346   347   348

349   350   351   352   353   354

355   356   357   358   359   360

361 362 363 364 365 366

367 368 369 370 371 372

373 374 375 376 377 378

379 380 381 382 383 384

385 386 387 388 389 390

391 392 393 394 395 396

397

398

399

400

401

402

403

404

405

406

407

408

409

410

411

412

413

414

415

416

417

418

419

420

421

422

423

424

425

426

427

428

429

430

431

432

433

434

435

436

437

438

439

440

441

442

443

444

445

446

447

448

449

450

451

452

453

454

455

456

457

458

459

460

461

462

463

464

465

466

467

468

505

506

507

508

509

510

511

512

513

514

515

516

517

518

519

520

521

522

523

524

525

526

527

528

529

530

531

532

533

534

535

536

537

538

539

540

577 MIKE HEGAN 1B-OF PILOTS

578 DON BOSCH Outfield EXPOS

579 DAVE NELSON 2nd Base INDIANS

580 JIM NORTHRUP Outfield TIGERS

581 GARY NOLAN Pitcher REDS

582 TOPPS BASEBALL 7th SERIES CHECK LIST

589 Joe Pepitone	605 Dick Ellsworth
590 Rico Carty	606 Gene Mauch
591 Mike Hedlund	607 Dick Bosman
592 Padres Rookies	608 Dick Simpson
593 Don Nottebart	609 Phil Gagliano
594 Dooley Womack	610 Jim Hardin
595 Lee Maye	611 Braves Rookies
596 C. Hartenstein	612 Jack Aker
597 A.L. Rookies	613 Jim Beauchamp
598 Ruben Amaro	614 Houston Rookies
599 John Boozer	615 Len Gabrielson
600 Tony Oliva	616 Don McMahon
601 Tug McGraw	617 Jesse Gonder
602 Cubs Rookies	618 Ramon Webster
603 Joe Keough	619 Royals Rookies
604 Bobby Etheridge	620 Dean Chance

583 CLYDE WRIGHT Pitcher ANGELS

584 DON MASON Infield GIANTS

585 RON SWOBODA Outfield METS

586 TIM CULLEN 2B-SS SENATORS

587 JOE RUDI Outfield ATHLETICS

588 BILL WHITE 1st Base CARDS

589 JOE PEPITONE 1st Base YANKEES

590 RICO CARTY Outfield BRAVES

591 MIKE HEDLUND Pitcher ROYALS

592 1969 ROOKIE STARS PADRES AL SANTORINI P RAFAEL ROBLES SS

593 DON NOTTEBART Pitcher CUBS

594 DOOLEY WOMACK Pitcher HOUSTON

595 LEE MAYE Outfield INDIANS

596 CHUCK HARTENSTEIN Pitcher PIRATES

597 1969 ROOKIE STARS AMERICAN LEAGUE ROLLIE FINGERS LARRY BURCHART BOB FLOYD

598 RUBEN AMARO SS-1B ANGELS

599 JOHN BOOZER Pitcher PHILLIES

600 TONY OLIVA Outfield TWINS

601 TUG McGRAW Pitcher METS

602 1969 ROOKIE STARS CUBS JIM QUALLS DON YOUNG ALEC DISTASO

603 JOE KEOUGH Outfield ROYALS

604 BOBBY ETHERIDGE 3rd Base GIANTS

605 DICK ELLSWORTH Pitcher INDIANS

606 GENE MAUCH Manager EXPOS

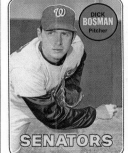

607 DICK BOSMAN Pitcher SENATORS

608 DICK SIMPSON Outfield YANKEES

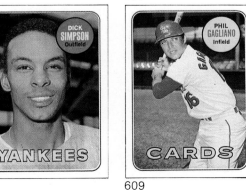

609 PHIL GAGLIANO Infield CARDS

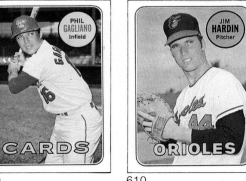

610 JIM HARDIN Pitcher ORIOLES

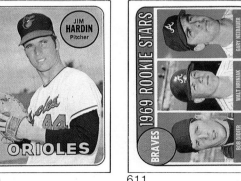

611 1969 ROOKIE STARS BRAVES GARY NEIBAUER WALT HRINIAK BOB DIDIER

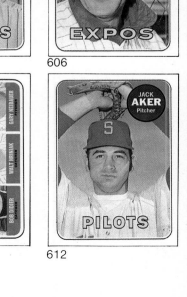

612 JACK AKER Pitcher PILOTS

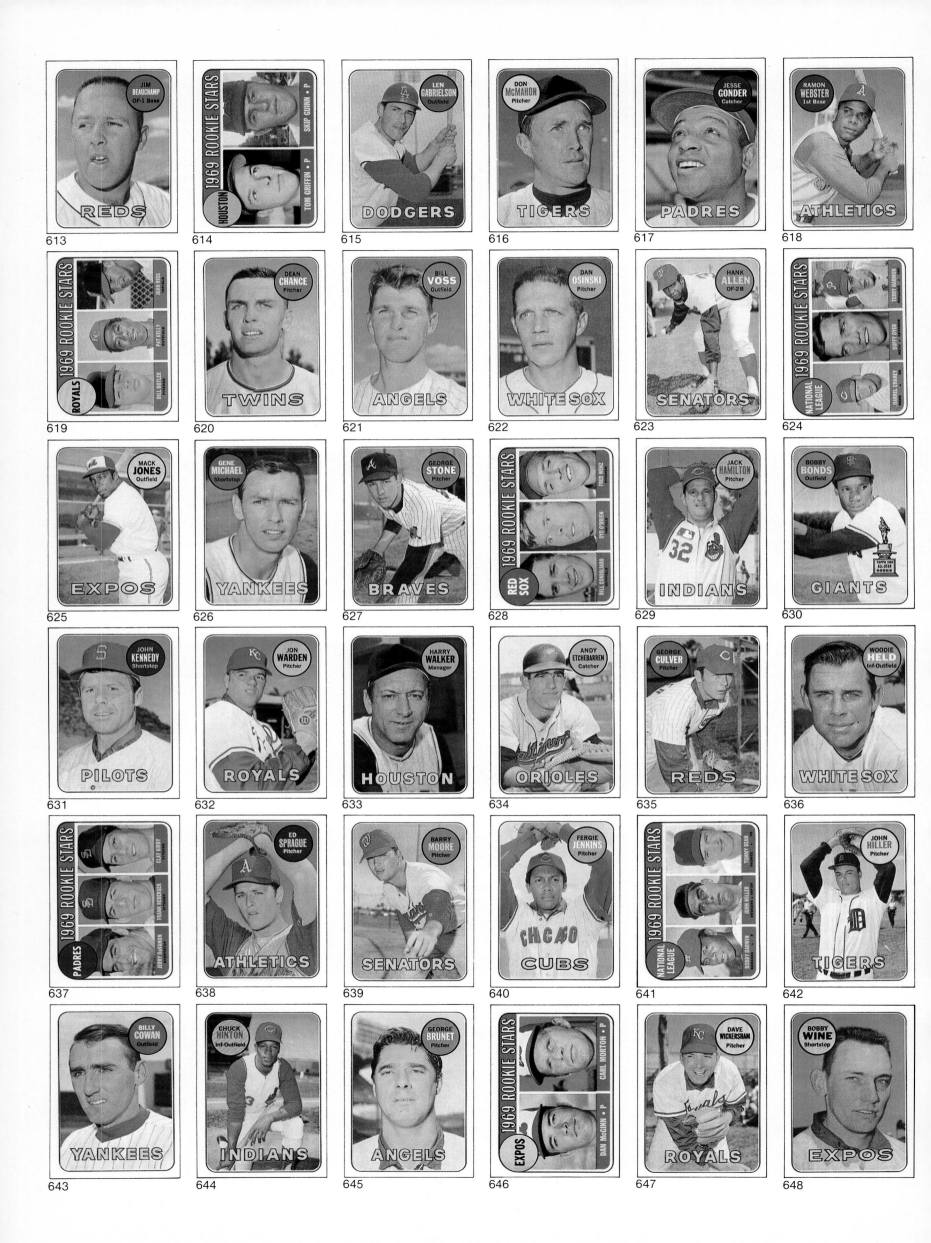

649

650

651

652

653

654

655

656

657

658

659

660

661

662

663

664

AARON, HANK, 60/300, 60/566, 61/43, 61/415, 61/484, 61/577, 62/320, 62/394, 63/1, 63/1, 63/3, 63/242, 63/390, 64/7, 64/9, 64/11, 64/300, 64/423, 65/2, 65/170, 66/215, 66/500, 67/242, 67/244, 67/250, 68/3, 68/5, 68/110, 68/370, 69/100
AARON, TOMMY, 63/46, 64/454, 65/567, 68/394, 69/128
ABARBANEL, MICKEY, 68/287
ABERNATHY, TED, 60/334, 64/64, 65/332, 66/2, 67/597, 68/264, 69/483
ACKER, TOM, 60/274
ACKLEY, FRITZ, 64/368, 65/477
ADAIR, JERRY, 61/71, 62/449, 63/488, 64/22, 65/231, 66/533, 67/484, 68/346, 69/159
ADAMSON, MIKE, 69/66
ADCOCK, JOE, 60/3, 61/245, 62/265, 63/170, 67/563
ADLESH, DAVE, 67/51, 68/576, 69/341
AGEE, TOMMY, 65/166, 66/164, 67/455, 68/465, 69/364
AGUIRRE, HANK, 60/546, 61/324, 62/407, 63/6, 63/257, 64/39, 65/522, 66/113, 67/263, 68/553, 69/94
AKER, JACK, 66/287, 67/110, 68/224, 69/612
ALCARAZ, LUIS, 69/437
ALLEN, BERNIE, 62/596, 63/427, 64/455, 65/237, 66/327, 67/118, 68/548, 69/27
ALLEN, BOB, 61/452, 62/543, 63/266, 64/209, 66/538, 67/24, 68/176
ALLEN, HANK, 67/569, 68/426, 69/623
ALLEN, RICHIE, 64/243, 65/460, 66/80, 67/242, 67/244, 67/309, 67/450, 68/225, 69/6, 69/350
ALLEY, GENE, 64/509, 65/121, 66/336, 67/283, 68/53, 68/368, 69/436
ALLISON, BOB, 60/320, 61/355, 62/180, 63/75, 64/10, 64/290, 65/180, 66/345, 67/194, 67/334, 68/335, 69/30
ALOMAR, SANDY, 65/82, 66/428, 67/561, 68/541, 69/283
ALOU, FELIPE, 60/287, 61/565, 62/133, 63/270, 64/65, 65/383, 66/96, 67/240, 67/530, 68/55, 69/2
ALOU, JESUS, 64/47, 65/545, 66/242, 67/332, 68/452, 69/22
ALOU, MATTY, 61/327, 62/413, 63/128, 64/204, 65/318, 66/94, 67/10, 67/240, 68/1, 68/270, 69/2, 69/490
ALSTON, WALT, 60/212, 61/136, 62/217, 63/154, 64/101, 65/217, 66/116, 67/294, 68/472, 69/24
ALTMAN, GEORGE, 60/259, 61/551, 62/240, 63/357, 64/95, 65/528, 66/146, 67/87
ALUSIK, GEORGE, 62/261, 63/51, 64/431
ALVARES, ROGELIO, 63/158
ALVIS, MAX, 63/228, 64/545, 65/185, 66/415, 67/520, 68/340, 69/145
ALYEA, BRANT, 66/11, 69/48
AMADO, SAMUEL, 62/597, 64/129
AMALFITANO, JOE, 60/356, 61/87, 62/456, 63/199, 64/451, 65/402
AMARO, RUBEN, 61/103, 62/284, 63/455, 64/432, 65/419, 66/186, 67/358, 68/138, 69/598
AMOROS, SANDY, 60/531
ANDERSON, BOB, 60/412, 61/283, 62/557, 63/379
ANDERSON, CRAIG, 62/593, 63/59
ANDERSON, GEORGE, 60/34
ANDERSON, HARRY, 60/285, 61/76
ANDERSON, JOHN, 62/266
ANDREWS, MIKE, 67/314, 68/502, 69/52
ANTONELLI, JOHNNY, 60/80, 60/572, 61/115
APARICIO, LUIS, 60/240, 60/559, 61/440, 61/574, 62/325, 62/469, 63/205, 64/540, 65/410, 66/90, 67/60, 68/310, 69/75
APPLING, LUKE, 60/461
ARCHER, JIM, 61/552
ARCIA, JOSE, 68/258, 69/473A, 69/473B
ARRIGO, GERRY, 64/516, 65/39, 66/357, 67/488, 68/302, 69/213
ARROYO, LUIS, 61/142, 62/455, 63/569
ASHBURN, RICHIE, 60/305, 61/88, 62/213, 63/135
ASPROMONTE, KEN, 60/114, 61/176, 62/563, 63/464, 64/252
ASPROMONTE, BOB, 60/547, 61/396, 62/248, 63/45, 64/467, 65/175, 66/273, 66/352, 67/274, 68/95, 69/542
AUST, DENNIS, 66/179
AVERILL, EARL, 60/39, 61/358, 62/452, 63/139
AVILA, BOBBY, 60/90
AZCUE, JOE, 62/417, 63/501, 64/199, 65/514, 66/452, 67/336, 68/443, 69/176
BAHNSEN, STAN, 67/93, 68/214, 69/380
BAILEY, BOB, 63/228, 64/91, 65/412, 66/485, 67/32, 68/580, 69/399
BAILEY, ED, 60/411, 61/418, 62/459, 63/368, 64/437, 65/559, 66/246
BAKENHASTER, DAVE, 64/479
BAKER, DEL, 60/456
BAKER, GENE, 60/539, 61/339
BALDSCHUN, JACK, 62/46, 63/341, 64/520, 65/555, 66/272, 67/114
BALDWIN, DAVE, 68/231, 69/132
BALES, WES, 67/51
BANDO, SAL, 67/33, 68/146, 69/371, 69/556
BANKS, ERNIE, 60/10, 60/560, 61/43, 61/350, 61/485, 61/575, 62/25, 63/3, 63/242, 63/380, 64/55, 65/510, 66/110, 67/215, 68/355, 69/6, 69/20
BANKS, GEORGE, 63/564, 64/223, 65/348, 66/488
BARBER, STEVE, 60/514, 61/125, 62/57, 62/355, 63/12, 64/450, 65/113, 66/477, 67/82, 68/316, 69/233
BARBIERI, JIM, 67/76
BARKER, RAY, 61/428, 65/546, 66/323, 67/583
BARNES, FRANK, 60/538
BARNOWSKI, ED, 66/442, 67/507
BARRAGAN, CUNO, 62/66, 63/557
BARTON, BOB, 66/511, 67/462, 68/351, 69/41
BASS, NORM, 62/122, 63/461
BATEMAN, JOHN, 63/386, 64/142, 65/433, 66/86, 67/231, 68/592, 69/138
BATTEY, EARL, 60/328, 61/315, 61/582, 62/371, 63/306, 63/410, 64/90, 65/490, 66/240, 67/15
BAUER, HANK, 60/262, 61/119, 61/398, 62/127, 62/463, 64/178, 65/323, 66/229, 67/1, 67/534, 68/513, 69/124
BAUMANN, FRANK, 60/306, 61/46, 61/550, 62/161, 63/381, 64/453, 65/161
BAUMER, JIM, 61/292
BAUTA, ED, 62/344, 63/336
BAXES, JIM, 60/318
BEARNARTH, LARRY, 63/386, 64/527, 65/258, 66/464
BEAUCHAMPS, JIM, 64/492, 65/409, 66/84, 67/307, 69/613
BECK, RICH, 66/234
BECKER, JOE, 60/463
BECKERT, GLENN, 65/549, 66/232, 67/296, 69/171
BECQUER, JULIO, 60/271, 61/329
BEDELL, HOWIE, 61/353, 62/76
BELANGER, MARK, 67/558, 68/118, 69/299
BELINSKY, BO, 62/592, 63/33, 64/315, 65/225, 66/506, 67/447, 69/366
BELL, GARY, 60/441, 61/274, 62/273, 63/129, 64/234, 65/424, 66/525, 67/479, 68/43, 69/377
BELL, GUS, 60/235, 60/352, 61/25, 61/215, 62/408, 63/547, 64/534
BENCH, JOHNNY, 68/247, 69/95, 69/430
BENNETT, DAVE, 64/561, 65/521
BENNETT, DENNIS, 63/56, 64/396, 65/147, 66/491, 67/206
BERBERET, LOU, 60/6
BERRA, YOGI, 60/480, 61/425, 61/472, 62/360, 63/340, 64/21, 65/470
BERRES, RAY, 60/458
BERRY, KEN, 65/368, 66/127, 67/67, 68/485, 69/494
BERTAINA, FRANK, 65/396, 66/579, 68/131, 69/554
BERTELL, DICK, 61/441, 63/287, 64/424, 65/27, 66/587
BERTOIA, RENO, 60/297, 61/392
BETHKE, JIM, 65/533
BEVAN, AL, 61/456
BILKO, STEVE, 60/396, 61/184, 62/422
BILLINGHAM, JACK, 68/228, 69/92
BLACKBURN, RON, 60/209
BLAIR, PAUL, 65/473, 66/48, 67/319, 68/135, 69/506
BLANCHARD, JOHN, 60/283, 61/104, 62/93, 63/555, 64/118, 65/388, 66/268
BLANCO, GIL, 65/566, 67/303
BLASINGAME, DON, 60/397, 61/294, 62/103, 63/518, 64/327, 65/21, 65/44, 67/119
BLASINGAME, WADE, 66/355, 68/507, 69/308
BLASS, STEVE, 65/232, 66/344, 67/562, 68/499, 69/104
BLEFARY, CURT, 65/49, 66/460, 67/180, 67/521, 68/312, 69/458
BLOOMFIELD, BUD, 64/532
BOCCABELLA, JOHN, 64/192, 66/482, 67/578, 68/542, 69/466
BOEHMER, LEN, 69/519
BOLES, CARL, 63/428
BOLIN, BOB, 61/449, 62/329, 63/106, 64/374, 65/341, 66/61, 67/252, 68/169, 69/8, 69/505A, 69/505B
BOLLING, FRANK, 60/482, 61/335, 62/130, 62/211, 63/570, 64/115, 65/269
BOLLO, GREG, 65/541, 66/301
BOND, WALT, 60/552, 61/334, 63/493, 64/339, 65/109, 66/431, 67/224
BONDS, BOBBY, 69/630
BONIKOWSKI, JOE, 62/592
BOONE, RAY, 60/281
BOOZER, JOHN, 63/29A, 63/29B, 64/16, 65/184, 66/324, 68/173, 69/599
BORK, FRANK, 65/592, 66/123
BORLAND, TOM, 60/117, 61/419
BOROS, STEVE, 61/348, 62/62, 62/72, 63/532, 64/131, 65/102
BOSCH, DON, 68/572, 69/578
BOSMAN, DICK, 67/459, 68/442, 69/607
BOSWELL, DAVE, 67/575, 68/322, 69/459
BOSWELL, KEN, 69/402
BOUCHEE, ED, 60/347, 61/196, 62/497
BOULDIN, CARL, 63/496, 64/518
BOUTON, JIM, 62/592, 63/401, 64/4, 64/219, 64/470, 65/30, 66/276, 67/393, 68/562
BOWENS, SAM, 64/201, 65/188, 66/412, 67/491, 68/82
BOWMAN, ERNIE, 63/61, 66/302
BOWSFIELD, TED, 60/382, 61/216, 62/369, 63/339, 64/447
BOYD, BOB, 60/207, 61/199
BOYER, CLETE, 60/109, 61/19, 62/163, 62/490, 63/361, 64/69, 65/475, 66/9, 67/328, 68/550, 69/489
BOYER, KEN, 60/160, 60/485, 61/43, 61/375, 61/573, 62/52, 62/370, 62/392, 63/375, 64/11, 64/160, 65/6, 65/100, 66/385, 67/105, 68/259, 69/379
BRABENDER, GENE, 66/579, 67/22, 68/163, 69/393
BRADFORD, BUDDY, 68/142, 69/97
BRAGAN, BOBBY, 60/463, 63/73, 64/506, 65/346, 66/476
BRAND, RON, 64/326, 65/212, 66/394, 68/317, 69/549
BRANDON, DARRELL, 66/456, 67/117, 68/26, 69/301
BRANDT, JACKIE, 60/53, 61/515, 62/165, 63/65, 64/399, 65/33, 66/383, 67/142
BRAUN, JOHN, 65/82
BRECHEEN, HARRY, 60/455
BREEDEN, DANNY, 69/536
BREEDING, MARV, 60/525, 61/321, 62/6, 63/149
BRESSOUD, EDDIE, 60/253, 61/203, 62/504, 63/188, 64/352, 65/525, 66/516, 67/121
BRETT, KEN, 69/476A, 69/476B
BREWER, JIM, 62/191, 63/309, 64/553, 65/416, 66/158, 67/31, 68/298, 69/241
BREWER, TOM, 60/439, 61/317, 61/434
BRICKELL, FRITZ, 61/333
BRIDGES, ROCKY, 60/22, 61/508
BRIGGS, JOHN, 60/376, 64/482, 65/163, 66/359, 67/268, 68/284, 69/73
BRIGHT, HARRY, 60/277, 61/447, 62/551, 63/304, 64/259, 65/584
BRILES, NELSON, 65/431, 66/243, 67/404, 68/540, 69/60
BRINKMAN, ED, 63/479, 64/46, 65/417, 66/251, 67/311, 68/49A, 68/49B, 69/153
BRISTOL, DAVE, 67/21, 68/148, 69/234
BRITTON, JIM, 64/94, 68/76, 69/154
BROCK, LOU, 62/387, 63/472, 64/29, 65/540, 66/125, 67/63, 67/285, 68/372, 68/520, 69/85, 69/428
BROGLIO, ERNIE, 60/16, 61/45, 61/47, 61/49, 61/420, 61/451, 62/507, 63/131, 64/59, 65/565, 66/423
BROSNAN, JIM, 60/449, 61/513, 62/2, 63/116
BROWN, DICK, 60/256, 61/192, 62/438, 63/112
BROWN, GATES, 64/471, 65/19, 66/362, 67/134, 68/583, 69/256
BROWN, HAL, 60/89, 61/46, 61/218, 62/488, 63/289, 64/56
BROWN, LARRY, 64/301, 65/468, 66/16, 67/145, 68/197, 69/503
BROWN, OLLIE, 66/524, 67/83, 68/223, 69/149
BROWN, PAUL, 62/181, 63/478, 64/319
BROWN, TOM, 64/311
BROWN, WINSTON, 61/391
BROWNE, BYRON, 66/139, 67/439, 68/296
BRUBAKER, BRUCE, 65/493, 67/276
BRUCE, BOB, 60/118, 61/83, 62/419, 63/24, 64/282, 65/240, 66/64, 67/417
BRUMLEY, MIKE, 64/167, 65/523, 66/29
BRUNET, GEORGE, 63/538, 64/322, 65/242, 66/393, 67/122, 68/347, 69/645
BRUTON, BILL, 60/37, 61/251, 62/335, 63/437, 64/98
BRYAN, BILLY, 63/236, 65/51, 66/332, 67/601, 68/498
BRYANT, DON, 69/400
BUCHEK, JERRY, 62/439, 64/314, 65/397, 66/454, 67/574, 68/277
BUDDIN, DON, 60/520, 61/99, 62/332
BUFORD, DON, 64/368, 65/81, 66/465, 67/143, 67/232, 68/194, 69/478
BUHL, BOB, 60/230, 60/374, 61/145, 62/458A, 62/458B, 63/175, 64/96, 65/264, 66/185, 67/68
BUNKER, WALLY, 64/201, 65/9, 65/290, 66/499, 67/585, 68/489, 69/137
BUNNING, JIM, 60/502, 61/46, 61/50, 61/490, 62/57, 62/59, 62/460, 63/8, 63/10, 63/218, 63/365, 64/6, 64/265, 65/20, 66/435, 67/238, 67/560, 68/7, 68/9, 68/11, 68/215, 69/175
BURBACH, BILL, 69/658
BURCHART, LARRY, 69/597
BURDA, BOB, 69/392
BURDETTE, FRED, 64/408
BURDETTE, LOU, 60/70, 60/230, 61/47, 61/320, 62/380, 63/429, 64/523, 65/64, 66/299, 67/265
BURGESS, SMOKEY, 60/393, 61/461, 62/388, 63/18, 63/425, 64/37, 65/198, 66/354, 67/506
BURGMEIER, TOM, 69/558
BURKE, LEO, 63/249, 64/557, 65/202
BURNSIDE, PETE, 60/261, 61/507, 62/207, 63/19
BURRIGHT, LARRY, 62/348, 63/174
BURTON, ELLIS, 60/446, 63/262, 64/269
BURWELL, BILL, 60/467
BUSBY, JIM, 60/232
BUSCHHORN, DON, 65/577
BUTLER, BILL, 69/619
BUTLER, CECIL, 62/239, 63/201
BUTTERS, TOM, 63/299, 64/74, 65/246
BUZHARDT, JOHN, 60/549, 61/3, 62/555, 63/35, 64/323, 65/458, 66/245, 67/178, 68/403
BYERLY, BUD, 60/371
CAIN, LES, 69/324
CALLISON, JOHNNY, 60/17, 61/468, 62/17, 63/434, 64/135, 65/4, 65/310, 66/52, 66/230, 67/85, 67/309, 68/415, 69/133
CALMUS, DICK, 64/231, 68/427
CAMILLI, DOUG, 62/594, 63/196, 64/249, 65/77, 66/593, 67/551
CAMPANELLA, ROY, 61/480
CAMPANERIS, BERT, 65/266, 66/175, 67/515, 68/109, 69/423, 69/495, 69/556
CAMPANIS, JIM, 67/12, 68/281, 69/396
CAMPBELL, DAVE, 69/324
CAMPBELL, JIM, 63/373, 64/303
CAMPBELL, RON, 67/497
CANNIZZARO, CHRIS, 61/118, 62/26, 65/61, 66/497, 69/131
CARDENAL, JOSE, 65/374, 66/505, 67/193, 68/102, 69/325
CARDENAS, CHICO, 60/119, 61/244, 62/381, 63/203, 64/72, 65/437, 66/370, 67/325, 68/23, 68/480, 69/265
CARDINAL, RANDY, 63/562
CARDWELL, DON, 60/384, 61/393, 61/564, 62/495, 63/575, 64/417, 65/502, 66/235, 67/555, 68/437, 69/193
CAREW, ROD, 67/596, 68/80, 68/363, 69/419, 69/510
CAREY, ANDY, 60/196, 61/518, 62/418
CARLOS, CISCO, 68/287, 69/54
CARLTON, STEVE, 65/477, 67/146, 69/255
CARMEL, DUKE, 60/120, 63/544, 64/44, 65/261
CARPIN, FRANK, 66/71
CARREON, CAMILO, 60/121, 61/509, 62/178, 63/308, 64/421, 65/578, 66/513
CARROLL, CLAY, 65/461, 66/307, 67/219, 68/412, 69/26
CARTER, DICK, 60/466
CARTY, RICO, 64/476, 65/2, 65/305, 66/153, 67/35, 67/240, 68/455, 69/590
CASALE, JERRY, 60/38, 61/195
CASANOVA, PAUL, 67/115, 68/560, 69/486A, 69/486B
CASH, NORM, 60/488, 61/95, 62/51, 62/250, 62/466, 63/4, 63/445, 64/331, 64/425, 65/153, 66/218, 66/315, 67/216, 67/540, 68/256, 69/80
CATER, DANNY, 64/482, 65/253, 66/398, 67/157, 68/535, 69/1, 69/44, 69/556
CAUSEY, WAYNE, 62/496, 63/539, 64/75, 65/425, 66/366, 67/286, 68/522, 69/33
CECCARELLI, ART, 60/156
CEPEDA, ORLANDO, 60/450, 61/435, 62/40, 62/54, 62/390, 62/401, 63/3, 63/520, 64/9, 64/306, 64/390, 65/4, 65/360, 66/132, 67/20, 68/3, 68/200, 68/362, 69/385
CERV, BOB, 60/415, 61/563, 62/169
CHACON, ELIO, 60/543, 62/256
CHANCE, BOB, 64/146, 65/224, 66/564, 67/349, 69/523
CHANCE, DEAN, 62/194, 63/6, 63/355, 64/32, 65/7, 65/9, 65/11, 65/140, 66/340, 67/380, 68/10, 68/12, 68/255, 69/620
CHANEY, DARREL, 69/624
CHARLES, ED, 62/595, 63/67, 64/475, 65/35, 66/422, 67/182, 68/564
CHARLTON, PETE, 64/459, 66/329
CHAVARRIA, OSSIE, 67/344
CHENEY, TOM, 61/494
CHESBRO WINS 41, 61/407
CHITI, HARRY, 60/339, 61/269, 62/253
CHITTUM, NELSON, 60/296
CHRISLEY, NEIL, 60/273, 62/308
CHRISTIAN, BOB, 69/173
CHRISTOPHER, JOE, 61/82, 63/217, 64/546, 65/495, 66/343
CICOTTE, AL, 60/473, 61/241, 62/126
CIMINO, PETE, 66/563, 67/34, 68/143
CIMOLI, GINO, 60/58, 61/165, 62/402, 63/321, 64/26, 65/569
CIPRIANI, FRANK, 62/333
CISCO, GALEN, 62/301, 63/93, 64/202, 65/364, 67/596, 69/211
CLARK, RON, 67/137, 68/589, 69/561
CLARKE, HORACE, 66/547, 67/169, 68/263, 69/87
CLARY, ELLIS, 60/470
CLEMENS, DOUG, 67/489
CLEMENTE, ROBERTO, 60/326, 61/41, 61/388, 62/10, 62/52, 63/18, 63/540, 64/7,61/388, 62/10, 62/52, 63/18, 63/540, 64/440, 65/2, 65/160, 66/215, 66/300, 67/242, 67/400, 68/1, 68/3, 68/150, 68/374, 68/480, 69/50
CLENDENON, DONN, 62/86, 63/477, 64/163, 65/325, 66/99, 66/375, 67/266, 67/535, 68/343, 69/208A, 69/208B
CLEVENGER, TEX, 60/392, 61/291, 63/457
CLINE, TY, 61/421, 62/362, 63/414, 64/171, 65/63, 66/306, 67/591, 68/469, 69/442
CLINTON, LOU, 60/533, 62/457, 63/96, 64/526, 65/229, 67/426
CLONINGER, TONY, 62/63, 63/367, 64/575, 65/520, 66/10, 66/223, 67/396, 67/490, 68/93, 69/492
CLOSTER, AL, 66/549, 69/114
COATES, JIM, 60/51, 61/531, 62/553, 63/237, 67/401
COGGINS, FRANK, 68/96
COHEN, ANDY, 60/466
COKER, JIM, 60/438, 61/144, 63/456, 64/211, 65/192, 66/292, 67/158
COLAVITO, ROCKY, 60/260, 60/400, 61/44, 61/330, 62/20, 62/314, 62/472, 63/4, 63/240, 64/320, 65/380, 66/150, 66/220, 67/109, 67/580, 68/99
COLBERT, NATE, 66/596, 69/408
COLEMAN, CHOO CHOO (CLARENCE), 61/502 63/27, 64/251
COLEMAN, GORDY, 60/257, 61/194, 62/508, 63/90, 64/577, 65/289, 66/494, 67/61
COLEMAN, JOE, 66/333, 67/167, 68/573, 69/246
COLEMAN, RIP, 60/179
COLLINS, KEVIN, 65/581, 69/127
COLTON, LARRY, 68/348, 69/454A, 69/454B
COMER, WAYNE, 69/346
CONIGLIARO, BILLY, 69/628
CONIGLIARO, TONY, 64/287, 65/55, 66/218, 66/380, 67/280, 68/140, 69/330
CONLEY, GENE, 60/293, 61/193, 62/187, 63/216, 64/571
CONNOLLY, ED, 65/543
CONNORS, BILL, 67/272
CONSOLO, BILLY, 60/508, 61/504
CONSTABLE, JIM, 63/411
COOK, CLIFF, 61/399, 62/41, 63/566
COOMBS, DAN, 65/553, 66/414, 67/464, 68/547, 69/389
COONEY, JOHNNY, 60/458
COOPER, WALKER, 60/462
CORRALES, PAT, 65/107, 66/137, 67/78, 69/382
COSMAN, JIM, 67/384
COTTIER, CHUCK, 60/417, 61/13, 62/27, 63/219, 64/397, 69/252
COUGHTRY, MARLAN, 62/595
COURTNEY, CLINT, 61/342
COVINGTON, WES, 60/158, 61/296, 62/157, 63/529, 64/208, 65/583, 66/52, 66/484
COWAN, BILLY, 64/192, 65/186, 69/643
COX, BOBBY, 69/237
COX, CASEY, 66/549, 67/414, 68/66A, 68/66B, 69/383
CRAFT, HARRY, 62/12, 63/491, 64/298
CRAIG, PETE, 65/466, 66/11, 67/459
CRAIG, ROGER, 60/62, 61/543, 62/183, 63/197, 64/295, 65/411, 66/543
CRANDELL, DEL, 60/170, 60/568, 61/390, 61/583, 62/351, 62/443, 63/460, 64/169, 65/68, 66/339
CRAWFORD, WILLIE, 65/453, 68/417, 69/327

CRIDER, JERRY, 69/491A, 69/491B
CROSETTI, FRANK, 60/465
CROWE, GEORGE, 60/419, 61/52
CUCCINELLO, TONY, 60/458
CUELLAR, MIKE, 60/398, 65/337, 66/566, 67/97, 67/234, 68/274, 69/453, 69/532
CULLEN, JACK, 63/54A, 63/54B, 66/31
CULLEN, TIM, 67/167, 68/209, 69/586
CULP, RAY, 63/29A, 63/29B, 64/412, 65/505, 66/4, 67/168, 68/272, 69/391
CULVER, GEORGE, 65/166, 67/499, 68/319, 69/635
CUMBERLAND, JOHN, 69/114
CUNNINGHAM, JOE, 60/40, 60/562, 61/520, 62/195, 63/100, 64/340, 65/496, 66/531
CURRY, TONY, 60/541, 61/262
CURTIS, JACK, 61/533, 62/372
DABOLL, DENNIS, 65/561
DAILEY, BILL, 63/391, 64/156
DAL CANTON, BRUCE, 69/468A, 69/468B
DALEY, BUD, 60/8, 61/48, 61/422, 62/376, 63/38, 64/164, 65/262
DALEY, PETE, 60/108, 61/158
DALKOWSKI, STEVE, 63/496
DALRYMPLE, CLAY, 60/523, 61/299, 62/434, 63/192, 64/191, 65/372, 66/202, 67/53, 68/567, 69/151A, 69/151B
DANIELS, BENNIE, 60/91, 61/368, 62/378, 63/497, 64/587, 65/129
DARK, ALVIN, 60/472, 61/220, 62/322, 63/258, 64/529, 66/433, 67/389, 68/237, 69/91
DARWIN, BOBBY, 69/641
DAVALILLO, VIC, 63/324, 64/435, 65/128, 66/216, 66/325, 67/69, 68/397, 69/275
DaVANON, JERRY, 69/637
DAVENPORT, JIM, 60/154, 61/55, 62/9, 63/388, 64/82, 65/213, 66/176, 67/441, 68/525, 69/102
DAVIDSON, TED, 65/243, 66/89, 67/519, 68/48
DAVIE, JERRY, 60/301
DAVIS, BILL, 65/546, 66/44, 67/253, 68/432, 69/304
DAVIS, BOB, 61/246
DAVIS, BROCK, 63/553
DAVIS, JACKE, 62/521, 63/117
DAVIS, RON, 67/298, 68/21, 69/553
DAVIS, TOMMY, 60/509, 61/168, 62/358, 63/1, 63/310, 64/7, 64/180, 65/370, 66/75, 67/370, 68/265, 69/135
DAVIS, WILLIE, 61/506, 62/108, 63/229, 64/68, 65/435, 66/535, 67/160, 68/208, 69/65
De La HOZ, MIKE, 61/191, 62/123, 63/561, 64/216, 65/182, 66/346, 67/372
DEAL, COT, 60/459
DEAN, TOMMY, 69/641
DeBUSSCHERE, DAVE, 63/54A, 63/54B, 64/247, 65/297
DEES, CHARLIE, 64/159
DEL GRECO, BOBBY, 60/486, 61/154, 62/548, 63/282
DELOCK, IKE, 60/336, 61/268, 62/201, 63/136
DeMAESTRI, JOE, 60/358, 61/116
DeMERIT, JOHN, 61/501, 62/4
DEMETER, DON, 60/234, 61/23, 62/146, 63/268, 64/58, 65/429, 66/98, 67/572
DENEHY, BILL, 67/581, 68/526
DENNIS, DON, 66/142, 67/259
DICKEY, BILL, 60/465
DICKSON, JIM, 64/524, 65/286, 66/201
DIDIER, BOB, 69/611
DIERKER, LARRY, 65/409, 66/228, 67/498, 68/565, 69/411
DIETZ, DICK, 67/341, 68/104, 69/293
DILLARD, DON, 60/122, 61/172, 63/298
DILLMAN, BILL, 67/558, 68/466, 69/141
DILLON, STEVE, 64/556
DISTASO, ALEC, 69/602
DITMAR, ART, 60/430, 61/46, 61/48, 61/510, 62/246
DOBBECK, DAN, 60/123, 61/108, 62/267
DOBSON, CHUCK, 66/588, 67/438, 68/62, 69/397
DOBSON, PAT, 67/526, 68/22, 69/231
DONALDSON, JOHN, 68/244, 69/217
DONOHUE, JIM, 60/124, 61/151, 62/498
DONOVAN, DICK, 60/199, 61/414, 62/15, 62/55, 63/8, 63/370
DOTTER, GARY, 65/421
DOTTERER, DUTCH, 60/21, 61/332
DOWLING, DAVE, 65/116, 66/482, 67/272
DOWNING, AL, 62/219, 64/86, 64/219, 65/11, 65/598, 66/384, 67/308, 68/105, 69/292
DRABOWSKY, MOE, 60/349, 61/364, 62/331, 64/42, 65/439, 66/291, 67/125, 68/242, 69/508
DRAGO, DICK, 69/662
DRAKE, SAMMY, 62/162
DRESSEN, CHUCK, 60/213, 61/137, 64/443, 65/538, 66/187
DROPO, WALT, 60/79, 61/489
DROTT, DICK, 60/27, 61/231
DRYSDALE, DON, 60/475, 60/570, 61/45, 61/49, 61/260, 62/60, 62/340, 62/398, 63/5, 63/7, 63/9, 63/360, 63/412, 64/5, 64/120, 65/8, 65/12, 65/260, 66/223, 66/430, 67/55, 68/145, 69/400
DUFFALO, JIM, 62/578, 63/567, 64/573, 65/159
DUKES, TOM, 68/128, 69/223
DULIBA, BOB, 60/401, 62/149, 63/97, 64/441, 66/53, 67/599
DUNCAN, DAVE, 64/528, 68/261, 69/68
DUREN, RYNE, 60/204, 61/356, 62/388, 63/17, 64/173, 65/339
DUROCHER, LEO, 67/481, 68/321, 69/147
DUSTAL, BOB, 63/299
DYER, DUFFY, 69/624
DYKES, JIMMY, 60/214, 61/222
EARLEY, ARNOLD, 67/388
EDWARDS, DOC, 62/594, 63/296, 64/174, 65/239
EDWARDS, JOHNNY, 62/302, 63/178, 64/507, 65/418, 66/507, 67/202, 68/558, 69/186
EGAN, DICK, 63/169, 64/572, 66/536, 67/539
EGAN, TOM, 65/486, 66/263, 67/147, 69/407
EILERS, DAVE, 66/534
ELIA, LEE, 66/529, 67/406, 68/561, 69/312
ELLIOT, BOB, 60/215
ELLIOT, LARRY, 63/407, 64/536, 67/23
ELLIS, DOCK, 69/286
ELLIS, SAMMY, 63/29A, 63/29B, 64/33, 65/507, 66/250, 67/176, 68/453, 69/32
ELLSWORTH, DICK, 60/125, 61/427, 62/264, 63/399, 64/1, 64/220, 65/165, 66/447, 67/359, 68/406, 69/605
ELSTON, DON, 60/233, 61/169, 62/446, 63/515, 64/111, 65/436
EPSTEIN, MIKE, 67/204, 68/358, 69/461A, 69/461B, 69/539
ERMER, CAL, 68/206
ESPOSITO, SAMMY, 60/31, 61/323, 62/586, 63/181
ESSEGIAN, CHUCK, 60/166, 61/384, 62/379, 63/103
ESTELLE, DICK, 65/282, 66/373
ESTRADA, CHUCK, 60/126, 61/48, 61/395, 62/560, 63/465, 64/263, 65/378, 67/537
ETCHEBARREN, ANDY, 66/27, 67/457, 68/204, 69/634
ETHERIDGE, BOB, 68/126, 69/604
FACE, ROY, 60/20, 60/115, 61/250, 61/370, 62/210, 62/423, 63/409, 64/539, 65/347, 66/461, 67/49, 68/198, 69/207
FAIREY, JIM, 68/228, 69/117
FAIRLY, RON, 60/321, 61/492, 62/375, 63/105, 64/490, 65/196, 66/330, 67/94, 68/510, 69/122
FANOK, HARRY, 63/54A, 63/54B, 64/262
FARLEY, BOB, 62/426
FARREL, TURK, 65/80, 66/377, 67/190, 68/217
FARRELL, DICK, 60/103, 61/522, 62/304, 63/9, 63/277, 64/560, 69/531
FAUL, BILL, 63/558, 64/236, 66/322
FERNANDEZ, CHICO, 60/314, 61/112, 62/173, 63/278
FERNANDEZ, FRANK, 66/584, 68/214, 69/557
FERRARA, AL, 64/337, 65/331, 66/487, 67/557, 68/34, 69/452A, 69/452B
FERRARO, MIKE, 68/539, 69/83
FERRASE, DON, 60/477, 61/558, 62/547
FERRICK, TOM, 60/461
FINGERS, ROLLIE, 69/597
FIORE, MIKE, 69/376
FISCHER, BILL, 60/76, 61/553, 63/301, 64/409
FISCHER, HANK, 63/554, 64/218, 65/585, 66/381, 67/342
FISHER, EDDIE, 60/23, 61/366, 63/6, 63/223, 64/66, 65/328, 66/85, 66/222, 67/434, 68/418, 69/315
FISHER, FRITZ, 64/312, 66/209
FISHER, JACK, 60/399, 61/463, 62/203, 63/474, 64/422, 65/93, 66/316, 67/533, 68/444, 69/318
FISHER, JERRY, 60/46
FITZGERALD, ED, 60/423
FITZSIMMONS, FRED, 60/462
FLOOD, CURT, 60/274, 61/438, 62/590, 63/505, 64/103, 65/415, 66/60, 67/63, 67/245, 68/180, 69/426, 69/540
FLOYD, BOB, 69/597
FOILES, HANK, 60/77, 61/277, 62/112, 63/326, 64/554
FORD, WHITEY, 60/35, 61/160, 61/586, 62/57, 62/59, 62/310, 62/315, 62/475, 63/6, 63/142, 63/446, 64/4, 64/380, 65/330, 66/160, 67/5
FORNIELES, MIKE, 60/54, 61/113, 62/512, 63/28
FOSNOW, JERRY, 65/529
FOSSE, RAY, 69/244
FOSTER, ALAN, 69/266
FOWLER, ART, 62/128, 63/454A, 63/454B, 64/349
FOX, NELLIE, 60/100, 60/429, 60/555, 61/30, 61/477, 61/570, 62/73, 63/525, 64/81, 64/205, 65/485
FOX, TERRY, 61/458, 62/196, 63/44, 64/387, 65/576, 66/472, 67/181
FOY, JOE, 66/456, 67/331, 68/387, 69/93
FOYTACK, PAUL, 60/364, 61/171, 62/349, 63/327, 64/149
FRANCIS, EARL, 61/54, 62/252, 63/303, 64/117
FRANCONA, TITO, 60/30, 60/260, 61/503, 62/97, 63/248, 63/392, 64/583, 65/256, 66/163, 67/443, 68/527, 69/398
FRANKS, HERMAN, 65/32, 66/537, 67/116, 68/267
FREEHAN, BILL, 63/466, 64/407, 65/390, 66/145, 67/48, 68/375, 68/470, 69/390, 69/431
FREESE, GENE, 60/435, 61/175, 62/205, 63/133, 64/266, 65/492, 66/319
FREGOSI, JIM, 62/209, 63/167, 64/97, 65/210, 66/5, 67/385, 68/170, 68/367, 69/365
FRENCH, JIM, 66/333, 69/199
FRIEND, BOB, 60/437, 61/45, 61/270, 61/585, 62/520, 63/450, 64/1, 64/20, 65/392, 66/519
FRISELLA, DAN, 68/191, 69/343
FRYMAN, WOODY, 66/498, 67/221, 68/112, 69/51
FUENTES, TITO, 66/511, 67/177
FULLER, VERN, 68/71, 69/291
FUNK, FRANK, 61/362, 62/587, 63/476, 64/289
FURILLO, CARL, 60/408
GABRIELSON, LEN, 63/253, 64/198, 65/14, 66/395, 67/469, 68/357, 69/615
GAGLIANO, PHIL, 64/568, 65/503, 66/418, 67/304, 68/479, 69/609
GAGLIANO, RALPH, 65/501
GAINES, JOE, 62/414, 63/319, 64/364, 65/594, 66/122
GARCIA, MIKE, 60/532
GARDNER, BILLY, 60/106, 61/123, 62/163, 62/338, 63/408
GARDNER, ROB, 66/534, 67/217, 68/219
GARRETT, PAT, 66/553
GARRIDO, GIL, 64/452, 69/331
GARVER, NED, 60/471, 61/331
GASTON, CLARENCE, 69/304
GATEWOOD, AUBREY, 64/127, 65/422, 66/42
GEHRIG, LOU, 61/405, 62/140
GEIGER, GARY, 60/184, 61/33, 62/117, 63/513, 64/93, 65/452, 66/286, 67/566, 69/278
GELNAR, JOHN, 65/143, 67/472
GENTILE, JIM, 60/448, 61/559, 62/53, 62/290, 63/4, 63/260, 64/196, 65/365, 66/45
GENTRY, GARY, 69/31
GERNERT, DICK, 60/86, 61/284, 62/536
GIBBON, JOE, 60/512, 61/523, 62/448, 63/101, 64/307, 65/54, 66/457, 67/541, 68/32, 69/158
GIBBS, JAKE, 62/281, 64/281, 65/226, 66/117, 67/375, 68/89, 69/401
GIBSON, BOBBY, 60/73, 61/211, 62/530, 63/5, 63/9, 63/415, 64/460, 65/12, 65/320, 66/225, 67/210, 67/236, 68/100, 68/378, 69/8, 69/10, 69/12, 69/200, 69/432
GIBSON, JOEL, 65/368
GIBSON, RUSS, 67/547, 68/297, 69/89
GIEL, PAUL, 60/526, 61/374
GIGON, NORM, 67/576
GIL, GUS, 67/253, 69/651
GILBERT, BUDDY, 60/359
GILE, DON, 61/236, 62/244
GILLIAM, JIM, 60/255, 61/238, 62/486, 63/80, 64/310
GILSON, HAL, 68/162, 69/156
GINSBERG, JOE, 60/304, 61/79
GIUSTI, DAVE, 62/509, 63/189, 64/354, 65/524, 66/258, 67/318, 68/182, 69/98
GLADDING, FRED, 64/312, 65/37, 66/337, 67/192, 68/423, 69/58
GOLDEN, JIM, 61/298, 62/568, 63/297
GOLDY, PURNELL, 63/516
GOMEZ, PRESTON, 69/74
GOMEZ, RUBEN, 60/82, 61/377, 67/427
GONDER, JESSE, 63/29A, 63/29B, 64/457, 65/423, 66/528, 67/301, 69/617
GONZALES, PEDRO, 63/537, 64/581, 65/97, 66/266, 67/424
GONZALEZ, TONY, 60/518, 61/93, 62/534, 63/32, 64/379, 65/72, 66/478, 67/548, 68/1, 68/245, 69/501A, 69/501B
GOODMAN, BILLY, 60/69, 61/247
GOOSSEN, GREG, 67/287, 68/386
GORDON, JOE, 60/216, 61/224, 69/484
GORYL, JOHN, 62/558, 63/314, 64/194
GOSGER, JIM, 63/553, 66/114, 67/17, 68/343, 69/482A, 69/482B
GOSS, HOWIE, 62/598, 63/364
GOTAY, JULIO, 62/489, 63/122, 65/552, 68/41
GRAMMAS, ALEX, 60/168, 61/64, 62/223, 63/416
GRANGER, WAYNE, 69/551
GRANT, JIM, 60/14, 61/18, 62/307, 63/227, 64/133, 65/432, 66/40, 66/224, 67/545, 68/398, 69/306
GRAY, DAVE, 64/572
GRAY, DICK, 60/24
GRBA, ELI, 60/183, 61/121, 62/96, 63/231
GREEN, DALLAS, 60/366, 61/359, 62/111, 63/91, 64/464, 65/203
GREEN, DICK, 64/466, 65/168, 66/545, 67/54, 68/303, 69/515
GREEN, FRED, 60/272, 61/181
GREEN, GENE, 60/269, 61/206, 62/78, 63/506
GREEN, LENNY, 60/99, 61/4, 62/84, 63/198, 64/386, 65/588, 66/502
GREEN, PUMPSIE, 60/317, 61/454, 62/153, 63/292, 64/442
GRIFFIN, TOM, 69/614
GRIFFITH, DERRELL, 65/112, 66/573, 67/502
GRIGGS, HAL, 60/244
GRILLI, GUIDO, 66/558
GRIM, BOB, 60/78, 62/564
GRIMM, CHARLEY, 60/217
GROAT, DICK, 60/258, 61/1, 61/41, 61/486, 62/270, 63/130, 64/7, 64/40, 65/275, 66/103A, 66/103B, 67/205
GROSS, DON, 60/284
GROTE, JERRY, 64/226, 65/504, 66/328, 67/413, 68/582, 69/55
GROTH, JOHNNY, 60/171
GRUNWALD, AL, 60/427
GRZENDA, JOE, 69/121
GUINDON, BOB, 65/509
GUINN, SKIP, 69/614
GUTIERREZ, CESAR, 69/16
GUTTERIDGE, DON, 60/458
HAAS, BILL, 63/544, 64/398
HADDIX, HARVEY, 60/340, 61/100, 61/410, 62/67, 63/239, 64/439, 65/67
HADLEY, KENT, 60/102
HAGUE, JOE, 69/559
HALE, BOB, 60/309, 61/532
HALL, DICK, 60/308, 61/197, 62/189, 63/526, 67/508, 68/17
HALL, JIMMY, 64/73, 65/580, 66/190, 67/432, 68/121, 69/61
HALL, TOM, 69/658
HALLER, TOM, 62/356, 63/85, 64/485, 65/465, 66/308, 67/64, 67/65, 68/185, 69/310
HAMILTON, JACK, 62/593, 63/132, 65/288, 66/262, 67/2, 68/193, 69/629
HAMILTON, STEVE, 63/171, 64/206, 65/309, 66/503, 67/567, 68/496, 69/69
HAMLIN, KEN, 60/542, 61/263, 62/296, 66/69
HANDS, BILL, 66/392, 67/16, 68/279, 69/115
HANEY, LARRY, 67/507, 68/42, 69/209
HANNAN, JIM, 63/121, 64/261, 65/394, 66/479, 67/291, 69/106
HANSEN, RON, 60/127, 61/240, 62/245, 63/88, 64/384, 65/146, 66/261, 67/9, 68/411, 69/566
HARDER, MEL, 60/460
HARDIN, JIM, 68/222, 69/532, 69/610
HARDY, CARROLL, 60/341, 61/257, 62/101, 63/468
HARGAN, STEVE, 66/508, 67/233, 67/440, 68/35, 69/348
HARKNESS, TIM, 62/404, 63/436, 64/57
HARMON, TERRY, 69/624
HARPER, TOMMY, 64/330, 65/47, 66/214, 67/392, 68/590, 69/42
HARRELL, BILLY, 61/354
HARRELSON, BILL, 69/224
HARRELSON, BUD, 67/306, 68/132, 69/456
HARRELSON, KEN, 64/419, 65/479, 66/55, 67/188, 68/566, 69/3, 69/5, 69/240, 69/417
HARRIS, ALONZO, 67/564, 68/128
HARRIS, BILL, 60/128, 69/569
HARRIS, GAIL, 60/152
HARRIS, LUMAN, 60/455, 65/274, 66/147, 68/439, 69/196
HARRISON, CHUCK, 66/244, 67/8, 69/116
HARSHMAN, JACK, 60/112
HART, JIM RAY, 64/452, 65/4, 65/395, 66/295, 67/220, 68/73, 69/555
HARTENSTEIN, CHUCK, 68/13, 69/596
HARTMAN, BOB, 60/129
HARTMAN, J.C., 63/442
HATTON, GRADY, 66/504, 67/347, 68/392
HAWKINS, WYNN, 60/536, 61/34, 63/334
HEATH, BILL, 66/539, 67/172
HEBNER, RICH, 69/82
HEDLUND, MIKE, 65/546, 69/591
HEFFNER, BOB, 65/199, 66/432
HEFFNER, DON, 60/462, 64/79, 66/269
HEGAN, MIKE, 67/553, 68/402, 69/577
HEIST, AL, 61/302, 62/373
HELD, WOODY, 60/178, 61/60, 62/215, 63/435, 64/105, 65/336, 66/136, 67/251, 68/290, 69/636
HELMS, TOMMY, 65/243, 66/311, 67/505, 68/405, 69/70, 69/418
HEMUS, SOLLY, 60/218, 61/139
HENDERSON, KEN, 65/497, 66/39, 67/383, 68/309
HENDLEY, BOB, 61/372, 62/361, 63/62, 64/189, 65/444, 66/82, 67/256, 68/345, 69/144
HENDRICKS, ELROD, 69/277
HENRY, BILL, 60/524, 61/66, 62/562, 63/378, 64/49, 65/456, 66/115, 67/579, 68/239, 68/384
HEPLER, BILL, 66/574, 67/144
HERBEL, RON, 63/208, 64/47, 65/84, 66/331, 67/156, 68/333, 69/251
HERBERT, RAY, 60/252, 61/498, 62/8, 63/8, 63/560, 64/215, 65/399, 66/121
HERMAN, BILLY, 60/456, 65/251, 66/37
HERNANDEZ, JACKIE, 68/352, 69/258
HERNANDEZ, RAMON, 67/576, 68/382
HERNANDEZ, RUDY, 61/229
HERRERA, FRANK, 60/130, 61/569
HERRERA, JOSE, 69/378
HERRMANN, ED, 69/439
HERRNSTEIN, JOHN, 63/553, 64/243, 65/534, 66/304
HERSHBERGER, MIKE, 62/341, 63/254, 64/465, 65/89, 66/236, 67/323, 68/18, 69/655
HERTZ, STEVE, 64/544
HERZOG, WHITEY, 60/92, 61/106, 62/513, 63/302
HIATT, JACK, 65/497, 66/373, 67/368, 68/419, 69/204
HICKMAN, JIM, 62/598, 63/107, 64/514, 65/114, 66/402, 67/346, 69/63
HICKS, JIM, 67/532, 69/559
HICKS, JOE, 61/386, 62/428
HIGGINS, DENNIS, 66/529, 67/52, 68/509, 69/441A, 69/441B
HIGGINS, MIKE, 61/221, 62/559
HILLER, CHUCK, 61/538, 62/188, 63/145, 63/185, 64/313, 65/531, 66/154, 67/198, 68/461
HILLER, JOHN, 66/209, 68/307, 69/642
HILLMAN, DAVE, 60/68, 61/326, 62/282
HINSLEY, JERRY, 64/567, 65/449
HINTON, CHUCK, 62/347, 63/2, 63/330, 64/52, 65/235, 66/391, 67/189, 68/531, 69/644

HIPPAUF, HERB, 66/518
HISLE, LARRY, 68/579, 69/206
HITCHCOCK, BILLY, 60/461, 62/121, 63/213, 67/199
HOAK, DON, 60/373, 61/230, 62/95, 63/305, 64/254
HOBAUGH, ED, 60/131, 61/129, 62/79, 63/423
HOBBIE, GLEN, 60/182, 61/264, 61/393, 62/585, 63/212, 64/578
HODGES, GIL, 60/295, 61/460, 62/85, 63/68, 63/245, 64/547, 65/99, 66/386, 67/228, 68/27, 69/564
HOEFT, BILLY, 60/369, 61/256, 62/134A, 62/134B, 63/346, 64/551, 65/471, 66/409
HOERNER, JOE, 64/544, 66/544, 67/41, 68/227, 69/522
HOLMAN, GARY, 69/361
HOLTZMAN, KEN, 67/185, 68/60, 68/380, 69/288
HOOK, JAY, 60/187, 61/162, 62/94, 63/469, 64/361
HORLEN, JOE, 62/479, 63/332, 64/584, 65/7, 65/480, 66/560, 67/107, 67/233, 68/8, 68/125, 68/377, 69/328
HORNSBY, 61/404
HORTON, WILLIE, 64/512, 65/206, 66/20, 66/218, 66/220, 67/465, 68/360, 69/5, 69/180, 69/429
HOUK, RALPH, 60/465, 61/133, 62/88, 63/382, 67/468, 68/47, 69/447A, 69/447B
HOUSE, FRANK, 60/372
HOUSE, TOM, 69/331
HOWARD, BRUCE, 64/107, 65/41, 66/281, 67/159, 68/293, 69/226
HOWARD, ELSTON, 60/65, 61/495, 62/51, 62/400, 62/473, 63/60, 63/306, 64/100, 65/1, 65/450, 66/405, 67/25, 68/167
HOWARD, FRANK, 60/132, 61/280, 62/175, 63/123, 64/371, 65/40, 66/515, 67/255, 68/6, 68/320, 69/3, 69/5, 69/170
HOWSER, DICK, 61/416, 62/13, 63/124, 64/478, 65/92, 66/567, 67/411, 68/467
HRINIAK, WALT, 69/611
HUBBS, KEN, 62/461, 63/15, 64/550
HUGHES, DICK, 67/384, 68/253, 69/39
HUMPHREYS, BOB, 65/154, 66/342, 67/478, 68/268, 69/84
HUNDLEY, RANDY, 66/392, 67/106, 68/136, 69/347
HUNT, KEN, 60/522, 61/156, 61/556, 62/68, 62/364, 63/207, 64/294
HUNT, RON, 63/558, 64/235, 65/285, 66/360, 67/525, 68/15, 69/664
HUNTER, JIM, 65/526, 66/36, 67/369, 68/385, 69/235
HUNTZ, STEVE, 69/136
HUTCHINSON, FRED, 60/219, 61/135, 62/172, 63/422, 64/207
HUTTON, TOM, 67/428, 69/266
HYDE, DICK, 60/193
JACKSON, AL, 62/464, 63/111, 64/494, 65/381, 66/206, 67/195, 68/503
JACKSON, GRANT, 66/591, 67/402, 69/174
JACKSON, LARRY, 60/492, 61/75, 61/535, 62/83, 62/306, 63/95, 64/444, 65/10, 65/420, 66/595, 67/229, 68/81
JACKSON, LOU, 64/511
JACKSON, REGGIE, 69/260
JACKSON, RON, 60/426
JACKSON, SONNY, 65/16, 66/244, 67/415, 68/187, 69/53
JAECKEL, PAUL, 65/386
JAMES, CHARLEY, 60/517, 61/561, 62/412, 63/83, 64/357, 65/141
JAMES, JEFF, 69/477
JAMES, JOHNNY, 60/500, 61/457
JARVIS, PAT, 67/57, 68/134, 69/282
JASTER, LARRY, 67/356, 68/117, 69/496
JAVIER, JULIAN, 61/148, 62/118, 63/226, 64/446, 65/447, 66/436, 67/226, 68/25, 69/497
JAVIER, MANUEL, 60/133
JAY, JOEY, 60/266, 61/233, 62/58, 62/263, 62/440, 63/7, 63/225, 64/346, 65/174, 66/406
JENKINS, FERGUSON, 66/254, 67/333, 68/9, 68/11, 68/410, 69/10, 69/12, 69/640
JENSEN, JACKIE, 61/173, 61/476, 61/540
JERNIGAN, PETE, 63/253
JIMENEZ, ELVIO, 65/226, 69/567
JIMENEZ, MANNY, 62/598, 63/195, 64/574, 66/458, 67/586, 68/538
JOHN, TOMMY, 64/146, 65/208, 66/486, 67/609, 68/72, 69/465
JOHNSON, ALEX, 65/352, 66/104A, 66/104B, 67/108, 68/441, 69/280
JOHNSON, BEN, 60/528
JOHNSON, BOB, 62/519, 63/504, 64/304, 65/363, 66/148, 67/38, 68/338, 69/261
JOHNSON, DARRELL, 60/263, 62/16
JOHNSON, DAVE, 65/473, 66/579, 67/363, 68/273
JOHNSON, DERON, 60/134, 61/68, 62/82, 64/449, 65/75, 66/219, 66/440, 67/135, 68/323, 69/297
JOHNSON, ERNIE, 60/228
JOHNSON, FRANK, 69/227
JOHNSON, JERRY, 69/253
JOHNSON, KEN, 60/135, 61/24, 61/401, 62/278, 63/352, 64/158, 65/359, 66/466, 67/101, 68/342, 69/238
JOHNSON, LOU, 60/476, 63/238, 66/13, 67/410, 68/184, 69/367
JOHNSON, OWEN, 66/356
JOHNSTONE, JAY, 67/213, 68/389, 69/59
JONES, CLARENCE, 68/506
JONES, CLEON, 65/308, 66/67, 67/165, 68/254, 69/512
JONES, DALTON, 64/459, 65/178, 66/317, 67/139, 68/106, 69/457
JONES, DEACON, 63/253
JONES, GORDON, 60/98, 61/442
JONES, HAL, 62/49
JONES, MACK, 62/186, 63/137, 65/241, 66/446, 67/435, 68/353, 69/625
JONES, SAM, 60/410, 61/49, 61/555, 62/92
JONES, SHERMAN, 61/161
JONES, STEVE, 69/49A, 69/49B
JONES, WILLIE, 60/289, 61/497
JOSEPH, RICARDO, 68/434, 69/329
JOSEPHSON, DUANE, 67/373, 68/329, 69/222
JOYCE, MIKE, 63/66, 64/477
JURGES, BILLY, 60/220
KAAT, JIM, 60/136, 61/63, 62/21, 63/10, 63/165, 64/567, 66/224, 66/445, 67/235, 67/237, 67/300, 68/450, 69/290
KALINE, AL, 60/50, 60/561, 61/429, 61/580, 62/51, 62/150, 62/470, 63/25, 64/8, 64/250, 64/331, 65/130, 66/410, 67/30, 67/216, 67/239, 68/2, 68/240, 69/410
KANEHL, ROD, 62/597, 63/371, 64/582
KASKO, EDDIE, 60/61, 61/534, 62/193, 63/498
KATT, RAY, 60/468, 65/62
KEALEY, STEVE, 69/224
KEANE, JOHNNY, 60/468, 62/198, 63/166, 64/413, 65/131, 66/296
KEEGAN, BOB, 60/291
KEEGAN, ED, 61/248, 62/249
KEKICH, MIKE, 65/561, 69/262
KELLEY, DICK, 64/476, 66/84, 67/138, 67/214, 68/203, 69/359
KELLEY, TOM, 64/552, 66/44
KELLY, PAT, 69/619
KELSO, BILL, 65/194, 67/367, 68/511
KEMMERER, RUSS, 60/362, 61/56, 62/576, 63/338
KENNEDY, BOB, 65/457, 68/183
KENNEDY, JOHN, 64/203, 64/486, 65/119, 66/407, 67/111, 69/631
KENNEY, GERRY, 69/519
KENWORTHY, DICK, 68/63
KEOUGH, JOE, 69/603
KEOUGH, MARTY, 60/71, 61/146, 62/258, 63/21, 64/166, 65/263, 66/334
KERNEK, GEORGE, 66/544
KESSINGER, DON, 66/24, 68/159, 69/225, 69/422
KIELY, LEO, 60/94
KILKENNY, MIKE, 69/544
KILLEBREW, HARMON, 60/210, 61/80, 62/53, 62/70, 62/316, 63/4, 63/500, 64/10, 64/12, 64/81, 64/177, 65/3, 65/5, 65/400, 66/120, 67/243, 67/334, 67/460, 68/4, 68/6, 68/220, 68/361, 68/490, 69/375
KINDALL, JERRY, 60/444, 61/26, 62/292, 63/36
KING, CLYDE, 69/274
KING, JIM, 61/351, 62/42, 63/176, 64/217, 65/38, 66/369, 67/509
KIPP, FRED, 60/202
KIRBY, CLAY, 69/637
KIRKLAND, WILLIE, 60/172, 61/15, 62/447, 63/187, 64/17, 65/148, 66/434
KIRKPATRICK, ED, 63/386, 64/296, 65/393, 66/102, 67/293, 68/552, 69/529
KLAGES, FRED, 67/373, 68/229
KLAUS, BILLY, 60/406, 61/187, 62/571, 63/551
KLAUS, BOBBY, 64/524, 65/227, 66/108, 69/387
KLEIN, LOU, 60/457
KLESSINGER, DON, 67/419
KLIMCHOCK, LOU, 60/137, 61/462, 62/259, 63/542, 65/542
KLINE, RON, 60/197, 61/127, 62/216, 63/84, 64/358, 65/56, 66/453, 67/133, 68/446, 69/243
KLIPPSTEIN, JOHNNY, 60/191, 61/539, 62/151, 63/571, 64/533, 65/384, 66/493, 67/588
KLUSZEWSKI, TED, 60/505, 61/65
KNOOP, BOBBY, 64/502, 65/26, 66/280, 67/175, 68/271, 69/445
KNOWLES, DAROLD, 64/418, 65/577, 66/27, 67/362, 68/483
KOLB, GARY, 64/119, 65/287, 68/407, 69/307
KOLSTAD, HAL, 62/276, 63/574
KONSTANTY, JIM, 61/479
KOONCE, CAL, 65/34, 66/278, 67/171, 68/486, 69/303
KOOSMAN, JERRY, 68/177, 69/90, 69/434
KOPLITZ, HOWIE, 62/114, 63/406, 64/372, 66/46
KOPPE, JOE, 60/319, 61/179, 62/39, 63/396, 64/279
KORCHECK, STEVE, 60/56
KORINCE, GEORGE, 67/72, 67/526, 68/447
KOSCO, ANDY, 66/264, 67/366, 68/524, 69/139
KOSTRO, FRANK, 63/407, 65/459, 68/44, 69/242
KOUFAX, SANDY, 60/344, 61/49, 61/207, 61/344, 62/5, 62/60, 63/5, 63/9, 63/210, 63/412, 64/1, 64/3, 64/5, 64/200, 65/8, 65/300, 66/100, 66/221, 66/223, 66/225, 67/234, 67/236, 67/238
KRALICK, JACK, 61/36, 62/346, 63/448, 64/338, 65/535, 66/129, 67/316
KRANEPOOL, ED, 63/228, 64/393, 65/144, 66/212, 67/186, 67/452, 68/92, 69/381
KRAUSSE, LEW, 63/104, 64/334, 65/462, 66/256, 67/565, 68/458, 69/23
KRAVITZ, DANNY, 60/238, 61/166
KRESS, RED, 60/460
KREUTZER, FRANK, 64/107, 65/371, 66/211
KROLL, GARY, 65/449, 66/548
KRSNICH, MIKE, 62/289
KRUG, CHRIS, 66/166
KUBEK, TONY, 60/83, 61/265, 62/311, 62/430, 63/20, 64/415, 65/65
KUBIAK, TED, 68/79, 69/281
KUCKS, JOHNNY, 60/177, 61/94, 62/241
KUENN, HARVEY, 60/330, 60/429, 61/500, 62/480, 63/30, 64/242, 65/103, 66/372
KUNKEL, BILL, 61/322, 62/147A, 62/147B, 63/523
KUTYNA, MARTY, 60/516, 61/546, 62/566
LABINE, CLEM, 60/29, 61/22
LABOY, JOSE, 69/524
LACHEMANN, RENE, 65/526, 66/157, 67/471, 68/422
LAHOUD, JOE, 69/189
LAMABE, JACK, 62/593, 63/251, 64/305, 65/88, 66/577, 67/208, 68/311
LANDIS, BILL, 68/189, 69/264
LANDIS, JIM, 60/550, 61/271, 62/540, 63/485, 64/264, 65/376, 66/128, 67/483
LANDRITH, HOBIE, 60/42, 61/114, 63/209
LANDRUM, DON, 61/338, 62/323, 63/113, 64/286, 65/596, 66/43
LANIER, HAL, 65/118, 66/156, 66/271, 67/4, 68/436, 69/316
LARKER, NORM, 60/394, 61/41, 61/130, 62/23, 63/536
LaROSE, VIC, 69/404
LARSEN, DON, 60/353, 61/177, 61/402, 62/33, 63/163, 64/513, 65/389
LaRUSSA, TONY, 64/244, 68/571
LARY, FRANK, 60/85, 61/48, 61/50, 61/243, 62/57, 62/474, 63/140, 63/218, 64/197, 65/127
LASHER, FRED, 68/447, 69/373
LATMAN, BARRY, 60/41, 61/560, 62/37, 62/145, 63/426, 64/227, 65/307, 66/451, 67/28
LAU, CHARLEY, 60/312, 61/261, 62/533, 63/41, 64/229, 65/94, 66/368
LAUZERIQUE, GEORGE, 69/358
LAVAGETTO, COOKIE, 60/221
LAVAGETTO, HARRY, 61/226
LAW, VERN, 60/453, 61/47, 61/250, 61/400, 62/295, 63/184, 64/472, 65/515, 66/15, 66/221, 67/351
LAWRENCE, BROOKS, 60/434
LAZAR, DAN, 69/439
LEE, BOB, 64/502, 65/46, 66/481, 67/313, 68/543
LEE, DON, 60/503, 61/153, 62/166, 63/372, 64/493, 65/595
LEE, MIKE, 60/521
LEEK, GENE, 61/527
LEFEBVRE, JIM, 65/561, 66/57, 67/260, 68/457, 69/140
LeJOHN, DON, 66/41
LEMASTER, DENNY, 63/74, 64/152, 65/441, 66/252, 67/288, 68/491, 69/96
LeMAY, DICK, 62/71, 63/459
LEMON, BOB, 60/460
LEMON, JIM, 60/440, 61/44, 61/450, 62/510, 63/369, 68/341, 69/294
LEONHARD, DAVE, 68/56, 69/228
LEPICO, TED, 60/97, 61/234
LEPPERT, DON, 62/36, 63/243, 64/463
LERSCH, BARRY, 69/206
LEWIS, JOHNNY, 64/479, 65/277, 66/282, 67/91
LILLIS, BOB, 60/354, 61/38, 62/74, 63/119, 64/321
LINDBLAD, PAUL, 66/568, 67/227, 68/127, 69/449
LINES, DICK, 67/273, 68/291
LINZ, PHIL, 62/596, 63/264, 64/344, 65/369, 66/522, 67/14, 68/594
LINZY, FRANK, 65/589, 66/78, 67/279, 68/147, 69/345
LIPSKI, BOB, 63/558
LOCK, DON, 63/47, 64/114, 65/445, 66/165, 67/376, 68/59, 69/229
LOCKE, BOBBY, 60/44, 61/537, 62/359, 65/324, 68/24
LOCKE, RON, 64/556, 65/511
LOCKER, BOB, 65/541, 66/374, 67/338, 68/51, 69/548
LOCKMAN, WHITEY, 60/535
LOCKWOOD, SKIP, 65/526
LOES, BILLY, 60/181, 61/237
LOGAN, JOHNNY, 60/205, 61/524, 62/573, 63/259
LOLICH, MICKEY, 64/128, 65/335, 66/226, 66/455, 67/88, 68/414, 69/270
LOLLAR, SHERM, 60/495, 60/567, 61/285, 62/514, 63/118
LONBORG, JIM, 65/573, 66/93, 67/371, 68/10, 68/12, 68/460, 69/109
LONG, DALE, 60/375, 61/117, 62/228, 63/484
LONG, JEOFF, 64/497
LOOK, BRUCE, 69/317
LOPAT, ED, 60/465, 63/23, 64/348
LOPATA, STAN, 60/515
LOPEZ, AL, 60/222, 61/132, 61/337, 62/286, 63/458, 64/232, 65/414, 69/527
LOPEZ, ART, 65/566
LOPEZ, HECTOR, 60/163, 61/28, 62/502, 63/92, 64/325, 65/532, 66/177
LOPEZ, MARCELINO, 63/549, 65/537, 66/155, 67/513
LOUN, DON, 65/181
LOVRICH, PETE, 63/549, 64/212
LOWN, TURK, 60/57, 60/313, 61/424, 62/528
LUM, MIKE, 68/579, 69/514
LUMENTI, RALPH, 61/469
LUMPE, JERRY, 60/290, 61/119, 61/365, 62/127, 62/305, 63/256, 64/165, 65/353, 66/161, 67/247
LUPOW, AL, 62/598, 63/351, 64/184, 66/188, 67/433
LYLE, SPARKY, 69/311
LYNCH, JERRY, 60/198, 60/352, 61/97, 62/487, 63/37, 64/193, 65/291, 66/182
MAAS, DUKE, 60/421, 61/387
MABE, BOB, 60/288
MacKENZIE, KEN, 60/534, 61/496, 62/421, 63/393, 64/297
MAGLIE, SAL, 60/456
MAGRINI, PETE, 66/558
MAHAFFEY, ART, 60/138, 61/433, 62/550, 63/7, 63/385, 64/104, 65/446, 66/570
MALKMUS, BOB, 60/251, 61/530
MALONEY, JIM, 61/436, 63/444, 64/3, 64/5, 64/420, 65/530, 66/140, 67/80, 68/42 69/362
MALZONE, FRANK, 60/310, 60/557, 61/173, 61/445, 62/225, 63/232, 64/60, 65/315, 66/152
MANTILLA, FELIX, 60/19, 61/164, 62/436, 63/447, 64/228, 65/29, 66/557, 67/524
MANTLE, MICKEY, 60/160, 60/350, 60/563, 61/44, 61/300, 61/406, 61/475, 61/57 62/18, 62/53, 62/200, 62/318, 62/471, 63/2, 63/173, 63/200, 64/50, 64/331, 65/3, 65/5, 65/350, 66/50, 67/103, 67/150, 68/280, 68/490, 69/500A, 69/500
MANZANT, RAY, 60/338
MARANDA, GEORGES, 60/479
MARICHAL, JUAN, 61/417, 62/505, 63/440, 64/3, 64/280, 65/10, 65/50, 66/221, 66/420, 67/234, 67/236, 67/500, 68/205, 69/10, 69/370, 69/572
MARIS, ROGER, 60/377, 60/565, 61/2, 61/44, 61/478, 61/576, 62/1, 62/53, 62/313 62/401, 63/4, 63/120, 63/144, 64/225, 64/331, 65/155, 66/365, 67/45, 68/33
MARSHALL, DAVE, 69/464A, 69/464B
MARSHALL, JIM, 60/267, 61/188, 62/337
MARSHALL, MIKE, 68/201, 69/17
MARTIN, BILLY, 60/173, 61/89, 62/208, 69/547
MARTIN, J.C., 60/346, 61/124, 62/91, 63/499, 64/148, 65/382, 66/47, 67/538, 68/211, 69/112
MARTINEZ, MARTY, 69/337
MARTINEZ, ORLANDO, 67/504, 68/578
MARTINEZ, TONY, 63/466, 64/404, 66/581
MASON, DON, 66/524, 69/584
MASON, HENRY, 60/331
MATCHICK, JOHN (TOM), 67/72, 68/113, 69/344
MATHEWS, EDDIE, 60/420, 60/558, 61/43, 61/120, 62/30, 63/275, 64/35, 65/500, 66/200, 67/166, 68/58
MATHEWS, NELSON, 63/54A, 63/54B, 64/366, 65/87
MATHEWSON FANS 267, 61/408
MATHIAS, CARL, 60/139
MAUCH, GENE, 61/219, 62/374, 63/318, 64/157, 65/489, 66/411, 67/248, 68/122, 69/606
MAXIE, LARRY, 64/94
MAXVILL, DAL, 63/49, 64/563, 65/78, 66/338, 67/421, 68/141, 69/320
MAXWELL, CHARLEY, 60/443, 61/37, 62/506, 63/86, 64/401
MAY, CARLOS, 69/654
MAY, DAVE, 68/56, 69/113
MAY, JERRY, 65/143, 66/123, 67/379, 68/598`, 69/263
MAY, LEE, 66/424, 68/487, 69/405
MAY, RUDY, 65/537
MAYE, LEE, 60/246, 61/84, 62/518, 63/109, 64/416, 65/407, 66/162, 67/258, 68/94 69/595
MAYS, WILLIE, 60/7, 60/200, 60/564, 61/41, 61/150, 61/482, 61/579, 62/18, 62/54 62/300, 62/395, 63/3, 63/138, 63/300, 64/9, 64/150, 64/306, 64/423, 65/4, 65/6, 65/250, 66/1, 66/215, 66/217, 66/219, 67/200, 67/244, 67/423, 68/50, 68/490, 69/190
MAZEROSKI, BILL, 60/55, 61/430, 61/571, 62/353, 62/391, 63/323, 64/570, 65/95 66/210, 67/510, 68/390, 69/335
McANDREW, JIM, 69/321
McAULIFFE, DICK, 62/527, 63/64, 64/363, 65/53, 66/495, 67/170, 68/285, 69/305
McBEAN, AL, 62/424, 63/387, 64/525, 65/25, 66/353, 68/514, 69/14
McBRIDE, KEN, 60/276, 61/209, 62/268, 63/510, 64/405, 65/268
McCABE, JOE, 64/564, 65/181
McCARVER, TIM, 62/167, 63/394, 64/429, 65/294, 66/275, 67/485, 68/275, 68/37 69/475
McCLAIN, JOE, 61/488, 62/324, 63/311
McCLURE, JACK, 65/553
McCOOL, BILL, 64/356, 65/18, 66/459, 67/353, 68/597, 69/129
McCORMICK, MIKE, 60/530, 61/45, 61/305, 61/383, 62/56, 62/107, 62/319, 63/56 64/487, 66/118, 67/86A, 67/86B, 68/9, 68/400A, 68/400B, 69/517
McCOVEY, WILLIE, 60/316, 60/554, 61/517, 62/544, 63/490, 64/9, 64/41, 64/350, 65/176, 66/217, 66/550, 67/423, 67/480, 68/5, 69/4, 69/6, 69/416, 69/440A, 69/440B, 69/572
McCRAW, TOM, 64/283, 65/586, 66/141, 67/29, 68/413, 69/388
McCREA, HAL, 68/384
McDANIEL, LINDY, 60/195, 61/75, 61/266, 62/306, 62/522, 63/329, 64/510, 65/24 66/496, 67/46, 68/545, 69/191
McDEVITT, DANNY, 60/333, 61/349, 62/493
McDOUGALD, GIL, 60/247
McDOWELL, SAM, 62/591, 63/317, 64/391, 65/76, 66/222, 66/226, 66/470, 67/23 67/295, 67/463, 68/12, 68/115, 69/7, 69/11, 69/220, 69/435
McFADDEN, LEON, 69/156
McFARLANE, JESUS, 62/229
McFARLANE, ORLANDO, 64/509, 66/569, 67/496
McGAHA, MEL, 62/242, 65/391
McGINN, DAN, 69/646
McGLOTHLIN, JIM, 66/417, 67/19, 68/493, 69/386
McGRAW, TUG, 65/533, 66/124, 67/348, 68/236, 69/601
McKNIGHT, JIM, 62/597
McLAIN, DENNY, 65/236, 66/226, 66/540, 67/235, 67/420, 68/40, 69/9, 69/150, 69/433
McLISH, CAL, 60/110, 61/157, 62/453, 63/512, 64/365
McMAHON, DON, 60/189, 61/278, 62/483, 63/395, 64/122, 65/317, 66/133, 67/7, 68/464, 69/616
McMILLAN, ROY, 60/45, 61/465, 62/211, 62/393, 63/156, 64/238, 65/45, 66/421
McMULLEN, KEN, 63/537, 64/214, 65/319, 66/401, 67/47, 68/116, 69/319
McNALLY, DAVE, 63/562, 64/161, 65/249, 66/193, 67/382, 68/478, 69/7, 69/9, 69/340, 69/532
McNERTNEY, JERRY, 68/14, 69/534
MEJIAS, ROMAN, 60/2, 62/354, 63/432, 64/186

MELE, SAM, 60/470, 62/482, 63/531, 64/54, 65/506, 66/3, 67/418
MELTON, BILL, 69/481
MENKE, DENIS, 62/597, 63/433, 64/53, 65/327, 66/184, 67/396, 67/518, 68/232, 69/487
MERRITT, JIM, 66/97, 67/523, 68/64, 69/661
MESSERSMITH, ANDY, 69/296
METCALF, TOM, 64/281
MEYER, BOB, 64/488, 65/219
MEYER, JACK, 60/64, 61/111
MICHAEL, GENE, 67/428, 68/299, 69/626
MIKKELSEN, PETE, 64/488, 65/177, 66/248, 67/425
MILES, JIM, 69/658
MILLAN, FELIX, 67/89, 68/241, 69/210
MILLER, BOB, 60/101, 61/314, 62/293, 62/572, 63/261, 64/394, 65/98, 66/208, 67/461, 68/534, 69/403
MILLER, JOHN, 63/208, 65/49, 66/427, 67/141, 69/641
MILLER, LARRY, 65/349, 69/323
MILLER, NORM, 67/412, 68/161, 69/76
MILLER, STU, 60/378, 61/72, 62/155, 63/286, 65/499, 66/265, 67/345
MINCHER, DON, 60/548, 61/336, 62/386, 63/269, 64/542, 65/108, 66/388, 67/312, 68/75, 69/285
MINGORI, STEVE, 69/339
MINOSO, MINNIE, 60/365, 61/42, 61/380, 62/28, 63/190, 64/538
MITTERWALD, GEORGE, 68/301, 69/491A, 69/491B
MOELLER, JOE, 63/53, 64/549, 65/238, 66/449, 67/149, 68/359, 69/444A, 69/444B
MOELLER, RON, 61/466, 63/541
MONBOUQUETTE, BILL, 60/544, 61/562, 62/580, 63/480, 64/25, 65/142, 66/429, 67/482, 68/234, 69/64
MONDAY, RICK, 67/542, 68/282, 69/105
MONEY, DON, 69/454A, 69/454B
MONROE, ZACK, 60/329
MONTEAGUDO, AURELIO, 64/466, 65/286, 66/532, 67/453
MOON, WALLY, 60/5, 61/325, 62/52, 62/190A, 62/190B, 63/279, 64/353, 65/247
MOORE, ARCHIE, 64/581
MOORE, BARRY, 67/11, 68/462, 69/639
MOORE, JACKIE, 65/593
MOORE, RAY, 60/447, 61/289, 62/437, 63/26
MOORHEAD, BOB, 62/593
MOOSE, BOB, 68/36, 69/409
MORALES, RICH, 69/654
MORAN, AL, 63/558, 64/288
MORAN, BILLY, 62/539, 63/57, 64/333, 65/562
MOREHEAD, DAVE, 63/299, 64/376, 65/434, 66/135, 67/297, 68/212, 69/29
MOREHEAD, SETH, 60/504, 61/107
MORGAN, JOE, 65/16, 66/195, 67/337, 68/144, 68/364, 69/35
MORGAN, JOE M., 60/229, 61/511
MORGAN, TOM, 60/33, 61/272, 62/11, 63/421
MORHARDT, MOE, 62/309
MORRIS, DANNY, 69/99A, 69/99B
MORRIS, JOHNNY, 69/111
MORTON, BUBBA, 62/554, 63/164, 67/79, 68/216, 69/342
MORTON, CARL, 69/646
MORYN, WALT, 60/74, 61/91
MOSCHITTO, ROSS, 65/566
MOSES, GERRY, 65/573, 69/476A, 69/476B
MOSES, WALLY, 60/459
MOSSI, DON, 60/418, 61/14, 62/55, 62/105, 63/218, 63/530, 64/335, 66/74
MOTA, MANNY, 63/141, 64/246, 65/463, 66/112, 67/66, 68/325, 69/236
MOTTON, CURT, 68/549, 69/37
MUFFETT, BILLY, 61/16, 62/336
MULLEAVY, GREG, 60/463
MURAKAMI, MASANORI, 65/282
MURCER, BOBBY, 66/469, 69/657
MURPHY, BILL, 66/574
MURPHY, DANNY, 62/119, 63/272
MURPHY, TOM, 69/474
MURRELL, IVAN, 68/569, 69/333
MURTAUGH, DANNY, 60/223, 61/138, 61/567, 62/503, 63/559, 64/144, 64/268
MUSIAL, STAN, 60/250, 61/290, 62/50, 62/317, 63/1, 63/138, 63/250
MYATT, GEORGE, 60/464
NAPOLEON, DAN, 65/533, 66/87
NARAGON, HAL, 60/231, 61/92, 62/164
NARLESKI, RAY, 60/161
NARRON, SAM, 60/467
NARUM, LES (BUSTER), 64/418, 65/86, 66/274
NASH, JIM, 67/90, 68/324, 69/546
NAVARRO, JULIO, 60/140, 63/169, 64/489, 65/563, 66/527
NEAL, CHARLIE, 60/155, 60/556, 61/423, 62/365, 63/511, 64/436
NEEMAN, CAL, 60/337
NEIBAUER, GARY, 69/611
NEIGER, AL, 61/202
NELSON, DAVE, 69/579
NELSON, MEL, 63/522, 64/273, 65/564, 66/367, 69/181
NELSON, ROCKY, 60/157, 61/304
NELSON, ROGER, 68/549
NEN, DICK, 64/14, 65/466, 66/149, 67/403, 68/591
NETTLES, GRAIG, 69/99A, 69/99B
NEVILLE, DAN, 65/398
NEWCOMBE, DON, 60/345, 61/483
NEWMAN, FRED, 63/496, 64/569, 65/101, 66/213, 67/451, 69/543
NICHOLS, CHET, 61/301, 62/403, 63/307
NICHOLSON, DAVE, 61/182, 62/577, 63/234, 64/31, 65/183, 66/576, 67/113, 69/298
NIEKRO, JOE, 67/53, 64/75, 69/43
NIEKRO, PHIL, 64/541, 65/461, 66/28, 67/456, 68/7, 68/257, 69/355
NIEMAN, BOB, 60/149, 61/178, 62/182
NISCHWITZ, RON, 62/591, 63/152, 66/38
NIXON, RUSS, 60/36, 61/53, 62/523, 63/168, 64/329, 65/162, 66/227, 67/446, 68/515, 69/363
NOLAN, GARY, 68/196, 69/581
NOLD, DICK, 68/96
NOREN, IRV, 60/433
NORMAN, FRED, 64/469, 65/386
NORTHRUP, JIM, 65/259, 66/554, 67/408, 68/78, 69/3, 69/580
NOSSEK, JOE, 64/532, 65/597, 66/22, 67/209, 69/143
NOTTEBART, DON, 60/351, 61/29, 62/541, 63/204, 64/434, 65/469, 66/21, 67/269, 68/171, 69/593
NUNN, HOWIE, 61/346, 62/524
NUXHALL, JOE, 60/282, 61/444, 63/194, 64/106, 65/312, 66/483, 67/44
NYE, RICH, 67/608, 68/339, 69/88
NYMAN, GERRY, 69/173
O'BRIEN, SYD, 69/628
O'CONNELL, DANNY, 60/192, 61/318, 62/411
O'DELL, BILLY, 60/303, 61/383, 62/429, 63/7, 63/9, 63/235, 64/18, 65/476, 66/237, 67/162
O'DONOGHUE, JOHN, 64/388, 65/71, 66/501, 67/127, 68/456
O'TOOLE, JIM, 60/32, 60/325, 61/328, 62/56, 62/58, 62/60, 62/450, 63/70, 64/185, 65/60, 66/389, 67/467
OCEAK, FRANK, 60/467
ODOM, JOHNNY, 65/526, 67/282, 68/501, 69/195
OGIER, MOE, 68/589
OLDIS, BOB, 60/361, 61/149, 62/269, 63/404
OLIVA, TONY, 64/116, 65/1, 65/340, 66/216, 66/220, 66/450, 67/50, 67/239, 68/165, 68/371, 68/480, 69/1, 69/427, 69/600
OLIVARES, ED, 62/598
OLIVER, AL, 69/82
OLIVER, BOB, 69/662
OLIVER, GENE, 60/307, 61/487, 62/561, 63/172, 64/316, 65/106, 66/541V18, 68/449, 69/247
OLIVER, NATE, 63/466, 65/59, 66/364, 68/124, 69/354
OLIVO, PEDRO, 63/228, 66/578
OLLUM, JIM, 67/137, 68/91
ORSINO, JOHNNY, 62/377, 63/418, 64/63, 65/303, 66/77, 67/207
ORTEGA, PHIL, 62/69, 63/467, 64/291, 65/152, 66/416, 67/493, 68/595, 69/406
OSBORNE, LARRY, 60/201, 61/208, 62/583, 63/514
OSINSKI, DAN, 63/114, 64/537, 65/223, 66/168, 67/594, 68/331, 69/622
OSTEEN, CLAUDE, 60/206, 62/501, 63/374, 64/28, 65/570, 66/270, 67/330, 68/9, 68/440, 69/528
OSTEEN, DARRELL, 66/424, 67/222, 68/199
OTERO, REGGIE, 60/459
OTIS, AMOS, 69/31
OTT, BILLY, 65/354
OWENS, JIM, 60/185, 61/341, 62/212, 63/483, 64/241, 65/451, 66/297, 67/582
OYLER, RAY, 65/259, 66/81, 67/352, 68/399, 69/178
PAFKO, ANDY, 60/464
PAGAN, JOSE, 60/67, 62/565, 63/545, 64/123, 65/575, 66/54, 67/322, 68/482, 69/192
PAGLIARONI, JIM, 61/519, 62/81, 63/159, 64/392, 65/265, 66/33, 67/183, 68/586, 69/302
PALMER, JIM, 66/126, 67/475, 68/575, 69/573
PAPPAS, MILT, 60/12, 60/399, 61/48, 61/295, 62/55, 62/75, 63/358, 64/45, 66/105, 67/254, 68/74, 69/79
PARKER, SALTY, 60/469
PARKER, WES, 64/456, 65/344, 66/134, 67/218, 68/533, 69/493A, 69/493B
PARSONS, TOM, 62/326, 65/308
PASCUAL, CAMILO, 60/483, 60/569, 61/235, 62/59, 62/230, 63/8, 63/10, 63/220, 64/2, 64/4, 64/6, 64/500, 65/11, 65/255, 66/305, 67/71, 68/395, 69/513
PATEK, FREDDIE, 69/219
PATTERSON, DARYL, 68/113, 69/101
PATTIN, MARTIN, 69/563
PAUL, MIKE, 69/537
PAVLETICH, DON, 62/594, 65/472, 66/196, 67/292, 68/108, 69/179
PEARSON, ALBIE, 60/241, 61/288, 62/343, 63/182, 64/110, 65/358, 66/83
PENA, JOSE, 69/339
PENA, ORLANDO, 63/214, 64/124, 65/311, 66/239, 67/449, 68/471
PENA, ROBERTA, 65/549, 66/559, 69/184
PENDLETON, JIM, 62/432
PEPITONE, JOE, 62/596, 63/183, 64/360, 65/245, 66/79, 67/340, 68/195, 69/589
PEREZ, TONY, 65/581, 66/72, 67/476, 68/130, 69/295
PERRANOSKI, RON, 61/525, 62/297, 63/403, 64/30, 65/484, 66/555, 67/197, 68/435, 69/77A, 69/77B
PERRY, BOB, 64/48
PERRY, GAYLORD, 62/100, 63/169, 64/468, 65/193, 66/598, 67/236, 67/320, 68/11, 68/85, 69/485A, 69/485B
PERRY, JIM, 60/324, 61/48, 61/385, 61/584, 62/37, 62/405, 63/535, 64/34, 65/351, 66/283, 67/246, 68/393, 69/146
PESKY, JOHNNY, 63/343, 64/248
PETERS, FRANK, 68/409
PETERS, GARY, 60/407, 61/303, 63/522, 64/2, 64/130, 65/9, 65/430, 66/111, 67/233, 67/310, 68/8, 68/210, 68/379, 69/34
PETERSON, CAP, 64/568, 65/512, 66/349, 67/387, 68/188, 69/571
PETERSON, FRITZ, 66/584, 67/495, 68/246, 69/46
PETROCELLI, RICO, 65/74, 66/298, 67/528, 68/430, 69/215
PFISTER, DAN, 62/592, 63/521, 64/302
PHILLEY, DAVE, 60/52, 61/369, 62/542
PHILLIPS, ADOLPHO, 66/32, 67/148, 68/202, 69/372
PHILLIPS, BUBBA, 60/243, 61/101, 62/511, 63/177, 64/143, 65/306
PHILLIPS, DICK, 63/544, 64/559
PHILLIPS, TAYLOR, 60/211
PHOEBUS, TOM, 67/204, 68/97, 69/185, 69/532
PICHE, RON, 61/61, 62/582, 63/179, 65/464
PIERCE, BILLY, 60/150, 60/571, 61/260, 63/50, 63/147, 63/331, 64/222
PIERCE, TONY, 67/542, 68/38
PIERSALL, JIM, 60/159, 61/345, 62/51, 62/90, 63/443, 64/586, 65/172, 66/565, 67/584
PIGNATANO, JOE, 60/292, 60/442, 61/74, 62/247
PILARCIK, AL, 60/498, 61/62
PINIELLA, LOU, 64/167, 68/16, 69/394
PINSON, VADA, 60/32, 60/176, 61/25, 61/110, 62/52, 62/80, 63/265, 64/80, 64/162, 65/355, 66/180, 67/550, 68/90, 69/160
PIZARRO, JUAN, 60/59, 61/227, 62/59, 62/255, 63/10, 63/160, 64/2, 64/430, 65/9, 65/125, 66/335, 67/602, 68/19, 69/498
PLASKETT, ELMO, 63/549
PLEIS, BILL, 62/124, 63/293, 64/483, 65/122
PODRES, JOHNNY, 60/425, 61/109, 61/207, 62/280, 63/150, 63/412, 64/580, 65/387, 66/468, 67/284, 69/659
POINTER, AARON, 67/564
POLLET, HOWIE, 60/468
POPOVICH, PAUL, 67/536, 68/266, 69/47A, 69/47B
PORTCARRERO, ARNIE, 60/254
POSADA, LEO, 61/39, 62/168
POSEDEL, BILL, 60/469
POST, WALLY, 60/13, 61/378, 62/148, 63/462, 64/253
POWELL, GROVER, 64/113
POWELL, JOHN (BOOG), 62/99, 63/398, 64/89, 65/3, 65/560, 66/167, 67/230, 67/241, 67/243, 67/521, 68/381, 69/15
POWER, VIC, 60/75, 61/255, 62/445, 63/40, 64/355, 65/442, 66/192
POWERS, JOHN, 60/422
PRICE, JIM, 67/123, 68/226, 69/472
PRIDDY, BOB, 64/74, 65/482, 66/572, 67/26A,, 67/26B, 68/391, 69/248
PROCTOR, JIM, 60/141
PURDIN, JOHN, 65/331, 68/336, 69/161
PURKEY, BOB, 60/4, 61/9, 62/120, 62/263, 63/5, 63/7, 63/350, 65/214, 66/551
QUALLS, JIM, 69/602
QUEEN, MEL, 64/33, 66/556, 67/374, 68/283, 69/81
QUILICI, FRANK, 66/207, 68/557, 69/356
QUIRK, ART, 62/591, 63/522
RADATZ, DICK, 62/591, 63/363, 64/170, 65/295, 66/475, 67/174, 69/663
RADER, DOUG, 67/412, 68/332, 69/119
RAKOW, ED, 60/551, 61/147, 62/342, 63/82, 64/491, 65/455
RAMOS, PEDRO, 60/175, 61/50, 61/528, 63/14, 64/562, 65/13, 66/439, 67/187
RANEW, MERRITT, 62/156, 64/78, 66/623, 66/62B
RATLIFF, GENE, 65/553
RATLIFF, PAUL, 63/549
RAY, JIM, 68/539, 69/257
RAYDON, CURT, 60/49
RAYMOND, CLAUDE, 63/519, 64/504, 65/48, 66/586, 67/364, 68/166, 69/446
REBERGER, FRANK, 69/637
REED, HOWIE, 65/544, 66/387
REED, RON, 68/76, 69/177
REESE, RICH, 65/597, 67/486, 68/111, 69/56
REGAN, PHIL, 61/439, 62/366, 63/494, 64/535, 65/191, 66/347, 67/130, 68/88, 69/535
REICHARDT, RICK, 65/194, 66/321, 67/40, 68/570, 69/205
REISER, PETE, 60/463
RENICK, RICK, 68/301
RENIFF, HAL, 62/139B, 62/139/C, 62/159, 63/546, 64/36, 65/413, 66/68, 67/201
REPOZ, ROGER, 66/138, 67/416, 68/587, 69/103
REPULSKI, RIP, 60/265, 61/128
RETTENMUND, MERV, 69/66
RETZER, KEN, 62/594, 63/471, 64/277, 65/278
REYNOLDS, TOMMIE, 64/528, 65/333, 67/487, 69/467
RIBANT, DENNIS, 65/73, 66/241, 67/527, 68/326, 69/463
RICE, DEL, 60/248, 61/448
RICHARDS, PAUL, 60/224, 61/131, 61/566
RICHARDSON, BOBBY, 60/405, 61/180, 62/65, 63/173, 63/420, 64/190, 65/115, 66/490
RICHARDSON, GORDON, 66/51
RICHERT, PETE, 62/131, 63/383, 64/51, 65/252, 66/95, 67/590, 68/354, 69/86
RICKETTS, DAVE, 65/581, 67/589, 68/46, 69/232
RICKETTS, DICK, 60/236
RIDZIK, STEVE, 60/489, 64/92, 65/211, 66/294
RIGNEY, BILL, 60/7, 60/225, 61/225, 62/549, 63/294, 64/383, 65/66, 66/249, 67/494, 68/416, 69/182
RIOS, JUAN, 69/619
RIPPELMEYER, RAY, 61/276, 62/271
RITCHIE, JAY, 65/494
RITTWAGE, JIM, 65/501
RIVERA, JIM, 60/116, 61/367
RIZZUTO, PHIL, 61/471
ROACH, MEL, 60/491, 61/217, 62/581
ROARKE, MIKE, 61/376, 62/87, 63/224, 64/292
ROBERTS, DAVE, 63/158, 66/571, 69/536
ROBERTS, ROBIN, 60/264, 61/20, 62/243, 63/6, 63/125, 64/285, 65/15, 66/530
ROBERTSON, BOB, 68/36, 69/468A, 69/468B
ROBERTSON, HUMBERTO, 60/416
ROBERTSON, JERRY, 69/284
ROBERTSON, RICH, 69/16
ROBINSON, BILL, 67/442, 68/337, 69/313
ROBINSON, BROOKS, 60/28, 61/10, 61/572, 62/45, 62/468, 63/345, 64/230, 65/1, 65/5, 65/150, 66/390, 67/1, 67/600, 68/20, 68/365, 68/530, 69/421, 69/550
ROBINSON, EARL, 61/343
ROBINSON, EDDIE, 60/456
ROBINSON, FLOYD, 62/454, 63/2, 63/405, 64/195, 65/345, 66/8, 66/199, 67/120, 68/404
ROBINSON, FRANK, 60/352, 60/490, 61/25, 61/360, 61/581, 62/54, 62/350, 62/396, 63/1, 63/3, 63/400, 64/260, 65/120, 66/219, 66/310, 67/1, 67/61, 67/100, 67/239, 67/241, 67/243, 68/2, 68/4, 68/373, 68/500, 68/530, 69/250
ROBINSON, JERRY, 63/466
ROBLES, RAFAEL, 69/592
RODGERS, ANDRE, 60/431, 61/183, 62/477, 63/193, 64/336, 65/536, 66/592, 67/554
RODGERS, BOB, 62/431, 63/280, 64/61, 64/426, 65/342, 66/462, 67/281, 68/433, 69/157
RODRIGUEZ, AURELIO, 69/653
RODRIGUEZ, E., 69/49A, 69/49B
RODRIQUEZ, ROBERTO, 68/199, 69/358
ROEBUCK, ED, 60/519, 61/6, 62/535, 63/295, 64/187, 65/52
ROGAN, PAT, 65/486
ROGGENBURK, GARRY, 63/386, 64/258, 66/582, 67/429, 68/581
ROHR, BILL, 67/547, 68/314
ROHR, LES, 68/569
ROJAS, COOKIE, 63/221, 64/448, 65/474, 66/170, 67/104, 67/595, 68/39, 69/507
ROJAS, MINNIE, 68/305, 69/502
ROLAND, JIM, 63/522, 64/341, 65/171, 69/336
ROLLINS, RICH, 62/596, 63/110, 64/8, 64/270, 65/90, 66/473, 67/98, 68/243, 69/451A, 69/451B
ROMAN, BILL, 65/493
ROMANO, JOHN, 60/323, 61/5, 62/330, 63/72, 63/392, 64/515, 65/17, 66/199, 66/413, 67/196
ROMO, VICENTE, 69/267
ROMONOSKY, JOHN, 60/87
ROOF, PHIL, 64/541, 65/537, 66/382, 67/129, 68/484, 69/334
ROOKER, JIM, 69/376
ROOT, CHARLIE, 60/457
ROSE, PETE, 63/537, 64/125, 65/207, 66/30, 67/430, 68/230, 69/2, 69/120, 69/424
ROSEBORO, JOHN, 60/88, 60/292, 61/363, 62/32, 62/397, 63/487, 64/88, 65/405, 66/189, 67/365, 68/65, 69/218
ROSELLI, BOB, 61/529, 62/363
ROSEN, AL, 61/474
ROSS, GARY, 69/404
ROWE, DON, 63/562
ROWE, KEN, 63/562, 65/518
ROZNOVSKY, VIC, 65/334, 66/467, 67/163, 68/428, 69/368
RUDI, JOE, 69/587
RUDOLPH, DON, 62/224, 63/291, 64/427
RUIZ, CHICO, 63/407, 64/356, 65/554, 66/159, 67/339, 68/213, 69/469
RUNNELS, PETE, 60/15, 61/42, 61/210, 62/3, 63/2, 63/230, 64/121
RUSH, BOB, 60/404
RUTH, BABE, 61/401, 62/135, 62/136, 62/137, 62/138, 62/139A, 62/142, 62/143, 62/144
RYAN, MIKE, 65/573, 66/419, 67/223, 68/306, 69/28
RYAN, NOLAN, 68/177, 69/533
SADECKI, RAY, 60/327, 61/32, 62/383, 63/486, 64/147, 65/10, 65/230, 66/26, 67/409, 68/494, 69/125
SADOWSKI, BOB, 62/595, 63/568, 64/271, 65/156, 66/523
SADOWSKI, ED, 60/403, 61/163, 62/569, 63/527, 64/61
SADOWSKI, TED, 61/254
SALMON, CHICO, 64/499, 65/105, 66/594, 67/43, 68/318, 69/62
SAMFORD, RON, 60/409
SANCHEZ, RAUL, 60/311
SANFORD, JACK, 60/165, 61/258, 61/383, 62/538, 63/7, 63/143, 63/325, 64/414, 65/228, 66/23, 67/549, 67/549
SANGUILLEN, MANNY, 68/251, 69/509
SANTIAGO, JOSE, 65/557, 66/203, 67/473, 68/123, 69/21
SANTO, RON, 61/35, 62/170, 63/252, 64/375, 65/6, 65/110, 66/290, 67/70, 68/5, 68/235, 68/366, 69/4, 69/420, 69/570
SANTORINI, AL, 69/592

SATRIANO, TOM, 63/548, 64/521, 65/124, 66/361, 67/343, 68/238, 69/78
SAUER, HANK, 61/481
SAVAGE, TED, 62/104, 63/508, 64/62, 67/552, 68/119, 69/471A, 69/471B
SAVERINE, BOB, 63/158, 64/221, 65/427, 66/312, 67/27149
SAWATSKI, CARL, 60/545, 61/198, 62/106, 63/267, 64/24
SAWYER, EDDIE, 60/226
SCHAAL, PAUL, 65/517, 66/376, 67/58, 68/474, 69/352
SCHAFFER, JIM, 62/579, 63/81, 64/359, 65/313, 68/463
SCHAFFERNOTH, JOE, 61/58, 63/463
SCHAIVE, JOHN, 61/259, 62/529, 63/356
SCHEFFING, BOB, 60/464, 61/223, 62/72, 62/416, 63/134
SCHEINBLUM, RICHIE, 65/577, 68/16, 69/479
SCHILLING, CHUCK, 61/499, 62/345, 62/467, 63/52, 64/182, 64/481, 65/272, 66/6
SCHLESINGER, BILL, 65/573, 68/258
SCHMIDT, BOB, 60/501, 61/31, 62/262, 63/94, 65/582
SCHNEIDER, DAN, 63/299, 64/351, 65/366, 67/543, 68/57, 69/656
SCHOENDIENST, RED, 60/335, 61/505, 62/575, 65/556, 66/76, 67/512, 68/294, 69/462
SCHOFIELD, DICK, 60/104, 61/453, 62/485, 63/34, 64/284, 65/218, 66/156, 66/474, 67/381, 68/588, 69/18
SCHRODER, BOB, 65/589
SCHROLL, AL, 60/357, 62/102
SCHULT, ART, 60/93
SCHULTZ, BARNEY, 62/89, 65/28
SCHULTZ, BUDDY, 63/452
SCHULTZ, JOE, 69/254
SCHURR, WAYNE, 64/548, 65/149
SCHWALL, DON, 62/35, 63/344, 64/558, 65/362, 66/144, 67/267
SCHWARTZ, RANDY, 67/33
SCORE, HERB, 60/360, 61/185, 61/337, 62/116
SCOTT, GEORGE, 66/558, 67/75, 68/233, 69/574
SEAVER, TOM, 67/581, 68/45, 69/480
SECRIST, DON, 69/654
SEGUI, DIEGO, 63/157, 64/508, 65/197, 66/309, 68/517, 69/511A, 69/511B
SELMA, DICK, 66/67, 67/386, 68/556, 69/197
SEMBERA, CARROLL, 66/539, 67/136, 68/207, 69/351
SEMPROCH, RAY, 60/286, 61/174
SEVCIK, JOHN, 65/597
SEYFRIED, GORDON, 64/499
SHAMSKY, ART, 65/398, 66/119, 67/96, 68/292, 69/221
SHANNON, MIKE, 64/262, 65/43, 66/293, 67/605, 68/445, 69/110
SHANTZ, BOBBY, 60/315, 61/379, 61/473, 62/177, 63/533, 64/278
SHAW, BOB, 60/380, 61/352, 62/109, 63/5, 63/255, 64/328, 65/428, 66/260, 67/470
SHAW, DON, 67/587, 68/521, 69/183
SHEA, STEVE, 69/499
SHELDON, ROLAND, 61/541, 62/185, 63/507, 65/254, 66/18, 68/276, 69/413
SHELLENBACK, JIM, 67/592, 69/567
SHEPARD, LARRY, 68/584, 69/384
SHERRY, LARRY, 60/105, 61/412, 61/521, 62/435, 63/565, 64/474, 65/408, 66/289, 67/571, 68/468
SHERRY, NORM, 60/529, 61/521, 62/238, 63/316
SHETRONE, BARRY, 60/348, 63/276
SHIPLEY, JOE, 60/239
SHIRLEY, BART, 66/591, 67/287, 69/289
SHOCKLEY, COSTEN, 65/107
SHORT, BILL, 60/142, 61/252, 62/221, 67/577, 68/536, 69/259
SHORT, CHRIS, 67/395, 68/7, 68/139, 69/395
SIEBERN, NORM, 60/11, 61/119, 61/267, 62/127, 62/275, 63/2, 63/430, 64/145, 66/14, 67/299, 68/537
SIEBERT, SONNY, 64/552, 65/96, 66/197, 66/222, 66/226, 67/95, 67/463, 68/8, 68/295, 69/455
SIEBLER, DWIGHT, 64/516, 65/326, 66/546, 67/164
SIEVERS, ROY, 60/25, 61/470, 62/220, 63/283, 64/43, 65/574
SILVESTRI, KEN, 60/466
SIMMONS, CURT, 60/451, 61/11, 62/56, 62/285, 63/22, 64/385, 65/373, 66/489, 67/39
SIMPSON, DICK, 63/407, 64/127, 65/374, 66/311, 67/6, 68/459, 69/608
SIMS, DUKE, 66/169, 67/3, 68/508, 69/414
SIMS, GREG, 66/596
SINGER, BILL, 66/288, 67/12, 68/249, 69/12, 69/575
SISK, TOMMIE, 63/169, 64/224, 65/558, 66/441, 67/84, 68/429, 69/152
SISLER, DAVE, 60/186, 61/239, 62/171, 63/284, 64/162
SISLER, DICK, 65/158
SIZEMORE, TED, 69/552
SKEEN, ARCHIE, 64/428
SKINNER, BOB, 60/113, 61/204, 62/115, 63/18, 63/215, 64/377, 65/591, 66/471, 69/369
SKOWRON, BILL (MOOSE), 60/370, 60/553, 61/42, 61/371, 61/568, 62/110, 63/180, 64/445, 65/70, 66/199, 66/590, 67/357
SLAUGHTER, STERLING, 64/469, 65/314
SMITH, AL, 60/428, 61/42, 61/170, 62/410, 63/16, 64/317
SMITH, BOB, 63/241
SMITH, BOBBY GENE, 60/194, 61/316, 62/531
SMITH, CHARLEY, 62/283, 63/424, 64/519, 65/22, 66/358, 67/257, 68/596, 69/538
SMITH, DICK, 64/398, 65/579
SMITH, GEORGE, 65/483, 66/542, 67/444
SMITH, HAL R., 60/84, 61/549, 63/153, 64/233
SMITH, HAL W., 60/48, 61/242, 62/492
SMITH, JACK, 63/496, 64/378
SMITH, MAYO, 67/321, 68/544, 69/40
SMITH, PETE, 64/428
SMITH, REGGIE, 67/314, 68/61, 69/660
SMITH, WILLIE, 65/85, 66/438, 67/397, 68/568, 69/198
SNIDER, DUKE, 60/493, 61/443, 62/500, 63/68, 63/550, 64/155
SNYDER, RUSS, 60/81, 61/143, 62/64, 63/543, 64/126, 65/204, 66/562, 67/405, 68/504, 69/201
SORRELL, BILL, 66/254, 67/341
SPAHN, WARREN, 60/230, 60/445, 61/48, 61/200, 61/589, 62/56, 62/58, 62/100, 62/312, 62/399, 63/320, 64/3, 64/400, 65/204
SPANGLER, AL, 60/143, 61/73, 62/556, 63/77, 64/406, 65/164, 66/173, 68/451, 69/268
SPANSWICK, BILL, 64/287, 65/356
SPARMA, JOE, 64/512, 65/587, 66/267, 67/13, 68/505, 69/488
SPECKENBACH, PAUL, 64/548
SPENCER, DARYL, 60/368, 61/357, 61/451, 62/197, 63/502
SPIEZIO, ED, 67/128, 68/349, 69/249
SPIEZIO, WAYNE, 65/431
SPRAGUE, ED, 69/638
SPRIGGS, GEORGE, 67/472, 68/314, 69/662
SPRING, JACK, 62/257, 63/572, 64/71
STAEHLE, MARV, 65/41, 66/164, 69/394
STAFFORD, BILL, 61/213, 62/55, 62/570, 63/155, 63/331, 64/299, 65/281
STAHL, LARRY, 66/107, 69/271
STALEY, JERRY, 60/57, 60/510, 61/90
STALLARD, TRACY, 61/81, 62/567, 63/419, 64/176, 65/491, 66/7
STANEK, AL, 64/99, 65/302, 66/437
STANGE, LEE, 62/321, 63/246, 64/555, 65/448, 66/371, 67/99, 68/593, 69/148
STANKY, EDDIE, 66/448, 67/81
STANLEY, MICKEY, 66/198, 67/607, 68/129, 69/13
STARGELL, WILLIE, 63/553, 64/342, 65/377, 66/99, 66/255, 67/140, 67/266, 68/86, 69/545
STARRETTE, HERM, 64/239, 65/539
STAUB, RUSTY, 63/544, 64/109, 65/321, 66/106, 67/73, 68/300, 69/230
STENGEL, CASEY, 60/227, 62/29, 63/43, 63/233, 64/324, 64/393, 65/187
STENHOUSE, DAVE, 62/592, 63/263, 64/498, 65/304
STEPHENS, GENE, 60/363, 61/102, 62/38, 64/308, 65/498
STEPHENSON, JERRY, 65/74, 66/396, 68/519, 69/172
STEPHENSON, JOHN, 64/536, 66/17, 67/522, 68/83
STEVENS, MORRIE, 65/521
STEVENS, R. C., 61/526
STEWART, JIM, 64/408, 65/298, 66/63, 67/124
STIEGLITZ, AL, 60/144
STIGMAN, DICK, 60/507, 61/77, 62/37, 62/532, 63/89, 64/6, 64/245, 65/548, 66/512
STOBBS, CHUCK, 60/432, 61/431
STOCK, WES, 60/481, 61/25, 62/442, 63/438, 64/382, 65/117, 67/74
STONE, DEAN, 62/574, 63/271
STONE, DON, 68/409
STONE, GEORGE, 69/627
STONE, ROD, 66/568
STONE, RON, 69/576
STONEMAN, BILL, 68/179, 69/67
STOTTLEMYRE, MEL, 65/550, 66/224, 66/350, 67/225, 68/120, 69/9, 69/470A, 69/470B
STOWE, HAL, 62/291
STRICKLAND, GEORGE, 60/63
STRIKER, JAKE, 60/169
STROUD, ED, 67/598, 68/31, 69/272
STUART, DICK, 60/402, 61/126, 62/160, 63/18, 63/285, 64/10, 64/12, 64/410, 65/5, 65/280, 66/580
STURDIVANT, TOM, 60/487, 61/293, 62/179, 63/281, 64/402
SUAREZ, KEN, 66/588, 68/218, 69/19
SUDAKIS, BILL, 69/552
SUKLA, ED, 66/417
SULLIVAN, FRANK, 60/280, 61/281, 62/352, 63/389
SULLIVAN, HAYWOOD, 60/474, 61/212, 62/184, 63/359
SULLIVAN, JOHN, 65/593, 66/597, 67/568
SUTHERLAND, DARRELL, 66/191, 68/551
SUTHERLAND, GARY, 67/587, 68/98, 69/326
SUTTON, DON, 66/288, 67/445, 68/103, 69/216
SWIFT, BOB, 60/470
SWOBODA, RON, 65/533, 66/35, 67/186, 67/264, 68/114, 69/585
TALBOT, FRED, 65/58, 66/403, 67/517, 68/577, 69/332
TALTON, TIM, 67/603
TANNER, CHUCK, 60/279
TAPPE, ELVIN, 60/457
TARTABULL, JOSE, 62/451, 63/449, 64/276, 66/143, 67/56, 68/555, 69/287
TASBY, WILLIE, 60/322, 61/458, 62/462A, 62/462B
TAUSSIG, DON, 62/44
TAYLOR, BILL, 63/481
TAYLOR, BOB, 61/446, 62/406, 64/381, 69/239
TAYLOR, CARL, 68/559, 69/357
TAYLOR, HAWK, 65/329, 68/52
TAYLOR, RON, 62/591, 63/208, 64/183, 65/568, 66/174, 67/606, 68/421, 69/72
TAYLOR, SAMMY, 61/253, 62/274, 63/273
TAYLOR, TONY, 60/294, 61/411, 62/77, 63/366, 64/585, 65/296, 66/585, 67/126, 68/327, 69/108
TEBBETTS, BIRDIE, 62/588, 63/48, 64/462, 65/301, 66/552
TEMPLE, JOHNNY, 61/155, 62/34, 63/576
TERRY, RALPH, 60/96, 61/389, 62/48, 63/8, 63/10, 63/148, 63/315, 64/458, 65/406, 66/109, 67/59
TERWILLIGER, WAYNE, 60/26
THACKER, MOE, 61/12, 62/546
THIBODEAU, JOHN, 69/189
THOENEN, DICK, 68/348
THOMAS, FRANK, 60/95, 61/382, 62/7, 63/495, 64/345, 65/123
THOMAS, GEORGE, 61/544, 62/525, 63/98, 64/461, 65/83, 66/277, 67/184, 69/521
THOMAS, LEE, 62/154, 63/441, 64/255, 65/111, 66/408, 67/458, 68/438
THOMAS, LEROY, 61/464
THOMAS, VALMY, 60/167, 61/319
THOMSON, BOBBY, 60/153
THRONEBERRY, FAYE, 60/9, 60/436, 61/57, 61/282
THRONEBERRY, MARV, 63/78
TIANT, LUIS, 65/145, 66/285, 67/377, 68/532, 69/7, 69/9, 69/11, 69/560
TIEFNAUER, BOB, 62/227, 64/522, 65/23, 68/269
TILLMAN, BOB, 62/368, 63/384, 64/112, 65/222, 66/178, 67/36, 69/374
TILLOTSON, THAD, 67/553
TOLAN, BOB, 65/116, 66/179, 67/474, 68/84, 69/448
TOMPKINS, RON, 66/107, 68/247
TORBORG, JEFF, 64/337, 65/527, 66/257, 67/398, 68/492, 69/353
TORGESON, EARL, 60/299, 61/152
TORRE, FRANK, 60/478, 62/303, 63/161
TORRE, JOE, 62/218, 62/351, 63/347, 64/70, 65/200, 66/130, 67/350, 68/30, 69/460
TORRES, FELIX, 62/595, 63/482
TORRES, HECTOR, 69/526
TORREZ, MIKE, 68/162, 69/136
TOTH, PAUL, 63/489, 64/309
TOVAR, CESAR, 65/201, 66/563, 67/317, 69/530
TRACEWSKI, DICK, 64/154, 65/279, 66/378, 67/559, 68/488, 69/126
TRESH, TOM, 62/31, 63/146, 63/173, 63/470, 64/395, 65/440, 66/205, 67/289, 68/69
TRIANDOS, GUS, 60/60, 61/140, 62/420, 63/475, 64/83, 65/248
TROWBRIDGE, BOB, 60/66
TSITOURIS, JOHN, 60/497, 63/244, 64/275, 65/221, 66/12, 68/523
TURLEY, BOB, 60/270, 61/40, 62/589, 63/322
TURNER, JIM, 62/263
TUTTLE, BILL, 60/367, 61/536, 62/298, 63/127
UECKER, BOB, 62/594, 63/126, 64/543, 65/519, 66/91A, 66/91B, 67/326
UHLAENDER, TED, 66/264, 67/431, 68/28, 69/194
UMBACH, ARNIE, 66/518
UMBRICHT, JIM, 60/145, 63/99, 64/389
UNSER, DEL, 69/338
UPHAM, JOHN, 67/608
UPSHAW, CECIL, 67/179, 68/286, 69/568
VALDESPINO, SANDY, 65/201, 66/56, 68/304
VALDIVIELSO, JOSE, 60/527, 61/557, 62/339
VALENTINE, FRED, 64/483, 66/351, 67/64, 68/248
VALLE, HECTOR, 65/561314
VALO, ELMER, 60/237, 61/186
VAUGHAN, CHARLES, 67/179
VEAL, COOT, 61/432, 63/573
VEALE, BOB, 62/593, 63/87, 64/501, 65/12, 65/195, 66/225, 66/425, 67/238, 67/335, 68/70, 69/8, 69/520
VERBANIC, JOE, 67/442, 68/29, 69/541
VERNON, MICKEY, 60/467, 61/134, 62/152, 63/402
VERSALLES, ZOILO, 61/21, 62/499, 63/349, 64/15, 65/157, 66/400, 67/270, 68/315, 69/38
VEZENDY, GERRY, 65/509
VIDAL, JOSE, 67/499, 68/432, 69/322
VINEYARD, DAVE, 65/169
VINSON, CHUCK, 68/328
VIRDON, BILL, 60/496, 61/70, 62/415, 63/55, 64/268, 64/495, 65/69
VIRGIL, OSSIE, 61/67, 62/327, 65/571, 67/132
VON HOFF, BRUCE, 68/529
VOSS, BILL, 66/529, 68/142, 69/621
WAGNER, GARY, 66/151, 67/529, 68/448, 69/276
WAGNER, LEON, 60/383, 61/547, 62/491, 63/4, 63/335, 64/41, 64/530, 65/367, 66/65, 67/109, 67/360, 68/495, 69/187
WAKEFIELD, BILL, 65/167, 66/443
WALKER, HARRY, 60/468, 65/438, 66/318, 67/448, 69/633
WALKER, JERRY, 60/399, 60/540, 61/85, 62/357, 63/413, 64/77
WALKER, LUKE, 66/498, 67/123, 68/559, 69/36
WALLACE, DON, 67/367
WALLS, LEE, 60/506, 61/78, 62/129A, 62/129B, 63/11, 64/411
WALTERS, KEN, 60/511, 61/394, 62/328, 63/534
WARD, JAY, 64/116, 65/421
WARD, PETE, 63/324, 64/85, 65/215, 66/25, 67/143, 67/436, 68/33, 69/155
WARD, PHIL, 63/324
WARDEN, JON, 69/632
WARNER, JACK, 65/354, 65/517, 66/553
WARWICK, CARL, 62/202, 63/333, 64/179, 65/357, 66/247
WASHBURN, RAY, 62/19, 63/206, 64/332, 65/467, 66/399, 67/92, 68/388, 69/41
WASLEWSKI, GARY, 69/438
WATSON, BOB, 69/562
WATT, EDDIE, 66/442, 67/271, 68/186, 69/652
WEAVER, EARL, 69/516
WEAVER, FLOYD, 65/546, 66/231
WEAVER, JIM, 68/328
WEBSTER, RAMON, 67/603, 68/164, 69/618
WEBSTER, RAY, 60/452
WEEKLY, JOHNNY, 62/204, 64/256
WEGENER, MIKE, 69/284
WEIS, AL, 63/537, 64/168, 65/516, 66/66, 67/556, 68/313, 69/269
WENZ, FRED, 69/628
WERHAS, JOHN, 64/456, 65/453, 67/514
WERT, DON, 62/299, 64/19, 65/271, 66/253, 67/511, 68/178, 69/443
WERTZ, VIC, 60/111, 61/173, 61/340, 62/481, 63/348
WESTRUM, WES, 60/469, 66/341, 67/593
WHISENANT, PETE, 60/424, 61/201
WHITAKER, STEVE, 67/277, 68/383, 69/71
WHITBY, BILL, 67/486
WHITE, BILL, 60/355, 61/232, 61/451, 62/14, 63/1, 63/290, 64/11, 64/240, 65/19 66/397, 67/290, 69/588
WHITE, JO-JO, 60/460
WHITE, MIKE, 64/492, 65/31
WHITE, ROY, 66/234, 68/546, 69/25
WHITE, SAMMY, 60/203, 62/494
WHITFIELD, FRED, 63/211, 64/367, 65/283, 66/88, 67/275, 68/133, 69/518
WICKER, FLOYD, 69/524
WICKERSHAM, DAVE, 61/381, 62/517, 63/492, 64/181, 65/9, 65/375, 66/58, 67/112, 68/288, 69/647
WIEAND, TED, 60/146
WILHELM, HOYT, 60/115, 60/395, 61/545, 62/423, 62/545, 63/108, 64/13, 65/27 66/510, 67/422, 68/350, 69/565
WILL, BOB, 60/147, 61/512, 62/47, 63/58
WILLEY, CARLTON, 60/107, 61/105, 62/174A, 62/174B, 63/528, 64/84, 65/401, 68/408
WILLHITE, NICK, 64/14, 65/284, 66/171, 67/249
WILLIAMS, BILLY, 61/141, 62/288, 63/353, 64/175, 65/4, 65/220, 66/217, 66/58 67/315, 68/37, 69/4, 69/450
WILLIAMS, DICK, 60/188, 61/8, 62/382, 63/328, 64/153, 67/161, 68/87, 69/349
WILLIAMS, DON, 60/414
WILLIAMS, GEORGE, 63/324, 64/388
WILLIAMS, JIMMY, 66/544
WILLIAMS, STAN, 60/278, 61/45, 61/190, 62/60, 62/515, 63/42, 64/505, 65/404, 68/54, 69/118
WILLIAMS, TED, 69/539, 69/650
WILLIAMS, WALT, 67/598, 68/172, 69/309
WILLIS, RON, 67/592, 68/68, 69/273
WILLS, MAURY, 67/570, 68/175, 69/45
WILLS, TED, 61/548, 62/444, 65/488
WILSON, BILLY, 67/402, 69/576
WILSON, DON, 68/77, 69/202
WILSON, EARL, 60/249, 61/69, 63/76, 64/503, 65/42, 66/575, 67/235, 67/237 67/305, 68/10, 68/160, 69/525
WILSON, RED, 60/379
WINDHORN, GORDON, 62/254
WINE, BOBBY, 63/71, 64/347, 65/36, 66/284, 67/466, 68/396, 69/648
WISE, CASEY, 60/342
WISE, RICK, 64/561, 65/322, 67/37, 68/262, 69/188
WITT, GEORGE, 60/298, 61/286, 62/287
WOJCIK, JOGN, 63/253
WOLF, WALLY, 63/208
WOMACK, DOOLEY, 66/469, 67/77, 68/431, 69/594
WOOD, JAKE, 61/514, 62/72, 62/427, 63/453, 64/272, 65/547, 66/509, 67/394
WOOD, WILBUR, 64/267, 65/478, 67/391, 68/585, 69/123
WOODESHICK, HAL, 60/454, 61/397, 62/526, 63/517, 64/370, 65/179, 66/514, 67/324
WOODLING, GENE, 60/190, 61/275, 62/125, 63/43, 63/342
WOODS, JIM, 61/59
WOODS, RON, 69/544
WOODSON, GEORGE, 69/244
WOODWARD, WOODY, 64/378, 65/487, 66/49, 67/546, 68/476, 69/142
WORTHINGTON, AL, 60/268, 63/556, 64/144, 65/216, 66/181, 67/399, 68/473
WRIGHT, CLYDE, 69/583
WYATT, JOHN, 63/376, 64/108, 65/590, 66/521, 67/261, 68/481
WYATT, WHITLOW, 60/464
WYNN, EARLY, 60/1, 61/50, 61/37, 61/455, 62/385
WYNN, JIM, 64/38, 65/257, 66/520, 67/390, 68/5, 68/260, 69/360
YASTRZEMSKI, CARL, 60/148, 61/287, 62/425, 63/115, 64/8, 64/182 , 64/210, 65/385, 66/70, 66/216, 67/355, 68/2, 68/4, 68/6, 68/250, 68/369, 69/1, 69/130, 69/425
YELLEN, LARRY, 64/226, 65/292
YORK, RUDY, 60/456
YOST, EDDIE, 60/245, 61/413, 62/176A, 62/176B
YOUNG, DON, 66/139, 69/602
ZACHARY, CHRIS, 64/23, 66/313, 67/212
ZANNI, DOM, 62/214, 63/354, 66/233
ZIMMER, DON, 60/47, 61/493, 62/478, 63/439, 64/134, 65/233
ZIMMERMAN, JERRY, 62/222, 63/186, 64/369, 65/299, 66/73, 67/501, 68/181
ZIPFEL, BUD, 63/69